*The*

# GLADIATORY ART

*The*

## LIVES, WRITINGS,

### *and* TECHNIQUES

*of the*

### EIGHTEENTH CENTURY

## STAGE GLADIATORS.

*a*

## SOURCE-BOOK.

WRITTEN BY
BEN MILLER

HOLLY–WOOD,
*Hudson Society Press.*
*Anno* MM. XXIV.

Front cover image of "A Ticket for James Figg the Prize-fighter" in Samuel Ireland, *Graphic Illustrations Of Hogarth, From Pictures, Drawings, And Scarce Prints In The Possession Of Samuel Ireland* (London: R. Faulder & J. Egerton, 1794).

Back cover images of John Laguerre, *Hob's Defence*, ca 1725, Oil on canvas, Yale Center for British Art, Paul Mellon Collection, and Claude Du Bosc, *Hob triumphs over Sr. Thomas / Plate VIII* [1760], Courtesy of The Lewis Walpole Library, Yale University.

Cover art and book design by Bronwyn Frazier-Miller.

Printed in the United States of America and the United Kingdom.

DISCLAIMER: The author, publisher, creators, and distributors of this book are not responsible, in any way whatsoever, for any loss, damage, injury, or any other adverse consequences that may result from the study, practice, or improper use made by anyone of the information or techniques contained in this book. All use of the information contained in this book must be made in accordance with what is permitted by law, and any damage liable to be caused as a result thereof will be the exclusive responsibility of the user. Many of the techniques described herein could lead to serious injury if not practiced under the guidance and training of a qualified instructor using appropriate safety equipment. This book is not a substitute for formal training. It is the sole responsibility of every person planning to train in the techniques described in this book to consult with a licensed physician before beginning.

*Publisher's Cataloging-in-Publication data*

Miller, Ben.

The Gladiatory Art: The Lives, Writings, & Techniques of the Eighteenth Century Stage Gladiators. A Sourcebook. / Ben Miller.

pages cm.

*Paperback:* ISBN 978-0-9990567-7-6

*Hardcover:* ISBN 978-0-9990567-8-3

1. Fencing. 2. Dueling. 3. Swordplay. 4. Martial arts—History—18th century. 5. Britain—History. I. Miller, Ben. II. Title.

FIRST EDITION

10 9 8 7 6 5 4 3 2 1

Dedicated to Jack Richard Frazier, Jr.

*Engraving by George Bickham, Jr., after Gravelot, 1737.*

# CONTENTS

# PREFACE

Since childhood, like nearly every boy, I grew up hearing legends, tales, and references to the ancient Roman gladiators who famously fought to the death in the Coliseum. Completely unknown to me, however, was the resurgence of bloody gladiatorial combat that took place in the British Isles during the late seventeenth and early eighteenth centuries—a shockingly violent and popular phenomenon that existed during the pinnacle of the so-called Age of Reason. Although some of these eighteenth century gladiators had been famous enough to become household names at the time, by the late nineteenth century their existence was nearly forgotten, and they fell into almost complete obscurity during the twentieth century.

I first learned of the existence of these eighteenth century "stage gladiators" about nineteen years ago, after my initiation into the world of classical fencing. Dissatisfied with my martial arts instruction at the time, and searching for something new, I stumbled upon the atmospheric New York City *salle d'armes* of Maestros Ramón Martínez and Jeannette Acosta-Martínez, two of the last masters in the world still teaching authentic living traditions of the older, martial methods of European swordsmanship connected to dueling and self-defence. The various fencing systems taught at the Academy—passed down to the Maestros by their own fencing master, *Maître d'Armes* Frederick Rohdes (a German born in 1897)—included a vast, almost countless number of techniques that had completely vanished from the modern sport, and from other surviving fencing lineages. Additionally, the usage of ancient European weapons such as the rapier, sword and dagger, single dagger, cloak, staff, cane, military saber, and others were being taught. From the very beginning, I was hooked—and the study of traditional classical fencing has since become a lifelong pursuit.

After commencing study at the academy, my interest in the history of fencing was naturally piqued. Upon expressing my desire to learn more about this history to Maestro Martínez, he unhesitatingly recommended the classic fencing books of Egerton Castle and Captain Alfred Hutton. Both of these gentlemen's major works contained short sections pertaining to the eighteenth century stage gladiators, who fought before large audiences with a variety of sharp weapons to win fame, glory, and prize money. These accounts and descriptions captured my imagination with all of their drama, excitement, sensationalism, larger-than-life personalities, and nearly superhuman exploits. I was keen to learn more, and the works of fencing scholar J. D. Aylward provided some further study. However, as far as I knew, no book devoted *solely* to the subject of the stage gladiators yet existed. Much of the reason for this, as I came to later learn, was that known firsthand accounts and additional source material concerning the stage gladiators was scant and extremely difficult to find.

In the following years, in tandem with my training as a classical fencer, I went on to author a number of texts pertaining to fencing history, several of which touched upon the subject of the stage gladiators. These included the foreword to the republication of Donald McBane's *Expert Sword-Man's Companion*, presented by Maestro Jared Kirby. McBane, a prolific Scottish duelist, had fought as a gladiator following his amazing career as a soldier. Through much research, I was able to unearth a number of contemporary accounts of, and primary sources for, McBane's challenges and exploits, thereby confirming the amazing truth of what had heretofore been considered by some to be a preposterous and unbelievable autobiography. I also authored the massive book *Irish Swordsmanship* (ten years in the writing), which contained a lengthy chapter all about the Irish stage gladiators. In researching the subjects of these books, I collected thousands of challenges and firsthand accounts of stage gladiators from a disparate range of sources, from between the years 1650 and 1760. I also made some surprising discoveries, such as the existence of a significant number of female gladiators, the fact that gladiatorial combats had taken place in the Americas, and the additional fact that black, Jewish, and Native American gladiators had traveled across the sea to England to take part in stage combats.

It certainly seemed like fertile material for a book. There were, however, a few obstacles. The first was that the source material was so vast as to make a "complete history" of the stage gladiators an extremely daunting task, likely requiring a one-thousand page tome. Moreover, with hundreds of different personalities, and thousands of combats with little connection or through-line, constructing any sort of engaging and coherent narrative history would be extremely challenging to say the least. Between personal duties and the other writing projects that I was engaged in, this was simply not going to be feasible for any time in the foreseeable future. The other obstacle to the task was that the vast bulk of the challenges themselves were brief, sparsely written, and became rather tedious when read in succession *en masse*.

Perhaps one day, I will find the time and leisure to write such a massive narrative history. In the meantime, I have decided to publish the present "sourcebook", which collates what I believe to be the most descriptive and interesting accounts and challenges that I have come across, as well as material on the most famous gladiators and "masters". I have also included a selection of the poetry, literature, satire, and song pertaining to the stage gladiators, in order to give the reader an idea of the impact and influence that the phenomenon had on the culture of the British Isles. Additionally, contained herein is a collection of historical images relating to the gladiators, a significant portion of which are likely unknown even to long-time enthusiasts of the history of fencing. Aside from the introduction, I have kept my own prose and insertions to a minimum, leaving the reader to draw his or her own conclusions about the nature of these combats, and about the gladiators themselves. Perhaps, one day, someone else will take the time to write a massive narrative history of the gladiators (and I encourage anyone so interested to do so!). In that case, this book may also serve as a valuable resource.

Until then, however, I hope this sourcebook will be enjoyed with the spirit in which it is presented.

For their help in preparing the current work for publication, I would like to thank the following people:

My wife, Bronwyn Frazier-Miller, for her consummate work in restoring numerous antique images included herein, for her book cover design, and for her ever-steadfast love and support.

Maestro Ramón Martínez and Maestro Jeannette Acosta-Martínez, for their invaluable guidance, insight, feedback, and encouragement, and continued mentorship on and off the *salle* floor.

My parents, David and Pam Miller, and Jack and Pam Frazier, for their generous support throughout the years.

Maestro Jared Kirby, for his immense help in research, and for allowing me to include James Miller's plates.

Maestro Paul Macdonald, for answering my numerous questions relating to this project.

David Bretherton, of the Thame Museum in Oxfordshire, for sharing his advertisements of stage-fights.

Christopher Scott Thompson, for first giving me the idea to publish this project in the form of a sourcebook, and for informing me of the existence of gladiator-turned-pirate William Lewis.

Heiko Große, for his assistance with sourcing historical images.

Sarah Hobbs, Archives Officer at Manchester Central Library, for assistance with locating the rare engraving of Irish gladiator Thomas Barrett, and facilitating its inclusion in this book.

Glenn Dunne, National Library Ireland, for facilitating the inclusion of gladiator Felix MacGuire's broadside.

Stephen Kilbane, for inviting me to lecture on Donald McBane for "McBane Night" 2020, which prompted me to further research Donald McBane and Scottish gladiators—research which has now been included in this book.

Carl Massaro, David Mastro, Robert Brooks, and Mike Smith, for their feedback regarding the manuscript.

Ben Miller
Hollywood, January 2024

# INTRODUCTION

Fearsome, brash, bold, grotesque, flamboyant, humorous, and wonderful, the stage gladiators, as they came to be known, appeared in England just after the midpoint of the seventeenth century, risking life and limb while utilizing a variety of antiquated weapons to fight for fame, glory, and prize-money. In 1672, a Frenchman named Josevin de Rocheford visited the London amphitheater known as the "Bear Garden", and observed the dramatic pomp and ritual preceding such combats:

> We went to the 'Bergiardin', where combats are fought by all sorts of animals, and sometimes men, as we once saw. Commonly, when any fencing-masters are desirous of showing their courage and great skill, they issue mutual challenges, and before they engage parade the town with drums and trumpets sounding, to inform the public there is a challenge between two brave masters of the science of defence, and that the battle will be fought on such a day.

What followed these processions was violent and often gruesome. On the appointed day, to the sound of trumpets and beating drums, the two combatants would ascend the stage, strip to their chests, and, on a signal from the drum, draw their weapons and commence fighting. The combat would continue until one participant conceded the match, or was unable to continue. In de Rocheford's account, the combatants continue fighting while enduring horrific wounds, including severed ears, cut scalps, and half-severed wrists.[1] Sometimes both combatants' feet were purposely strapped to the floor of the stage, forcing the fencers to hold their ground no matter the cost. During these particular contests, combatants were often wounded so that they were, to use their own term, "*made a devil of;* that is, cloven in the foot."[2] Bouts occurred with different types of weapons, including the two-handed sword, backsword, single rapier, rapier and dagger, sword and buckler, sword and targe, sword and gauntlet, falchion, flail, pike, halberd, smallsword, and quarterstaff.[3]   Although such fights were not intended to end in death, the wounds received were often serious enough to incur it.[4] In 1729, it was reported that "the *Irishman* who had a piece taken out of his Skull at Mr. *Fig*'s Ampitheatre last Week, in a Battle with a Gladiator, was thought last Thursday to be at the Point of Death."[5]

---

1   Egerton Castle, *Schools and Masters of Fence* (London: George Bell and Sons, 1885), 189-190, 201-204. Walter Thornbury, *Old and New London, a Narrative of Its History, Its People, and Its Places* (London: Cassell, Petter, Galpin & Co.,1881), 308.

2   *Ipswich Journal*, June 10, 1727.

3   Josias Maynard and William Swinnow. *A Tryall [of] Skill, Betwen Josias Maynard Citizen, and Cutler of London, and Master of the Noble Science of Defence ... of the House of White Friers, and William Swinow, Alias Scot, Citizen and Cooke of London, and Master of the Noble Science of Defence, of the House of Tower Royall.* 1652.

4   Examples of notable prize-fighters who died as a result of wounds incurred while contesting include "Norfolk Champion" William Emmerson, Timothy Buck of Clare-Market, Michael Butler of Kilkenny, and the celebrated "famous gladiator" William Sherlock (killed by Edward "Ned" Sutton in 1735). *Ipswich Journal*, April 15, 1721. *Derby Mercury*, January 15, 1735.

5   *Universal Spectator and Weekly Journal*, July 26, 1729.

Despite their sensational nature, and the considerable fame they enjoyed at the time, the gladiators of the eighteenth century have received virtually no examination in modern cultural histories of Britain, being instead relegated to a chapter or two in the works of the nineteenth century fencing scholars Egerton Castle and Alfred Hutton, and later, in the works of J.D. Aylward.[6] Up until now, no book devoted solely to the subject of the stage gladiators had ever been written; instead, authors and historians have been content to study the "prize players" which preceded the gladiators[7], and, when treating of famous gladiators such as James Figg, to focus almost exclusively on their connection to boxing—a connection which in some aspects may actually be erroneous[8]. Much of the reason for this can undoubtedly be attributed to the fact that known firsthand accounts and source material for the stage gladiators has been extremely scant and scattered to the four winds. As a result, some myths and misconceptions about the stage gladiators have endured. Likewise, the historians of Victorian England—though they deserve immense credit for the work they accomplished with the resources available to them—were unaware of some important aspects of the stage gladiator phenomenon, such as the existence of certain female, African American, and Native American champions, as well as the fact that gladiatorial combats took place in many places outside of England, including Ireland, the Caribbean, New England, and South America.

Some misconceptions were also propagated during the gladiators' own heyday. For instance, although observers at the time loftily claimed that their practice was directly descended from that of the ancient Romans, nineteenth and twentieth century historians claimed that the stage gladiators likely had their origins in the "playing of prizes" by the "corporations of defence" in Renaissance England. In contrast to the bloody, rowdy combat of the stage gladiator, this earlier "playing for a prize" was a regulated public examination used to determine a fencer's rank within the major houses (or guilds) of fencing masters. The fencing historian and antiquarian, Captain Alfred Hutton, described the origins of these corporations as follows:

> In the days of chivalry the art of fencing was confined to the lower orders; hence, the men who practised and taught what of art there was in it were of a very rough stamp indeed, and were ready to make use of any unseemly trick to get the better of an opponent, whether in play or in earnest; the exuberance of their spirits required curbing.
>
> Where there is a demand there is sure soon to be a supply. Accordingly, in the reign of Henry VIII, we find the most respectable men of the profession organizing themselves into a corporate body, with distinct rules for the maintenance of fair play and decent behaviour, and as a punishment for the breach of these rules they agreed upon a system of fines and other penalties...
>
> To become a member of the association, the simple "Scholler" had to pass an examination, which usually took place in one of the schools kept by the "Maisters." This consisted of bouts at certain weapons, in which he had to encounter a given number of young men who had already passed that ordeal. It was known as "Playing his Prize"; it was, in fact,

---

6    Egerton Castle, *Schools and masters of fence, from the Middle Ages to the eighteenth century* (London: G. Bell & Sons, 1885). *Sword and the Centuries* (London: G. Richards, 1901). J.D. Aylward, *The English Master of Arms* (London: Routledge & Paul [1956]). I also devoted a chapter to Irish stage gladiators in my own book, *Irish Swordsmanship*.

7    For instance, see Jay P. Anglin, "The Schools of Defense in Elizabethan London" in *Renaissance Quarterly*, Vol. 37, No. 3 (Autumn, 1984), 393-410; Herbert Berry, *The Noble Science: A Study and Transcription of Sloane Ms. 2530, Papers of the Masters of Defence of London, Temp. Henry VIII to 1590* (Newark, DE: University of Delaware Press, 1991); Ian Borden, "The Blackfriars Gladiators: Masters of Fence, Playing a Prize, and the Elizabethan and Stuart Theater", *Inside Shakespeare* (Penn.: Susquehanna University Press, 2006), *Faculty Publications and Creative Activity, School of Theatre and Film*, 1; Mary McElroy & Kent Cartwright, "Public Fencing Contests on the Elizabethan Stage", *Journal of Sport History*, Vol. 13, No. 3 (Winter, 1986), 193-211.

8    In numerous 19th and 20th century books on the history of boxing, James Figg is lauded as a "boxing champion" and the "father of modern boxing." He was also inducted into the International Boxing Hall of Fame, and *Encyclopedia Britannica* has described him as the "first recognized bare-knuckle boxing champion." However, in our exhaustive survey of hundreds of accounts and advertisements pertaining to Figg that were printed during his lifetime, we have not been able to find a single reference to Figg actually boxing. In the 1790s, a trade card attributed to Hogarth mentioned that Figg taught boxing. However, this trade card is now believed by scholars and museum curators to be falsely attributed to Hogarth, the earliest known copy being from 1794. Additionally, there is an advertisement which appears in later histories (and reprinted in this book), supposedly set down during his lifetime, which mentions the "Valiant FIG, who will exhibit his knowledge in various Combats—with the Foil, Back-sword, Cudgel, and Fist." However, this advertisement does not appear in the known published literature until 1812, and the location of the original (if it actually exists) is unknown. See Henry Pierce Egan, *Boxiana; Or Sketches of Ancient and Modern Pugilism* (London: G. Smeeton, 1812), 44. Considering all of the aforementioned, it must be stated that Figg may still well have boxed, or taught boxing. However, the available evidence for him doing so is extraordinarily slim, and not currently verifiable.

his matriculation, and when successful he was received as a "Free Scholler."... This Association of Masters of Defence arrived at its zenith in the time of Queen Elizabeth...[9]

The format for these tests usually involved a single fencer (that is, the subject being tested) facing two or more expert fencers in succession. Sometimes the list of opponents could be long; in one example, a certain Richard White was required to face "23 schollers" with the longsword. And in 1561, a prize played before Queen Elizabeth lasted for a duration of two days.[10] In 1617, Joseph Swetnam published a massive list of the weapons that "have beene plaied at in Challenges, here in England at severall times." They included the two handed sword, backsword, sword and dagger, sword and buckler, short sword and gauntlet, bastard sword, single rapier, rapier and dagger, half pike, long pike, long staff, quarterstaff, case of rapiers, rapier and cloak, rapier and target, rapier and gauntlet, rapier and pike, falchion, poleaxe, battle axe, single dagger, double daggers, welsh hook, and halberd. He also lists additional combinations of weapons that were used against each other, such as "Sword and Dagger against a Staffe or Haulbert" and "the Staffe against a Flaile."[11]

The exact reason as to why these academic "prize players" were replaced by the subsequent, brutal stage gladiators remains uncertain. Hutton, however, suggests that it may have been due to the civil and religious conflicts between parliament and the monarchy that took place in England during the seventeenth century. This thesis is seemingly supported by the existence of an official writ issued in May of 1653 during Cromwell's reign, which ordered "bear baiting, bull baiting, and playing for prizes by fencers hitherto practised in Southwark and other places, which have caused great evils and abominations, to be suppressed from this time."[12] Ten years later, in 1663, following the Restoration, it was proclaimed that the "Ancient Honour of the Famous City of London" had been restored, and that "there is none so pregnant and great a proof as the Restauration of those manly English Exercises of Wrestling, Archery, and Sword and Dagger, revived by the pious Care and Wisdom of [Mayor] Sir John Robinson..."[13]

The fencing historian J. D. Aylward offers some additional speculation on this transition in his seminal history, *The English Master of Arms*. He summarizes the rise of the new gladiators, or "prize fighters," after the Restoration as follows:

Hardly was King Charles reseated on his throne [in 1660] than clamour arose for the revival of the trials of skill and endurance which had broken the tedium of workaday life in the not-so-distant past. But there were material difficulties. The ancient guild of Masters of Defence had disappeared, there was no longer a governing body with a centuries-old experience of organization, there were no trained aspirants to present themselves for examination, and if there were, nobody now had the power to confer degrees or to issue official licenses.

All this was of little moment to a generation which had never learned to look upon arms as one of the fine arts. It got exactly what it deserved. Disbanded soldiers, mean tradesmen, all the curious heirs to the "very unskilfull and insufficient" pretenders set free by the Monopolies Act to "illude" the public, seized their opportunity. With that unerring instinct for the value of tradition which is innate in the Englishman, they assumed the honoured title of Masters of Defence, for there was no one to say them nay. Heedless of anachronism, they refurbished the discarded weapons of their predecessors, and they posted their Bills of Challenge to which, however, they gave a new and magniloquent turn. But the "good and laudable" Rules and Orders of the departed gild, to which bygone monarchs and bygone masters had paid tribute, were thought too inconvenient for adoption.

Those Rules defined prizes as tests of the competence of students of arms. They forbade admitted Masters to challenge other Masters "being Englishmen", an exception provided, no doubt, to meet the case of the Italian interlopers of the end of the sixteenth century. The ancient Rules laid down as a fundamental law that prizes, as examinations of aspi-

---

9   Alfred Hutton, *Sword and the Centuries* (London: G. Richards, 1901), 259, 261, 285.
10  Ibid., 276.
11  Joseph Swetnam, *The schoole of the noble and worthy science of defence* (London: Printed by Nicholas Okes, 1617), 186-187.
12  Mary Anne Everett Green, *Calendar of State Papers, Domestic Series 1652-1653, Volume 5.* London: Longman & Co., 1878. p. 307.
13  *The ancient honour of the famous city of London restored and recovered by the noble Sir John Robinson knight & baronet, Lord Maior for this year 1663, in the truly English and manly exercises of wrestling, archery, and sword & dagger: with the speeches of Mr. William Smee (master of the game pro hac vice, and clerk of the market) upon this solemn occasion* (London: Printed for R.L., 1663).

rants, must be played openly in the presence of all who chose to attend them, the new prizes were challenges between self-styled Masters, fought for stakes put up either by themselves or by their backers, and a charge was made for admission to the event. The old prizes were severe tests of academic skill and competence in which the examinees played with foiled or blunted weapons, the new ones were exhibitions of valour and endurance performed by men armed with sharp swords. In short, the revival of the prize resulted in its degradation to the level of a gladiatorial show.[14]

Captain Hutton further states,

> The prize-player must not be confounded with the prize-fighter. The two did not co-exist; the hundred years during which the prize-player flourished had ended before the hundred years (for they both lasted about the same time) of the prize-fighter commenced.[15]

It should be noted that although the above-quoted authors take great pains to delineate the stark differences between the earlier age of the "academic" prize-players and that of the later stage gladiators, while nevertheless positing that the latter were inspired by, or descended from, the former, a closer perusal of the historical evidence indicates that this evolution is not so simple. Both Aylward and Hutton, for instance, ignored another form of combat outside of the academic "prize playing" world, which may well have inspired, or given rise to, that of the stage gladiators. These were challenges arising from personal insults or injuries, and settled in a (presumably) dangerous but (probably) non-lethal public contest with various weapons on a stage. The earliest such example we have been able to find comes from fencing master George Silver, who wrote during the sixteenth century:

> These two *Italian* Fencers...said that Englishmen were strong men, but had no cunning, and they would go backe too much [i.e., retreat] in their fight, which was great disgrace unto them. Upon these words of disgrace against Englishmen, my brother *Toby Silver* and my selfe, made challenge against them both, to play with them at the single Rapier, Rapier and Dagger, the single Dagger, the single Sword, the Sword and Target, the Sword and Buckler, & two hand Sword, the Staffe, battell Axe, and Morris Pike, to be played at the Bell Savage upon the Scaffold, where he that went in his fight faster backe then he ought, of Englishman or Italian, shold be in danger to breake his necke off the Scaffold. We caused to that effect, five or six score Bils of challenge to be printed, and set up from *Southwarke* to the Tower, and from thence through *London* unto *westminster*, we were at the place with all these weapons at the time apointed, within a bow shot of their Fence schoole: many gentlemen of good accompt, caried manie of the bils of chalenge unto them, telling them that now the *Silvers* were at the place appointed, with all their weapons, looking for them, and a multitude of people there to behold the fight, saying unto them, now come and go with us (you shall take no wrong) or else you are shamed for ever. Do the gentlemen what they could, these gallants would not come to the place of triall.[16]

Although no copy of Silver's "bill of challenge" is known to survive, the "triall" he describes in the above passage does not constitute an academic test for rank, or a "playing for a prize". Rather, he presents a public combat fought on a personal quarrel—that is, over an insult to Englishmen *en masse*—and used to determine martial supremacy, on both a personal and national level in the eyes of the public. Moreover, this combat was to be fought on a "scaffold" or stage. Likewise, a surviving broadside from early in the next century, published in 1629, contains no mention of "playing for a prize", and bears many striking similarities to the later gladiatorial stage fights:

A Challenge,

From *Richard Gravener*, Gentleman and Souldier, Scholler to *Thomas Musgrove*, & Servant to Robert Battell, Provis Masters of the Noble Sience of Defence, against *Thomas Blunne*, Shoo-maker, and Scholler to *Thomas Turpin*, Master

---

14  J.D. Aylward, *The English Master of Arms* (London: Routledge & Paul [1956]), 116-117.
15  Hutton, 259, 286.
16  George Silver, *Paradoxes of Defence* (London: Edvvard Blount, 1599), 66-67.

of the Noble Science of Defence this to be performed at the Red Bull in St. Johns street, on Tuesday next, being the 20. of October, 1629. If God permit.

Judicious Gentlemen and others, I being a Souldier, from me expect no complementall phrases, for in my opinion that more stuffes the eare, then please the eye; then to leave off this empty outside of verball threatenings, I in plaine termes challenge the said *Thomas Blunne* at these eight severall weapons hereunder named, wishing him to bring his best skill and resolution with him. This to be performed at the time and place above named, desiring from the specta-tors stage-room, and from him his uttermost of his malice, while then I rest.

*The names of the Weapons.*

Long Picke, Half Picke, Backe Sword, Sword and Buckler, Single Rapier, Rapier and Dagger, Sword and Dagger, Holberd.

And I the said *Thomas Blunne* will be ready at the time and place appointed, to answer this Challenge, If God permit. *Vivat Rex.*[17]

In the above challenge, one can observe the public airing of a "grievance" (whether real or concocted) regarding a personal insult or injury that might otherwise lead to a potentially deadly duel, as well as the same vaunting, melodramatic language and bravado utilized by the later stage gladiators. Indeed, the only major difference between this challenge, and those subsequently issued at the turn of the following century, may be the absence of specific mention of financial recompense (in the form of gate money)—which, for ought we know, could still have possibly existed, the combat taking place in a popular theatre (the Red Bull). Likewise, many decades later, in 1663, Samuel Pepys recorded the following combat:

[We] walked to the New Theatre, which, since the King's players are gone to the Royal one, is this day begun to be employed by the fencers to play prizes at. And here I came and saw the first prize I ever saw in my life: and it was between one Mathews, who did beat at all weapons, and one Westwicke, who was soundly cut several times both in the head and legs, that he was all over blood: and other deadly blows they did give and take in very good earnest, till West-wicke was in a most sad pickle.[18]

The above account clearly depicts a brutal gladiatorial combat of the later mold, yet nevertheless describes the event as "playing" for a "prize"—i.e., using the old terminology—once again, suggesting that the transition between prize players and stage gladiators was not as stark or simplistic as earlier historians have claimed.

We now arrive at the subject of our book: the bloody gladiatorial contests of the late seventeenth and early eighteenth century. Fencing scholar and antiquarian Egerton Castle described this newer form of combat as follows:

The stage-fight of the eighteenth century, although the outcome of those "prizes" played in public by the old "Maisters of Defence," or their scholars, was a prize-fight in another sense. Its object was to win, not merely glory, but likewise the stakes deposited on the wager, as well as the gate-money, which became the property of the gladiator who "kept the stage to the last."[19]

These combats generally took place on the outskirts of London, in a rough area known as Hockley in the Hole, described during the period as "a wretched Bottom, between the North End of Hatton-Garden and Townsend-Lane, remarkable for having been the Scene of numberless Battles between Dogs, Bulls and Bears, and their no less brutish Masters the Butchers and Prize-Fighters..."[20] Another author of the era described Hockley in the Hole

---

17  *A Challenge, from Richard Gravener Gentleman and Souldier, Against Thomas Blunne Shoomaker, to be Performed at the Red Bull in St. Johns Street, on Tuesday Next, the 20. of October, 1629.* Eliot's Court Press, 1629

18  See page 3 of this book for the full account.

19  Castle, 201.

20  Thomas Salmon, *Modern History: or the Present State of all Nations. Describing Their Respective Situations, Persons, Habits, Buildings, Manners, Laws and Customs, Religion and Policy, Arts and Sciences, Trades, Manufactures and Husbandry, Plants, Animals and Minerals* (Dublin: Geo. Grierson, Printer to the King's Most Excellent Majesty, at the King's Arms and Two Bibles in Essex-Street, 1733), 118.

in even harsher terms, stating that it was "the Place where the Bear-Garden is situated, famous for sheltring Thieves, Pick-pockets, ordinary Whores, &c. and for breeding Bull-Dogs."[21]

Several major arenas, or "amphitheaters" are mentioned as settings for these gladiatorial combats. The most renowned, by far, was that run by James Figg, a central figure in this book. A contemporary account of Figg's business described it thus:

> FIGG'S-AMPHITHEATRE, Formerly a Place for the rude Diversion of Bear and Bull-Baiting by Bull-Dogs; which Dogs are in their Kind the fierce Animals, not to be matched in the World: But this at present (under the Direction of Figg a great Prize-Fighter) is changed into a Diversion of a different Nature, not more polite, otherwise than in the Name of Amphitheatre. Here, commonly once or twice a Week, is a Challenge between two Champions, who, like the Roman Gladiators, fight at Back-Sword and other Weapons, and very often cruelly wound one another. Here is also Wrestling and playing at Cudgels; and what is still more to be admired, Women often, like intrepid Amazons, appear upon the Stage, and with equal Skill and Courage fight with the same Weapons Men use. This commonly draws much Company; and in the lowest Part of Life here is seen the Skill, Generosity, and Courage of the English Nation.[22]

Contrary to what is claimed in the above account, brutal combats between bears, bulls, and dogs were frequent occurrences at the Bear Garden throughout its heyday. These animal-fights, while undoubtedly cruel, were not without severe danger to the attending humans; in one particular incident

> the Bull had toss'd a Poor Fellow that went to save his Dog: There was a mighty Bustle about him, with Brandy and other Cordials to bring him to Himself again; but when the College found there was no Good to be done on't. Well go thy ways Jaques, says a Jolly Member of that Society, There's the best Back-Sword Man in the Field gone. Come, Play Another Dog.[23]

In September of 1709, in yet another "tragic" occurrence, "Christopher Preston, keeper of the [Bear] Garden, had taught his Bears every thing but forgiveness of injuries; and this he experienced, at an unguarded moment, by an attack from one, who not only killed, but almost devoured him, before his friends were aware of the fact."[24] Another author later recounted, "Preston, the present Marshal, was the Son of Preston the Great, the first Founder of the rough Game, who unhappily falling into the Paws of his own Bear, was cruelly slain, and almost devour'd before he was discover'd by his Son, who immediately slew the Bear, and so succeeded his Father in Honour, Post and Authority."[25]

James Figg was not only the most famous of all the gladiators, but he also played a major role in the popularization and dissemination of gladiatorial combat. As one of his Irish rivals explained:

> Hearing that Mr. James Figg excels so much all other Masters, that no one is able to put themselves in Competition with him, the great Report of which is spreading itself all over the aforesaid Parts [of the British Isles], excited me to come over [from Ireland], to dispute with him that Character, in order for which, I hereby invite him to meet me...[26]

Other noted amphitheaters included those run by Edward Sutton, James Stokes, and Thomas Sibblis. Occasionally, these combats would take place in lavish theatres, where they were often attended by members of the British nobility. Smaller, humbler settings for gladiators also existed—places where neophytes could hone their skills

---

21 Preston, *Æsop. At the Bear-Garden: a Vision. By Mr. Preston. In Imitation of the Temple of Fame, a Vision, by Pope* (London: Sold by John Morphew near Stationers-Hall, 1715), 35.

22 *The foreigner's guide: both for the foreigner and native, in their tour through the cities of London and Westminster* (London: Joseph Pote, 1729), 120.

23 *Fables of Æsop and Other Eminent Mythologists: with Morals and Reflections. By Sir Roger L'Estrange, Kt. The Sixth Edition Corrected, Volume 1* (London: R. Sare, 1714), 285.

24 James Peller Malcolm, *Anecdotes of the Manners and Customs of London during the Eighteenth Century; Vol. II* (London: Longman, Hurst, Rees, and Orme, 1810), 126.

25 Preston, 34.

26 From a copy in the Westminster Archives, dated Sept. 4, 1723.

before eventually securing a place on the stage before the masses. These included the so-called "Great Booths" maintained in various parts of the city, by individuals such as the Irish gladiatorial couple, Thomas and Sarah Barrett, as well as others in Smithfield, Moorfields, Tottenham Court, and St. George's Fields. Gladiatorial combats also took place at festivals and country fairs, some of which were immortalized in the etchings of William Hogarth (a few of which are reprinted in this book). At the very bottom of this hierarchy were combats fought behind hedges and in ditches—venues vehemently disdained by more celebrated gladiators such as Francis Sherlock, who wrote in response to one such challenge: "your Hedge and Ditch fighting I scorn and detest..."[27]

The bravado and vulgarity that characterized these gladiatorial combats is well-illustrated in the following challenge by the Irish couple, Robert Barker and Mary Welsh:

We Robert Barker and Mary Welsh, from Ireland, having often contaminated our swords in the abdominous corporations of such antagonists as have had the insolence to dispute our skill, do find ourselves once more necessitated to challenge, defy, and invite Mr. Stokes and his bold Amazonian virago to meet us on the stage, where we hope to give a satisfaction to the honourable Lord of our nation who has laid a wager of twenty guineas on our heads. They that give the most cuts to have the whole money, and the benefit of the house; and if swords, daggers, quarter-staff, fury, rage, and resolution, will prevail, our friends shall not meet with a disappointment.[28]

Or the following colorful response by an English gladiatorial couple:

We James and Elizabeth Stokes, rather admiring the Vanity of the above presumptuous Challenge, than what Consequence must be drawn therefrom, assure our Opponents, not a single Fault shall escape our watchful Eyes, without due Correction from our vindictive Swords; and that they might as well have attempted the Chariot of the Sun, as to invade those Arms which nothing but Time itself can subdue, by paying that Debt of Nature to which Monarchs must submit, as well the meanest Subject: Being satisfied in this, we condescend to devote ourselves wholly at their Service as above, resolving to give them a final Answer in the most authentick Manner our Art can study, or Mankind desire, &c.[29]

Often these bloody combats would be preceded, or followed, by non-lethal (but still dangerous) contests of single-stick, boxing, and wrestling. The referee or manager of these events was often referred to as "Captain Vinegar", although it is unclear if this represented a single individual, or was a title and position adopted by several.[30] Typically, seconds would stand near each respective combatant with staves in hand, in case the fighters needed to be separated, as can be seen in numerous woodcuts of the era. Witnesses often remarked on the emotional intensity and shocking nature of these combats. After attending a match between the famous champions James Figg and Edward Sutton, John Byrom recorded in his diary that one "gentleman" in the audience was so affected by the violence that he passed out cold; Byrom further remarked—concerning a sensitive friend of his who departed the event early—that "Tom B. I believe would have done so too [i.e., fainted], if he had stayed."[31]

Contrarily, a number of skeptical writers of the period suggested that these gladiatorial combats might have been "faked" or staged. For instance, one early account by a visiting Frenchman mentions that: "I fancy there is some sort of Collusion between [the combatants], to make the Sport last, for they presently give over at the first Drawing of Blood; besides, the Swords are blunt..."[32] Whereas Samuel Pepys, around the exact same time, contrarily reports:

27 *Daily Advertiser,* September 2, 1745.
28 Castle. Thornbury. W. R. Chambers, *W. R. Chambers's journal of popular literature, science and arts, Volume 59* (London: W. R. Chambers, 1882). Samuel Palmer, *St. Pancras: being antiquarian, topographical, and biographical memoranda, relating to the extensive metropolitan parish of St. Pancras, Middlesex* (London: S. Palmer, 1870).
29 *Weekly Journal or British Gazetteer,* July 11, 1730.
30 John Edwin Wells, "Fielding's 'Champion' and Captain Hercules Vinegar", *The Modern Language Review,* Vol. 8, No. 2 (Apr., 1913), 165-172.
31 John Byrom, *The private journal and literary remains of John Byrom* ([Manchester]: Chetham Society, 1854), 117.
32 Samuel Sorbière, *A voyage to England: containing many things relating to the state of learning, religion, and other curiosities of that kingdom. Done into English from the French original.* (London: J. Woodward, 1709), 71-72. (French original from 1666).

I did till this day think that it has only been a cheat; but this being upon a private quarrel, they did it in good earnest; and I felt one of their swords, and found it to be very little, if at all blunter on the edge, than the common swords are.[33]

Yet another witness of a stage combat between females observed:

Their weapons were a sort of two-handed sword, three or three and half feet in length; the guard was covered, and the blade was about three inches wide and not sharp—only about half a foot of it was, but then that part cut like a razor.[34]

Probably the passage most often cited by authors to "prove" that gladiatorial combats were fake appeared in the popular journal *The Spectator* in 1712. In it, an anonymous letter-writer stated:

I was the other day at the *Bear-Garden,* in hopes to see your short face; but not being so fortunate, I must tell you by way of Letter, That there is a Mystery among the Gladiators which has escaped your Spectatorial Penetration. For being in a Box at an Ale-house, near the renowned Seat of Honour above-mentioned, I over-heard two Masters of the Science agreeing to quarrel on the near Opportunity. This was to happen in the Company of a Set of Fraternity of Basket-Hilts, who were to meet that Evening. When this was settled, one asked the other, Will you give Cuts, or receive? The other answered, Receive. It was replied, Are you a passionate Man? No, provided you cut no more nor no deeper than we agree. I thought it my Duty to acquaint you with this, that the People may not pay their Money for fighting and be cheated.

    *Your humble Servant,*

        Scabbard Rusty.[35]

Although it is tempting to accept the above letter at face value (as some previous historians have done), a wider reading of the gladiatorial literature inspires greater caution. There is no doubt that the elaborate, melodramatic challenges between gladiators contained a strong element of theatricality—such braggadocio being a common feature of the stage-fights, designed to whip up partisan sentiment and enhance publicity. It is also possible, as hinted in the above-quoted letter, that secret agreements between gladiators existed. However, it is notable that without exception, all such insinuations of fakery originate from outside parties. The writings of former gladiators such as Donald McBane and James Miller, for instance, contain no mention of such chicanery. Although one might counter that these men were personally invested in maintaining the aura of their own martial prowess, McBane's memoir has been rightly described as one of the most ingenuous memoirs in the English language[36], and is full of self-deprecating accounts of his roguish escapades and occasional martial failures. Likewise, John Godfrey, in his lengthy, personal 1747 account of the major gladiators (some of whom he had trained with), expresses nothing but reverence for their skill, courage, and fighting ability. Perhaps the greatest testament, however, to the seriousness of gladiatorial combats comes from one of their greatest critics, the Scottish fencing master William Hope. Although Hope was unsparing in his polemic against the gladiators, his main critique was that their combats were *too* dangerous and aggressive:

There is a Cunning and Subtilty, as well as Dexterity, which belongs to the true Art of the Sword, and which but few, professing the Art, are Masters of; Thrusts and Blows being to be avoided several other Ways, by a judicious and agile Artist, than by always meeting with, and obstinately opposing the Adversary's Sword; a Thing not known in the Bear-Gardens, where, at first engaging they come commonly close up to one another, and there with Fury discharge repeated

33 Samuel Pepys, *The Diary of Samuel Pepys, M.A., F.R.S., Clerk of the Acts and Secretary to the Admirality, Volume 3, Part 1* (New York: Croscup & Sterling Company, 1893), 143-144.

34 Cesar de Saussure, *A foreign view of England in the reigns of George I and George II: The letters of Monsieur Cesar de Saussure to his family* (London: John Murray, 1902), 277-279.

35 *Spectator,* August 5, 1712.

36 Aylward, 162.

Blows, whereby ensue Contretemps* and grievous Wounds; which does indeed please the ignorant Mob, but ought to be abominate by all good Artists and Men of Judgment, seeing it is a most scandalous Disparagement to all true Art; which ought to be perform'd, not only with Calmness, but with a cautious Vigour and Judgment, otherwise such fool-hardy Persons run headlong to their own Destruction...[37]

It must also, of course, be noted that all of the above accounts may, in a sense, be "true", and that the reality of the eighteenth century gladiator could have been somewhat complex. Just as the ancient classical world exhibited both legitimate athletics and cheating[38], and just as the world of twentieth century combat sports featured both corruption, doping, "fixed" matches, as well as honestly and genuinely-fought contests by amazingly skilled combatants, the same may have been true regarding the stage gladiators. Individuals are, after all, individuals.

Whatever the case, a perusal of the many firsthand accounts in this book will reveal that, while some aspects of the stage fights (such as blunted points, and lack of intent to kill) may have indeed made these fights "safer" than an earnest duel to the death, the stage-combats were still extremely dangerous to those who took part in them, as evinced by the number of severe injuries and deaths that occurred in the arena. The famous gladiators that we know of who were mortally wounded on the stage (in often gruesome ways) include Timothy Buck (Figg's master), "Norfolk Champion" William Emmerson, Michael Butler of Kilkenny, William Sherlock of Dublin, and Thomas Barrett of Dublin, as well as many lesser-known, anonymous fighters.[39] The fatal nature of these fights was somewhat facilitated by English law at the time, which specified that "if two Masters of Defence, playing at their prizes, kill one another, it is not a Felony."[40] This aspect of the law proves both the potential deadliness of these combats, as well as the fact that their highly dangerous nature was condoned by the British legal system, and by British society at large—most public criticisms of the gladiators coming strictly from the *literati*. Most of these deaths occurred not instantaneously on the stage, but in the hours or days following the combats, as the result of serious wounds received. It is thus difficult to know if such wounds were the result of mere accident, or if they were intended to be mortal by those who dealt them. This is something that rival gladiators publicly argued over in print, when such fatal incidents took place.

Veteran prize fighters were typically described as being severely scarred and frightening to behold. A Londoner who witnessed a group of gladiators passing in the street described them as

A parcel of Scarified Ruffians, whose Faces seem'd to be as full of Cuts as a Plow'd Field is of Furrows; some their Countenances chop'd into the Form of a *Good-Fryday* Bun, with Cuts cross one another, as if they were Markt out for Christian Champions: Others having as many scars in their Bear-Garden Physiognamies, as there are Marks in a Chandlers Cheese, Scor'd out into Penniworths.[41]

Yet another foreign witness to a prize fight noted that the combatants "were hideous to look at, their faces being all seamed and scarred."[42]

As shall be shown in this book, contemporaries of the period judged the gladiators in a wide variety of ways. As one harsh critic lamented: "What is it but a degree of *Self-Murther,* when Men out of Frolick or Humour, out of low Ambition of Honour or for the Gain of a little Pelf, challenge each other to these brutal Combats? Their

---

* "Indeed, nothing discovers more a Man's Ignorance in Fencing, than to be frequently guilty of offering *Thrusts* in *Contre-temps*, when himself hath neither forced, nor his Adversary given any opportunity or *Open*[ing]; or by alwise *Thrusting* upon his Adversary's *Thrust*, without offering first to Parie [parry]; whereby *Contre-temps* and *Exchanged* [simultaneous] *Thrusts*, do most frequently follow." In short, Hope is warning about the dangers of *contre-temps*, which can result in suicidal actions or simultaneous deaths. William Hope, *A New, Short, and Easy Method of Fencing* (Edinburgh: James Watson, 1707), 107.

37 [Sir William Hope], *A Few Observations Upon the Fighting for Prizes in the Bear Gardens* (London: 1715), 6.
38 For examples of fixed matches and bribery in ancient pugilistic contests, see Charles Stocking, *Ancient Greek Athletics* (Oxford: Oxford University Press, 2021), 190-192.
39 *Ipswich Journal,* April 15, 1721. See also pages 34-35, 82, 101, 144, and 197.
40 Michael Dalton, *The Countrey Justice: Containing the Practice of the Justices of the Peace* (London: G. Sawbridge, 1677), 356.
41 Edward Ward, *The London-Spy Compleat, in eighteen-parts* (London: J. How, 1703).
42 Saussure, 277-9.

Flesh is hack'd and hew'd with many a Wound... their Blood is spilt upon a publick Stage, and Life it self sometimes pays for their Folly."[43] Yet another claimed that the resurgence of such a brutal practice associated with Ancient Rome was a sign that the apocalyptic "end times" had arrived.[44] Contrarily, others described the practice as a highly useful—and even necessary—tradition, which "toughened" British youth, and cultivated a brave and valiant national spirit inured to danger and hardship. In 1747, John Godfrey opined, circumspectly:

> It must be allowed that those amphitheatrical Practices were productive of some ill, as they gave some Encouragement to Idleness and Extravagance among the Vulgar. But there is hardly any good useful Thing, but what leaves an Opening for Mischief, and which is not liable to Abuse. Those Practices are certainly highly necessary, and the Encouragement of Back-Sword Fighting, and Boxing, I think commendable; the former for the Uses which have been mentioned; the latter, and both, to feed and keep up the British Spirit. Courage I allow to be chiefly natural, probably owing to the Complexion and Constitution of our Bodies, and flowing in the different Texture of the Blood and Juices; but sure it is, in a great measure, acquired by Use, and Familiarity with Danger. Emulation and the Love of Glory are great Breeders of it. To what Pitch of daring do we not see them carry in Men? And how observable it is in Miniature among the Boys, who, almost as soon as they can go alone, get into their Postures, and bear their little bloody Noses, rather than be stigmatized for Cowards?[45]

Other critics (such as fencing master Sir William Hope) considered the gladiators to be little better than criminals, the very rabble of society. We may, of course, choose to trust in such opinions. However, it is important to note that although there are a few scattered reports of crimes committed by gladiators (such as in the sad cases of Thomas Cook[46], and the pirate William Lewis[47]), the record shows that these men (and women) overwhelmingly were not described as career criminals, but as farmers, butchers, tailors, shoe-makers, felt-makers, weavers, printers, cooks, carpenters, tobacconists, woolcombers, sailors, soldiers, and members of other working class professions.[48] Therefore, one cannot rule out the possibility that classism may well account for some of the more disparaging accusations leveled at the gladiators.

Whatever the true nature of the gladiators' morals, one cannot claim that they lacked for wit or humor. Much like the medieval monks who frequently inserted grotesque cartoons into the margins of their manuscripts, we find that the gladiators never squandered an opportunity to include a joke in one of their challenges or advertisements, such as the final line of the following specimen—appearing almost as an after-thought: "N.B. There will be a Match of Cudgel-playing between 7 Countrymen and 7 Londoners, for 7 Guineas."[49] Or another poem, included as part of a challenge, which was the final exchange between two particularly boastful gladiators:

> Know, base Slave, that I am one of those,
> Can fight a Man as well in Verse as Prose:
> And when thou'r dead, write this upon thy Hearse,
> Here lies a Swordsman that was slain in Verse.[50]

---

43  Isaac Watts, *A Defense Against the Temptation to Self-murther* (London: J. Clark and R. Hett, 1726), 127.

44  "How doth the Apostle express his Design in it, 1 Cor. 4.9. I think (says he) that God hath set forth us the Apostles [left] as it were Men appointed to Death, for we are made a Spectacle unto the World, and to Angels, and to Men. Alluding to these Gladiators, brought up last upon the Stage, as a Spectacle to the People. The thing I cite it for, is, that the greatest Work in that kind, he appointed to be at last: As also, was that which immediately preceded it, the coming of his Son in the lasts Days." Thomas Goodwin, *The Works of T. G. [With Preface to Vol. 1. by T. Owen and J. Barron.], Volume 3* (London: J. Darby, 1692).

45  Capt. John Godfrey, *A Treatise Upon the Useful Science of Defence, Connecting the Small and Back-Sword, And showing the Affinity between them* (London: T. Gardner, 1747), 39.

46  See Chapter 1, pages 9, 10, and 12-15 for the challenges and case of Thomas Cook.

47  In a description of his trial at Nassau, Dec. 9-10, 1718: "William Lewis aged about 34 Years, as he had been an hardy Pyrate & a Prize fighter, Scorn'd to shew any Fear to dye, but heartily desired Liquors enough drink with his fellow sufferers on the Stage, & with the Standers by." Baylus C. Brooks, *Dictionary of Pyrate Biography* (Lulu Press [S.l.], 2020), 290.

48  Ben Miller, *Irish Swordsmanship: Fencing and Dueling in Eighteenth Century Ireland* (N.Y.: Hudson Society Press, 2017), 148-149.

49  *Daily Journal*, June 18, 1729.

50  *Derby Mercury*, October 22, 1730.

# I.

## EARLIEST ACCOUNTS: 1652 – 1703

*T*he following challenges and firsthand accounts are among the earliest that we have been able to find pertaining to the stage gladiators, and offer a window into their origin and development during the late seventeenth century, as well as their transition into the beginning of the eighteenth century.

The earliest such document comes from 1652, and involved Josias Maynard, of London, and William Swinnow, alias "Scot" (see Figure 1 on next page). The mention of these men belonging to "houses" gives rise to the possibility that historian J. D. Aylward was wrong in his declaration that the old tradition of "playing for a prize" had disappeared by 1631. If so, this would appear to be one of the last such challenges in existence.

Here follow the rest of the surviving accounts from this time that we have been able to find, in sequential order.

### BURGES vs. TUBB, 1660

Copy of a Warrant granted to Fencers.

With the favour and priviledge of his Highnes the Duke of Yorke, it is agreed upon, by and betweene Francis Burges and William Tubb, to play a tryall of skill at eight severall weapons, which are hereunder expressed, on the thirteenth day of August next, being Monday, at the Red Bull Playhouse. 30th July. l660.

| *The Weapons of Francis Burges* | *The Weapons of Wm. Tubb* |
|---|---|
| Backe Sword | Single Rapier |
| Sword and Gantlet | Rapier and Dagger |
| Sword and Dagger | Halfe Pike |
| Sword and Buckler. | Quarter Staffe. |

## A Tyrall Skill,

BEtwen *Josias Maynard Citizen*, and Cutler of *London*, and Master of the *Noble Science* of *defence* at the *Black Swan* in *Holborne*, & of the House of *White-Friers*. And *William Swinow*, alias *Scot*, *Citizen* and Cooke of *London*, and Master of the *Noble Science* of *defence*, of the House of *Tower Royall*.

GENTLEMEN,

ACcording to the ancient custome heretofore used, & practised in the use of weapons by way of Tryalls of Skill, where the Members of the said two Houses are to play one House against the other, and not to play two Members of one House against one another ; Therefore for example sake, and avoyding of such disorder hereafter. I the said *Josias Maynard* do invite the said *William Swinnow*, alias *Scot*, to meet at the *Hope* on the *Banck side* on *Munday* next being the twenteith of this instant *September* 1652, betweene one and two of the Clock in the afternoon at the firthest. at these fourteene weapons

### The Names of the Weapons,

| | |
|---|---|
| Long Sword, | Short Sword and Gauntlet, |
| Back Sword, | Halbert, |
| Single Rapier, | Case of Rapiers, |
| Sword & Dagger, | Mall, |
| Rapier & Dagger, | Single Faulchion, |
| Sword & Buckler, | Flayle, |
| Halfe Pike, | Quarter-staffe, |

KNOW GENTLEMEN,

THat I William Swinnow, alias Scot, shall dare to meet the afore named Josias Maynord if God permitt, at the time and place appointed, where according to the the ancient custom above mentioned: I shall without question give that content unto all, deserning Spectators as shall bee, both to my credit, and the whole House of Tower Royall.

GENTLEMEN.

*If any accident may chance to happen, as you may conjecture easily may be, in playing of so many weapons; there shall be as formerly mentio-*ned, Bengimon Dobson, and Francis Burgis, *Professors of the Noble Science of defence, ready to performe what shall be wanting in my Person. Thus desiring nothing more then a cleare stage & from him no favour.* God preserve the Commonwealth of England.

*Figure 1. Josias Maynard vs. William Swinnow, September 20, 1652. Beinecke Rare Book and Manuscript Library, Yale University.*

Whereas his Highnes the Duke of Yorke hath been pleased to comende unto me Francis Burges and Wm. Tubb, for a warant to playe a prize.

These are to authorise the said Frances Burges and William Tubb to playe a prize at the weapons above named, at the House called the Red Bull, and for so doinge this shall be their warant.

Dated the 30th July, 1660.

H. HERBERT.

## SAMUEL PEPYS: WESTWICKE vs. MATHEWS, 1663

We walked away to White Hall and there took coach, and I with Sir J. Minnes to the Strand May-pole; and there 'light out of his coach, and walked to the New Theatre, which, since the King's players are gone to the Royal one, is this day begun to be employed by the fencers to play prizes at. And here I came and saw the first prize I ever saw in my life: and it was between one Mathews, who did beat at all weapons, and one Westwicke, who was soundly cut several times both in the head and legs, that he was all over blood: and other deadly blows they did give and take in very good earnest, till Westwicke was in a most sad pickle. They fought at eight weapons, three bouts at each weapon. It was very well worth seeing, because I did till this day think that it has only been a cheat; but this being upon a private quarrel, they did it in good earnest; and I felt one of their swords, and found it to be very little, if at all blunter on the edge, than the common swords are. Strange to see what a deal of money is flung to them both upon the stage between every bout. But a woful rude rabble there was, and such noises, made my head ake all this evening. So, well pleased for once with this sight, I walked home, doing several businesses by the way.[51]

## SHARD vs. SAWKINS, 1664

A Triall of Skill.

To be performed betwixt *Thomas Shard* Citizen and Merchant-Taylor of *London*, Scholler to Mr. *Benja. Dobson* Gent, Master of the Noble Science of Defence, and *Richard Sawkins*, Citizen and Butcher of *London*, Schollar to Mr. *William Wright*, Master of the aforesaid Science. At the *Red-Bull* at the upper end of St. *John-Street*, on Whitson Munday the 30th of *May*, 1664. Beginning exactly at Three of the clock in the after-noon, *and the best Man is to take all the Money.*

GENTLEMEN. I *Thomas Shard* do invite *Richard Sawkins* to meet me at the time and place aforesaid, to try him at these Eight severall Weapons undernamed, *VIZ.:*

|  |  |
|---|---|
| *Back Sword* | *Sword* and *Buckler,* |
| *Single Rapier* | *Halfe Pike,* |
| *Sword* and *Dagger* | *Sword* and *Gauntlet,* |
| *Rapier* and *Dagger,* | *Single Faulchion.* |

I *Richard Sawkins* will not fail to meet this fair inviter at this time and place aforesaid, if GOD permit.

VIVAT REX[52]

---

51 Pepys, 143-144.
52 John Eliot Hodgkin, *Rariora; being notes of some of the printed books, manuscripts, historical documents, medals, engravings, pottery, etc., collected, 1858-1900* (London: S. Low, Marston & Co., Ltd., 1902), 53-54.

*Fig. 2. Woodcut from "The Unfortunate Fencer".*

A SONG OF A STAGE-FIGHT
*(undated, late 17th century)*

THE Unfortunate Fencer;
OR, *The Couragious Farmer* of Gloucester-shire.

SHEWING How this huffing Spark went down into those Parts, Challenging any one at all sorts of Weapons; and
at length shamefully Conquer'd by a Country Farmer.

To the Tune of, *The Spinning Wheel.* Licensed according to Order.

You that delight in merriment,
be pleased to attend a while,
I hope to give you all content,
this very Song will make you smile;
'Tis of a Fencer, brave and bold,
Adorn'd with rich embroider'd Gold.

This Spark in pomp, and rich array,
from *London* rid with right good will,
That he young Lords might learn to play
all sorts of Weapons by his skill;
And wheresoever this Fencer came,
the drum, and trumpet, blaz'd his fame.

This huffing Fencer, fierce and stout,
to *Glocester* City did repair,

4

*The Spinning Wheel. See p. 241.*

*Fig. 3. Music to which "The Unfortunate Fencer" was to be sung.*

The which a Farmer did espy,
As he by chance was passing by.

The jolly Farmer, brisk and bold,
as soon as he the Sword beheld,
He cry'd, what is there to be sold?
what is your Room with Rapiers fill'd?
The valiant Fencer did reply,
I come my Valour here to try.

With that he did his Rapier shake,
and said let whose will here arrive,
I do a noble Challenge make,
to fight the stoutest Man alive:
The Farmer said, I'll answer thee,
If that you dare to Cope with me.

The Fencer cry'd you sorry slave,
here by this Rapier in my hand,
I'll send thee to thy silent Grave,
against my force no Clown can stand:
It shall be try'd the Farmer cry'd,
I value not your huffing Pride.

Next Morning they a Stage prepare,
the drums did beat, and trumpets sound,
Right joyfull tydings to declare,
this Gallant trac'd the City round,
Dress'd in his Shirt of Holland fine,
With Sword which did like Silver shine.

5

The Stage he mounted brisk and gay,
and eke the Farmer straight likewise;
To whom the Huffing Spark did say,
of you I'll make a Sacrifice,
This work in short, I shall compleat,
You should have brought a Winding-sheet.

No more that, but let's fall too,
I hope to make my party good
And e'er this World I bid adieu,
who knows but I may let you blood;
With that he cut him o'er the Face,
And thus began the Spark's Disgrace.

But when they came to Quarter-staff,
the Farmer bang'd the Spark about;
Which made all the Spectators laugh
and with Huzzas they all did shout;
He made his Head and Shoulders sore,
He ne'er had been so thrash'd before.

Thus fairly did he win the day,
which put the Fencer in a Rage,
Who through the crowd did sneak away,
while the stout Farmer kept the Stage;
Huzzas of joy, did echo round,
While he with Victory was Crown'd.

FINIS.[53]


## THE GREAT BOOBEE, 1663

(excerpt)

The Bearward went to save me then,
The People flock'd about;
I told the Bear-Garden-Men,
My Guts they were almost out:
They said I stink most grievously,
No Man would pity me;
They call'd me witless Fool and Ass,
*And a great Boobee.*[54]

---

53 *THE Unfortunate Fencer; OR The Couragious Farmer of Gloucester-shire* (P. Brooksby, J. Deacon, J. Blare, J. Back, [1675-1696]).
54 Thomas D'Urfey, *Wit and mirth: or, Pills to purge melancholy* (London : W. Pearson, 1720).

## AN ACCOUNT BY SAMUEL SORBIERE, 1666

Among the Diversions of the City of *London*, I am not to forget the *Bear-Garden* Prize-fighters; they are usually Fencing-masters, or their Ushers, who to gain themselves Reputation, and something else besides Blows, put out a Challenge, and lay a Wager of Twenty or Thirty Pounds against any that will fight them: The Money is deposited and delivered to him that accepts the Challenge; the Challenger takes up the Money that is received at the Door, which, amounts sometimes to more than Twice or Thrice the Sum he gave his Opponent, as there are more or less People there to see the Sport: They fight with Sword and Buckler, and Back-Sword. But I fancy there is some sort of Collusion between them, to make the Sport last, for they presently give over at the first Drawing of Blood; besides, the Swords are blunt: However, they sometimes give one another terrible Hacks and Slashes, so that half a Cheek hangs down; but this is done by chance, and happens not often, tho' there is always something that is fierce in this Brutish Exercise.[55]

## THE DIARY OF SAMUEL PEPYS, 1667 - 1669

*Monday, May 27, 1667:* So to my chamber, and there did some little business, and then abroad, and stopped at the Bear-garden-stairs, there to see a prize fought. But the house so full there was no getting in there, so forced to go through an alehouse into the pit, where the bears are baited; and upon a stool did see them fight, which they did very furiously, a butcher and a waterman. The former had the better all along, till by and by the latter dropped his sword out of his hand, and the butcher, whether not seeing his sword dropped I know not, but did give him a cut over the wrist, so as he was disabled to fight any longer. But, Lord! to see how in a minute the whole stage was full of watermen to revenge the foul play, and the butchers to defend their fellow, though most blamed him; and there they all fell to it to knocking down and cutting many on each side. It was pleasant to see, but that I stood in the pit, and feared that in the tumult I might get some hurt. At last the rabble broke up, and so I away to White Hall and so to St. James's...

*Monday, September 9, 1667:* Up; and to the office, where all the morning, and at noon comes Creed to dine with me. After dinner, he and I and my wife to the Bear-Garden, to see a prize fought there. But, coming too soon, I left them there and went on to White Hall, and there did some business with the Lords of the Treasury...Thence I by water to the Bear-Garden, where now the yard was full of people, and those most of them seamen, striving by force to get in, that I was afeard to be seen among them, but got into the ale-house, and so by a back-way was put into the bull-house, where I stood a good while all alone among the bulls, and was afeard I was among the bears, too; but by and by the door opened, and I got into the common pit; and there, with my cloak about my face, I stood and saw the prize fought, till one of them, a shoemaker, was so cut in both his wrists that he could not fight any longer, and then they broke off: his enemy was a butcher. The sport very good, and various humours to be seen among the rabble that is there.[56]

*Monday, April 12, 1669:* Thence I [went] to St. James's, but there was no musique, but so walked to White Hall, and, by and by to my wife at Unthanke's, and with her was Jane, and so to the Cocke, where they, and I, and Sheres, and Tom dined, my wife having a great desire to eat of their soup made of pease, and dined very well, and thence by water to the Bear-Garden, and there happened to sit by Sir Fretcheville Hollis, who is still full of his vain-glorious and prophane talk. Here we saw a prize fought between a soldier and country fellow, one Warrell, who promised the least in his looks, and performed the most of valour in his boldness and evenness of mind, and

---

55 Sorbière, 71-72.
56 Samuel Pepys, *Diary and correspondance of Samuel Pepys, F.R.S.,secretary to the admiralty in the Reigns of Charles II and James II, Vol. III* (London: H.G.Bohn,York Street,Convent Garden, 1858), 137, 246.

smiles in all he did, that ever I saw and we were all both deceived and infinitely taken with him. He did soundly beat the soldier, and cut him over the head. Thence back to White Hall, mightily pleased, all of us, with this sight, and particularly this fellow, as a most extraordinary man for his temper and evenness in fighting.[57]

## JOSEVIN DE ROCHFORD, 1672

We went to see the Bergiardin, which is a great amphitheatre, where combats are fought between all sorts of animals, and sometimes men, as we once saw. Commonly, when any fencing masters are desirous of shewing their courage and their great skill, they issue mutual challenges, and before they engage, parade the town with drums and trumpets sounding, to inform the public there is a challenge between two brave masters of the science of defence, and that the battle will be fought on such a day. We went to see this combat, which was performed on a stage in the middle of this amphitheatre, where, on the flourishes of trumpets and the beat of drums, the combatants entered, stripped to their shirts. On a signal from the drum, they drew their swords, and immediately began the fight, skirmishing a long time without any wounds. They were both very skilful and courageous. The tallest had the advantage over the least: for, according to the English fashion of fencing, they endeavoured rather to cut than push in the French manner, so that by his height he had the advantage of being able to strike his antagonist on the head, against which the little one was on his guard. He had in his turn an advantage over the great one, in being able to give him the jarnac stroke, by cutting him on his right ham, which he left in a manner quite unguarded. So that, all things considered, they were equally matched. Nevertheless, the tall one struck his antagonist on the wrist, which he almost cut off: but this did not prevent him from continuing the fight, after he had been dressed, and taken a glass of wine or two to give him courage, when he took ample vengeance for his wound: for a little afterwards, making a feint at the ham, the tall man, stooping in order to parry it, laid his whole head open, when the little one gave him a stroke, which took off a slice of his head, and almost all of his ear. For my part I think there is an inhumanity, a barbarity and cruelty, in permitting men to kill each other for diversion. The surgeons immediately dressed them, and bound up their wounds: which being done, they resumed the combat, and both being sensible of their respective disadvantages, they therefore were a long time without giving or receiving a wound, which was the cause that the little one, failing to parry so exactly, being tired with this long battle, received a stroke on his wounded wrist, which dividing the sinews, he remained vanquished, and the tall conqueror received the applause of the spectators. For my part I should have had more pleasure in seeing the battle of the bears and dogs, which was fought the following day on the same theatre.[58]

## SWAINSTON vs. WOOD, 1683

1683. Two men fought a prize in the New Place, upon a stage—Swainston and Wood—but Wood wounded Swainston with back sword, although Swainston got the better.[59]

## DESCRIPTION OF A GLADIATOR, 1694

'Tis the wild Extravagance of some Women to be in love with Filth... some can be pleas'd with nothing but the strutting of a Prize-Fighter with a Hackt-face, and a Red Ribbon in his Shirt...[60]

---

57 Samuel Pepys, *Diary and correspondance of Samuel Pepys, F.R.S., secretary to the admiralty in the Reigns of Charles II and James II, Vol. IV* (London: H.G.Bohn, York Street, Convent Garden, 1858), 150.

58 *The Antiquarian Repertory: A Miscellany, Intended to Preserve and Illustrate Several Valuable Remains of Old Times; Adorned with Elegant Sculptures* (London: F. Blyth, 1779), 37-38.

59 Surtees Society, *Six North Country Diaries* (Durham: Andrews & Co., 1910), 46.

60 Petronius Arbiter [Mr. Burnaby], *The Satyr of Titus Petronius Arbiter* (London: S. Briscoe, 1694), 100. Note: although this purports to be a translation of the ancient Roman *Satyricon*, the author has replaced a vague reference to a "Gladiator" with the quoted passage.

## A SERIES OF CHALLENGES FROM 1699

AT His Majesty's Bear-Garden in Hockley in the Hole, A Trial of Skill is to be Performed (without Beat of Drum) between these following Masters, on Wednesday the 26th of July, 1699, by Three of the Clock precisely. I George Cary, of Taunton Dean, Master of the Noble Science of Defence, doth invite you Henry Worly, to meet me, and Fight at these several Weapons Following, viz. Back-Sword, Quarter-Staff, Sword and Dagger, Single Falchon, Sword and Gauntlet, Case of Falchons, Sword and Buckler, Quarter-Staff. I Henry Worly, Master of the said Science of Defence, formerly of Tame, now Living at the Flaming Sword at the Corner of St. James's-street, will not Fail; God Willing, to meet this Fair Inviter at the Time and Place appointed, desiring a clear Stage, and from him no Favour.[61]

AT His Majesty's Bear-Garden, in Hockley in the Hole, A Tryal of Skill is to be Performed (without Beat of Drum) between these following Masters, on Wednesday the 25th Instant, by one of the Clock precisely. I Francis Gorman, Master of the Noble Science of Defence, doth Invite you Thomas Cook, the famous Butcher of Gloucester, to meet me, and Exercise at these following Weapons, viz. Back-Sword, Sword and Dagger, Sword and Buckler, Single Falchon, Case of Falchons, Quarter-Staff, and 3 Bouts at what the Company pleases. I Thomas Cook, Butcher of Gloucester, Master of the said Science of Defence, God willing, Will not fail to meet this fair Inviter at the Time and Place appointed, desiring a clear Stage, and from him no favour. William Cross, and Thomas Brown, to fight 6 Bouts at Sword.[62]

ON Wednesday next, November the 8th will be perform'd a Trial of Skill, at the Bear Garden in Hockley the Hole, between Anderson, the famous Highlander, and John Terrewest, of Oundle, in Northamptonshire, with sharp Edges. At Two of the Clock exactly.[63]

## VARIOUS CHALLENGES, 1700

On Monday next, at the Play-house in Salisbury Court, is to be a Tryal at Back Sword, Sword and Dagger, &c. between the famous Thomas Hesgate, (who Cut down Old Bush last Summer) and Mr. George Cary; both of them Masters of the Noble Science of Defence. They are to begin at Two of the Clock precisely, being obliged to fight out their Weapons by Four.[64]

At his Majesty's Bear Garden in Hockley in the Hole, a Tryal of Skill is to be performed between these following Masters, to Morrow being the 10 Instant, by 3 of the Clock precisely. I, John Bowler of the City of Norwich, and Champion of Norfolk, Master of the Noble Science of Defence, do Invite You, bold Edgecombe of the West, to Meet me, and Fight these following Weapons, viz., Back Sword, Sword and Dagger, Sword and Buckler, Single Falchon, Case of Falchons, and Quarter-Staff. I, Will of the West, from the City of Salisbury, Master of the said Science of Defence, will not fail, God Willing, to meet this Brave and Bold Champion of Norfolk, at the time and place, appointed, desiring a Clear Stage, and from him no favour.[65]

---

61 *Post Boy*, July 25, 1699.
62 *Post Boy*, Oct. 21, 1699.
63 *Post Boy*, Nov. 4, 1699.
64 *Post Boy*, May 11, 1700.
65 *Post Boy*, July 9, 1700.

## VARIOUS CHALLENGES and ACCOUNTS, 1701

A tryal of Skill to be performed at his Majesty's Bear Garden in Hockley in the Hole, on Thursday next being the 9th instant, betwixt these following Masters, Edward Butler, Master of the Noble Science of Defence, who has lately cut down Mr Hasget, and the Champion of the West, and 4 besides, and James Harris a Herefordshire man Master of the Noble Science of Defence, who has fought 98 Prizes, and never was worsted, to exercise the usual Weapons. At 2 a Clock in the afternoon precisely.[66]

AT His Majesties Bear-Garden, in Hockley in the Hole, on Wednesday next, being the 19th of March, 1701. A Tryal of Skill will be performed between Joseph Sanderson, the Valiant Trooper, and Francis Gorman, who lately cut down four brave Men, Masters of the Noble Science of Defence: Who will fight, whether a full House or not, for 30 1. the best Man at the sharp Weapons. Beginning exactly at 3 of the Clock in the Afternoon.[67]

Tomorrow being Wednesday the 26th instant, Twill be Tryal of Skill performed with the usual weapons, between these following Masters, viz. Robert Robins, the Plow-man of Monmouth, Master of the Noble Science of Defence, also Master to Thomas Hesgate; and John Davis, Champion of the West, and Master of the Noble Science of Defence. There are also 4 men to fight at Sword for a Hat of half a Guinea price, and 6 to Wrestle for three pair of Gloves, at half a Crown price each pair. To begin at 3 a Clock precisely.[68]

AT His Majestys Bear Garden in Hockley in the Hole, a Tryal of Skill will be performed between these following Masters, to morrow being the 16th instant, viz, John White, who has fought 30 Prizes, besides three bouts at Sword with Mr Edward Bush, and never lost the Stage, and Will of the West, from the City of Salisbury, both Masters of the Science of Defence. Also Mr Gold and Mr Joseph Thomas, have agreed to fight 3 bouts at Sword at the same time. To begin at 3 of the Clock precisely.[69]

This Majesty's Bear Garden in Hockley in the Hole, on Friday next, being the 19th of this instant September, 1701. At three of the Clock precisely, (without beat of Drum) will be performed a Tryal of Skill between these following Masters, *Thomas Cook*, Butcher of Gloucester, at the request of several Gentlemen, and in vindication of my self, being reported a Coward by this *John Munslow*, who fought Mr *John Worly* at the *George Inn* in *Holbourn* for 20 Guineas; and *John Munslow*, Needlemaker from Chichester, both Masters of the Noble Science of Defence, to exercise the usual Weapons. After which two Scholars are to fight 4 bouts at Sword in vindication of their matters.[70]

## "ALMOST CHOP'D ONE ANOTHER to MINC'D MEAT", 1701

The Envoy from *Morocco* with his Lacquer'd-fac'd Attendance, has lately done his Majesty's Bear-garden the Honour of his Presence, in order to see a Tryal of Skill perform'd between two eminent Masters of the Noble Science of Defence; who, for the Credit of the English Nation, almost chop'd one another to minc'd Meat, giving such a bloody Entertainment to the Barbarian Spectators, that they hoop'd and hollow'd to express their Satisfaction, as if they had been Hunting an Estrich...As the two Fellows were thus Dialoguing, one of the Gladiators gave his Adversary such a Chop in the Noddle, as if he had design'd to have cleft it, as a Boiling-cook does a Sheep's Head for the Porridge-pot, which occasion'd such a Shout, that had a Regiment of City-cuckolds, upon a grand

66 *The Post Man and The Historical Account*, January 4, 1701.
67 *The Post Man and The Historical Account*, March 17, 1701.
68 *The Post Man and The Historical Account*, March 22, 1701.
69 *The Post Man and The Historical Account*, April 12, 1701.
70 *The Post Man and The Historical Account,* September 16, 1701.

Training-day, taken the Dunghill in *Bunhil-fields*, to show the Mob the Policy of War, they could not have exprest more Joy for their mighty Success over the Heap of Sir-reverence, than was shown here in Contempt of the Victim, and Honour of the Conqueror.[71]

## A PROCESSION of SCARRED GLADIATORS, and a POEM, 1703

No sooner had these [coaches] dispersed themselves towards the several Places they were Bound to by their Fares, but one of the Prize-Fighting Gladiators from *Dorset Garden* Theatre, where he had been exercising the several Weapons of Defence with his Bold Challenger upon a clear Stage, without Favour, was Conducted by in Triumph, with a couple of Drums to Proclaim his Victory, Attended with such a parcel of Scarified Ruffians, whose Faces seem'd to be as full of Cuts as a Plow'd Field of Furrows; some of their Countenances chop'd into the Form of a *Good-Fryday* Bun, with Cuts cross one another, as if they were Markt out for Christian Champions: Others having as many Scars in their Bear-Garden Physiognomies, as there are Marks in a Chandler's Cheese, Scor'd out into Penniworths. These were hem'd in with such a cluster of *Journeymen Shooemakers*, Weavers and Taylors, that no Bayliff from an Inns-of-Court Bog-House, or a Pickpocket carrying to be Pump'd, could have been Honour'd with a greater Attendance. Tho' this, the Victorious Combatant, came off with Flying [colours], yet 'twas with Bloody Colours; for by the Report of the Mob, like a true Cock, he won the Day after he had lost an eye in the Battle. They mauld one another stoutly, to the great satisfaction of the Spectators. I think, it will not be amiss, if in this place I present the Reader with a Character of a Prize-Fighter, it being properly enough introduced, I have therefore thought fit to put it into Lyrick Verse, as follows.

> Bred up in th' Fields near Lincolns-Inn,
> Where Vinegar Reigns Master;
> The forward Youth does there begin,
> A Broken-Head to Lose or Win,
> For Shouts or for a Plaister.
>
> For North, or West, he does Contend,
> Sometimes his Honour Loses,
> Next Night his Credit is regain'd,
> Thus Fights till harden'd in the End,
> To Bloody Cuts and Bruises.
>
> When at his Weapons grown expert,
> By Bangs and rough Instruction,
> To make a Tryal of his Heart,
> At Sharps he doth himself exert,
> And Dallies with Destruction.
>
> Proud of his Courage and his Skill,
> No Champion can out-Brave him,
> He dares to Fight, yet Scorns to Kill,
> He Guards so Well, and Lives so Ill,
> That few know where to have him.

71 *A Pacquet from Will's: or a New collection of original letters on several subjects. Written and collected by several hands.* (London: Sam. Briscoe, 1701), 21-22.

He Glories in his Wounds and Scars,
Like any Flanders Souldier,
And as one Talks of Forreign Wars,
The t'other Boasts of Hockly Jars,
Wherein no Man was bolder.

He Fought before some Duke or Lord,
With hardy Tom the Weaver:
And Cut him off the Stage at Sword,
The Duke his Manhood to reward,
Presented him a Beaver.

With Lies he tells his Bloody Feats,
And Bounces like a Bully,
Tho' all his Prizes were but Cheats,
Yet when he with a Coward meets,
He knows he has a Cully.

Thus backs in Jest, and finds at best,
But little Money coming,
And when his Youthful Days are pass,
His only Refuge is at last,
To follow Theft, or Bumming.[72]

## A GLADIATOR TRIED for MURDER, 1703

*The Trial and Behaviour of* THOMAS COOK *who was executed for the Murder of* JON COOPER,
*a Constable, in May-Fair.*

At the sessions held at the Old Bailey, on the 2nd of May, 1703, Thomas Cook was indicted for the murder of John Cooper, a constable, by giving him a wound with a rapier, in his body, near the left pap, on the 12th of May, 1702; of which wound he languished till the 16th of the same month, and then died.

Some of the evidences swore that, in pursuance of her Majesty's proclamation for the suppressing vice and immorality, the justices issued their warrants to the high constable, and he sent his summons the other constables, who accordingly assembled, and going to May Fair, a great disturbance arose; and some of the constables having seized the prisoner's wife, while he was at his own house, it came to his knowledge, and he swore that he would have the blood of some of them before he left the fair: hereupon he shut up his house, and going into the fair, he, with a drawn sword in his hand, and a mob of about thirty soldiers, and other persons, got over a bank, and stood in defiance of the constables, huzzaing, and throwing brickbats at them: they then pursued the constables to the sheep-pens, and Mr. Cooper being behind the rest, they overtook him, and cut and wounded him so that he died.

They deposed that the prisoner, had, after the sword, a constable's staff in his hand, and that the mob, over-powering the constables, had an opportunity of escaping; but that the constables having information that the prisoner was the person who killed Cooper, went in search of him, and three days afterwards met him in their way to

---

72 Edward Ward, *The london-Spy compleat, in eighteen-parts, By the author of The trip to Jamaica* (London: Printed and sold by J. How [etc.], 1703), 426-428.

the fair, when he drew his sword, made several passes at them, waved his sword over his head, ran into the fair, and made his escape.

The prisoner now went over to Ireland; and an evidence deposed, that while he was there, talking in a public house, with a person who taught the use of the small sword, he swore very profanely; upon which the publican censured him, and told him there were persons in the house who would take him up for it; whereupon the prisoner said, "Are there any of the informing dogs in Ireland? We in London drive them; for at a fair called May-fair, there was a noise which I went out to see: there were six soldiers and myself; the constables played their parts with their staves, and I played mine; and when the man dropped, I wiped my sword, put it up, and went away."

Cook having several times told of this exploit in a boasting manner, was at length apprehended and sent to Chester, from whence he was removed, by *Habeas Corpus*, to London, and brought to his trial.

The evidence against him being finished, he in his defence said, that at the time of the murder, he was disabled, having fought a prize on the 29th of April preceding, in which he was so much wounded, that it was extremely unlikely he should be concerned in such an affair. With regard to the woman whom they called his wife, he disowned her, saying she was only his bar-keeper, and that as soon as she returned, she shut up his house, and went to another. Notwithstanding all he could say, as the evidences swore positively that he was the man who committed the murder, the Jury brought him in guilty.

Thomas Cook, the prize-fighter, who was generally known by the name of the Gloucester Butcher, said he was about thirty-five years of age, and born of honest parents, in the city of Gloucester; from whence he came up to London, where, being bound apprentice to a Barber-Surgeon, he served two years, and then running away, went into the service of Mr. Needham, but did not stay long with him, for his mother sent for him down into the country, telling him that a gentleman's service was no inheritance.

He now set up the trade of a butcher in Gloucester, after which he kept an inn, and then turned grazier, being very much unsettled in his mind what employment to follow. At length he turned prize-fighter, a profession which he said the pride of his heart led him to, as he apprehended that there was not in the world a more courageous man than himself.

As to the crime for which he was to die, he positively denied it; saying that he had no sword in his and on the day the constable was killed, nor was in the company of those who killed him. While under sentence of death he gave signs of the utmost contrition for the sins of his past life, and acknowledged that upon the whole he had been very wicked, that he had been an adulterer, a profane swearer, a drunkard, and a sheep-stealer. Having, at his own desire, received the sacrament, on Wednesday the 21st of July, he was carried from Newgate towards Tyburn, with the rest of the criminals who were then to suffer: but when he was got as far as Bloomsbury, there came reprieve for him till the Friday following; upon which he was carried back to Newgate, and when the Ordinary returned from attending the execution of the other prisoners, he went to visit him in the condemn'd-hold, where he found him at prayers, in which he appeared to be very earnest and devout. He told he Ordinary that he was not affected with this temporal life, and that he would have been well contented to have died with his fellow-prisoners; but as it appeared otherwise, he was very desirous of having attended them to the place of execution, that he might have joined in prayer with them; but this the officers would not permit. His friends now flocked to Newgate to visit him, and would have made merry with him on his reprieve but he would not indulge the least levity, and would accept of no company but such as could assist him in his devotions, being earnestly desirous of improving is time to the purpose of his eternal salvation.

On the Friday morning a farther reprieve was brought till Wednesday, the 11th of August, on which day he was attended to the place of execution by the Ordinary, where he read the following speech and prayer, and sung the hymn.

*His Speech, Prayer, and Verses.*

Gentlemen, I thought it convenient to give you an account of my life and conversation, which is as followeth.

"Gentlemen,

"I was a young man that was well educated, and well brought up, and come of very honest parents, and about the age of 15, was put apprentice to a barber-surgeon in London; and after the serving of two Years, or, thereabouts, I ran away from my trade, and afterwards lived with Esquire Needham, who was page of hononur to the late King William; but my dear mother told me, that a gentleman's service was no inheritance, and so desired me to come home and settle. Accordingly I went to Gloucester, and there set up the trade of a butcher, which was the calling of my forefathers; and I followed that trade for several years, and served master of the company of butchers, in the said city of Gloucester. But being too much emboldened with courage, I thought no man a better man than myself; I took up the sword, and followed the sport of prize-playing for several years, which practice has proved prejudicial to me. And I desire all young men to take warning by me, and never meddle with any such idle practice; but let their honest calling be whatever it will, mind that they serve God, and keep good company. For here I shall give you an account of the ill consequence and tendency of such idle and wicked practices. First, it is displeasing to God, to have his image scarified after such a manner. Secondly, it brings a man to a correspondence with ill company, and ill company takes a man off from his duty of serving God, and makes him to follow those vices that I have been guilty of myself; as, breaking the Sabbath, swearing, cursing, drunkenness, lewdness, and other like debaucheries. But as to what I die for, I do declare before God, and all the world, I die innocent. There was one witness deposed, on oath, that he saw me lock up my doors, and go down towards the fair with a sword in my hand: and there was one Jonathan Sheppard declared upon oath, that he saw me in the middle of the mob, with a naked sword in my hand: and there was a beadle declared also upon oath, that he saw me with a sword in my hand, bloody: and there was one Mr. Deering, who, in like manner, declared upon oath, that I told him in Ireland, that when the constable dropt, I wip'd my sword, put it up, and went away, which I declare, I never said, nor spoke any such words to him in all my life. And furthermore I do declare, as I expect mercy from God, I had no sword in my hand in the fair that day, and did not so much as lift up my hand, either for, or against any person, when the constable was kill'd.

"Gentlemen, I must desire you not to reflect on Mr. Gorman, for he is very innocent of what they have charged him with, concerning me. But since it is my misfortune to die this shameful death, I must look upon it as an affliction from God Almighty, for my worldly sins. As for those false witnesses that swore my life away, I do freely forgive them with all my spirit; and I hope God will forgive them also. And, as for all whom I ever wrong'd in my life, I do hope they will freely forgive me, as I do freely forgive all the world. So gentlemen, I bid you an eternal farewell, and shall now conclude with this my prayer."

*His Prayer.*

"Almighty God! I humbly beseech thee to bless our most gracious sovereign lady Queen Anne, and guide her by thy good spirit, that the may do always that which is righteous in thy sight. And I beseech thee, O Heavenly Father, that thou wouldst be pleas'd to give her that sight; as that the may foresee her enemies; and arm her so with thy defence, that the may not fear the power of any adversaries: and I beseech thee, O Lord! give unto her a long and happy reign, and after this life, a crown of glory with thee in thy Heavenly Kingdom. And I likewise beseech thee, O Lord! to bless thy Holy Catholic Church, and especially that purest part of it, the Church of England, and give unto it the same honour, power, and glory, as it had heretofore; and let not those who dissent from it, ever have that power to trample it down: And furthermore I beg of thee, O Lord! that if any of those dissenters should in any wise ever rise in rebellion against our gracious Queen and Church, that thou wouldst abate their pride, asswage their malice, and confound their devices: and so let the Church of England remain and flourish unto the world's end. And finally, I beseech thee, O Lord, to pour down thy blessing upon my whole family, and enable them to bear my death, (as by thy grace I do) with patience and resignation; and grant that this my death may be a joy and comfort to them, and a warning to the world. And Lord Jesus! I beseech thee to forgive all my enemies, especially those who swore false against me; for thou knowest, O Lord! I die innocent of that bloody fact, for which I am condemned. But my sins have provok'd thee to deliver me up a prey to the enemy. Lord! I beseech thee, that this my shameful death may, through the merits of the blood of Christ, and Sanctification of thy grace, make an attonement to thee for my worldly sins; that as I die here, so I may live eternally with thee hereafter. And now I come again to beg mercy for myself, intreating thee, O Heavenly Father! to have mercy on my poor soul, for thy dear Son's sake, my Lord and Saviour JESUS CHRIST: into whose hands I commend my spirit. Amen."

*His Verses in Answer to the Bell-Man's, the Night before the Execution.*

THOU art the bell-man for this night,
Who com'st to let me know,
That on to-morrow I'm to die,
And be a public show.

*What follows was sung by him at the Tree.*

I Hope my death will warning give,
  To all that here attend,
And by my sad example may,
  Your lives learn to amend.
Amend your lives, young men, I pray,
  And do no more offend,
That great and mighty God above,
  Whose kingdom has no end.
He's a God that merciful is,
  To all that do believe,
In Jesus Christ his only son;
  Who will our sins forgive.
Pray do repent of all your sins,
  Before it be too late;
And beg the help of God above,
  For Jesus Christ his sake.
Who suffer'd death upon the cross;
  To make a recompence,
To all that do in him believe,
  Before he did go hence.
In him I do put all my trust,
  Whose mercy is full sure,
Hoping my soul with him shall dwell;
  Henceforth for evermore.   Amen.

"This I writ as my last farewell;
Hoping my soul with Christ shall dwell." Amen.
    THOMAS COOK.

He was executed at Tyburn on Wednesday the 11th of August, 1703.[73]

73 *The Tyburn chronicle: or, villainy display'd in all its branches. Containing an authentic account of the lives, adventures, tryals, of the most notorious male factors. From the year 1700, to the present time. Vol. 1* (London: J. Cooke, [1768]), 50-57.

*Fig. 4. 19th century engraving of the 1689 Boston revolt in New England, showing the colonists' arrest of Governor Sir Edmund Andros.*

# II.

## GLADIATORS *in the* AMERICAS: 1687 – 1720

### NEW ENGLAND

*T*he Puritan government of New England did not look fondly upon recreational activities that involved combat or violence of any kind. However, the extant evidence shows that the general populace frequently failed to live up to those sentiments. In 1680, a Dutch visitor named Jasper Danckaerts observed, "Drinking and fighting occur [in New England] not less than elsewhere; and as to truth and godliness, you must not expect more of them than of others."[74]

Perhaps, then, it should come as little surprise that the practice of the stage gladiators appeared in Massachusetts during the late 1680s. This was undoubtedly due to the influx of British soldiers who accompanied Sir Edmund Andros to the colony, during the latter's brief tenure as Governor of the short-lived "Dominion of New England in America" (1686-1689), which was an attempt by England to re-assert control over the increasingly disobedient colonial populace.

During April of 1687, the Puritan firebrand and witch-hunter Increase Mather recorded in his diary that,

> Sword playing was this day openly practised on a Stage in Boston & that immediately after ye Lecture, so yt the Devil has begun a Lecture in Boston on a Lecture-Day which was set up for Christ...[75]

This combat took place only a few days after a massive celebration, by Andros's troops, of the anniversary of King James II's coronation, which involved fireworks and other festivities—celebrations which the Puritan clergy disapproved of. A Boston colonist and merchant named Samuel Sewall witnessed some of the events surrounding

---

74  Jasper Danckaerts, *Journal of Jasper Danckaerts, 1679-1680* (New York: Charles Scribner's Sons, 1913), 274- 275.
75  *Proceedings of the Massachusetts Historical Society, 2nd Series, Vol. XIII*, 411.

*this stage combat, and the colorful, ritualistic parade that preceded it:*

Friday, 22. Two persons, one array'd in white, the other in red, goe through the Town with naked Swords advanced, with a Drum attending each of them and a Quarter Staff, and a great rout following as is usual. It seems 'tis a chaleng to be fought at Capt. Wing's next Thorsday.[76]

*Sewall's comment that this parade was taking place "as usual" suggests that undocumented challenges to combats of the same nature had taken place previously in New England, and had become a frequent occurrence. Again, three days later, he resumed writing in his diary:*

Monday, Apr. 25. Another Challenge goes with his naked Sword through the Street with Hitchborn Drummer, and a person carrying a Quarter Staff.[77]

*And again, in another three days:*

Apr. 28. After the Stage-fight, in the even, the Souldier who wounded his Antagonist went accompanied with a Drumm and about 7 drawn Swords, Shouting through the streets in a kind of Tryumph.[78]

*The custom was not to endure in New England. In 1689, dissatisfied with Andros's pro-Anglican policies and oppressive reign, the local Puritans overthrew the governor in what became known as the Boston Revolt, which resulted in the Puritans reasserting local control. After this time, no further reports of gladiatorial combats appear in the records.*

CRESCENTIUS MATHERUS.
Ætatis Suæ 85. 1724.

Fig. 5. Increase Mather, the Puritan firebrand who wrote bitterly of gladiatorial fights in New England.

However, in 1794, a sensational story appeared in the annals of Massachusetts, looking back at an event that supposedly occurred during the late 1660s, prior to even the time of the Boston Revolt. The tale tells of a fencing master who erected a stage on Boston Common, "defying any one to a combat with swords." The somewhat fanciful account involves William Goffe, a regicide and former major-general in Cromwell's army, who had fled the restoration of Charles II to the relative anonymity of New England. Goffe, who had ventured out of hiding in disguise, now approached the stage and challenged the fencing master to fight. Wrapping a huge cheese in a napkin for a shield, and, arming himself with a mop, Goffe engaged the fencing master, skillfully receiving the thrusts of his opponent's sword into the cheese and thwarting the master's attacks one after another. Angry and humiliated, the fencing master took up a broadsword and charged, when Goffe exclaimed, in a serious tone,

---

76  Samuel Sewall, *The Diary of Samuel Sewall, 1674-1729. Newly edited from the ms. at the Massachusetts Historical Society by M. Halsey Thomas, Vol. 1* (New York: Farrar, Straus and Giroux, 1973), 173.
77  Ibid, 175.
78  Ibid, 175-176.

'Stop, sir; hitherto, you see, I have only played with you, and not attempted to harm you; but if you come at me now with the broad-sword, know that I will certainly take your life.' Goffe's firmness alarmed the fencing-master, who exclaimed, 'Who can you be? You must be either Goffe, Whalley, or the devil, for there was no other man in England could beat me.'[79]

*Although the accuracy of the Goffe tale is highly questionable, one is struck by the fact that such fencing-stages were indeed erected in late seventeenth century Boston, and that at the very least, this tale may have been inspired by an actual incident or stage-fights that had taken place during the period.*

## THE CARIBBEAN

*The tradition of the stage gladiators was exported to other British colonies in the Americas as well. Published in 1700, the following challenge indicates that gladiatorial combats had already taken place in the Caribbean in significant numbers:*

Tomorrow being *Wednesday* the 4th of this instant *September*, a Tryal of Skill is to be performed at his Majesty's Bear Garden in Hockley in the Hole, between *Thomas Steeper,* lately come from the *West Indies,* and who fought several Prizes there, Master of the Noble Science of Defence, and *Edward Gadbee* of *London*, Salesman, well-wisher to the said Science of Defence. Also ten young men to fight to divert the company.[80]

*In 1709, a stage-fighter named George Gray, skilled at multiple weapons, appeared at the Bear Garden in London. It was announced:*

At the Bear Garden in Hockley in the Hole.
   A Tryal of Skill to be Performed between two Profound Masters of the Noble Science of Defence on Wednesday next, being this 13th of the instant July at Two of the Clock precisely.
   I, George Gray, born in the City of Norwich, who has Fought in most Parts of the West Indies viz. Jamaica, Barbadoes, and several other Parts of the World; in all Twenty five times, upon a Stage, and was never yet Worsted, and now lately come to London; do invite James Harris, to meet and Exercise at these following Weapons...[81]

*Although we have been unable to find firsthand accounts of such combats in the Caribbean, these challenges strongly suggest a widespread presence of stage combats there. The final such challenge we have been able to find (that is, mentioning gladiatorial combats in the Caribbean) comes from 1730, and involved one Robert Carter of the West Indies, who brought with him an Ironwood staff from St. Dominico\*, with the intention of it being used against an Irish shillelagh:*

At Mr. FIGG's GREAT ROOM, At his House, the Sign of the City of Oxford, in Oxford Road, this present Wednesday, the 22d of July, will be a Trial of Skill by the following Masters.
   Robert Carter, lately arrived from the West Indies, Master of the Science of Defence, who formerly fought Mr. Figg, and most of the approved Gentlemen then in Being, with a Bravery and success equal to their mighty Titles, and much improv'd my Talent that way in the Western Islands, by a frequent Exercise of the usual Weapons fought on the Stage; no sooner arrived than I invited the said James Figg to a second Rencounter, at the Time and Place abovementioned,

79  Stiles, Ezra, *A history of three of the judges of King Charles I. Major-General Whalley, Major-General Goffe, and Colonel Dixwell: who, at the restoration, 1660, fled to America; and were secreted and concealed, in Massachusetts and Connecticut, for near thirty years. With an account of Mr. Theophilus Whale, of Narragansett, supposed to have been one of the judges* (Hartford: Elisha Babcock, 1794).
80  *Post Man and the Historical Account,* September 3, 1700.
81  George Thornbury, *Old and new London: a narrative of its history, its people and its places, Volume 2* (London: Cassel, Petter & Galpin, 1880), 308.
\*   Probably a reference to Santo Domingo ("Saint Dominic"), the oldest European city in the Americas, and today the capital of the Dominican Republic. During the eighteenth century, it was often referred to as "Hispaniola."

when he thought himself obliged to decline the Acceptance, by Reason of an Accident in a late Journey in Oxford, whereby his Scapula, or Shoulder-Bone, was dislocated, and recommended me to Mr. Edward Sutton, as the next Man fit to engage me; to which I condescended, and expect him to go through the Weapons, having brought a Staff of Iron-Wood with me from St. Dominico, of such foreign Virtue, that if his Performances be not well corrected by the Sword, its ponderous Weight will bear down all his Courage, a Kentish Man being no more able to survive its touch, than an English Snake can endure the Stroke of an Irish Hazle, &c.

> ROBERT CARTER.

I Edward Sutton, of Gravesend in Kent, who never yet submitted to the Power of any For, Foreign or Domestick, find I have now a Challenge from a Man of War, bearing a Flag of Defiance at his Fore-top-mast Head, which I am afraid he will be obliged to strike upon the first Broadside. I allure him I shall lye by till the Time appointed, and attack him upon a close Wind, when he may expect no Quarter. Were his Staff that of St. Jago, I have a Kentish Crab-tree, which like that of Ar-thar-a-Bland knocks down all before it, making no Difference between a Calf and a Man, but renders its Master, like Robin Hood, chief Ranger of the sword, Britannia's Pride, and Europe's Glory, &c.

> EDWARD SUTTON.[82]

*Once again, Carter's statement that he had "much improv'd my Talent that way in the Western Islands" suggests the presence of a vibrant gladiatorial culture in the Caribbean during the early eighteenth century. Such a culture evidently also produced a number of gladiators of African descent, who traveled to England to fight in the Bear-Garden, as will be seen in detail in Chapter VIII.*

## SOUTH AMERICA

*Though it was likely an anomaly, British stage gladiators also made their way to Peru, the land of the Incas, around the year 1720. The following unusual account appears in William Betagh's* A voyage round the world. Being an account of a remarkable enterprize, begun in the year 1719, chiefly to cruise on the Spaniards in the great South ocean:

They [the Peruvians] have a sort of a play-house where the young gentlemen and students divert themselves after their fashion; for what performances they have in the dramatical way are so mean, that they are hardly worth mentioning, being scripture stories interwoven with romance and obscenity.

It was at this theatre that two English sailors of monsieur Martinet's squadron, fought a prize a little before I came to Lima. They first obtained leave of the viceroy to exercise at the usual weapons; and after the shew-day was fixt, most of the preceding time was taken up with preparatory ceremonies to bring a good house. They each traversed the town by beat of drum in their holland shirts and ribands, saluting the spectators at their windows with a learned flourish of the sword; so that by the extraordinary novelty and manner of the thing, the whole city came to see the trial of skill: some gave gold, but a few less than a dollar. When the company male and female was close packt up together, the masters mounted the stage: and after the usual compliment peculiar to the English nation of shaking hands before they quarrel, they retired in great order and stood upon their guard. Several bouts were playd without much wrath or damage: the design of this meeting being more to get money than cuts or credit, one of the masters had the seasonable fortune to receive a small harm on the breast, which having blooded his shirt began to make the combat look terrible: whereupon the company fearing from such a dreadful beginning that the zele of the combatants might wax too intemperate; and till they were reconciled, no man in the house was safe, unanimously cried out, *basta, basta,* which signifys enough, enough; and so the house broke up. The sailors finding this a better prize than any they ever made at sea, humbly besought his excellency for another trial of skill: but the viceroy and people were all against it, from a religious objection that could never be got over; and that was, lest the fellows should kill one another, die without absolution and be damnd.[83]

---

82  *Daily Post*, July 22, 1730.
83  William Betagh, *A voyage round the world. Being an account of a remarkable enterprize, begun in the year 1719, chiefly to cruise on the Spaniards in the great South ocean* (London: Printed for T. Combes [etc.] 1728), 274-276.

To all Gladiators, and such that Delight in
Scars, Scuffles, *and* Wars, Bloody Hacking *and* Fighting,
*Whose Faces are Honour'd with* Scars *and with* Patches,
*At the* Bear-Garden *won, or in* Drunken Debauches:
*Who value no Danger, at nothing will shrink,*
And sell their own Bloods to get Money for Drink...[84]

84 Edward Ward, *The London-spy compleat, in eighteen parts. The second volume of the author's writings.* (London: J. How, 1709), 105.

## THE BEAR GARDEN.

This was of an irregular form, and probably, before it was used for the purpose of sports, had been literally a garden.—We are not informed when this building was erected, though this and the Circus, denominated the Bull Baiting, appear in Aggas's plan, as well as in Braunii Civitates Orbis Terrarum, both published about the year 1574.—The sports of Bull and Bear baiting were very different among our ancestors, compared with those of the ancient Romans.—The former were contented to enjoy the ingenuity of the victim when chained to a stake, in eluding the attacks and manœuvres of the worrying dogs; whilst the polished Romans enjoyed the sight of their human bestiarii, engaged with wild beasts, and uttering shouts of joy when a limb was torn from either of the devoted combatants.

London, Published Oct.r 11.th 1810, by Rob.t Wilkinson, N.o 58, Cornhill.

*Fig. 6. Engraving of the Bear Garden, ca. 1810. Yale Center for British Art, Paul Mellon Collection.*

# III.

## A DESCRIPTION *of the* BEAR GARDEN: 1715

from *ÆSOP AT THE BEAR-GARDEN*

(excerpts)

In that soft Season when each Hedge and Field,
The Violet, Cowslip, and the Primrose yield;
When the Sun's Heat the Ground so dry had made,
That we might safely sleep beneath a Shade.

I took a Walk my self to disengage,
From all my Cares, Love, and Poetick Rage;
Till growing weary, then it came to pass,
I laid me down on the RELENTING Grass;
Where I fell fast asleep, and as I slept,
The following VISION in my Fancy, crept.

I thought that I was hurry'd through the Air,
To that fam'd Place where Dogs assail the Bear[*];

---

[*] Original note reads: "The Bear-Garden is an ancient Place, dedicated originally to Bull-baiting, Bear-baiting, Prize-fighting, and all other Sorts of Rough Game, and not only attended by Butchers and Drovers, and great Crowds of all Sorts of Mob, but like-wise by Dukes, Lords, Knights, Squires, &c." Preston, 33n.

*Fig. 7. The Bear Garden (at left), shown opposite the Globe Theatre, by Edward John Roberts, 1825. Yale Center for British Art, Paul Mellon Collection.*

Huge Crowds of Mob the Yard incircle round,
And with fierce Mopsticks make the Boards resound.
Promiscuous Yelps of Dogs and Men I heard,
Some from without, some from within the Yard.
Here stood the valiant Masters of Defence,
Who fight with equal Rage for Fame and Pence:
And there the sturdy Butchers in a Ring,
Leading their four-leg'd Champions in a String.
Whilst I this INTELLECTUAL SCENE survey,
A sudden Voice was heard, Make Way, make Way.
Here comes the Duke, with the Embassador,
And this the Voice repeated o'er and o'er.

At this I turn'd about, and staring round,
A Place distinguish'd from the rest I found,[†]
Where none Admittance gain but only those,
That have most Money and the finest Clothes,
There I methought beheld a blazing Star,
Incompass'd round with dreadful Men of War.
The Place was antique, and to make it more,
An *Indian* Carpet cover'd it all o'er.

Next this methought I saw another Place,
Which none but Heroes have a Right to grace,
Inscriptions here of various Names I view'd,[*]
The greater Part by hostile Time subdu'd;
For as the Planks and Posts of Deal decay,
So must these Names of Heroes wast away.
On ev'ry Board and Rail about the Place,
I plainly could some Marks of Worthies trace:
Some old, some new, for all that hither came,
Haggl'd at least two Letters of their Name.
With Charcoal some, but more with Chalk had writ
Their Names, and interspers'd & them with their Wit:
But these I saw the next that came deface,
And scribble their own Nonsence in their Place...

A Quarrel rose, and the two Champions strip'd,
Naked as Thieves and Whores at Cart's-Arse whip'd,
Fierce was the Combat, and so long it lasted,
'Till the whole Strength and Breath of both was wasted:
When smeer'd with Blood and Dirt all black and blue,
They breath awhile, and then the Fight renew;
With Head and Fist and ev'ry other Way,
That ancient Boxers held to be fair Play.[‡]
These two young hardy Warriours strove so long,
Till diff'rent Fears and Hopes divide the Throng:
Some for the Honour of *Clare-Market* bawl,
And some as loud for that of Leaden-Hall,
'Till the whole Crowd promiscuously engage
The Poor, the Rich, the Valiant, and the Sage...[85]

---

†   Original note reads: "This Place is peculiar to the Persons of Quality, and distinguish'd by an old Piece of Tapestry-Hangings, into which none are admitted under Half a Crown, and some pay more." Preston, 33n.

*   Original note reads: "The Posts all over the Gallery are haggled full of the Names of ancient and modern Spectators, and seem, according to Mr. *Pope*'s Description, not much unlike the Walls of his Temple of Fame, upon which Account I have ventured to make use of the Expression." Preston, 34n.

‡   In 1713, Sir Thomas Parkyns, who lectured at Figg's Amphitheatre, describes "boxing" as involving head butting, punching, grappling, and eye-gouging. Sir Thomas Parkyns, Προγυμνάσματα. *The Inn-play: Or, Cornish-hugg Wrestler* (Nottingham: William Ayscouh, 1713), 27. See also Chapter XVI of the present book, page 200.

85   Preston, 1-12, 18.

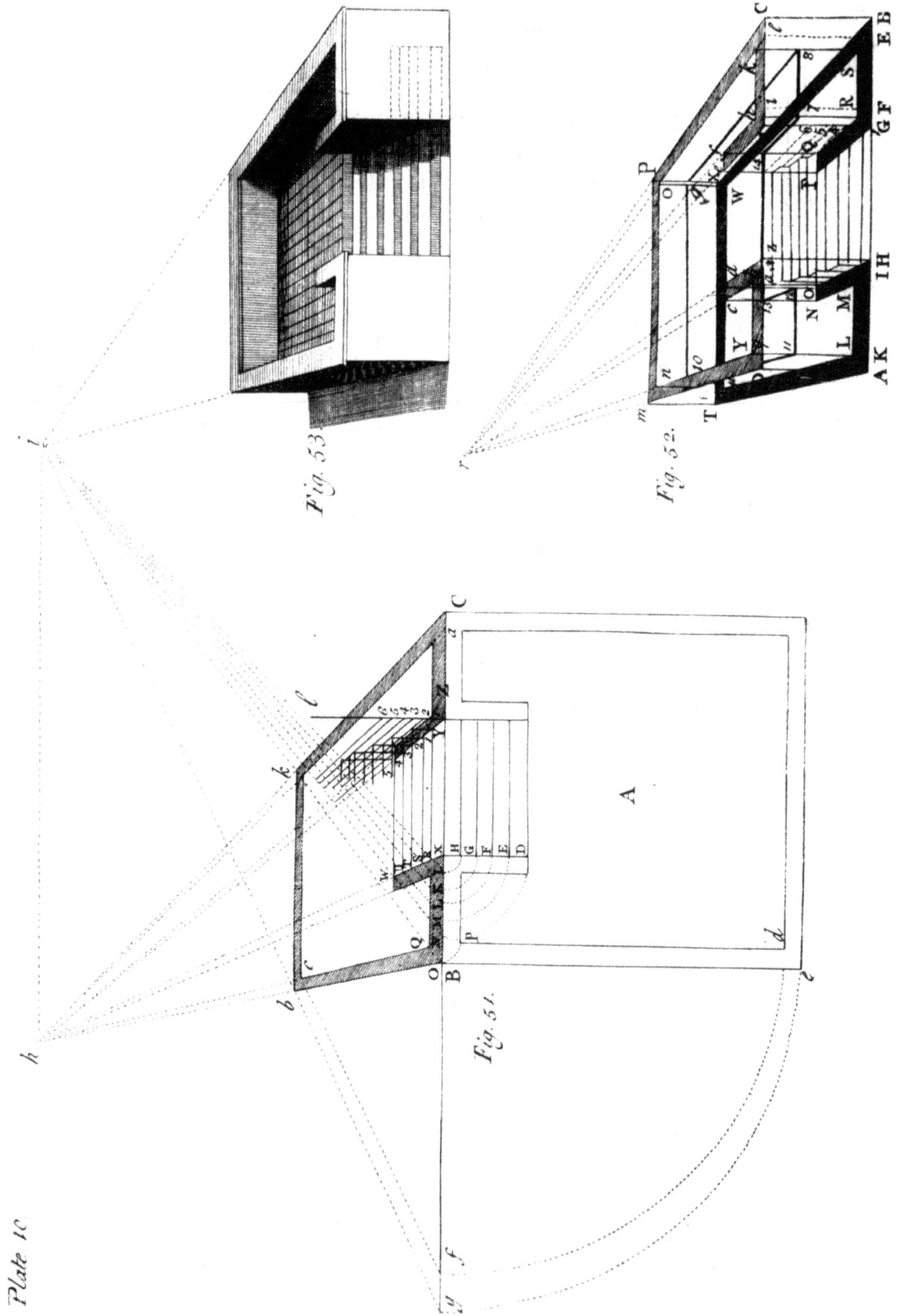

*Fig. 8. William Halfpenny's Plate 10, containing the design for a gladiatorial stage, 1731.*

# IV.

## PLAN *of a* STAGE *for the* MASTERS OF DEFENCE

### PLATE X.

*F*IG. LI. is the Plan of a stage for Masters of Defence to decide their Combats in. To find its Perspective Plan; first, draw the Geometrical Plan A, fix the Points of sight, and Distance $h$ and $i$; draw the occult Lines B$h$= N$h$=I$h$=X$h$=Y$h$=Z$h$=$ah$ and C$h$; take B$e$, and set it to $g$, draw the Line $gi$, which gives the Point $b$, draw the Line $bk$; take N$d$, and set it to $f$; draw the Line $fi$, which cuts the Line $h$N, at $c$, and gives the Perspective Width of the back Wall. Take NP, set it to O, draw the Line B$i$, which cuts the Line N, at Q, and gives the Width of the front Wall. To draw the steps, take XH, and set it to I. XG, to K. = XF, to L, = XE, to M, and XD, to N, draw the Lines I$i$=K$i$=L$i$=M$i$, and N$i$; and where they cut the Line $h$X, as at RSTU and W, gives the Perspective Widths of the steps, which draw parallel to the Base BC, and the Plan is finish'd.

*To draw the Perspective Elevation of the stage.*

*FIG.* LII. Draw the Ground-Plan (which in the Example is colour'd Black) by the Rule laid down in the foregoing Example; and set up the intended Heights AD and BC. Draw a Line from C, to D, with a Pencil, or the like; then draw the Perpendiculars BC, and E$l$, as far distant from each other as the Geometrical Thickness of the Wall; also F$i$, and G$g$, =HZ, and I$a$, =K$q$, and AD; draw the occult Lines C$r$, =$lr$, =$ir$, =$gr$, =$zr$, =$ar$, =$qr$, and D$r$; then from S, raise a perpendicular Line to touch the Line $lr$, at k; also from R, to touch the Line $ir$, at $h$; from M, to touch the Line $ar$, at b; from L, to touch the Line $qr$, at $y$; from Q, to touch the Line $ir$, at $f$; from P, to touch the Line $gr$, at e; from O, to touch the Line $zr$, at $d$; from N, to touch the Line $ar$, at $c$; from X, to touch the Line $cr$, at $p$; from W, to touch the Line $lr$, at $o$; from U, to touch the Line $qr$, at $n$; and from T, to touch the Line D$r$, at $m$: then draw the Ink Lines $egcpm$DZ$dcbynokhfe$, which represents the Top of the Wall.

To draw the steps, first draw their Plan between G$p$, and H$o$, then set up their intended Heights, 123456, from G, on the Line G$g$, and draw occult Lines I$r$ =2$r$ =3$r$ =4$r$ =5$r$, and 6$r$; then from the first Division I, draw the upper front Line of the first step, parallel to the bottom Line GH; and from one end of the second Line in the Plan, raise a Perpendicular to cut the Line I$r$, which gives the Perspective Width of the first step; from which, draw a Line parallel to GH, which is the bottom front Line of the second step: continue that Perpendicular Line to touch the Line 2$r$; from which, draw the upper front Line of the second step, and so on. But for the better Explanation, see *Fig.* 5I. where being less crouded with Lines, is laid down more plainly, First, draw $yl$, (which represents G$g$ in Fig. 52.) on which set the six Risings of the steps; and draw the occult Lines I$h$ —2$h$=3$h$=4$h$=5$h$ and 6$h$, then from 12345 on the Plan, raise Perpendiculars, which give the Perspective height and Width of every step; (observe this Example in all kinds of Steps.) The Steps being raised, I am to shew a Line for the Top of the Pavement, which must be level with the upper step; (see Fig. 52.) Continue the upper front Line of the upper step, to touch the Lines Q$f$, and N$c$, (which you see mark'd 13=14) then lay a Ruler on the Points $r$, and 14, and draw the Line 7=14; from 7, draw a Line to 8, parallel to the Base BG; on 8 and $r$, lay a Ruler, and draw the Line 8=9, draw the Line 9—10, parallel to the Base; then lay a Ruler on $r$10, draw the Line 10=11, and the Line 11=12, parallel to the Base AH; then lay a Ruler on 12$r$, draw the Line 12 =13, then will the Lines 7—8—9=10=11=12=13=14, represent the upper Face of the Pavement. See *Fig.* 53. the, finish'd Object.[86]

---

86 William Halfpenny, *Perspective made easy: or, a new method for practical perspective. Shewing the use of a new-invented senographical protractor; together with the draughts of several remarkable places, in and about the cities of Bristol and Bath; in twenty-six copper plates* (London: John Oswald, 1731), 23-25.

# V.

# THE MASTERS

Fig. 9. Trade card depicting Figg's Amphitheatre. The authorship of this etching is uncertain and has been attributed to both William Hogarth and Joseph Sympson. From Samuel Ireland's Graphic Illustrations of Hogarth (1794).

# i.

## TIMOTHY BUCK

*A*lthough not many accounts of—or challenges concerning—Timothy Buck of Clare-market have survived, the available evidence suggests that he was a most renowned and venerable master, having faced the greatest gladiators of his time well into middle and old age. More importantly, he was the mentor of James Figg, widely regarded as the greatest and most celebrated gladiator of all time.

### ACCOUNT BY JOHN GODFREY, 1747

TIMOTHY BUCK was a most solid Master, it was apparent in his Performances, even when grown decrepit, and his old Age could not hide his uncommon Judgement. He was the Pillar of the Art, and all his Followers, who excelled, built upon him.[87]

### BUCK vs. JAMES MILLER, 1712

A Tryal of Skill to be fought at the Bear-Garden in Hockley in the Hole, to Morrow being Wednesday the 16th of July, at 2 of the Clock precisely, between James Miller, Serjeant, (lately come from the Frontiers in Portugal) Master of the Noble Science of Defence, and Timothy Buck, Master of the said Science.[88]

---

87  Capt. John Godfrey, *A Treatise Upon the Useful Science of Defence: Connecting the Small and Back-sword, and Shewing the Affinity Between Them* (London: Printed for the Author, 1747), 40.
88  *Daily Courant*, July 15, 1712.

# CHAPTER V

--------------------------------*Verso pollice vulgi*
*Quemlibet occidunt Populariter.*------------
Juv. Sat. 3. v. 36.
*With Thumbs bent back they popularly kill.*   DRYDEN.

Being a Person of insatiable Curiosity, I could not forbear going on *Wednesday* last to a Place of no small renown for the Gallantry of the lower Order of *Britons*, namely, to the Bear-Garden at *Hockley in the Hole*; where (as a whitish brown Paper, put into my Hands in the Street, informed me) there was to be a Tryal of Skill to be exhibited between two Masters of the Noble Science of Defence, at two of the Clock precisely. I was I was not a little charm'd with the Solemnity of the Challenge, which ran thus:

*I* James Miller, *Serjeant, (lately come from the Frontiers of* Portugal) *Master of the noble Science of Defence, hearing in most Places where I have been of the great Fame of* Timothy Buck *of* London, *Master of the said Science, do invite him to meet me, and exercise at the several Weapons following,* viz.

|                    |                      |
|--------------------|----------------------|
| *Back-Sword,*      | *Single Falchion,*   |
| *Sword and Dagger,*| *Case of Falchions,* |
| *Sword and Buckler,*| *Quarter Staff.*    |

If the generous Ardour in *James Miller* to dispute the Reputation of *Timothy Buck*, had something resembling the old Heroes of Romance, *Timothy Buck* return'd Answer in the same Paper with the like Spirit, adding a little Indignation at being challenged, and seeming to condescend to fight *James Miller*, not in regard to *Miller* himself, but in that, as the Fame went out, he had fought *Parks* of Coventry. The Acceptance of the Combat ran in these Words:

*I* Timothy Buck *of* Clare-Market, Master *of the Noble Science of Defence, hearing he did fight* Mr. Parkes *of* Coventry, *will not fail (God willing) to meet this fair Inviter at the Time and Place appointed, desiring a clear Stage and no Favour.*

Vivat Regina.

I shall not here look back on the Spectacles of the *Greeks* and *Romans* of this kind, but must believe this Custom took its Rise from the Ages of Knight-Errantry; from those who lov'd one Woman so well, that they hated all Men and Women else; from those who would fight you, whether you were or were not of their Mind; from those who demanded the Combat of their Contemporaries, both for admiring their Mistress or discommending her. I cannot therefore but lament, that the terrible Part of the ancient Fight is preserv'd, when the amorous Side of it is forgotten. We have retained the Barbarity, but lost the Gallantry of the old Combatants. I could wish, methinks, these Gentlemen had consulted me in the Promulgation of the Conflict. I was obliged by a fair young Maid whom I understood to be called *Elizabeth Preston*, Daughter of the Keeper of the Garden, with a Glass of Water; whom I imagined might have been, for Form's sake, the general Representative of the Lady fought for, and from her Beauty the proper *Amarillis* on these Occasions. It wou'd have ran better in the Challenge, *I* James Miller, *Serjeant, who have travelled Parts abroad, and came last from the Frontiers of* Portugal, *for the Love of* Elizabeth Preston, *do assert, That the said* Elizabeth is the Fairest of Women. Then the Answer; *I* Timothy Buck, *who have stay'd in* Great Britain *during all the War in Foreign Parts, for the Sake of* Susannah Page, *do deny that* Elizabeth Preston *is so fair as the said* Susannah Page. *Let* Susannah Page *look on, and I desire of* James Miller *no Favour.*

This would give the Battle quite another Turn; and a proper Station for the Ladies, whose Complexion was disputed by the Sword, would animate the Disputants with a more gallant Incentive than the Expectation of

Money from the Spectators; tho' I would not have that neglected, but thrown to that Fair One, whose Lover was approved by the Donor.

Yet, considering the Thing wants such Amendments, it was carried with great Order. *James Miller* came on first; preceded by two disabled Drummers, to shew, I suppose, that the Prospect of maimed Bodies did not in the least deter him. There ascended with the daring *Miller* a Gentleman, whose Name, I could not learn, with a dogged Air, as unsatisfy'd that he was not Principal. This Son of Anger lower'd at the whole Assembly, and weighing himself as he march'd around from Side to Side, with a stiff Knee and Shoulder, he gave Intimations of the Purpose he smother'd till he saw the Issue of this Encounter. Miller had a blue Ribbon tied round the Sword Arm; which Ornament I conceive to be the Remain of that Custom of wearing a Mistress's Favour on such Occasions of old.

*Miller* is a Man of six Foot eight Inches Height, of a kind but bold Aspect, well-fashion'd, and ready of his Limbs: and such Readiness as spoke his Ease in them, was obtained from a Habit of Motion in Military Exercise.

The Expectation of the Spectators was now almost at its Height, and the Crowd pressing in, several active Persons thought they were placed rather according to their Fortune than their Merit, and took it in their Heads to prefer themselves from the open Area or Pitt, to the Galleries. This Dispute between Desert and Property brought many to the Ground, and raised others in proportion to the highest Seats by Turns for the Space of ten Minutes, till *Timothy Buck* came on, and the whole Assembly giving up their Disputes, turned their Eyes upon the Champions. Then it was that every Man's Affection turned to one or the other irresistibly. A judicious Gentleman near me said, I could methinks be *Miller*'s Second, but I had rather have *Buck* for mine. *Miller* had an audacious Look that took the Eye; *Buck* a perfect Composure, that engaged the Judgment. *Buck* came on in a plain Coat, and kept all his Air till the Instant of Engaging; at which time he undress'd to his Shirt, his Arm adorned with a Bandage of red Ribbon. No one can describe the sudden Concern in the whole Assembly; the most tumultuous Crowd in Nature was as still and as much engaged, as if all their Lives depended on the first Blow. The Combatants met in the middle of the Stage, and shaking Hands as removing all Malice, they retired with much Grace to the Extremities of it; from whence they immediately faced about, and approached each other, *Miller* with an Heart full of Resolution, *Buck* with a watchful untroubled Countenance; *Buck* regarding principally his own Defence; *Miller* chiefly thoughtful of annoying his Opponent. It is not easy to describe the many Escapes and imperceptible Defences between two Men of quick Eyes and ready Limbs; but *Miller*'s Heat laid him open to the Rebuke of the calm *Buck*, by a large Cut on the Forehead. Much Effusion of Blood covered his Eyes in a Moment, and the Huzzas of the Crowd undoubtedly quickened the Anguish. The Assembly was divided into Parties, upon their different ways of Fighting; while a poor Nymph in one of the Galleries apparently suffered for *Miller*, and burst into a Flood of Tears. As soon as his Wound was wrapped up, he came on again with a little Rage, which still disabled him further. But what brave Man can be wounded into more Patience and Caution? The next was a warm eager Onset which ended in a decisive Stroke on the left Leg of *Miller*. The Lady in the Gallery, during this second Strife, covered her Face; and for my part, I could not keep my Thoughts from being mostly employed on the Consideration of her unhappy Circumstance that Moment, hearing the Clash of Swords, and apprehending Life or Victory concerned her Lover in every Blow, but not daring to satisfy her self on whom they fell. The Wound was exposed to the View of all who could delight in it, and sewed up on the Stage. The surly Second of *Miller* declared at this Time, that he would that Day Fortnight fight Mr. *Buck* at the same Weapons, declaring himself the Master of the renowned *Gorman*; but Buck denied him the Honour of that courageous Disciple, and asserting that he himself had taught that Champion, accepted the Challenge.

There is something in Nature very unaccountable on such Occasions, when we see the People take a certain painful Gratification in beholding these Encounters. Is it Cruelty that administers this Sort of Delight? Or is it a Pleasure which is taken in the Exercise of Pity? It was methought pretty remarkable, that the Business of the Day being a Trial of Skill, the Popularity did not run so high as one would have expected on the Side of *Buck*. Is it that People's Passions have their Rise in Self-Love, and thought themselves (in Spite of all the Courage they had) liable to the Fate of *Miller*, but could not so easily think themselves qualified like *Buck*?

*Tully* speaks of this Custom with less Horror than one would expect, though he confesses it was much abused in his Time, and seems directly to approve of it under its first Regulations, when Criminals only fought before the People, *Crudele Gladiatorum spectaculum & inhumanum nonnullis videri solet; & haud scio annon ita fit ut nunc fit; cum vero sontes ferro depugnahant, auribus fortasse multa, oculis quidem nulla, poterat esse fortior contra dolorem & mortem disciplina.* \* *'The Shows of Gladiators may be thought barbarous and inhuman, and I know not but it is so as it is now practised; but in those Times when only Criminals were Combatants, the Ear perhaps might receive many better Instructions, but it is impossible that any thing which affects our Eyes, should fortify us so well against Pain and Death.'*[89]

## BUCK vs. DONALD McBANE, 1713 & 1714

A Tryal of Skill to be fought at the Bear-Garden in Marrow-Bone-Fields, at the Boarded House, near Tyburn-Road, on Wednesday, next, being the 20th of May, beginning exactly at 2 a Clock, between Daniel Beane [Donald McBane] from Flanders, Master of the Noble Science of Defence, who lately fought Mr. Miller; and Timothy Buck of Clare-Market, Master of the said Science.[90]

A Tryal of Skill to be fought at the Bear- Garden in Marrow-Bone-Fields the Backside of Soho-Square, at the Boarded-House, this present Wednesday, being the 28th of April, beginning at 3 of the Clock precisely, between Timothy Buck of Clare-Market, Mafter of the Noble Science of Defence, and Daniel Baine [Donald McBane], North Britain, Master of the said Science, without seconds.[91]

## BUCK vs. JOHN PARKES, 1714

A Tryal of Skill to be fought at the Bear-Garden in Marrow-Bone-Fields, the Backside of Soho-Square, at the Boarded House, this present Friday, being the 15th of October, beginning at 3 of the Clock precisely, between John Parkes, and his Brother, Masters of the Noble Science of Defence, against Timothy Buck of Clare-Market and his Scholar James Figg, Masters of the said Science. Note. It was at the Request of several Persons of Quality, who were obliged to attend the Reception of the Princess on Wednesday last, that this Prize was adjourned to this Day. N. B. They begin by times, by reason the Days are short.[92]

## REFERENCES TO BUCK'S DEATH IN THE ARENA, 1729-30

*At some point prior to the publication of the advertisements below, Buck was mortally wounded during a stage-fight against Irish gladiator Rowland Bennet. In 1729, it was noted that Bennet had merely "disabled [Figg's] Master Mr. Buck."[93] The wound appears to have been fatal, however, as the next year, Bennet was described as the one "by whose unfortunate Hand fell that ever memorable Gladiator, Mr. Timothy Buck." At the same time, Figg publicly paid "the greatest Deference and Respect to the Name of my deceased Master, and in Compliance with his surviving Victor, will not fail being as punctual in every Article, as he is in nominating the Hand which gave that fatal Blow; which shall not be forgot..."[94] That June, Bennet was described as "the Demolisher of the*

---

89 *The Spectator,* July 21, 1712.
90 *Daily Courant,* May 18, 1713.
91 *Daily Courant,* April 28, 1714.
92 *Daily Courant,* Oct 16, 1714.
93 *Daily Journal,* May 31, 1729.
94 *Weekly Journal,* April 25, 1730.

*renown'd Mr. Buck.*"[95] *As we have been unable to find a report in print of the fatal combat, its circumstances remain unclear. Below are the complete challenges containing references to this event.*

At Mr. STOKES's AMPITHEATRE, Islington Road, on Monday next, being the 2d of June, will be a Trial of Skill by the following Masters.

Whereas I Rowland Bennet, from the Kingdom of Ireland, Master of the Noble Science of Defence, having fought Mr Figg 19 times, and disabled his Master Mr. Buck; and likewise fought Mr. Sutton two Years ago, and gave him a Cut on the Forehead, and only receiving a small Cut in the Leg, which was by Accident, was to have fought him the second Battle, but he declining, and left the Kingdom and went to North Britain, and made an Excuse he was sent for, I believe more for fear of my Sword than any thing else: I therefore desire him to meet me at the Place above specified where I shall give him to understand, with the utmost Severity, that I am not to be deem'd as the rest of my Countrymen.

I Edward Sutton, from Gravesend, in the renown'd County of Kent, Master of the Science, never did, or will refuse any Master in Christendom, will not fail meeting him a the Place he mentions, and to let him know I never will fly my County for fear of the Sword, making no further Apology but I will endeavour to maintain my Character as I have hitherto gain'd, and to the intire Satisfaction of the Spectators.     Edward Sutton.

The Doors will be open'd at 3 o'clock, and the Masters mount at 5 precisely.

There will be Cudgel-playing as usual.[96]

At Mr. FIGG's Great Room,

*At his House, at the Sign of the City of* Oxford *in* Oxford Road *To-morrow being Wednesday the 29th of* April, *will be a Trial of Skill by the following Masters.*

Rowland Bennet, lately arrived from the City of Dublin, in the Kingdom of Ireland, Master the Noble Science of Defence, by whose unfortunate Hand fell that ever memorable Gladiator, Mr. Timothy Buck, having fought Mr. James Figg One and Twenty Battles already, hereby invite him once more to exercise the usual Weapons of the Stage with me, at the Time and Place above appointed, and that with the utmost Severity he is capable of administring to One, who believes his own Judgment will run parallel, if not exceed, what Fame has reported of his said Antagonist, &c.

Rowland Bennet.

I James Figg, from Thame in Oxfordshire, Master of my Sword, with greatest Deference and Respect to the Name of my deceased Master, and in Compliance with his surviving Victor, will not fail being as punctual in every Article, as he is in nominating the Hand which gave that fatal Blow; which shall not be forgot, if that Fortune yet attends my Genius, which has signaliz'd itself in 264 remarkable Trials, since my first Appearance on the publick Stage, &c.

James Figg.

The Doors will be open at Three, and the Masters mount at Six.

There will be the usual Diversion of Cudgel playing.[97]

AT the Amphitheatre at Hockley in the Hole, To-morrow the 1st July, will be an Engagement between two Famous Lanisterians, Mr. Rowland Bennet from Ireland, and the celebrated inimitable Mr. James Figg, the former of which having been the Demolisher of the renown'd Mr. Buck, and taking a Disgust at the Dialect of the latter, as being disagreeable to the Hibernian Spirit, has summon'd him to prove the same by the language of the Sword; so that a very hot dispute is like to arise for sometime Except their Communication be cut off.[98]

---

95 *Daily Post,* June 30, 1730.
96 *Daily Journal,* May 31, 1729.
97 *Weekly Journal,* April 25, 1730.
98 *Daily Post,* June 30, 1730.

JAMES FIGG

The Mighty Combatant, the first in Fame,
The lasting Glory of his Native Thame.
Rash, & unthinking Men! at length be Wise:
Consult your Safety, and Resign the Prize:
Nor tempt Superior Force; but Timely Fly
The Vigour of his Arm, the Quickness of his Eye.

J. Ellys Pinx.                    J. Faber fecit.

Fig. 10. James Figg by John Ellys, circa 1727-1729. Courtesy of The Lewis Walpole Library, Yale University.

# ii.

## JAMES FIGG

The *Mighty Combatant*, the first in *Fame*,
The lasting *Glory* of his Native *Thame.*
Rash, & unthinking Men! at length be *Wise;*
Consult your *Safety*, and Resign the *Prize:*
Nor tempt Superior *Force*; but Timely *Fly*
The *Vigour* of his *Arm*, the Quickness of his *Eye*.[99]

### ACCOUNT BY JOHN GODFREY, 1747

FIG was the Atlas of the Sword, and may he remain the gladiating Statue! In him, Strength, Resolution, and unparalleled Judgement conspired to form a matchless Master. There was a Majesty shone in his Countenance, and blazed in all his Actions, beyond all I ever saw. His right Leg bold and firm, and his left which could hardly ever be disturbed, gave him the surprising Advantage already proved, and struck his Adversary with Despair and Panic. He had that peculiar way of stepping in, I spoke of, in a Parry; he knew his Arm and its just time of moving, put a firm Faith in that, and never let his Adversary escape his Parry. He was just as much a greater MASTER, than any other I ever saw, as he was the greater Judge of Time and Measure...

I have purchased my Knowledge in the Back-Sword with many a broken Head, and Bruise in every Part of me. I chose to mostly go to FIG, and exercise with him; partly, as I knew him to be the ablest Master, and partly, as he was of a rugged Temper, and would spare no Man, high or low, who took up a Stick with him. I bore his rough

---

99 From a portrait of James Figg by John Ellys. Mezzotint, Sold by Faber at the Green Door in [the] great Piazza Covent Garden and Sold by H. Overton & I. Hoole at the White Horse without Newgate London, [1727-1729].

Treatment with determined Patience, and followed him so long, that Fig, at least, finding he could not have the beating of me at so cheap a Rate as usual, did not show such Fondness for my Company. This is well known by Gentlemen of distinguished Rank, who used to be pleased in setting us together...[100]

## FIGG & BUCK vs. the PARKES BROTHERS, 1714

A Tryal of Skill to be fought at the Bear-Garden in Marrow-Bone-Fields, the Backside of Soho-Square, at the Boarded House, this present Friday, being the 15th of October, beginning at 3 of the Clock precisely, between John Parkes, and his Brother, Masters of the Noble Science of Defence, against Timothy Buck of Clare-Market and his Scholar James Figg, Masters of the said Science. Note. It was at the Request of several Persons of Quality, who were obliged to attend the Reception of the Princess on Wednesday last, that this Prize was adjourned to this Day. N. B. They begin by times, by reason the Days are short.[101]

## FIGG vs. BROADMEAD, 1719

At the Boarded-House in Marybone Fields: On Wednesday next, being the 24th of June, 1719, will be perform'd a Tryal of Skill, by two Masters.

I William Broadmead, lately Serjeant of Dragoons, born at Silverton near Exon in Devonshire, Master of the Noble Science of Defence, and have fought many good Masters in England and Ireland, hearing of the Character of this Brave and Bold Master James Figg, Master of the said Science, to be one of the best Masters in England, do invite him to exercise the usual Weapons with me for 20 Guineas, although I never fought in London, nor never seen him fight.

I James Figg, from Thame in Oxfordshire, Master of the said Science, never thought to mount the Stage any more, but hearing of the Character of this bold Master, will not refuse to fight him at the Time and Place appointed, for 20 Guineas above-mention'd, and do not doubt but to give him, and the Spectators, Satisfaction as usual.

N. B. Each Master finds his own Weapons, and him that giveth most Cuts shall have the 20 Guineas.[102]

## FIGG vs. "GRAY LOCK", 1719

At the Boarded-House in Marybone-Fields; On Wednesday, being the 26th of August, 1719, will be perform'd a Tryal of Skill.

Whereas I Richard Stinson, (commonly known by the Name of Gray Lock) from Dublin in Ireland, Master of the Noble Science of Defence, having a Difference upon the Stage with Mr. James Figg, and his insisting upon the Wound he received to be very foul, do therefore Invite him to fight me for the whole House, and to mount the Stage without Seconds.

I James Figg, Master of the said Science, from Thame in Oxfordshire, who fought the said Stinson, one Bout, and received a Wound, which I do still insist upon to be very foul, and a Report spread abroad, by many People, that I was dead of the said Wound, will therefore (God willing) meet him at the Place and Time appointed, to let him know that I have Life enough in me still to give him sufficient Satisfaction, and to fight upon no other Terms than for the whole House, and without Seconds.[103]

---

100 Godfrey, 40.
101 *Daily Courant,* Oct 16, 1714.
102 *The Original Weekly Journal,* June 20, 1719.
103 *The Original Weekly Journal,* August 22, 1719.

*Fig. 11. Figg entering on horseback at right. Detail from* Southwark Fair *by William Hogarth, 1733. Yale Center for British Art, Paul Mellon Collection.*

## FIGG vs. THOMAS ELLMER of DUBLIN, 1720

At the Boarded-House in Marybone-Fields, on Wednesday next, being the 13th of April, 1720, will be perform'd a Tryal of Skill.

I Thomas Ellmer from Dublin in Ireland, Master of the Noble Science of Defence, who have fought most of the best Masters in England, as Mr. Buck, Mr. Parkes, and several Others, which have been noted, and hearing of the great Character and Bravery of Mr. Figg, do invite him to meet me and exercise the usual Weapons fought on the Stage.

I James Figg from Thame in Oxfordshire, Master of the said Science, which is well known never refus'd the best of Masters that ever yet fought, will not fail (God willing) to meet this bold Inviter, at the Time and Place appointed, and don't doubt but to give as sufficient Proof of my Judgment, as I did on Wednesday last; and each Master finds his own Weapons.

The Doors will be open at Three, and the Master mount at Five.[104]

## FIGG vs. PHILIP MCDONALD, 1723

At the Boarded-House in Marybone-Fields to Morrow being Wednesday, the 4th Day of September, will be perform'd a Tryal of Skill by the following Masters.

Whereas I, PHILIP MCDONALD, Carpenter from Dublin, Master of the Noble Science of Defence, after having attack'd the most celebrated Masters of that Place with Universal Success and Applause, as also an Eminent Master of England, the Particulars of all which I forbear to Instance, because, that as I speak it of myself, it may be censured as Partial: But hearing that Mr. James Figg excels so much all other Masters, that no one is able to put themselves in Competition with him, the great Report of which is spreading itself all over the aforesaid Parts, excited me to come over, to dispute with him that Character, in order for which, I hereby invite him to meet me as above, and Exercise the usual Weapons fought on the Stage.

I JAMES FIGG, from Thame in Oxfordshire, Master of the said Science, who had declin'd Fighting any more, (but upon such emergent Occasions) as indeed I would have done this if. But seeing that no body else will further the Honour of Countries being concern'd, shall not fail to meet the said famous Mr. McDonald, as pre-mention'd, where I shall give him to understand what Character I have gain'd by my assiduous Care and Practice, he shall find no easy Matter to deprive me of, and hope thereby to give to all Spectators, entire Satisfaction.

At the Boarded-House in Marybone-Fields to Morrow being Wednesday, the 11th Day of September, will be perform'd a Tryal of Skill by the following Masters.

Whereas I PHILIP MCDONALD, Carpenter from Dublin, Master of the Noble Science of Defence, who Fought Mr. Figg last Wednesday, but under what Disadvantages (as being altogether a Stranger, and my late Arrival, which I confess was on purpose) I leave to the candid Censure of the Spectators: But for a further Specimen of my Skill (which hitherto has equall'd all I ever met with) that no Cut may be obscur'd, I do once more invite the said Mr. Figg to meet me as above, and exercise the usual Weapons fought on the Stage, in plain Buff, and he that gives the Majority of Cuts to have the whole House.

I JAMES FIGG, from Thame in Oxfordshire, Master of the said Science, who am always ready to acquiesce with any Master's Invitation from whence, or what Place soever they come, upon their own Terms, will not fail to meet the said famous Mr. McDonald, at the Place and Time above specify'd; where, as Skill consists in the Judg-

104 *The Original Weekly Journal,* April 9, 1720.

ment of the Sword, I only desire he will not, as before, Lurk, but exert himself to the utmost, that the Spectators may have an Opportunity of seeing all he is Master of, as also whose Judgment and Skill is superior, which that this Battle may fully determine, to the Satisfaction of all Encouragers and Lovers of the Science, shall (as has always been) be the utmost Care of their humble Servant, *James Figg.* [105]

## A MODEST CHALLENGE, 1723

At the Boarded-House in Marybone-Fields on Wednesday next, the 17th Instant April, will be perform'd a Tryal of Skill by the following Masters.

Encouraged by the Fame that he will acquire, that encounters with Success the famous Mr. James Figg, I WILLIAM FINN, of Ireland, do invite him to meet me at the Place and Time above appointed, and to Exercise with the usual Weapons of the Stage. I desire no favour, and hope to give a general Satisfaction.

I JAMES FIGG, from Thame in Oxfordshire, am ready to meet Mr. William Finn at the Time and Place appointed. I esteem well of him from the Modesty of his Invitation, and hope to behave as becomes me.[106]

## "ENTIRELY DISABLED HIS ANTAGONIST", 1723

Our Modern Gladiators at Marybone on Wednesday last seem'd to be more in Earnest with their Sharps than usual: for after Figg, a noted Master of the Science, had entirely disabled his Antagonist, as his farewell to the Bear-Garden, another of these useful Heroes mounted, and gave a voluntary Challenge to be immediately decided; which was accepted by a Person commonly call'd the Bold Brasier, and, in a few hearty Cuts, his Boldness was defeated.[107]

## FIGG vs. ROBERT CARTER of LONDON, 1724

At the usual Place at Hockley in the Hole, on Wednesday next, being the 29th inst. will be perform'd a Trial of Skill by the following Masters.

Whereas I Robert Carter of the City of London, Master of the Noble Science of Defence, having by Ocular Demonstration found, that our Nation doth afford as good Proficients of the Sword as any other; and for a Specimen of the same, did Invite the Famous Mr. Figg, at the Conclusion of his last Encounter, as the only Person capable of exhibiting a trial thereof; Accordingly, I do hereby Re-invite the said Mr. Figg, that all Encouragers of the Science may be sensible of my Allegations, to meet me as above, and Exercise the usual weapons fought on the Stage.

I James Figg, from Thame in Oxfordshire, Master of the said Science, being not insensible of the Truth of Mr. Carter's Assertions having had the like Demonstration of him, as he of others; as also hearing of his advantageous Improvements, as has not only exceeded all he has experienced of late, but has likewise Equaliz'd him with any, will not fail to meet the said Mr. Carter as above, in order to give him an Opportunity of exerting his utmost Endeavours; and for my own Part shall, as I have always hitherto, do the like, not to recede from my usual Custom, and to give all Spectators intire Satisfaction.

N. B. The Doors will be open at Three, and Masters mount at Six precisely.[108]

---

105 From a clipping in possession of the Westminster City Archives.
106 From a clipping in possession of the Westminster City Archives.
107 *Daily Journal,* August 9, 1723.
108 *The Daily Post,* April 28, 1724.

## FIGG vs. JOHN HOYLE of YORKSHIRE, 1724

At Figg's new Amphitheatre, joining to his House, the Sign of the City of Oxford, in Oxford Road, Marybone Fields, To-morrow the 9th of Sept. will be perform'd a Trial of Skill by the following Masters.

Whereas I John Hoyle, from Beverly in Yorkshire, Master of the Noble Science of Defence, when I disputed with Mr. Figg's Pupil last, the Preference in the Judgment of the Sword, seeing Mr. Figg at the same Time to be disgusted at what (I believe) most of the Spectators thought very reasonable; but that such sinister Means of depressing my Character may not add to the magnifying his own, and not thinking myself inferior to any Master, as also to make Mr. Figg sensible thereof, I do hereby invite him to meet me as above, and Exercise the Weapons in the following manner, i. e. four Bouts at each Order of the Sword, instead of three, and the Staff to be omitted, the Reason of which preceeds from my Incapability of wielding it, by receiving a Wound in my Left Hand in the Service Abroad.

I James Figg, from Thame in Oxfordshire, Master of the said Science, do, and shall always think that to be allowable which shall be thought so by the Encouragers of the Sword; and that it may not be thought that I take more Advantage of any Master than what the Judgment of the Sword affords, I will not fail to meet the said Mr. Hoyle on his own Terms; where, contrary to his above Assertion, I shall endeavour to be as Dextrous as may be, in giving him and all Spectators intire Satisfaction.

N. B. Attendance will be given at Two, and the Masters mount at Four precisely, by reason of a Dispute between two other Masters, Mr. Clarkson, the Old Soldier, and Mr. Stevenson, known by the name of Greylock; who, after the former Masters have ended, will entertain the Spectators with an Exhibition throughout all the Weapons, and which is to be left to their Decision.[109]

AT Figg's new Amphitheatre, joining to his House, the Sign of the City of Oxford, in Oxford Road, Marybone Fields, this Day the 9th of Sept. will be acted a Tragi-Comedy, call'd The Competitors. The principal Parts to be perform'd by the celebrated Mr. James Figg, Oxonian, and Mr. John Hoyle, Eborac, or Yorkshire Professor: The Master of Debate being which of them are the most Emphatical and Excellent in their Performances, it is to be left to (and they are to rise and fall by) the judgment of the then Assembly.

N. B. Attendance will be given at Two, and the Masters mount at Four precisely, by reason of a Dispute between two other Master, Mr. Clarkson the Old Soldier, and Mr. Stevenson, known by the Name of Greylock; who after the former Masters have ended, will entertain the Spectators with an Exhibition throughout all the Weapons, and which is to be left to their Decision.[110]

## "NOT TO BE CONQUER'D BY ANY OF WOMAN BORN", 1726

AT Mr. *FIGG*'s New Ampitheatre, joining to his House, the Sign of the City of *Oxford,* in *Oxford* Road, *Marybone-Fields*, on *Wednesday* next, being the 6th of *April*, will be performed a Tryal of Skill by the following Masters.

Whereas I *James Collins, Cambridge* Professor of the Noble Science of Defence, hearing how the World has been amus'd with the Terrible Name of Mr. *Figg*, which is so highly extolled, as it (*Mackbeth* like) he is not to be Conquer'd by any of Woman born; therefore to make it appear that this Terribleness is only Nominal, as also that there is a *Macduff* still left to attack him, I do hereby invite the said Mr. Figg to meet me as above, and Exercise all he is Master of, at the usual Weapons practis'd on the Stage.

I *James Figg*, Oxonian Professor of the said Science, for the better understanding the said Mr. *Collins*, as being amus'd with this manner of Elocution, will not fail meeting him according to his Invitation; where, if

---

109 *The Daily Post,* September 8, 1724.
110 *The Daily Post,* September 9, 1724.

*Fig. 13. Figg pictured at center, in wig, holding a pair of quarterstaffs, while looking at the fencing master Dubois. From* A Rake's Progress, Plate II *by William Hogarth, 1735. Yale Center for British Art, Paul Mellon Collection.*

instead of the Fate of *Macduff*, he should share that of *Lenox*, it is to be hoped it will be imputed to his own Inadvertency, rather than any Seeking of mine.

N. B. The Doors will be open'd at Two, and the Masters mount at Five exactly.[111]

## FIGG vs. ROBERT LUN, a MILITARY PROFESSOR, 1726

AT Mr. FIGG's New Amphitheatre, joining to his House, the Sign of the City of Oxford, in Oxford-Road, Mary-bone Fields, To-morrow, being Wednesday the 25th of May, will be perform'd a Tryal of Skill by the following Masters.

Whereas I Robert Lun, Military Professor of the Noble Science of Defence, having in all my Observations seen nothing preternatural in the Performances of the extolled Mr. James Figg, notwithstanding the mighty Appellations ascribed to him, which seems to render him infallible: I therefore, to give infallible Demonstration of the Contrary to all who imagine him so, as also to lower this Nautical Swords-man's Topsail, do hereby request him to meet as above, and Dispute the same with me at all he is Master of, or capable of Performing, at the usual Weapons practised the on the Stage.

I James Figg, Oxonian Professor of the said Science, will not fail meeting this Bold Militarian, as abovementioned, in order for a Proof of what he asserts; when, if I make him sensible of his Mistake, he may comfort himself with not being the first; and that every Thing may be agreeable to his Dignity, I shall take Care that nothing shall be acted contrary to the Law of Arms, as also that all may prove to the entire Satisfaction of all Spectators.

N. B. That whereas I James Figg was to have encountred Mr. Sutton as this Wednesday, with his Foot strap'd down, but he having incurr'd the Displeasure of several Noblemen and Gentlemen by his gross and scurrilous Behaviour, I have thought proper to decline having any more to say to him in a publick Way, till by acknowledging his Error he shall regain their Favour. N. B. The Doors will be open'd at four, and the Masters mount between six and seven exactly.[112]

## FIGG vs. ROBERT BARKER the BUTCHER, 1727

*At Mr. FIGG'S Great Room, at his House, the Sign of the City of Oxford, in Oxford-Road, Mary-bone Fields, To-morrow being the 8th of March, will be perform'd a Tryal of Skill by the following Masters.*

WHEREAS I ROBERT BARKER, Butcher, from Dublin, and Professor of the Noble Science of Defence, having in Eighty-five Engagements with the most celebrated Masters in the said Science, given such signal Proofs of my Ability therein, as as have oblig'd them to confess me their Superior: But the Fame of the great and surprizing Mr. FIGG having spread itself as it were universally, stiling him the Inimitable, the Invincible, and such like terrifying Characters, as has served rather to spirit me up with an Emulation of his Performances, than to prepossess me with any Dread of encountering this mighty Hero; for which Reason, and thro' the Instigation of several eminent Persons, as well Masters as others, I have been prevailed upon to come over, to lower the Pride of this hitherto unequal'd English Champion; which, that this Eighty-sixth Battle (as all other heretofore) may not fail of, I do hereby request him to meet as above specified, and try the same at all he is capable of performing at the usual Weapons practis'd on the Stage.

I JAMES FIGG, Oxonian Professor of the said Science, for the Honour of the English Performances rather than any Ambition of my own, or Self-Ostentation, will not fail according with the Request of this yet unparal-

---

111 *The Universal Mercury*, April, 1726.
112 *Daily Post*, May 24, 1726.

lel'd Hero, when I shall communicate to him, in as emphatical Terms as I can, the Difficulty of this Undertaking, and which I don't doubt will determine between him and me any more Debates, or future Controversies whatever.[113]

At Mr. FIGG's GREAT ROOM, at his House, the Sign of the City of Oxford, in Oxford-Road, Mary-bone Fields, To-morrow being Wednesday the 22d of March, will be perform'd a Tryal of Skill by the following Masters.

Whereas I ROBERT BARKER, Butcher from from Dublin, and Professor of the Noble Science of Defence, did, on Wednesday the Eighth Instant, engage the terrifying Mr. James Figg, when, tho' I had not the Superiority, yet I found him neither Inimitable, nor Invincible: Now to convince this unequall'd Hero, and all his Abettors that I am an equal Rival in the Celebracy, of this Noble Science, I do hereby invite him to a Second Performance at the Time and Place above-specify'd; when, if he doth not exhibit the utmost skill he is Master of, I shall show him his Error, by giving a Masterly Stroke to eclipse his Glory.

I JAMES FIGG, Oxonian Professor of the said Science, will not fail according with the Request of this Hibernian Goliath, when I shall communicate to him, in as emphatical Terms as I can, the Difficulty of his Underaking: and which I don't doubt will determine between him and me, any more Debates of Future Controversie whatever, as well as prove to the entire Satisfaction of all Spectators, which has always been my chief Aim.

N. B. Whereas the last three Bouts should be at Quarter-Staff, they will be at Back-Sword, the said Barker not knowing the Staff.

Note, In the last Battle, Mr. Figg gave Mr. Barker two Cuts on the Breast, and one on the Nose, and Mr. Barker gave Mr. Figg one on the head.

N. B. They fight in White Drawers, Shirts, Stockings, and Pumps.[114]

## "The INIMITABLE, the INVINCIBLE", 1727

At Mr. FIGG'S GREAT ROOM,

AT his House, the Sign of the City of Oxford, in Oxford-Road, Marybone Fields, this present Wednesday being the 19th of July, will be perform'd a Tryal of Skill by the following Masters.

Whereas I BRIAN LE BUNN, from Dublin, Master of the Noble Science of Defence, having in several Engagements with the most celebrated Masters in the said Science, given such signal Proofs of my Ability therein as has obliged them to confess me their Superior (particularly Seven Battles with the famous Mr. Parkes) But the Fame of the Heroick Mr. Figg having Spread itself as it were universally, styling him the Inimitable, the Invincible, and such great Characters, as has serv'd rather to Spirit me up with an Emulation of his Performances, than to prepossess me with any Dread of Encountering this mighty Hero: For which Reason, and thro' the Instigation of several Eminent Persons, as well Masters as others, I have been prevail'd upon to come over, to lower the Pride of this hitherto unequal'd English Champion, which, that this Battle (as all other heretofore) may not fail of, I do hereby request him to meet me as above specify'd, and try the fame as all he is capable of Performing at the usual Weapons practised on the Stage.

I JAMES FIGG, Oxonian Professor of the said Science, for the Honour of the English Performances rather than any Ambition of my own, or self Ostentation, will not fail According with the Request of this yet unparallel'd Hero; when I shall communicate to him, in as Emphatical Terms as I can, the Difficulty of this Undertaking, and which I don't doubt (if he won't lurk, but fight up briskly while you can tell Twenty) will determine between him and me any more Debates or future Controversies whatever.

Note, There will be Boxing and Cudgel-playing likewise.[115]

---

113 *Daily Journal,* March 7, 1727.
114 *Daily Post,* March 21, 1727.
115 *Daily Post,* July 19, 1727.

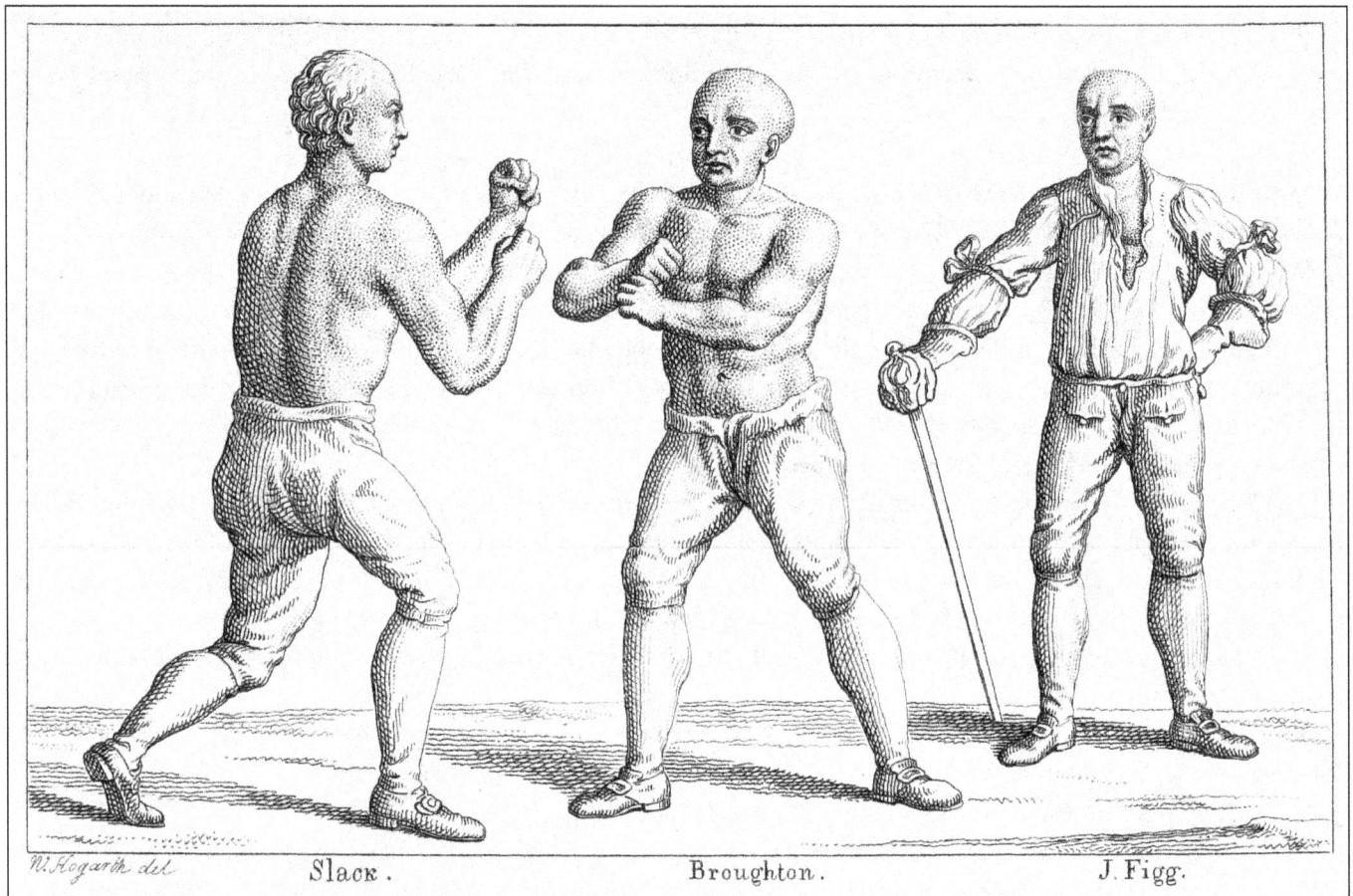

*Fig. 14. Figg shown on right, illustration circa 1750. Courtesy of The Lewis Walpole Library, Yale University.*

ADVERTISEMENT for FENCING & BOXING at the FAIR

(undated)

AT

FIG'S GREAT TIL'D BOOTH,
*On the* Bowling Green, Southwark,
During the Time of the *FAIR*,
(Which begins on SATURDAY, the 18th of SEPTEMBER),
The TOWN will be entertained with the
MANLY ARTS OF
Foil-play, Back-sword, Cudgelling, and Boxing,
in which
The noted PARKS, from Coventry, and the celebrated gentleman prize-fighter, Mr. MILLAR,
will display their skill in a tilting-bout, showing the advantages of *Time* and *Measure*:
ALSO
Mr. JOHNSON, the great Swordsman, superior to any man in the world for his unrivalled
display of the *hanging-guard*, in a grand attack of self-defence, against the all-powerful
arm of the renowned SUTTON.

DELFORCE, the finished Cudgeller, will likewise exhibit his uncommon feats with the *single-stick;* and who challenges any man in the kingdom to enter the lists with him for a *broken-head* or a *belly-full!*

BUCKHORSE, and several other *Pugilists*, will show the Art of Boxing.

To conclude

With a GRAND PARADE by the Valiant FIG, who will exhibit his knowledge in various Combats with the Foil, Back-sword, Cudgel, and Fist.

To begin each Day at Twelve o'clock, and close at Ten.

*Vivat Rex.*

N.B. The Booth is fitted up in a most commodious manner, for the better reception of Gentlemen, &c. &c.[116]

## "HE IS TERRIBLE", 1728

These celebrated Masters of Art are like the famous Mr. James Figg. He is terrible, not because others are weaker, but because They have not practised the same mischievous Weapons. Like Him, they wound and bruise their Fellow-Creatures, and make use of their Dexterity, as He does, though without his Excuse, for the vile Purpose of filling their own Pockets. Happy had it been for the Publick, if they had been confined to the narrow Compass of an Amphitheatre in Tyburn Road![117]

## FIGG vs. MICHAEL BUTLER of KILKENNY, 1728

At Mr. FIGG's GREAT ROOM, at his House, the Sign of the City of Oxford, in Oxford Road, Marybone-Fields, this present Wednesday the 11th of September, will be a Trial of Skill by the following Masters.

Whereas I MICHAEL BUTLER of Kilkenny in Ireland, Master of the noble Science of Defence, hearing of the great Fame Mr. Figg has established in disabling such Numbers of my Countrymen, oblig'd me in Justice to my Country to come over to have a Trial of Skill with him at the Weapons that are usuall practised on the Stage, thinking myself no Way in the least inferior to that terrible Champion, or any of his Countrymen that profess the Science; and do hereby invite him to fight me the Day above-mentioned, flattering myself, that whilst he is pusht up by his former Successes with an over-bearing Opinion of himself, it will be my lot to put a final Stop to his further Progress.

I JAMES FIGG, from Thame in Oxfordshire, Master of the said Science, will not fail meeting this bold Invitor at the Time and Place appointed, where I doubt not but to bestow some of my old Favours on him as well as the rest of his Countrymen, which I hope will give entire Satisfaction to all the Spectators.

N. B. Attendance will be given at Three, and the Masters mount at Five. There will be extraordinary Diversion of Cudgel-playing before the Battles.[118]

---

116 It should be noted that the earliest printing of this notice that we have been able to find is from 1812, therefore, its authenticity is in question. Pierce Egan, *Boxiana; Or Sketches of Ancient and Modern Pugilism; from the Days of the Reowned Broughton and Slack, to the Heroes of the Present Milling Æra! Volume 1* (London: G. Smeeton, 1812), 44.

117 *The Craftsman,* May 25, 1728.

118 *Daily Post,* September 11, 1728.

## FIGG vs. SGT. MASTERSON of GIBRALTAR, 1730

At Mr. Figg's GREAT ROOM, At his House, at the Sign of the City of Oxford in Oxford Road, on Wednesday next, being the 15th of April, will be a Trial of Skill by the following Masters.

MATTHEW MASTERSON, Serjeant, lately arriv'd from Gibraltar, whose Performances need an Encomiums to illustrate my Character, which first Shone in an Advantage over the famous Timothy Buck; then, in some Measure influenc'd Mr. James Fig, whose Judgment in those Days, I presume, might have been call'd in Question by a weaker Hand than mine; after which the pointed Rays of my rising Glory more sensibly affected Mr. John Sparks, Mr. Davenport, and Mr. Benjamin Jennings, three noted Masters, the Second of which I disabled in the Sword Arm, the first Bout at Back-Sword; the latter, whom I fought at Windsor, I must with Regret, own, tasted of such Severity, that the Quality then present seem'd apprehensive Death would have clos'd the Scene of a bloody Entertainment. However, Time having obliterated those Achievements, and, taking Fortune by the Hand, laid the Bays at the Feet of Mr. Figg aforesaid, believing I have a Seniority therein, hereby invite him once more to try his Success with me at the Time and Place above, laying aside the Staff, and deciding the Controversy by six Bouts at single Sword, which will enable me to judge of the Improvement he has made therein, &c.

MATTHEW MASTERSON.

I JAMES FIGG, from Thame in Oxfordshire, Master of my Sword, thinking it a Duty incumbent on every Professor thereof, to comply with the Request of a Gentleman, in Point of Honour, hereby assure the quondam Hero, I shall not fail to divert his Curiosity in so strenuous a Manner as shall compel him to own, that notwith-standing he may have gain'd a Halbert at Gibraltar, the Spanish Monarchy has neither qualified nor commission'd him for Generalissimo of the Sword in England; and that the tedious Catalogue in his vaunting Challenge, is the Product of an unlimited Ambition, which prompts him to this rash Attempt. If the steel of my just Refinement carry its usual Edge, he will find it so proportionate to his foreign Temerity, that he may live to repent it, and serve to adorn those Temples he envies, worthy of the Bays he has no share in, &c.

JAMES FIGG.

There will be a lac'd Hat Cudgel'd for by five Men of Hammersmith against the like Number of Londoners, the former scrutinying their bearing away the last Prize. The doors will be open at Three, and the Masters mount at Six.[119]


The same Day we went to see a Diversion very extraordinary and no where known but in *England*, I mean Combats of Gladiators which they call Prize-fighting, a *Roman* Custom kept up in this Island for near two thousand Years. We found assembled in the Place of Combat a Crowd of Persons of all Ranks. The Theatre where the Combatants fight is in the Middle of a large Hall, and surrounded on all Sides by the Spectators, seated upon Benches raised one above the other to the very Roof. The first Trial of skill was with Sticks, which the English call Cudgels. They use them after the Manner of Hangers, and the Strokes are given with so good Will, that I cannot conceive how they can give each other so many without breaking Arms or Heads, for they fight quite naked. Whoever draws Blood from his Antagonist's Head first, is Conqueror.

After cudgelling, comes boxing. The two Combatants strip, and are naked to the Belt, and the Strokes they give to one another are so violent, that they make the Blood sometimes spout out from the Mouth. I have seen some of them fall, and remain some Moments immoveable, but they soon recovered by the help of Vinegar put to their Nose. Upon which they get up, embrace their Adversary, and fall to Blows, till one or other has quite lost Strength, and sometimes Life itself. This Exercise seemed to me the most violent and dangerous; to which succeeds that of wrestling. You see two lusty well made Fellows approach one another softly, and with Precaution observing one another carefully for a few Minutes, turning round, as it were to discover the weak Part; touching Hough to Hough, and at last grapling, they squeeze and shake one another with a surprizing Force and Agility;

---

119*Daily Post*, April 13, 1730.

and sometimes it is a considerable Time before any Inequality is observed; at length, when Victory has declared itself in Favour of one, he lends a helping Hand to raise the vanquished, and then they fall to it anew, 'till one or other is quite spent.

The last Combat is with the Sword, which is commonly undertaken by *Irishmen*, who, by a publick Challenge, by Way of Advertisement in the News Papers, with a Rodomontade* that makes People laugh, engage themselves to fight with all who dare expose themselves to the cruel Edge of their terrible Sword; and then they give you a List of the rash Fools that have lost their Lives or been wounded by them; so that, take their own Word for it, they are so many *Cæsars* and *Alexanders*, and yet they are almost constantly beat by the *English*, particularly by a certain Prize fighter called *Figg*, who handles a broad Sword with the greatest Dexterity of any Man alive. I have been assured that he has fought publickly more than a hundred Times, without having received any considerable Wound. We were Witnesses that if he received none, he knew how to give.

His Antagonist was an Irish Serjeant, lately come from *Gibraltar*. They both appeared upon the Stage in their Shirts, and their Heads bare, and had a red Ribbon tied about their Arm to hold up the Sleeve of their Shirt. Boldness and Courage, with a Mixture of Calmness appeared in their Looks. *Figg* offered the Serjeant the Choice of Swords, of several that were brought upon the Stage, about two Inches in breadth, and the Points ground off. I had the Curiosity to take one of them in my Hand, and found that it was sharp edged enough to cut off an Arm or a Leg. The Combatants, after shaking Hands, as a Mark of Friendship and Esteem, put themselves in a Posture of Defence, crossed their Weapons, and began a furious Attack. We must not imagine that there was any foul Play in the Case, or that they were not serious, they let fly at one another so heartily, and with such Vigour and Rapidity, that the Spectacle became terrible, and the whole Assembly was in a profound Silence. The Serjeant made a Blow at *Figg*, which cut a pretty large Piece of his Stocking, without touching the Leg. *Figg*, whose Coolness and Judgment were surprizing, felt the Stroke; ho, ho! *said he*, I see thou hast a Mind to my Leg, but take Care of thy own, and with the same Breath whipped off a large Piece of the Calf of his Adversary's Leg, which fell upon the Stage; the general Applause was given to this clean Slash by clapping of Hands, and crying *bravo, bravo, encora, encora,* which is a sort of Approbation that they have learned from the *Italians*. The Serjeant, not able to support himself, sat down and looked at his Blood, which ran in Streams. I was told that they had Powders whose Effect operates a speedy Cure.

We saw several others fight afterwards, who gave and received several Wounds. This Diversion gave us an Opportunity to make several Reflections; it is certain that it has it's Utility, being a sort of School where Youth are formed to Intrepidity, and to the Contempt of Death and Wounds; but, on the other Hand, we agreed, that there was something cruel and barbarous in it. If the Effusion of human Blood is so looked upon as an Evil, even when it is just and necessary, it would seem contradictory to the Laws of Humanity and Nature to make a Diversion of spilling it. Nevertheless this Custom is authorised in *England*, and probably not without strong Reasons in so wise a Government, where every Thing is calculated for the publick Good.[120]


## FIGG vs. PHILIP MACDONALD of DUBLIN, 1730

At Mr. FIGG's Great Room,

At his House, at the Sign of the City of Oxford in Oxford Road, on Wednesday next being the 8th of April, will be a Trial of Skill by the following Masters.

I Philip Mac-Donald, of the City of Dublin, Carpenter, and Master of the Noble Science of Defence, who some Years agone signaliz'd myself in putting my Skill upon the Balance with the celebrated Mr. Figg, when we engag'd Naked, and with equal Ardency, for the Benefit of the whole House, twice facing him in like Manner in

---

* Boastful or inflated talk or behavior.
120 Antoine François Prévost d'Exiles, *The Memoirs and Adventures of the Marquis de Bretagne and Duc d'Harcourt: The wonderful Vicissitudes of Fortune, exemplified in the Lives of those Noblemen, To which is added The history of the chevalier de Grieu and Moll Lescaut. Translated from the Original French by Mr. Erskine, Volume II* (London: T. Cooper, 1743), 228-231.

Fig. 15. Sprawled figure alleged to be Figg, with cuts and patches on head. Detail from William Hogarth's Midnight Modern Conversation, 1733. Yale Center for British Art, Paul Mellon Collection.

the Space of eight Days, with a Bravery suitable to the boasted Vigour of my shining Antagonist; so that I cannot allow him the Superiority of the Sword, unless by a third Proof of his Judgment at the Time and Place above, I am convinc'd of Error by my Fall; it he is pleas'd to accept this Invitation, and it should so happen, my Glory will rise, in falling by his meritorious Arm, &c.

Philip Mac Donald.

I James Figg, from Thame in Oxfordshire, Master of my Sword, knowing the above Proficient, approve his Skill and generous Challenge, and most readily accept the same, being proud it is my Fortune to enter the Lists this Spring with a Person worthy of the Title he gives himself, and whom I look upon as the Flower of his Country; therefore shall not fail to answer him in every Point of his Request, as far as Honour will carry me, and my Sword permit, &c.,

James Figg.

Note, There is a Lac'd Hat to be play'd for by five Londoners, and from Hammersmith and Harrow-the-Hill, to divert the Quality before the Masters mount.

The Doors will be open'd at Three, and the Masters mount at Six.[121]

---

121 *Weekly Journal of British Gazetteer*, April 4, 1730.

## FIGG vs. WILLIAM HOLMES of IRELAND, 1730

We hear, that on Wednesday last, the celebrated Mr. James Figg, whose Courage and Genius in the Sword, has for many Years attracted the Eyes of Europe, fought one Mr. Holmes, the reputed principal Swordsman of Ireland, for 100 Guineas, on most Cuts at Sword and Blows at Staff. The Contest prov'd very sharp, Blood being drawn on both Sides; but, to decide the Odds, both Parties were oblig'd to strip, when the said Mr. Holmes was found to have received five Wounds, Mr. Figg but one, to whom the Money was deem'd fairly won. However, the Loss of the ready Rhino has so chagrin'd his Antagonist, that he has again challeng'd to fight him on Wednesday the 16th Instant, for a larger Sum; Mr. Figg has also accepted the said Challenge, and hopes such Gentlemen who think Mr. Holmes had not fair Play shewn him, or that he is able to obtain more Satisfaction in another Battle, will be pleas'd to back him with their Purses as far as he (Mr. Figg) is willing to answer them, &c.[122]

On Wednesday last a Battle was fought for a very considerable Sum of Money between the Celebrated Mr. James Figg, and Mr. Holmes, the reputed Champion of Ireland, who (before they well engaged) clos'd in with him, and palming his Sword, gave Mr. Figg a slight Wound near the Diaphragma, and another on the Head, which he return'd, by taking a large Oval Piece from the Irishman's Scalp, cutting him also deeply in the Wrist and Brawn of the Hand, and quite out-hilting him every other Way, insomuch that such of the Quality and Gentry who were present, and Judges of the Affair, declared the Conquest in Mr. Figg's Favour, which the opposite Party would have set aside by Mutiny; but Superior Force obliged them to submit to Reason, and they went off much discotented, and are spurring on Mr. Holmes to fight him once more, of which further Notice will be given in this Paper.[123]

## "The SHARPEST and MOST BLOODY TRIALS of SKILL KNOWN in the MEMORY of MAN"

At Mr. FIGG's GREAT ROOM, At his House, the Sign of the City of Oxford, in Oxford-street, this present Wednesday, the 14th Instant,

SUCH of the Nobility and Gentry who shall be pleas'd to honour the fame with their Appearance will be entertain'd in an extraordinary Manner, by a Third and Decisive Trial of Skill between the two first Masters in Europe, who are determin'd to discountenance all Pretenders, by an unprecedented Bravery, and such a matchless Genius, that it shall be no Question hereafter, whether Britannia or Hibernia be sole Mistress of the Science of Defence. The Persons who are to terminate this Affair, and Occasion for so doing, are as follows, viz.

Whereas two of the sharpest and most bloody Trials of Skill known in the Memory of Man, has lately been fought between one Mr. Holmes from Ireland, and Mr. James Figg from Thame in Oxfordshire, without admitting a compleat Conquest to either, by Reason of Claims and Disputes on both Sides: These are to give Notice, that several British and Irish Peers, as well as Gentlemen Commoners, have requested the said Champions to fight a third and final Battle; and in order to oblige them to exert themselves, a handsome Purse is collected for the Victor, which, added to the Benefit of the Box they are to fight for, will admit of no Favour and give the Conqueror a Name immortal. Therefore such as desire to sit easy, are requested to be timely in securing a Place, a full House being unquestionable, the Days short, and the Performance Likely to be the last of the Kind this Season.

Note, The last Time these Champions fought, several Noblemen being kept out of their proper Places, have requested the Upper Gallery Seats to be set at 5 s. each, the Lower at 1 s. 6 d. The Box will be set at Two and the Heroes mount at Four.[124]

---

122 *Read's Weekly Journal,* September 5, 1730.
123 *Daily Post,* September 21, 1730.
124 *Daily Post,* October 14, 1730.

Yesterday at Mr. Figg's Ampitheatre was fought a decisive battle between the said Mr. Figg and Mr. Holmes, the Irish Heroe: when at the second beat the latter, in defending his head, received such a desperate wound in his left arm, as obliged him to yield, without having been able to give his adversary one cut.[125]

## "THE 271st PRIZE Mr. FIG HAS FOUGHT"

Yesterday, the invincible Mr. James Figg fought at his Amphitheatre, Mr. Holmes, an Irishman, who keeps an Inn at Yaul near Waterford in Ireland, and came into England on purpose to fight this Champion, when Mr. Figg (fighting with his usual Bravery and Judgment) at the second Bout cut him over the left Wrist to the Bone, in so desperate a manner that he was disabled and went off the Stage; this being the Two Hundred and seventy-first Prize Mr. Fig has Fought, and was never conquer'd.

### F I G G's Triumphant: Or, Hibernia's Defeat.

Inspir'd with generous Thrift of Martial Fame,
Figg's early Years presag'd his future Name;
As Hannibal, e're grown to Manhood's Bloom,
Swore in his Blood fell Emnity with Rome,
Like Ardor did our Infant Hero grace,
Like dire Aversion to th' Hibernian Race:
Long in successful Fights both Champions view'd,
Their Oath accomplish'd, and their Foes subdu'd;
But here th' illustrious Parrallel must end,
And Africk's Warrior to Britania's bend,
Events unequal their last Fights attend;
The former loses what he earn'd before,
The latter closes all his past with one grand Triumph more.[126]

## "IF I SEE FLESH, I MUST CUT AWAY"
### (undated)

Mr. FIGG said one day to a gentleman of my acquaintance, who had the happiness to be at one of these suppers, *Sir, no man has more compassion than I for the poor and miserable: but once I am upon the stage, if I see flesh, I must cut away.* Such is the table discourse with which this celebrated man entertains those who admire his talents, and it must certainly make the treat very agreeable.[127]

## FIGG's METHOD of PROCURING SHIRTS

Mr. *Figg* informed me once, that he had not bought a Shirt for more than twenty Years, but had sold some Dozens. It was his Method, when he fought in his Amphitheatre (his Stage bearing that superb Title); he sent round to a select Number of his Scholars to borrow a Shirt for the ensuing Combat, and seldom failed of half a

---

125 *Grub Street Journal*, Oct. 22, 1730.
126 *Derby Mercury*, October 22, 1730
127 Mons. l'Abbé Le Blanc, *Letters on the English and French nations; containing curious and useful observations on their constitutions natural and political; Translated from the original French.* (London: J. Brindley, 1747), 138.

dozen of superfine Holland from his prime Pupils (most of the young Nobility and Gentry made it Part of their Education to march under his warlike Banner). This Champion was generally Conqueror, tho' his Shirt seldom failed of gaining a Cut from his Enemy, and sometimes his Flesh, tho' I think he never receiv'd any dangerous Wound. Most of his Scholars were at every Battle, and were sure to exult at their great Master's Victories, every Person supposing he saw the Wounds his Shirt received. Mr. *Figg* took his Opportunity to inform his Lenders of Linen, of the Chasms their Shirts received, with a Promise to send them home. *But*, said the ingenious, courageous *Figg, I seldom received any other Answer, than, Damn you, keep it.* I shall not enter into the Merits of this Method in procuring Linen; but, if it was a Fraud (as he told me), he was never found Guilty. For, as *Hudibras* says,

> For those that meddle with his Tools,
> Will cut their Fingers, if they're Fools.[128]

## FIGG vs. SPARKS, 1731

On the 3d Dec. 1731, a prize was fought (says a public Journal) at the French Theatre in the Haymarket, between Mr. Figg and Mr. Sparks, at which performance his Serene Highness the Duke of Lorrain, his Excellency Count Kinski, and several persons of distinction, were present; when the beauty and judgment of the sword was delineated in a very extraordinary manner by those two champions, and with very little blood-shed. His Serene Highness was extremely pleased, and expressed his intire satisfaction, and ordered them an handsome gratuity.[129]

## FIGG in COURT, 1732

On Tuesday there was a Tryal in the Court of King's Bench at Westminister, Between Mr. Warwick and Mr. Smith, Sheriffs Officers, Plaintiffs, and Mr. Figg, the famous Prize Fighter, Defendant, the Jury gave the Plantiffs 100l. Damage.

Afterwards a Tryal was had, in which said Mr. Figg was Plaintiff, and said Warwick and Smith Defendants, for a Trespass, in unlawfully entering his House; in which Case the Jury gave Mr. Figg 100 l. Damage.[130]

## The DEATH of FIGG, 1734

On Saturday Morning died Mr. James Figg, the famous Prize-Fighter, at his House in Oxford-Road.[131]

On Sunday died of a Lethargy the famous Mr. Figg, the most eminent Prize-fighter of this Age.[132]

Last Saturday there was a Trial of Skill between the unconquered Hero, Death, on the one side and till then the unconquered Hero, Mr. James Figg, the famous Prize-Fighter and Master of the Noble Science of Defense on the other. The battle was most obstinately fought on both sides, but at last the former obtained an Entire Victory and

---

128 William Chetwood, *A General History of the Stage* (London: W. Owen, 1749), 60-61n.
129 *Gentleman's Magazine*, March, 1822.
130 *Derby Mercury*, June 1, 1732.
131 *The Daily Advertiser*, December 9, 1734.
132 *Derby Mercury*, December 12, 1734.

the latter tho' he was obliged to submit to a Superior Foe yet fearless and with Distain he retired and that evening expired at his house in Oxford Road.[133]


*On Mr* James Figg *the Prize Fighter dying of a Lethargy.*

Brave Figg is conquer'd, who had conquer'd all,
Yet death can boast but little by his fall,
For half afraid, he threw a leaden dart,
And maim'd him, e'er he pierced his noble heart.
Th' undaunted hero, grimly as he fell,
Look'd for his arms, and swore by heav'n and hell,
Death never shou'd his conquest have secur'd
Had he fought fairly with a staff or sword.

HUMBLE BEE.[134]


## RECOLLECTION by JOHN GODFREY, 1747

If a Troop of FIGS were engaged with a Troop of Men, ignorant of the Back Sword, I would ask, which has the better Chance? I believe it will be granted, that a considerable superior Strength in the latter would not be an equivalent Advantage to the Skill and Judgement of the former.

We are allowed to be more expert in the Back Sword than any other Nation, and it would be a pity, if we were not to continue so. In Fig's Time, the Spirit of it was greatly kept up; but I have been often sorry to find it dwindle, and in a Manner, die away with him.[135]

---

133 From a clipping in possession of the Westminster City Archives, dated 1734.
134 *Gentleman's Magazine*, April 1835.
135 Godfrey, 39.

# iii.

## CHRISTOPHER PERKINS

*O*ne *of the earliest Irish gladiators to contest during the eighteenth century was also one of the most renowned. His name was Christopher Perkins, and his first extant printed challenge—published in 1724 — indicates that he was already a "celebrated" and "famous" master, evidently worthy of facing James Figg, and a veteran of numerous stage-fights in Ireland.*

### PERKINS vs. JAMES FIGG, 1724

AT the usual Place, at Hockley in the Hole, to Morrow the 22d of April, will be perform'd a Tryal of Skill by two of the most celebrated Masters of the Science of Defence that are now, or have been known in Europe, the famous Mr. PERKINS, Taylor, from Dublin in Ireland, and Mr. JAMES FIGG of Oxfordshire. The former of which having flourish'd in those Parts with equal Honour and Applause, as Mr. James Figg has in these; so that there is likely to be another strange Phenomenon, or Eclipse, which was not prognosticated by our Astrologers, but it is not yet known whether it will be Total.[136]

### JOHN GODFREY'S RECOLLECTION of PERKINS

I will anticipate my Characters of the MASTERS, by bringing in one Perkins an Irishman. The Man certainly was a true Swords-Man, but his Age made him so stiff and slow in his Action, that he could not execute all that his Judgement put him upon; yet, by Dint of that, he made up for his Inactivity, he always, at first setting out, pitched

---

136 *Daily Post*, April 21, 1724.

to this Posture, lying, as I said before, low to the Inside, so wide as to hide all the Outside, with his Wrist so ready raised, that nobody knew what to do with him. I have seen FIG, in Battles with him, stand in a kind of Confusion, not knowing which way to move: For as FIG offered to move, the old Man would also move so warily upon his Catch, that he would disappoint him in most of his Designs.[137]

## PERKINS vs. JAMES FIGG, 1724

At Figg's new Amphitheatre, joining to his House, the Sign of the City of Oxford, in Oxford Road, Marybone Fields, this Day the 19th Instant, will be perform'd a Trial of Skill by the following Masters.

Whereas I Christopher Perkins, from Ireland, Master of the Noble Science of Defence, who when I encountered Mr. Figg last, being, as it were, thereunto compell'd, notwithstanding the Impediment I then labour'd under, which rendered me unfit for that Purpose: Now these Disadvantages being removed, and that the said Mr. Figg, and all his Votaries, may see the Odds, I do hereby Invite him to meet me, as above, and Exercise by Inversion (i.e. beginning with the Staff, &c.) the usual Weapons practised on the Stage.

I James Figg, from Thame in Oxfordshire, Master of the said Science, that the said Mr. Perkins, or any body else, may not have it in their Power to assert, I ever made use of any other Advantage than that of the Judgment of the Sword, will not fail to be ready to receive him at the Time abovemention'd; where, notwithstanding his Inverting the Order, I shall endeavour to give him to understand, that let him take hold of what Little of the Chain he pleases, the same Consequences will follow.

Attendance will be given at Three, and the Masters mount at 5 precisely, by reason of the Decrease of the Days.

N. B. Mr. Figg gives a Hat to be plaid for (instead of a Pair of Gloves, as was said in our Paper on Monday) to divert the Company before the Masters mount.[138]

## PERKINS vs. SUTTON, 1725

AT Mr. Figg's New Amphitheatre, joyning to his House, the Sign of the city of Oxford, in Oxford Road, Marybone Fields, To-morrow being Wednesday the 21st of July, will be perform'd a Tryal of Skill by the following Masters.

Whereas I Christopher Perkins, from Ireland, Master of the Noble Science of Defence, having in my last Battle with the Opinionated Mr. Sutton, made it plainly appear that he is not that mighty Man as many (especially his Country Men) Esteem him to be, and seeing there is an Absolute Necessity once more of Unveiling their Eyes, do hereby Invite him to meet me as above, and Exercise the usual Weapons practis'd on the Stage.

I Edward Sutton Pipemaker, from Gravesend, Master of the said Science, am indeed Blind as to what this Famous Mr. Perkins means by this Manner of Expressing himself; but that he may have an Opportunity of Explaining it, I will not fail to meet him as Requested, where I shall endeavour, not only to Couch my Meaning in such Significant Terms, as will determine all future Disputes, but likewise to Create in all Spectators intire Satisfaction. Attendance will be given at Three, and the Masters mount at 6 exactly.[139]

Whereas I, Christopher Perkins, from Ireland, Master of the noble Science of Defence, have lately receiv'd three several Challenges from the triumphant Mr. Sutton, the Pipemaker of Gravesend; but when the Day of Trial has Come, he has refus'd to fight me, to the Disappointment of many worthy Gentlemen, who came, expecting to see

---

137 Capt. John Godfrey, *A Treatise Upon the Useful Science of Defence, Connecting the Small and Back-Sword, And showing the Affinity between them* (London: T. Gardner, 1747), 29-30.

138 *Daily Post*, August 19, 1724.

139 *Daily Post*, July 20, 1725.

him convinc'd; that he is not so good a Master, or so brave a man he pretends himself to be; from which refusals, I hope others will be of Opinion with me, that he is not that great Man he would be thought: Therefore, that Gentlemen may not be disappointed again of seeing a good Battle, I the said Christopher Perkins, and Thomas Elmore, both Masters of the noble Science of Defence, do invite the famous Hero Mr. James Figg, and his Companion John Wells, to meet as above, and exercise the usual Weapons practis'd on the Stage.[140]

## PERKINS and FIGG FIGHT as a TEAM, 1725

At the Desire of several Gentlemen:

At Mr. Figg's New Amphitheatre, joyning to his House, the Sign of the city of Oxford, in Oxford Road, Mary-bone Fields, this present Thursday, the 21st of October (Yesterday being His Majesty's Coronation-Day), will be perform'd a Tryal of Skill by the four following Masters.

We Edward Sutton and Robert Carter, Masters of the Noble Science of Defence, having been much insulted by Mr. Figg and Mr. Perkins; therefore, that such Things shall not be in Force, and to do our selves Justice, we do Invite them at the usual Weapons practised on the Stage; not Questioning in the least but to give entire Satisfaction to all Spectators with a general Applause.

We James Figg and Christopher Perkins, Masters of the said Science, are not a little pleas'd, that the abovesaid Combatants have at last work'd themselves into Courage enough to give us this publick Invitation; not doubting but to confute the many extravagant Bravadoes they have been guilty of, in a Manner, that they will shew, they are as great Strangers to Modesty, as to the true Judgment of the Sword: And since Mr. Carter affects to forget the Time when he begg'd Mr. Figg to decline the great Advantage he had over him, and not quite spoil him, Mr. Figg promises, in this Battle to refresh his Memory, and make him an Example to all others of the same insolent Behaviour: And Mr. Perkins questions not but to satisfy all Spectators, that there will be no occasion for Mr. Sutton to put himself to the Expence of erecting a Stage in the Field to decide their Superiority in the Science.

Note, No Cut to be ty'd up; and to fight with their own Swords.[141]

## "THERE is no EQUALITY BETWEEN his PERFORMANCE and MINE", 1726

AT Mr. FIGG's New Amphitheatre, joining to his House, the Sign of the City of Oxford, in Oxford-Road, Mary-bone-Fields, To-morrow being the 23d of March, will be perform'd a Trial of Skill by the following Masters.

Whereas I Robert Carter, of the City of London, Master of the Noble Science of Defence, have with repeated Success fought all the best Masters in England, except the famous Mr. Perkins; and being desirous to try his Judgment so much boasted of, do invite him to meet me as above, and exercise the usual Weapons fought on the Stage, where I doubt not of the Applause of the Judicious, in letting all Spectators see, that his Skill is not superiour to mine.

I Christopher Perkins, from the City of Dublin, Master of the said Science, shall endeavour to convince this bold Inviter, as well as the Gentlemen then present, that there is no Equality between his Performance and mine, which shall be demonstrated by such visible Proofs as will admit of no Contradiction; to determine which I will not fail meeting, hoping at the fame Time to give all Encouragers of of the Sword an entire Satisfaction, according to my usual Custom.

Note, There will be Blunts play'd at by Three from St. James's and Three from Moorfields, to divert the Gentlemen before the Masters mount. N. B. The Doors will be opened at Two, and the Masters mount ar Five exactly.[142]

---

140 From a clipping in possession of the Westminster City Archives.
141 *Daily Post*, October 21, 1725.
142 *Daily Post*, March 22, 1726.

## PERKINS & COLLINS vs. SUTTON & WELLS, 1726

At Mr. FIGG's New Amphitheatre, joining to his House, the Sign of the City of Oxford, in Oxford Road this Day being the 10th of August, will be perform'd a Trial of Skill by the following Masters.

We Christopher Perkins and James Collins, the one from the Kingdom of Ireland and the other from Cambridge, Professors of the Noble Science of Defence, hearing how the Town is puffed up with the famous Mr. Sutton and Mr. Wells, Kentish and Suffolk Champions; and we thinking our selves equal, if not superiour to these two Heroes, do invite them to meet and exercise us at the usual Weapons practis'd on the Stage; and are resolved to use the utmost Means and the Severity of the Sword, in hopes to please the Spectators with as intire Satisfaction as ever was given.

We Edward Sutton and John Wells, Kentish and Suffolk Professors of the said Science, making no Apology, will not fail meeting this Hibernian Bravo, and Cambridge Champion at the Place abovemention'd, to Answer them in every Article of their Request, doubting not but to give them as warm a reception as ever they met with; and to maintain our Characters; we design to please the Gentlemen to the utmost Care of their Humble Servants Edward Sutton, John Wells. Mr. Sutton Fights Mr. Collins, and Mr. Wells Mr. Perkins; this being the first Time they ever fought each other. To fight in white Cotton Stockings, Drawers, and Pumps as usual.

N. B. The Door will be open'd at Three, and the Masters mount between Five and Six exactly. Because four Masters perform.[143]

## "THEY SEEM DISPOSED for BLOOD and WOUNDS...", 1726

At Mr. FIGG's GREAT ROOM, at his House, the Sign of the City of Oxford, in Oxford-Road, Marybone-Fields, To-morrow being the 7th of September, will be perform'd a compleat Trial of Skill by the following Masters.

We Christopher Perkins, and Rowland Bennet, Champions from Ireland, having received several Affronts from the noted Mr. Edward Sutton and Mr. John Wells, with Regard not only to our Judgment in the Sword, but that of all the rest of our Countrymen; most arrogantly assuming to themselves a much better, and declaring that we ought not to appear upon the Stage but at Blunts; with several other Particulars that require the most publick Satisfaction, and for which in Honour and Vindication of ourselves and and Countrymen, we demand their Appearance at the Time and Place, abovesaid, to receive the just and due Reward of their Behaviour in Exercising the best they can at the usual Weapons practised or the Stage; either backwards or forwards, no Cuts ty'd up; that Side which gives most Wounds have half the Money in the Box; or as they and the Company please.

We Edward Sutton, from Gravesend, and John Wells from St. Edmonds Bury, Masters of the Science of Defence cannot understand by the Style of this Challenge whether it came from Ireland or Smithfield, but believe from the latter, because it exactly agrees with one we receiv'd there the other Day from two Merry Andrews[*]; however since the abovesaid Champions (as they call themselves) can be spared from thence; and as they seem disposed for Blood and Wounds, we will not fail to meet them as above, at our Countryman Mr. Figg's, (the Stage we hope they intended to invite us to, as the only Place within the Bills of Mortality proper for Gentlemen of the Sword to appear and exercise at,) and maintain our superior Judgment, upon any Terms as they or the worthy Spectators require, only desiring to insist upon having the best of Weapons, and if one of either Side be disabled, his Companion to perform the Remainder of both Battles, or else to leave us, as we usually are, Masters of the Stage; which we claim as our just Right, and shall always do our utmost to support.

Note, Mr. Bennet fights Mr. Sutton, they having never fought yet. The Spectators are earnestly desired not to interpose or interrupt the Masters in any kind while they are performing.[144]

---

143 *Daily Post*, August 10, 1726.
* "Merry Andrew is an old word of the Elizabethan era for a jester, or mountebank, not yet wholly obsolete." Charles Mackay, *New Light on Some Obscure Words & Phrases in the Works of Shakespeare and his Contemporaries* (London: Reeves & Turner, 1884), 50.
144 *Daily Post*, September 6, 1726.

## "A MIGHTY MAN", 1726

*This present* Wednesday *being the 28th of this Instant September,*
AT Mr. STOKES's New Amphitheatre, in Islington Road, near Sadler's-Wells, will be perform'd a Trial of Skill by the following Masters.

Whereas I Christopher Perkins from Dublin, Professor of the Noble and Laudable Science of Defence, having Been amus'd with the wonderful Exploits the Town has been entertained with by the celebrated Mr. Sutton, (who is stil'd the famous Champion of Kent) when any has been so bold as to oppose him; therefore, to let him see that I not only dare to engage him, but also even vie with him who shall be deem'd the most excellent in their Performance, hereby do invite him to meet me as above, and exercise the usual Weapons practised on the Stage, in order to let the Spectators see this Champion confuted, as to his Judgment in the Sword, of which he is pleased to stile himself Master.

I Edward Sutton, Pipe-maker from Gravesend in the County of Kent, Professor of the said Science, will not fail complying with the Demands of this Hector, in Order for a Specimen of his proving himself such a mighty Man as he boasts to be; where I shall convince him of the Mistake he has hitherto been under; in conceiving such a Notion of me as he pretends to vouch for Truth; and likewise maintain my superior Judgment upon any Terms as he or the worthy Spectators shall require, only insist upon having the best of Weapons, which is requisite to decide such a Controversy, not doubting but, I shall give him such an unwelcome Reception as formerly, which will give him Occasion to leave me, as I usually am, Master of the Stage, which I claim as my just Right, and shall always use my utmost Endeavour to support.

N. B. There will be Cudgel-playing by six Englishmen and six Irishmen.[145]

## FIGG CANCELS, and PERKINS vs. GILL, 1727

At Mr. FIGG's GREAT ROOM, at his House, the Sign of the City of Oxford, in Oxford-Road, Marybone-Fields, To-morrow being the Wednesday the 2d of August, will be perform'd a Trial of Skill by the following Masters.

I WILLIAM GILL, from Gloucester, Professor of the Noble Science of Defence, and Scholar to the celebrated Mr. Figg, in Behalf of my said Master (who was to have fought the noted Mr. Perkins on the above Day, but by Reason of an Impediment in his Right Arm is render'd as yet incapable of performing in that Way) do invite the said Mr. Perkins to meet me as above, and exercise the usual Weapons practised on the Stage.

I CHRISTOPHER PERKINS, from Dublin, Professor of the said Science, who have fought the best Masters in the Three Kingdoms with a general Applause, and never yet refused any, particularly the invincible Mr. Figg, as his Countrymen style him, am willing to accept of this Invitation, to cut off this Limb of Defence (for I can style him no otherwise) in order to come at the Head.

Note, Samuel Boulton and a Weaver of Spittlefields are to Box and fight at Blunts Naked afterwards for Ten Pounds.[146]

## PERKINS & COLLINS vs. WELLS & GILL, 1727

At Mr. FIGG'S GREAT ROOM, AT his House, the Sign of the City of Oxford in Oxford-Road, Marybone Fields, To-morrow being Wednesday the 16th of August, will be perform'd a Trial of Skill by the following Masters.

I CHRISTOPHER PERKINS of the City of Dublin and I JAMES COLLINS from Cambridge, both Masters of the Noble Science of Defence, having an earnest Intention and Desire to fight the two famous Champions Mr.

---

145 *Daily Post,* September 28, 1726.
146 *Daily Post,* August 1, 1727.

John Wells and Mr. William Gill; We do therefore invite them to meet as above, and exercise us at the usual Weapons practised on the Stage; desiring them to exert themselves with the best Judgment they are Masters of, and with the most Severity, which for the agreeable Satisfaction of the Gentlemen then present we likewise intend to do as our usual Custom is.

We JOHN WELLS and WILLIAM GILL, Masters of the said Science, are always ready to embrace the stoutest and most dangerous Invitation from any Masters of the Sword, and very readily accept of this, in order to give them a warmer Reception than ever they yet mer with, and will use the best Skill we are Masters of, according to our usual Custom; to give the Spectators an intire Satisfaction.

Notice, Mr. Collins fights Mr. Wells, and Mr. Perkins Fights Mr. Gill: And there will be the usual Diversion before the Masters mount.[147]

## IRISH vs. ENGLISH CHAMPIONS, 1727

At Mr. FIGG'S GREAT ROOM, AT his House, the Sign of the City of Oxford in Oxford-Road, Marybone Fields, this present Wednesday being the 4th of October, will be perform'd a Trial of Skill by the following Masters.

Whereas there have been a great many Reflections cast on the Irish Swordsmen by the English, declaring they would cut down all the Hibernian Race: We believe they will find it easier to talk than to perform, we being assur'd, we have as much Judgment in that Kingdom as in any Part of the World; and to prove our Character equal, we will fight them two on a Day, till there be a true Distinction: And to begin, We CHRISTOPHER PERKINS and BRYAN MACGENNY, do invite John Parkes, the Famous Coventry Champion, and James Collins from Cambridge, at the usual Weapons fought on the Stage; desiring those two Champions to exert their utmost Skill.

Note, We beg if any Gentlemen would ask a Question about the Battle, they would ask it publickly; for the English Swordsmen are free to tell what Cuts they give, but forget to tell what they receive.

We JOHN PARKES and JAMES COLLINS, jointly with the rest of the English Swordsmen. are fond of the Resolution of these Hibernian Champions; and although they are great in Number, let them take Care that most of them be not sent Home by Weeping Cross; The two abovenamed Masters will not fail to meet as above, and will endeavour to make their Swords decide the Battle apparently without whispering.

Note, Mr. Perkins fights Mr. Parkes, and Mr. Mac-genny fights Mr. Collins.[148]

## "THE LAST TIME OF MY FIGHTING...", 1728

At Mr. FIGG's GREAT ROOM, At his House, the Sign of the City of Oxford, in Oxford-street, this Day the 24th Instant, will be perform'd a Trial of Skill by the following Masters.

Whereas I CHRISTOPHER PERKINS...who have often fought Mr. Figg, and have always came off with great Applause; so now taking my last Farewell of him, do once more invite him to meet me and exercise the usual Weapons practised on the Stage, it being the last Time of my fighting in England, wherein I hope to give Mr. Figg, and all Gentlemen entire Satisfaction at my taking my Leave of England.

I JAMES FIGG, from Thame in Oxfordshire, Master of the said Science, who never yet refused any Master, let them come from what Part of the World soever they will, will not fail to meet this bold Inviter, at his Time and Place appointed, where I doubt not but to give him something to remember me, at Parting, he designing to leave England, wherein I hope to give all Gentlemen entire Satisfaction, as I have hitherto done.[149]

147 *Daily Post,* August 15, 1727.
148 *Daily Post,* October 4, 1727.
149 *Daily Post,* July 24, 1728.

*Provocatio Pugno*

# iv.

## DONALD MCBANE

*Donald McBane was a Highland Scot, born in Inverness around the year 1664. During his amazing military career, he served abroad throughout much of Europe, where he took part in sixteen battles, fifteen skirmishes, and nearly one hundred duels or single combats. He was, at least, twenty-seven times wounded—not counting the time when he was blown up by his own hand grenade. In addition to his career as a soldier, he also set himself up as a fencing master, gamester, and brothel manager. At about age fifty he commenced fighting as a gladiator at the Bear Gardens, where McBane claimed to have fought a total of thirty-seven such prizes, often appearing under a variety of pseudonyms and spellings such as Daniel Bane, Donald Bane, Daniel Bain, Daniel Baine, Daniel Bean, Daniel Beane, Daniel Beine, and Macbain.*

*The best source for McBane's life and career is his extraordinary memoir and fencing treatise,* The Expert Sword-Man's Companion, *first published in 1728 in Glasgow. Notably, some rare copies of this book contain a frontispiece with a portrait of McBane (see above fragment) in which he stands in a fencing guard position, dressed only in his shirt (i.e., with no coat or customary waistcoat), and has two ribbons or "armigers" tied around his elbows—the costume or uniform of a Bear-Garden gladiator. He seems to have primarily identified as a gladiator; even his terse obituary described him as "the celebrated Highland Prize fighter." Following are the many challenges and accounts of McBane's gladiatorial contests. For a more complete account of McBane's life, duels, career, and techniques, see our introduction to the 2017 republication of McBane's text.*[150]

---

150 Donald McBane, *The Expert Sword-man's Companion* (New York: Jared Kirby Rare Books, 2017), i-xi.

## MCBANE vs. JAMES MILLER, 1713

A Tryal of Skill to be fought at the Bear-Garden in the Hockley in the Hole on Wednesday next, being the 29th of April, beginning at 2 of the Clock precisely, between Daniel Bean, a North-Britain, lately come from Flanders, Master of the Noble Science of Defence, and James Miller, Serjeant, Master of the said Science.[151]

## MCBANE vs. TIMOTHY BUCK, 1713

A Tryal of Skill to be fought at the Bear-Garden in Marrow-Bone-Fields, at the Boarded-House, near Tyburn-Road, on Wednesday next, being the 20th of May, beginning exactly at 2 a Clock, between Daniel Beane from Flanders, Master of the Noble Science of Defence, who lately fought Mr. Miller, and Timothy Buck, Master of the said Science.[152]

## MCBANE vs. PARKES, 1713

A Tryal of Skill to be fought at the Bear-Garden in Marrow-Bone-Fields, the Backside of Soho-Square, at the Boarded-House, on Wednesday next, being the 7th of October, beginning precisely at 2 a Clock, between Daniel Bean, North-Britain, Master of the Noble Science of Defence, and John Parks from Coventry, Master of the said Science. Note, Box or no Box we Fight, by reason the Company shall not be disappointed.[153]

## MCBANE vs. JAMES MILLER, 1714

A Tryal of Skill to be fought at the Bear-Garden in Marrow-Bone-Fields the Backside of Soho-Square, at the Boarded-House, on Wednesday next, being the 10th of March, beginning at 2 of the Clock precisely, between Daniel Baine, North-Britain, Master of the Noble Science of Defence, and James Miller, Master of the said Science.[154]

## MCBANE vs. TIMOTHY BUCK, with NO SECONDS, 1714

A Tryal of Skill to be fought at the Bear-Garden in Marrow-Bone-Fields the Backside of Soho-Square, at the Boarded-House, this present Wednesday, being the 28th of April, at 3 of the Clock precisely, between Timothy Buck of Clare-Market, Master of the Noble Science of Defence, and Daniel Baine, North-Britain, Master of the said Science, without Seconds.[155]

## MCBANE vs. PARKES, 1714

A Tryal of Skill to be fought at the Bear-Garden in Marrow-Bone-Fields the Backside of Soho-Square, at the Boarded-House, this present Wednesday, being the 2d of June, beginning at 3 of the Clock precisely, between Daniel Baine, North-Britain, Master of the Noble Science of Defence, and John Parkes of Coventry, Master of the said Science. Note, For the Diversion of all Spectators, there will be two Couple Fight after the Prize is over[156]

151 *Daily Courant*, April 27, 1713.
152 *Daily Courant*, May 18, 1713.
153 *Daily Courant*, October 5, 1713.
154 *Daily Courant*, March 6, 1714.
155 *Daily Courant*, March 6, 1714.
156 *Daily Courant*, June 2, 1714.

## "with RAPIER and PONIARD", 1714

A Tryal of Skill to be fought at the Bear-Garden in Marrow-Bone-Fields the Backside of Soho-Square, at the Boarded-House, this present Wednesday, being the 7th of July, beginning at 3 of the Clock precisely, between Thomas Cummins, Dragoon, Master of the Noble Science of Defence, and Daniel Baine of North-Britain, Master of the said Science. Note, We shall fight with Rapier and Poniard, and the other Weapons as usual.[157]

## MCBANE vs. TIMOTHY BUCK, 1714

A Tryal of Skill to be fought at the Bear-Garden in Marrow-Bone-Fields the Backside of Soho-Square, at the Boarded-House, on Wednesday next, being the 28th of July, beginning at 3 of the Clock precisely, between Daniel Bane, North-Briton, Master of the Noble Science of Defence, and Timothy Buck of Clare-Market, Master of the said Science. Note, Two Masters fight after the Prize is over.[158]

## DAGGER, BUCKLER, FALCHION & QUARTERSTAFF, 1715

### *ADVERTISEMENT.*
### *At the Request of several Persons of Quality.*

At the Boarded-House in Mary-Bone-Fields, the Backside of Soho-Square; on Wednesday next, being the 20th of April, 1715. Will be perform'd a Trial of Skill, between Thomas Cummins, an Eniskillen Dragoon, and Daniel Beine, a Royal British Grenadier, to exercise the following Weapons, *viz.* Back-Sword, Sword and Dagger, Sword and Buckler, Falchon, Case of Falchons, and Quarter-Staff. They give a Hat to be fought for at Blunts, before they mount. The Boxes are set precisely at 3 a Clock, and shall begin exactly at Five.[159]

## MCBANE & CUMMINS vs. the PARKS BROTHERS, 1715

A Tryal of Skill to be fought at the Bear-Garden in Marrow-Bone-Fields the Backside of Soho-Square, at the Boarded-House, to Morrow, being Wednesday, the 13th of July, (Wet or Dry) Thomas Cummins and Daniel Baine, Masters of the Noble Science of Defence, against John Parks and his brother from Coventry, Masters of the said Science, for 20 l. The first two that begin, are to fight 3 bouts, the next the same, and so gradually the Weapons through. NB. The Doors will be open at 3 a Clock, and it being a particular Prize, the First Gallery is 5 s. and the 2d 2 s. 6 d.[160]

## MCBANE & FIGG vs. AYLMER & CUMMINS, 1715

A Tryal of Skill to be fought at the Bear-Garden in Marrow-Bone-Fields the Backside of Soho-Square, at the Boarded-House, to Morrow, on Wednesday next, being the 20th of July, between  Daniel Baine and James Figg, Masters of the Noble Science of Defence, and Mr. Aylmer and Mr. Cummins, Masters of the said Science. The first that begin, are to fight 3 bouts, the next the same, and so gradually the Weapons through. NB. The Doors will be open at 3 a Clock. The First Gallery 5 s. the 2d 2 s. 6 d.[161]

---

157 *Daily Courant,* July 8, 1714.
158 *Daily Courant,* July 26, 1714.
159 *Weekly Journal with Fresh Advices*, April 16, 1715.
160 *Daily Courant,* July 12, 1715.
161 *Daily Courant,* July 18, 1715.

## MCBANE vs. O'BRYAN, 1726

We hear that one Andrew Obryan, of the Kingdom of Ireland, Gladiator, having boldly challenged the whole Professors of that Science in North Britain; the same has been accepted by the famous Daniel Bain, *alias* Macbain, of the North of Scotland; and that a comparative Trial of their Skill, in the noble Art of Defence, is to be the 20<sup>th</sup> Inst.[162]

An Irish sword-player named O'Bryan, who had beaten all the combatants at the Bear-Garden, and various individuals in other parts of the kingdom, paid a visit to Edinburgh, where, according to his custom, he challenged the inhabitants to produce an antagonist, under the usual penalty. That a breach of the peace of this monstrous character was then tolerated, or such an exaction submitted to, in a populous and not unenlightened city, may well excite surprise; but if we only reflect on how much custom will reconcile us to, our wonder may in some measure cease. O'Bryan had been in the city for some weeks, daily parading through its streets to proclaim his challenge, when the Duke of Hamilton, then residing in Holyrood House, sent for Donald Bane, the teacher of the broadsword already mentioned, with the view of engaging him to take up the cause of the citizens. When Bane arrived at the palace, the Duke of Argyle happened to be present, and, as an old commander of the veteran swordsman, entered heartily into the project.

"Has he a drum?" said Bane.

"Yes," answered Argyle, "and a very clever stout fellow he is, I assure you."

"You may make yourself easy as to that," replied Bane, " for I have broken his drum already."

This was really the case; for meeting O'Bryan at the foot of the West Bow, where he was in no very courteous terms defying the whole of Scotland, the patriotic blood of the Caledonian had become excited, and he drove his foot through the one end of the drum, and his fist through the other, as a first intimation of his acceptance of the challenge. An agreement, indeed, had already been made between O'Bryan and Bane, to fight on that day week. It was nevertheless thought necessary that a reply to the challenge should be published in fair set terms, and in Latin verse*; a fact which strikingly proves the interest taken in these sanguinary proceedings by persons of the better order.

* This answer was entitled *"Donaldi Bani famigerati ad Andreæ O'Bryan chartam provocatoriam Responsum,"* and commenced as follows:-

*"Ipse ego Donaldus Banus, forma albus et altus, Non huic Andreæ thrasoni occurrere decro,"* &c.

It might be thus translated into English:—

I, Donald Bane, fair-complexioned and tall, shall not fail to enter the lists with this bully Andrew. With heaven's assistance, and as a friend to my country, I will go to meet him, who, unskillful in the art, daringly challenges me to the combat. In a short time, when we have entered upon the fight, brave men admitted to behold us will perhaps see that the pugilist O'Bryan is, as I believe, not so expert a master of the art of fencing. Whether he have a protection or a patron, my weapon will render him an idle capon.

Donald being now sixty-six years of age, some fears were entertained by his friends for his success in the encounter; and tradition represents his chief asking if he thought he were "yauld enough" for O'Bryan.<sup>†</sup> On this the veteran pulled out his claymore and made it whistle in the air over his head, a sufficiently expressive test of his strength of arm. As he passed along the street, some of the bystanders said, "Ah, Donald's failed; I doubt he'll no do;" whereupon he leaped up to a lamp iron far above the reach of ordinary men, hung by one hand for a moment, and springing down, exclaimed "She'll do yet."

---

162 *Caledonian Mercury*, June 9, 1726.
† *Yauld*—agile, with vigour.

The stage was erected in St Anne's yards, at the back of the cavalry green attached to the palace; and the conflict, which lasted several hours, and was tried with a variety of weapons, terminated in a declaration of victory in favour of the native combatant, who, at the conclusion, found the boards covered with gold and silver, thrown there for him by the admiring spectators.[163]

*Edinburgh, July 2.* Last Week here was a Trial of Skill in the noble Science of Defence (as it is call'd) between an Irishman and an Highlander: the latter, whose Name is Donald Bain, tho' old, almost cut the Irishman to Pieces, and beat him off the Stage, without receiving the least Hurt, so that he has enough of coming over Sea to challenge a bonny Scot.[164]

Whether in Private or in Publick Field,
He Victor was and made his Foes to yield.
Grown Old at length, and spent with Warlike Toil,
He did return unto his native Soil.
Resolved no more to Fight, when lo he's told,
An Irish raw Bravado stout and bold
Imperiously all Scotish did Defy,
He laid his former Resolution by,
And from great Distance came in haste to see
Who was the Man, and what a Spark was he.
He took the Challenge up, and modestly
He set a day, their Valour for to try.
When met, our Hero mov'd with generous Rage
Beat at first Time O'Bryan of the Stage;
His luck was good he fell, for had he stood,
He there had lost his life and Irish Blood.
Foolhardy he Appear'd on Stage again,
And all his Bragadocia Threats were vain;
For Valiant Bane like Lyon void of Fear,
With furious Blows did this the Youngster tear.
Seven Bloody Wounds he gave, but none he got,
And this the Tague was Vanquished by the Scot.[165]

## MCBANE'S OWN ACCOUNT, 1728

In 1726 I Fought a Clean Young Man at *Edinburgh*, I gave him Seven Wounds and broke his Arm with the *Fauchion*, this I did at the request of several *Noblemen* and *Gentle-men*, But now being Sixty-three Years of Age, resolves never to Fight any more, but to Repent of my former Wickedness.[166]

163 *Chambers' Edinburgh Journal*, No. 180, July 11, 1835.
164 *Mist's Weekly Journal,* July 9, 1726.
165 McBane, 7.
166 Ibid, 183.

*Fig. 16. Captain James Miller. From the frontipiece of his 1738 treatise.*

# V.

## CAPTAIN JAMES MILLER

*C*aptain James Miller was most notable for authoring the only book treating wholly and specifically of gladia-torial combat techniques, and the various weapons specific to stage fights, entitled A short Treatise of ye Gladiatory Art of Defence, *published in 1738 (see Chapter XVI). He was also the subject of one of the most descriptive accounts of a gladiatorial combat, written by Joseph Addison and published in the* Spectator, *wherein Miller is described as a "Serjeant, (lately come from the Frontiers of Portugal)" and "a Man of six Foot eight Inches Height, of a kind but bold Aspect, well-fashion'd, and ready of his Limbs: and such Readiness as spoke his Ease in them, was obtained from a Habit of Motion in Military Exercise." This account, in full, has already been reprinted on pages 32-34 of this book, in Chapter V.i..*

*Here follow the few additional challenges and accounts pertaining to Miller that we have been able to find.*

### ACCOUNT BY JOHN GODFREY

MR. MILLAR was the palpable Gentleman through the Prize-Fighter. He was a most beautiful Picture on the Stage, taking in all his Attitudes, and vastly engaging in his Demeanor. There was such an easy Action in him, unconcerned Behaviour and agreeable Smile in the midst of Fighting, that one could not help being prejudiced in his Favour.[167]

---

[167]Godfrey, 40.

## MILLER vs. TIMOTHY BUCK, 1712

A Tryal of Skill to be fought at the Bear-Garden in Hockley in the Hole, to Morrow being Wednesday the 16th of July, at 2 of the Clock precisely, between James Miller, Serjeant, (lately come from the Frontiers in Portugal) Master of the Noble Science of Defence, and Timothy Buck, Master of the said Science.[168]

## MILLER vs. ROBERT WALDERN, 1713.

A Tryal of Skill to be fought at the Bear-Garden in Marrow-Bone-Fields, at the Boarded-House, near Tyburn Road, to Morrow being Wednesday, the 24th of June, beginning precisely at 4 a Clock, between Robert Waldern, Master of the Noble Science of Defence, and James Miller, Serjeant, Master of the said Science. Note, They begin with the Quarter-Staff first.[169]

## MILLER vs. DONALD MCBANE, 1714

A Tryal of Skill to be fought at the Bear-Garden in Marrow-Bone-Fields the Backside of Soho-Square, at the Boarded-House, on Wednesday next, being the 10th of March, beginning at 2 of the Clock precisely, between Daniel Baine, North-Britain, Master of the Noble Science of Defence, and James Miller, Master of the said Science.[170]

## DUEL between MILLER and CAPT. PETER DRAKE, 1714-1726

This Summer I had an odd Adventure, odd I must call it, from its Circumstance, and the Manner it happened, to shew how rashly and inconsiderately some People contrive Diversions to amuse and divert themselves and others, which may endanger their Lives. This was the Case here, and happened thus: There was at this time in *London*, among many famous Prize-Fighters, one *James Miller*, mightily esteemed by the Quality and General Officers, who were Lovers of that Sport, on account of his smiling Countenance, even when warmly engaged on the Stage; I also liked him very well, and was often in Company with him. One Day I took a Walk to *Lambeth* Wells, a Place for Dancing, and other Diversions; as I was paying at the Gate, one of the Drawers came, and told me, there was a Gentleman wanted to speak with me; he shewed me to Mr. Miller, who was taking a Glass with some Company: He said, he saw me come in, which made him send for me to take a Glass, which I accepted of. In about half an Hour the Musick was ordered to the Gallery; the Company moving to re-assume the Dancing, I called for a Flask of Wine; Mr. Miller said, when the Dancing was over, the Company would join, and accept of my Flask; but by the Time the Diversion was ended, it began to rain Mr. Miller then bespoke a large Parlour, and brought the Company thither, about Eleven in Number, only one Lady, whose Name was Hopkins; she kept a Tavern in Earl's Court, and seemed to have some Knowledge of me. I am so particular in this, it being necessary to my Story. Mr. Miller was at this Time in the Horse Grenadiers. I knew none of the Company but him; we drank pretty briskly about, and began to be merry; Toasts went about, mine was called for; I toasted Mrs. Jolly; Mrs. Hopkins immediately got up, and uttering some indecent Expressions, bid me be the Messenger of them, and that her Name was Bess Hopkins; I told her, I never interfered in Ladies Quarrels. A Gentleman, in a laced Hat and Waistcoat, who sat near her, gave himself the Trouble to come round to me, with a seeming angry Countenance, to inform me, I must not take amiss any thing the Lady said, for if I did, he should be very angry: I assured him, I

---

168 *Daily Courant*, July 15, 1712.
169 *Daily Courant*, June 23, 1713.
170 *Daily Courant*, March 6, 1714.

was naturally inclined to be civil to the Fair Sex, and the Lady was at Liberty to say what she pleased; he swore by his Maker, shaking his Head, it was my best Way; I desired he would not ingross any Merit to himself from my Meekness, for if he had said half so much, it was fifty to one, he would not come off so cheap; he then returned to his Seat. I sat near a French Gentleman, who was Mr. Miller's Sergeant; we discoursed in French; Mr. Miller sat on one Side of Mrs. Hopkins, the Gentleman above spoke of on the other; I observed they were all three whispering and laughing, but did not imagine they were plotting against me. The Rain continuing very heavy, there was no Thoughts of going. We being all in a merry Mood, Mr. Miller obliged us with a Song, to which all the Company bore a Chorus, performed in this Manner; at the End of each Verse, the Company (no one to be excused) were to hum through the Nose, striking gently on it with his Finger all the Time; when any was out of Tune, Mr. Miller was to give it a light Squeeze with his Fingers to put it to rights; this was done, or repeated to every one three times. He had smeared the Inside of two of his Fingers with some Snuff and Candle Grease; with these he tuned my poor Nose; this caused a general Laugh in the Company, I joined with the rest, though I did not know the Cause, nor think that I was the Object of their Mirth. The Company being thus diverted at my Expence for some time, the French Gentleman, who sat near me, whispered me to go clean my Nose, which was all black; I was very much surprised, and went out of the Room to look in a Glass, and found both Sides of my Nose, from the Eyes to the Tip, as black as a Coal. I took no Notice, but returned to the Company in the same Pickle, and sat in my Place, as if I had known nothing of the Matter, which increased their Mirth the more; some talked of Faces, others were describing Features, but I fell to singing, though I knew all this was levelled at me. At length, I got up, and said, I had all those Features they spoke of, rough as they were; among the rest I had a Nose, that he who blacked it, if he did it with Intent to affront me, was a Rascal and Scoundrel; Mr. Miller, to shew the Cap fitted him, made a Stroke with his Cane across the Table at me; then the Company interfered to prevent further Mischief. He was struggling with some Gentlemen to get to me, swearing I should go out of the Room; I desired him to sit down, saying, he had done enough in blacking my Nose, and confirming his Intent of affronting me by a Blow; that if I bore all this he might be easy, and let the Company be so too. All would not do, I must quit the Room; I told him, though he was the Man who brought me in, and I knew no one in Company but himself, yet he, nor no single Man should, or was able to put me out; that I appealed to the Company, or the major Part of them, if I had given Offence to any; if I had, I would willingly withdraw; they all declared to the contrary, that no Man could behave civiller, and that Mr. Miller was in the wrong.

To shew my Disposition for the Peace of the Company, I proposed, that any Person who spoke one Word more of the Dispute, should forfeit a Flask of Wine; this was agreed on by all; Mr. Miller, in less than an Hour, forfeited three, for which he paid as they were brought in: I desired that he and I might go out to speak a few Words together; this was opposed by the Company, unless we left our Swords, and promised not to go to handy Grips (a Sport I am sure neither of us liked) this we promised. He and I went into another Room, and agreed to take an Opportunity to slip the Company, on a Signal to be made, and meet in the Walk as soon as the Rain was over; then we returned to the Company.

About Break of Day it held up, the Company were mostly dispersed about the Room, some snoring in Corners, others sleeping on Chairs, &c. and our Dispute forgot; in short, finding this favourable Opportunity, I walked close by Mr. Miller, then trod on his Foot (the Signal agreed on) and went to the Walk. I had no sooner got to the upper End, and sat down in an Alcove, than he appeared at the other; when he saw me, (tho' the whole Length of the Walk was between us) he clapped his Hand to his Sword, and came in that Posture within ten or twelve Yards of me. I immediately drew, and we both attacked smartly; he gave Ground almost as fast as he came up. In this Retreat he received two slight Wounds, or rather Scratches, in his Sword Arm, he got behind one of the Trees, and begged I would let him breath. I said, though you deserve no Favour, I would scorn to take the Advantage. I put my Sword under my Arm, bidding him to draw Breath. About this Time being missed, four of the Gentlemen came, and found us in this Posture, which prevented our going to it again, so we parted for that Time, and all went to their respective Homes. This Duel was talked of for some Time, especially among the military Gentlemen; it also gained me some Reputation for having engaged one of the principal Heroes of the Stage.

After this, I slept in a whole Skin for twelve Years, no Person challenging, or engaging me, in the many Disputes and Broils I had during that Time. Mr. Miller and I sought each other, but to no Purpose, for some Days. At length we met by the Persuasion of some Friends, but neither for that Time would own himself in the wrong, especially my Antagonist, who warmly insisted upon the Grossness of the Affront, from the Appellation of Rascal and Scoundrel before a whole Company; and I, on the other Hand, on the Baseness he was guilty of in causing me to be a Laughing-stock, especially as he knew he was the only Acquaintance I had there, and that it was by his Invitation I entered into their Company. The Blow he gave me with his Cane was sufficient to demand a Gentleman-like Satisfaction, which I requested of him the first Opportunity; he assured me I might depend upon it. As our Friends could not at this Meeting make the Breach up, we parted.

Some Days after, our Friends hit on this Method to satisfy us both, and make a friendly Conclusion of the Affair; viz, that the Company who were at Lambeth Wells that Night, or as many of them as could be got (Mrs. Hopkins excepted) should be invited to a Dinner at a Time and Place which should be appointed, there to state, and fairly lay the Matter in Debate before them, and whoever it was given against, should beg the others Pardon, and pay the Expence, not exceeding a Guinea, what might be more, to be equally clubbed by the Company: This was communicated, and agreed to, by Mr. Miller and me. The Company was invited on a certain Day, and my House, the Queens Arms, was proposed for the Meeting: This I rejected. Then the Fountain Tavern in Catherine-street was named, where the Company met, and dined: As soon as the Cloth was taken away, Wine and Glasses brought, and the Servants gone, the Cause was opened, debated, and given against Mr. *Miller* by all the Company, even his own Officers, there being two present. He chearfully submitted to the Verdict, paid his Guinea, and begged my Pardon; we embraced, and continued intimate Friends ever after.[171]

## REVIEW of MILLER's TREATISE on FENCING, by a FRIEND, 1739

*To* RALPH FREEMAN, *Esq.,*
  *SIR,*

I BEG the Favour of your giving to the Publick the best Recommendation in my Power of my worthy Friend Mr. *Miller*'s Works relating to the useful *Science* of *Defence.* Two things I can assert of this Performance which are sufficient to prove that it cannot be a bad one. The first, that it comes from a Person whom all the World allows to be a Master of the Subject he treats of; the second, that it hath not been hastily compos'd or transcrib'd from Observations made in the earlier, that is, in the rawer Part of Life, but is the Effect of mature Reflection in the cooler Season of Man's Age, when his Judgment is strongest, and his Passions have had their Edges taken off. I can also offer two other Reasons in its Favour, which perhaps may carry the thing farther, viz. That the Author is too modest to present any thing to the Publick unworthy of its Acceptance, and that it hath already stood the Test of the best Criticks without suffering at all in its Character.

ONE may easily foresee, Mr. *Freeman*, that you will be amaz'd at this Address. But pray, Sir, have Patience a little, and I do not doubt of my being able to convince you, that nothing can be properer than my Letter to fill up two or three Columns in the *Gazetteer.* You are a Friend to the Ancients; your Writings speak you so. Well, Sir, the Ancients understood, practis'd and admir'd the Science I commend. *Jacob* was an excellent Wrestler; *Jonathan* and *David* Brothers in their Exercises, which produced that Affection which surpasseth the Love of Women. What were the first Heroes of *Greece* but so many able *Masters* in this noble *Science*, who went about demolishing Bullies and abasing the the Pride of insolent Pretenders. For my Part, when I read the Fables recorded of *Mars*, I cannot help believing he was a clever Fellow at Back-sword; and when hear of *Hercules*'s Club, I shrewdly suspect it to have been a Quarter-Staff. Thus, Sir, you see I have made good my Point, and justi-

---

171 Peter Drake, *The Memoirs of Capt. Peter Drake: Containing, an Account of Many Strange and Surprising Events, which Happened to Him Through a Series of Sixty Years, and Upwards; and Several Material Anecdotes, Regarding King William and Queen Anne's Wars with Lewis XIV of France, Volume I* (Dublin: S. Powell, 1755), 186-90.

fied my Title to a Place in the *Gazetteer*, from your own Claim to that honourable Appellation *A Lover of Antiquity.*

You may indeed say, that many Things in high Esteem among the Ancients are now grown out of Date. True, Sir, Time preys on all Things, or at least changes all Things; yet Manhood, with Submission, Sir, can never be out of Date while there is a Man. The Bully is indeed a detestable Character; but from the Abuse of a Thing to argue against the Use of that Thing, is, as I am told, bad Reasoning. Besides, this Science does not beget Bullies, but it teaches us how to be safe from them. If it was not possible to supply Force by Skill, every strapping Fellow might set up for the King of his Company, and no Man would dare to speak his Mind freely who was under Stature. But, by Dint of my Friend's Rules, Mankind are set on a Par, and, if I may be allow'd the Expression, the Partiality of Nature towards People of Six Feet high is set aside In regard to Use, therefore, I join Issue with you and as I have proved the Premise, insist upon a Place.

As I am never sanguine in my Expectation, so I have been thinking of another Excuse you might make, and that is the Impropriety of stiling this Business a Science. To this I might easily answer, Call it what you will. But as I love to speak pertinently, I think I had better defend the Term. Look over the Work, Sir, and deny it to be a Science if you can? It is built upon just Principles, which Principles are deduced from the Consideration of Nature. All its Rules might be (were it not pedantical) demonstrated Geometrically; in itself it is a noble Commentary on Anatomy, and a most excellent as well as irrefragable Proof of the Wisdom of the Supreme Being in the Structure of Human Bodies.

LASTLY, Mr. *Freeman*, let me tell you there is no getting off by saying you are a Political Writer. No, no, Sir, this is a System of Politicks too. Ay how so? Why, mark me, Sir, you have many times told us, that there is no Comparison more apt than that between the Body Corporal and Body Politick. Now if you convert Rules given by my Friend for the Conservation of the former into Maxims for the Defence of the latter, it will become a System of Politicks, and not a bad one. I might add to this, our late Political Disputes, especially in the Papers, have smelt a little of the *Bear-garden*; and perhaps I might say, that a certain Honourable Person hath fought his Enemies the Weapons thro', and at length beat them quite off the Stage. But you will probably think me already tedious, and therefore I conclude myself,

*SIR,*

| | |
|---|---|
| *Tilt-Yard Coffee-house,* | *Your Friend, Reader, and very humble Servant,* |
| *April* 10, 1739. | Christopher Buff. |

P. S. As my Prose is short, I have sent you some Verses to fill up; for, to borrow a Phrase from my Friend, I love a Bout at Sword and Dagger.

*To Captain* JAMES MILLER, *on his Gladiatory Art of Defence, &c.*

Freedom with Truth compleat your just Design,
The Praise be *Scotins*, as the Praise is *Thine*;
Harmoniously your mutual Powers unite;
And well he executes what you indite;
Mature in Science, boldly taught to draw
Great Nature, in her first and Sovereign Law,
The noble Apparate of Self-Defence,
Which equal Prudence boasts, and equal Sense.
　　From this fam'd School, young *Rome* in ancient Days
Form'd their rough Virtue, and renown'd their Praise
Contemning Danger, and contemning Death,
Advanc'd in Valour, and subdue the Earth;
Learnt ne'er in Fame's pursuit to be deterr'd,

And taught how Glory was to Life preferr'd:
With active Force our *Britain* catch'd the Flame,
The same their Passion, and their Fire the same;
Each Villa brings her Hero on the Green,
Provokes the Combat, and enjoys the Scene:
A Hat and Feather, crowns the Rustick Wars,
And he most Honour gains, who gains most Scars;
Till by Degrees their Emulation rise,
And Kings, and Sovereign Princes own the Prize:
The ample Stage with Seats incircl'd round,
Spread its broad Front, and animates the Ground;
A different Interest, different Nations warms,
And yield the Empire to the Law of Arms.
For *One* St. *Patrick*, *One* St. *George* appears,
Shouts rise on Shouts, and Fears succeed to Fears,
While equal Skill support the doubtful Fray,
They place their All on one decisive Day;
So *Horace*, and so *Curie* bravely rose,
This chose for *Rome*, and that for *Alba* chose,
Prepar'd the glorious Labour to sustain,
And fix the Nation's Fate ordain'd to Reign.
So *Hector* and *Achilles* boldly stride,
Maintain the Centre and the Field divide,
While Sword to Sword flash frightful from on high,
The stout Contention feeds each adverse Eye,
Uncertain who shall sink, or who prevail,
While *Jove* as yet suspends the doubtful Scale,
Till Shouts, and Shrieks, and Groans, confound the Coast,
Great *Hector* falls, and *Ilion* is lost.
    To Fashion's Whim all human Things submit,
Religion, Learning, Politicks and Wit;
In Nature change, or alter in Degree,
Ev'n Fortitude hath had its Modes we see;
Else why, tho' rais'd so high, and swell'd so big,
Why shines *Alcides* more than *Jemmy Fig*,
Alike in Fame, tho' differently they drub,
Or with a Quarter-Staff, or with a Club.
To thee (my Friend) I consecrate these Lays,
Accept my Wish, tho' impotent my Praise;
Led by the Science which adorns a State,
Inclines the Fair and stimulates the Great:
May each brave Soul thy Interest imbibe,
Each Maid applaud, and every Man subscribe;
Reward proportion'd to such just Deferr,
The bravest Mind, and best good-natur'd Heart.[172]

---

172 *Daily Gazetteer,* April 24, 1739.

# vi.

## JOHN PARKES

*"HAVING FOUGHT 350 BATTLES..."*

To the memory of Mr. John Parkes,
A native of this City.
He was a man of mild disposition,
A Gladiator by profession;
Who after having fought 350 battles
in the principal parts of Europe,
With honour and applause,
At length quitted the stage, sheathed his sword,
And with Christian resignation,
Submitted to the Grand Victor,
In the 52d year of his age.
Anno 1733.[173]

---

173 William Reader, *New Coventry Guide: Containing the History and Antiquities of that City* (Coventry: Rollason and Reader, 1824), 93.

## ACCOUNT BY JOHN GODFREY

JOHN PARKS of Coventry was a thorough Swords-Man, and an excellent Judge of all its Parts. He was a convincing Proof of what I advanced about the natural Suppleness in some Men's Joints. No Man bid fairer for an acquired Spring than he; but notwithstanding the vast Exercise, through such Numbers of Battles fought for twenty Years, he never could arrive to it. He still remained heavy, slow, and inactive, and had no Friend to help him, but his staunch Judgement.[174]

## PARKES vs. THOMAS HESGATE, 1710

At the Bear Garden in Hockley in the Hole.

A Tryal of Skill to be Performed between these two following Masters of the Noble Science of Defence, on Wednesday, the Fifth of April, 1710, at Three of the Clock precisely.

I, John Parkes, from Coventry, Master of the Noble Science of Defence, do Invite you, Thomas Hesgate, to meet me, and Exercise at these following weapons, viz. Back Sword, Sword and Dagger, Sword and Buckler, Single Falchon, Case of Falchons, And Quarterstaff.

I, Thomas Hesgate, a Barkshire Man, Masters of the said Sience, will not fail (God Willing) to meet this brave and bold Inviter, at the Time and Place appointed; desiring Sharp Swords, and from him no Favour.

Note. No person to be upon the Stage but the Seconds. Vivat Regina.[175]

## "GOOD SPORT, HACKING & HEWING", 1713

Yesterday a trial of skill was fought at the Bear Garden, between Henry Clements and Parkes, of Coventry, where there was a good sport, hacking and hewing. It is thought they got £50 a piece, the French ambassador being there, and giving them money very liberally. Soon after three bouts 'at threshing flail' were announced, and a flourish of 'no cut—no bout.'[176]

## PARKES vs. DONALD MCBANE, 1713

A Tryal of Skill to be fought at the Bear-Garden in Marrow-Bone-Fields, the Backside of Soho-Square, at the Boarded-House, on Wednesday next, being the 7th of October, beginning precisely at 2 a Clock, between Daniel Bean, North-Britain, Master of the Noble Science of Defence, and John Parks from Coventry, Master of the said Science. Note, Box or no Box we Fight, by reason the Company shall not be disappointed.[177]

## PARKES vs. JOHN TERRYWEST, 1714

At the *Bear-Garden* in *Marrow-bone-Fields*, the Backside of *Soho Square*, at the Boarded House, *A Tryal of Skill to be perform'd, this present* Monday, the 17th of May, 1714, *by two Masters of the Noble Science of Defence, beginning at Three of the clock precisely.*

I, *John Terrywest*, Master of the said Science, who am Obliged not to Challenge any Man: But the Gentlemen present at the last Battel, desiring me and Mr. *John Parkes*, of *Coventry*, to Exercise the usual weapons; We, to

174 Godfrey, 42.
175 *British Library Harley MS 5931 (217)*, April 5, 1710.
176 *Dawks's News Letter*, April 2nd, 1713.
177 *Daily Courant*, October 5, 1713.

Oblige them, and for the Diversion of others, will not fail (God willing) to Exercise the several Weapons following, viz. :—

BACK-SWORD,       SWORD AND GAUNTLET,
SWORD AND DAGGER,   SINGLE FALCHION, AND
SWORD AND BUCKLER,  CASE OF FALCHIONS.

Vivat Regina.[178]

## PARKES vs. DONALD MCBANE, 1714

A Tryal of Skill to be fought at the Bear-Garden in Marrow-Bone-Fields the Backside of Soho-Square, at the Boarded-House, this present Wednesday, being the 2d of June, beginning at 3 of the Clock precisely, between Daniel Baine, North-Britain, Master of the Noble Science of Defence, and John Parkes of Coventry, Master of the said Science. Note, For the Diversion of all Spectators, there will be two Couple Fight after the Prize is over[179]

## PARKES vs. TIMOTHY BUCK, 1714

A Tryal of Skill to be fought at the Bear-Garden in Marrow-Bone-Fields, the Backside of Soho-Square, at the Boarded House, this present Friday, being the 15th of October, beginning at 3 of the Clock precisely, between John Parkes, and his Brother, Masters of the Noble Science of Defence, against Timothy Buck of Clare-Market and his Scholar James Figg, Masters of the said Science. Note. It was at the Request of several Persons of Quality, who were obliged to attend the Reception of the Princess on Wednesday last, that this Prize was adjourned to this Day. N. B. They begin by times, by reason the Days are short.[180]

## PARKES & his BROTHERS vs. BUCK & his SCHOLARS, 1714

A Tryal of Skill to be fought at the Bear-Garden in Marrow-Bone-Fields the Backside of Soho-Square, at the Boarded-House, to Morrow being Wednesday, the 9th of June, beginning at 3 of the Clock precisely, between John Parkes of Coventry, Master of the Noble Science of Defence, with his Brothers, and Mr. Buck and his two Scholars. Note, We shall Fight on the Day above-mentioned, with Mr. Buck of Clare-Market, Master of the said Science, Thomas Commins and James Figg, his two Scholars.[181]

## The PARKES BROTHERS vs. JAMES FIGG & TIMOTHY BUCK, 1714

A Tryal of Skill to be fought at the Bear-Garden in Marrow-Bone-Fields, the Backside of Soho-Square, at the Boarded House, this present Friday, being the 15th of October, beginning at 3 of the Clock precisely, between John Parkes, and his Brother, Masters of the Noble Science of Defence, against Timothy Buck of Clare-Market and his Scholar James Figg, Masters of the said Science. Note. It was at the Request of several Persons of Quality, who were obliged to attend the Reception of the Princess on Wednesday last, that this Prize was adjourned to this Day. N. B. They begin by times, by reason the Days are short.[182]

---

178 George Clinch, *Marylebone and St. Pancras: Their History, Celebrities, Buildings, and Institutions* (London: Truslove, 1890), 41.
179 *Daily Courant*, June 2, 1714.
180 *Daily Courant*, Oct 16, 1714.
181 *Daily Courant*, Tuesday, June 8, 1714.
182 *Daily Courant*, Oct 16, 1714.

## PARKES vs. JAMES FIGG, 1720

At the Boarded House, in Marybone Fields, on Wednesday next, March 16, will be performed a Trial of Skill between JOHN PARKES from Coventry, and JAMES FIGG from Thame in Oxfordshire, Master of the noble Science of Defence, at the usual Weapons fought on the Stage.

N. B. They never thought to have fought any more; but being desired by a great number of Gentlemen which were present when they fought Six Scholars of each Master's, at the Fountain Tavern in the Strand; and the Two Masters fought Three Bouts, and gave great Satisfaction.[183]

At the desire of several Persons of Quality, and Others,

At the Board House in Marybone-Fields, on Wednesday the 16th of March, 1720, was to have been fought a Tryal of Skill, between John Parkes from Coventry, and James Figg from Thame in Oxfordshire, Masters of the noble Science of Defence; but the Day being so very cold that the Gentlemen desired it might be put of till Wednesday the 30th instant, where the above named, Masters will not fail at the Time and Place appointed, to give a general Satisfaction to all Spectators.

N. B. They never design'd to have fought any more but the Sword has been so much a bur'd by pretended Masters, and Gentlemen deciev'd and have not seen the truth of it, which was the Occasion of this Battle; but for the future they will prevent all such coming on the Stage.[184]

## IRISH vs. ENGLISH CHAMPIONS, 1727

At Mr. FIGG'S GREAT ROOM, AT his House, the Sign of the City of Oxford in Oxford-Road, Marybone Fields, this present Wednesday being the 4th of October, will be perform'd a Trial of Skill by the following Masters.

Whereas there have been a great many Reflections cast on the Irish Swordsmen by the English, declaring they would cut down all the Hibernian Race: We believe they will find it easier to talk than to perform, we being assur'd, we have as much Judgment in that Kingdom as in any Part of the World; and to prove our Character equal, we will fight them two on a Day, till there be a true Distinction: And to begin, We CHRISTOPHER PERKINS and BRYAN MACGENNY, do invite John Parkes, the Famous Coventry Champion, and James Collins from Cambridge, at the usual Weapons fought on the Stage; desiring those two Champions to exert their utmost Skill.

Note, We beg if any Gentlemen would ask a Question about the Battle, they would ask it publickly; for the English Swordsmen are free to tell what Cuts they give, but forget to tell what they receive.

We JOHN PARKES and JAMES COLLINS, jointly with the rest of the English Swordsmen. are fond of the Resolution of these Hibernian Champions; and although they are great in Number, let them take Care that most of them be not sent Home by Weeping Cross; The two abovenamed Masters will not fail to meet as above, and will endeavour to make their Swords decide the Battle apparently without whispering.

Note, Mr. Perkins fights Mr. Parkes, and Mr. Mac-genny fights Mr. Collins.[185]

## "I TALK NOTHING BUT WHAT I CAN AND DARE PERFORM", 1727

AT Mr. FIGG'S GREAT ROOM at his House, the Sign of the City of Oxford in Oxford-Road, Marybone Fields, this present Wednesday being the 6th Instant, will be perform'd a Trial of Skill by the following Masters:

Whereas I FELIX MACGUIRE, lately arrived from the Kingdom of Ireland, Master of the Noble Science of

---

183 *Original Weekly Journal*, March 12, 1720.
184 *Original Weekly Journal*, March 26, 1720.
185 *Daily Post*, October 4, 1727.

Defence, having fought Mr. Parkes several Times in that Kingdom, and came off with Honour; and since my Arrival here have fought Mr. Figg and Mr. Sutton with the same Applause; Mr. Parkes being a Spectator at the Battle on Wednesday last, and he talking much of his Judgment of the Sword, I do do invite him to meet and exercise me at the usual Weapons practised on the stage, nor doubting but to give entire Satisfaction to all Gentlemen.

I JOHN PARKES from Coventry, thought I had given this bold Challenger Reason to believe me a Master of the same Weapons, but farther to convince him, will not fail to meet as above, to let him know, I talk nothing but what I can and dare perform.

Note, They fight in Pumps and Drawers.

N.B. The Moorfields Gamesters and Lincolns-Inn-fields play at Cudgels for a Lac'd Hat, for Diversion of the Gentlemen before the Masters mount.[186]


## "the FAMOUS Mr. PARKES" in IRELAND, 1732

### At Mr. SIBBLIS's Great Room, (late Mr. FIGG's)

*In Oxford Road, Tomorrow, being Wednesday the 14th of June 1732, a Trial of Skill in the Noble Science of Defence will be performed between the two following Masters, viz.*

WHEREAS I John Bernard, from the Kingdom of Ireland, commonly called the Champion of Londonderry, who have obliged most of my Countrymen to own me their Master bath at Sword and Staff, having fought the famous Mr. Parks several times in Dublin, and always with great Applause, and now come to London on Purpose to fight that well-known Champion Mr. Figg; but finding, to my great Disappointment, that he hath declined the Stage, and hearing of the Character of Mr. Johnson, so famed for Judgment and Courage, thought myself, in Honour to the Sword, obliged to give him the first Invitation: Therefore do invite him to exercise all the Weapons he is Master of, and do caution him to take more Care than he did of my Countryman Mr. Mac-Guire, lest my Sword should penetrate as deep as it is reported his has done. Those Gentlemen that will be pleased to be at the Performance, need not doubt of ample Satisfaction, from

*Their Humble Servant,*
*John Bernard.*

JOSEPH JOHNSON, from Stapleton in Yorkshire, who never thought to mount the Stage till with Mr. Mac-Guire; but having given him an Invitation on Wednesday last, which he refused, (for what Reason I shall leave to the Censure of the World) now being invited by this unknown Hibernian Hero, cannot decline, without forfeiting that Character which by great Expence of Blood I have endeavour'd to gain: Therefore will meet him at the Time and Place appointed, likewise thank him for his Caution, but am of the Opinion, that my Sword will penetrate as deep as his, and do assure the worthy Spectators, that it shall be the utmost Endeavour of

*Their Humble Servant,*
*Joseph Johnson.*

N. B. There will be Boxing and Cudgel-playing, as usual, by Capt. Vinegar's Company.[187]


## PARKES vs MILLER (undated)

AT FIG'S GREAT TIL'D BOOTH, *On the* Bowling Green, Southwark, During the Time of the *FAIR*, (Which begins on SATURDAY, the 18th of SEPTEMBER)...The noted PARKS, from Coventry, and the celebrated gentleman prize-fighter, Mr. MILLAR, will display their skill in a tilting-bout, showing the advantages of *Time* and *Measure*...[188]

186 *Daily Post*, September 6, 1727.
187 *Daily Journal*, June 13, 1732.
188 Egan, 44.

Fig. 17. Thomas Barrett, Irish "Master of the Science of Defence." Engraving by Thomas Barrit, courtesy of Manchester Libraries, Information and Archives, Manchester City Council, reference number BR MS f 399 B13.

# vii.

## THOMAS BARRETT

### "WHOM HAS FOUGHT 260 ODD PRIZES", 1719

AT the Old Bear-Garden in Hockley in the Hole, on Tuesday being the 1st of September, 1719, will be perform'd, between Thomas Barret, and John Magaffy, a Tryal of Skill.

I Thomas Barret, from Dublin, whom has Fought 260 odd Priz's, and having a Difference with Mr. Magaffy, upon the Account of his reporting, that when he Fought me last, that he could Cut me where he pleas'd, which I took in Disdain; upon the same Affront do Challenge him to Fight me for the whole House, without Shirt or Stockings.

| | |
|---|---|
| Back Sword, | Single Falchon, |
| Sword and Dagger, | Case of Falchion, And |
| Sword and Buckler, | Quarter Staff. |

I John Magaffy, Sailor, commonly known by the Name of the bold Indian, and Master of the said Science, will not fail, God willing, to meet this bold Challenger, at his Place and Time appointed, and upon the same Terms he proposes, and don't doubt but to make him know that the Indian will give him full Satisfaction as he requires. The Box will be set at Four, and the Masters mount at Six.[189]

---

189 *Original Weekly Journal*, August 29, 1719.

## "WHO HAS FOUGHT 600 and ODD BATTLES", 1728

At Mr. STOKES's Amphitheatre, in Islington Road, Monday next, being the 30th Instant, will be perform'd a Trial of Skill by the following Champion and Championesses. Whereas I Thomas Barret, from Dublin, who has fought six hundred and odd Battles, and travel'd the three Kingdoms through to find and fight the principal Masters in those Parts, and hearing of the Fame of Mr. Stokes and his Wife being profound, have brought my Wife on purpose to give them a fair Invitation: The said Sarah Barret has fought thirty five Battles in Ireland, Scotland and England, and was, never yet defeated, and does not in the least Doubt but to have as good Success with this European Championess. I James Stokes, and Elizabeth Stokes, of the City of London, thought not to fight in Publick any more, but being creditably informed both by Scotch and Irish Gentlemen of Note, of the Bravery of this new Irish Champion and Championess in North Britain; but I am no-ways surpriz'd at this Encounter, and will display the Judgment of the Sword to their Disadvantage, my Spouse not doubting but to do the same, and hopes to give a general Satisfaction to all Spectators. Attendance will be given at Eleven, and the Encounter begins at Two. There will be the usual Diversion of Cudgel-playing before the Encounter begins.[190]

## "AND THEIR ACCOMPLISHED WIVES", 1730

At Mr. STOKES's Amphitheatre,

*In* Islington Road, *on* Monday *the* 13*th of* July, 1730, *the Judgment of the Sward will be shown in the best Manner that has been perform'd in the Memory of Man, between two compleat Masters of the Science of Defence, and their accomplish'd Wives, who are not to be equall'd in Europe, viz.*

Thomas and Sarah Barrett, after a Tour of several Years abroad, on our Arrival in this Metropolitan City, having challeng'd and engag'd the famed Mr. James Stokes and his victorious Wife, at their own Seat of Valour, where our Arms gain'd Applause enough to recommend us to the Publick, considering the Fatigue we had under-gone, and the Advantage our Antagonists had over us, by mounting the Stage fresh at Home, against Persons faint and weary'd with Travel as aforesaid: Being now in a State of Health, sufficient to undertake such an Enterprize, once more invite them at the Time and place above to shew what superior Power they command; not doubting to prove They are more fallible than ourselves, and that Fame has too lavishly bestow'd that Character on them, which we are of Opinion, justly belongs to us, &c.

Thomas and Sarah Barrett.

We James and Elizabeth Stokes, rather admiring the Vanity of the above presumptuous Challenge, than what than what Consequence must be drawn therefrom, assure our Opponents, not a single Fault shall escape our watchful Eyes, without due Correction from our vindictive Swords, and that they might as well have attempted the Chariot of the Sun, as to invade those Arms which nothing but Time itself can subdue, by paying that Debt of Nature to which Monarchs must submit, as well the meanest Subject. Being satisfied in this, we condescend to devote ourselves wholly at their Service as above, resolving to give them a final Answer in me most authentick Manner our Art can study, or Mankind desire, &c.

James and Elizabeth Stokes.

Note, As a numerous Concourse is expected, and good Diversion procured for the Day, by Cudgel-playing, &c. The Doors will be open'd at Three, and the Combatants mount at Six.[191]

---

190 *Weekly Journal or British Gazetteer*, December 28, 1728.
191 *Weekly Journal or British Gazetteer,* July 11, 1730.

## "AN EQUALITY of BLOOD WAS LOST on BOTH SIDES", 1730

At Mr. BARRETT's Great Booth,

*In* Bird-Cage-Alley, *over-against* St. George*'s Church,* Southwark*; on* Tuesday *next being the 28th of July 1730, there will be a Tryal of Skill by the following Masters.*

Whereas on Tuesday the 21st Instant, I Thomas Barrett, Master of the Science of Defence, who ever fac'd the most imminent Dangers, and have reduc'd the greatest Masters of the Sword by a Power superior to those who have been dignify'd with Imperial Titles, fought the famous Mr. Michael Butler, in which Battle an equality of Blood was lost on both Sides, where by the Glory of an intended Conquest was dawn'd, and the Victor held doubtful; In order to know the Man, I hereby invite him once more to try his Fortune at the Time and Place first above mention'd, being determin'd to maintain that Character the Publick have been pleas'd to honour me with, and of which Time itself can only deprive me, &c.

Thomas Barrett.

I Michael Butler, from Kilkenny in the Kingdom of Ireland, having fought the above Champion, before a numerous Appearance at the Place above-mention'd. and attracted a general Applause by a Deportment becoming a Gentleman of the Sword, assure him I shall there again face him, and add to the Honours already done me by grateful and impartial Judges, or so fall as to render s Defeat glorious, and teach unthinking Man how dear his Judgment ought to be fold, and that true Honour cannot be forfeited, &c.

Michael Butler.

Note, There will be the usual Diversion of Cudgel playing, &c. before the Masters mount, and due Care taken to render the Passage as easy and commodious as may be. The Doors will be open'd at Three, and the Masters mount at Six.[192]

## THOMAS and SARAH BARRETT vs. FELIX and LÆTITIA MACGUIRE, 1733

At Mr. SIBBLIS's Great Room,

(Late Mr. FIGG's)

*In Oxford-Road, Mary-le-bone Fields, this present Wednesday, being the 8th Instant, will be perform'd a Trial of Skill in the noble Science of Defence, between the following Champions and Chapionesses, viz.*

Whereas I Thomas Barratt, and Sarah my Wife, Champion and Championess of Exeter, gave great Satisfaction to the Gentlemen that were present at our last Engagement which Felix Mac-Guire and his wife, which was then judg'd equal, we do a second Time invite them to fight us at the usual Weapons practis'd on the Stage, where they may expect to meet a warmer Reception than they ever yet had, which shall be the earnest Endeavour of their humble Servants.

THOMAS and SARAH BARRATT

I Felix Mac-Guire, and Lettice my Wife, well known by the name of the bold Quaker, will not fail meeting these daring Inviters at the Times and Place appointed, not doubting but to give Intire Satisfaction to the Spectators and them some Marks with our keen Weapons.

FELIX and LETTICE MAC-GUIRE.

Attendance will be given at Four and the Champions mount at Six precisely.

Cudgel-playing and Boxing as usual by Capt. Vinegar's Company.[193]

---

192 *Weekly Journal or British Gazetteer*, July 25, 1730.
193 *Daily Post*, August 8, 1733.

## ACCOUNT of BARRETT'S DEATH, 1753

When I was a boy about eight years old, a noted prize fighter came to Manchester, by name Thomas Barret, an old man, with his face cut and scarred all over, so that for the most part he went by the name of "Old Chopping-block." He taught the science of defence (or what I should think was sometimes offence), in a large room at the Old Boar's Head, Hyde's Cross. While in town he articled with a stranger to show their feats of arms in public, in a yard near Salford Chapel; at which place I attended to see the exhibition, which was performed upon a stage in manner following: First, the champions entered the lists in their shirts, and bare-headed, with each a quarter-staff, about two yards long and as thick as the handle of a pike. These they brandished and whirled about with surprising dexterity; not forgetting every now and then to reach each other a lusty souse upon the sides, shoulders, or head, which was no ways displeasing to the spectators. This exercise being ended, and a little time spent in refreshing, the combatants approached each other with basket-hilted broadswords, and each a target (*i.e.* a large shield or buckler) upon their left arm; seconds likewise being appointed and upon the stage with poles, to prevent them going to extremities. In a little while both targets, not being covered with leather, were slit in pieces; and Old Chopping-block after this received a cut upon the cheek, near the nose. He immediately returned the compliment, cutting his antagonist directly upon the brow; by which their faces were almost covered with blood. After some few flourishes with their weapons, old Barret received another wound on his face, near the former, which he did not seem to approve; and, spying an opening in his adversary, gave him such a slice on the forehead, and with such earnestness, that the seconds, thinking it not prudent that the business should be continued any longer, parted them. This affair, however, not subsiding, a second challenge was given and place appointed, which was the Old Boar's Head yard, where I again attended a few days later. The fellows again mounted the stage with swords; but old Barret taking the advantage, cut his antagonist in the side, which was declared unfair play. Thus this combat ended, and was the last sword-play I ever heard of in England. In some while after Thomas Barret went to Ireland, and there followed the same business, and in a combat received a cut in his belly, which let his bowels out and ended his days.[194]

## BARRETT'S EPITAPH

Thomas Barritt. From the many cuts in his face called Old Chopping Block, a noted Prize Fighter; lost his life in single combat in Dublin about the year 1753, supposed to have been the last man in these kingdoms who made prize fighting his profession, his weapons were the broad sword & quarter staff, & at times used the target, he taught the use of the broad sword for the army, and the quarter staff for Park Keepers, Woodmen, and others.[195]

---

194 John Harland, *Collectanea Relating to Manchester and Its Neighborhood, at Various Periods*, Vol. II (Printed for the Chetham Society, 1847), 91-92

195 Thomas Barritt, *Ancient Armour and Weapons in the possession of Thomas Barritt* [1793-1811], MS.

# viii.

## EDWARD SUTTON

### ACCOUNT by JOHN GODFREY

SUTTON was a Contrast to the other. As PARKS had a clear Head upon a clumsy Body and stiff Joints; so SUTTON had a nimble Body and very agile Joints under a heavy Head. He was a resolute, pushing, awkward Swords-Man; but by his busy intruding Arm, and scrambling Legs, there were few Judgements, but what were disordered and disconcerted. FIG managed him the best of any, by his charming Distinction of Time and Measure, in which he far excelled all, and sufficiently proved these to be the Sword's true Foundation.[196]

### SUTTON vs. JOHN PARKES, 1724

AT the usual Place at Hockley in the Hole, this present Tuesday being the 11th Instant, will be perform'd a Trial of Skill by the following Masters.

I Edward Sutton, from Gravesend, Pipemaker (commonly distinguish'd by that Name,) who often with Pleasure have seen Mr. Parkes Exercise the real and true Judgment of the Sword; and being willing to approve myself his Competitor therein, do give him this Invitation, to meet me at the accustomed Place and Time, in order to Exercise the Weapons us'd in common on a publick Stage.

---

[196] Godfrey, 42.

I John Parkes, from Coventry, first return Mr. Sutton Thanks for his kind Complement; nor will I fail to gratify his Request, as expres'd in his Invitation: And as I doubt not in the least his Abilities, so hope to give a just Satisfaction to all Gentlemen, especially those who are Lovers and Encouragers of the Sword.

After the above Diversion, Mr. Carter and Mr. Hamlen, two Masters of approved Judgment, resolve to divert the Gentlemen by a Trial of their Skill, in order to obtain the Gentlemen's Sentiments who is the most Regular in their Performance. And the Diversion of the Day is to be concluded with three Bouts at Sword, and three at Staff, by two Scholars, the one of Mr. Parkes's, the other of Mr. Figg's.

N. B. The Spectators may expect to be well diverted, in regard four Masters and two Scholars are to perform.

N. B. The Doors will be open at Three, and the Masters mount at Six precisely.[197]

## "NO ARMOR": SUTTON vs. PARKES, 1724

AT the usual Place at Hockley in the Hole, this present Tuesday being the 8th Instant, will be perform'd a Trial of skill by the following Masters. I Edward Sutton Pipemaker, from Gravesend, Master of the Noble Science of Defence, when the Battle was on Tuesday last between Stokes and Mr. Parkes the Famous Coventry Champion, did insert in the Publick Papers, I would fight any Master; but no one apposing me, I bid a Defiance but Mr. Parkes never refusing any Man, accepted my Invitation. This is therefore to Certifie, that for the Credit of the Sword I will, upon the publick Stage, show myself Naked, that I have no Armour to defend the Sword, insisting, that Mr. Parkes shall do the same; and am resolv'd to give the best Satisfaction as in my power lies, it being the last Time of my Fighting. I John Parkes, from Coventry, Master of the said Science, will meet Mr. Sutton as above; and do assure him, it is to Answer every Article of his Invitation with the utmost Severity. N. B. The Doors will be open at Three, and the Masters mount at Five precisely, by reason of the Decrease of the Days.[198]

## "for the CREDIT of the SWORD", 1724

At Figg's new Amphitheatre, joining to his House, the Sign of the City of Oxford, in Oxford Road, Marybone Fields, on Wednesday next, being the 16th of Sept. 1724. Will be perform'd a Tryal of Skill by the following Masters.

I Edward Sutton, Pipemaker, from Gravesend, in the County of Kent, Master of the Noble Science of Defence, am strangely surpriz'd that Mr. Figg should have a Character beyond any other Master. Therefore, for the Credit of the Sword, do desire him to meet me as above at the usual Weapons, knowing myself equaliz'd with any, desiring him to exert the utmost of his Skill with the greatest Severity, not questioning in the least, but to give as good Satisfaction as ever was given on the Stage.

I James Figg, from Thame in Oxfordshire, Master of the said Science, am under as great a Surprize, that the above Mr. Sutton should be ignorant of the Cause of my having that Character, having, as I thought, given both him and all others Demonstrations thereof, the which to repeat, I will not fail meeting him as appointed, in Order to see how far his Knowledge of Equality does extend, as also to undeceive him, if he imagines that through me he will advance it any farther.

N. B. Attendance will be given at 2, and the Masters mount between 4 and 5 at farthest, because of the Decrease of the Days: As also that the usual Diversion at Blunts will be exercis'd for a Silver Spoon.[199]

---

197 *Daily Post,* August 11, 1724.
198 *Daily Post,* September 8, 1724.
199 *Daily Post,* September 14, 1724.

## SUTTON vs. JAMES FIGG, 1724

This present Wednesday the 21st Instant, at Mr. Figg's Amphitheatre, will be decided a great Controversy between the said Mr. Figg, and the experienc'd famous Edward Sutton of Gravesend Pipemaker, who abhorring the Thoughts of an Equal, much more a Superior, has invited our Oxonian Hero, who has hitherto undoubtedly been unequal'd, to dispute with him that Character, at which Time this famous Man of Kent is resolv'd to maintain the Appellation of their being unconquerable, and by the said Country 'tis thought he will gain the Point; but most others are inclinable to believe, that he will not only miss of the same, but also suffer a Repique.[200]

## BYROM'S ACCOUNT of SUTTON vs. FIGG, 1725

*Wednesday:* I was at Richard's first, for I wanted somebody to go with me to Figg's amphitheatre, where I went, but came too late to get in, as did numbers besides; so I went through unknown streets and by-places to look for books and coins.

*Wednesday, April 14th:* rose after nine; Clowes knocked at my door and bid me get up, for he wanted to speak to me; when I let him in he told me he was going to Westminster, and would call on me to go to Figg's amphitheatre; I thought he had something else to have told me of, about my son or something, I told him I could not go, upon which he flung away in a passion, and said only, "What an odd fellow you are, I never saw such a man in my life."...

Mr. B. and I walked to George's coffeehouse, where Mr. Leycester was; thence we took coach to Figg's amphitheatre, where Mr. Leycester paid 2s. 6d. for me. Figg and Sutton fought; Figg had a wound, and bled pretty much; Sutton had a blow with a quarterstaff just upon his knee, which made him lame, so then they gave over; there came other fellows in, but Tom Brettargh being uneasy, I came away with him, and we coached it to the Widow's coffee-house; there was a gentleman fainted away; Tom B. I believe would have done so too, if he had stayed.

*Wednesday, April 21st [1725]:* I writ out my verses about Figg and Sutton in shorthand for Jemmy Ord, and gave him them at Richard's to-night...

*Monday [May 3rd, 1725] :* I went through the park to the Court of Requests, where I met Mr. Whitworth and Mr. Staples, Mr. Fr. Whitworth, walked together a little; he desired I would not let the shorthand hinder my long-hand, that he had shown my verses about Figg and Sutton to Mr. Young, Jacob, that Jacobs was there, and said the thing was as it was described...

*Monday [January] 24th [1726]:* I crossed the water to Lambeth about four; after evening prayers saw Walker, with whom I stayed a good while, he...told me how Sir Thomas Parkyns* had been pleased with my verses about Figg and Sutton.[201]

200 *Daily Post*, October 21, 1724.
* Sir Thomas Parkyns (1664–1741), wrestling instructor who lectured at Figg's amphitheatre, and author of the noted grappling treatise Προγυμνάσματα, *The Inn Play, or Cornish Hugg Wrestler* (Nottingham: printed by William Ayscough, 1713). For more on Parkyns, see pages 200 and 236-237 of the present book.
201 Byrom, 104, 116-117, 121, 128, 194.

*Extempore V E R S E S upon a Trial of Skill between the two great Masters of Defence,*

*Messieurs* FIGG *and* SUTTON.

By John Byrom.

### I.

LONG was the great *Figg*, by the prize-fighting swains,
Sole Monarch acknowledg'd of Marrowbone plains:
To the Towns, far and near, did his Valour extend,
And swam down the river from *Thame* to *Gravesend*;
Where liv'd Mr. *Sutton*, Piper-maker by Trade,
Who hearing that *Figg* was thought such a stout Blade,
Resolv'd to put in for a Share of his Fame,
And so sent to challenge the Champion of *Thame*.

### II.

With alternate Advantage two Trials had past,
When they fought out the Rubbers on *Wednesday* last.
To see such a Contest, the House was so full
There hardly was Room left to thrust in your Skull.
With a Prelude of Cudgels we first were saluted,
And two or three Shoulders most handsomely fluted;
Till wearied at last with inferior Disasters,
All the Company cry'd, *Come, The Masters, The Masters.*

### III.

Whereupon the bold *Sutton* first mounted the Stage,
Made his Honours as usual, and yearn'd to engage;
Then *Figg*, with a Visage so fierce, yet sedate,
Came, and enter'd the List, with his fresh-shaven *Pate*;
Their arms were encircled by Armigers Two,
With a red ribbon *Sutton*'s, and *Figg*'s with a Blue.
Thus adorn'd the two Heroes, 'twixt Shoulder, and Elbow,
Shook hands, and went to 't, and the word it was *Bilboe*.

### IV.

Sure such a Concern in the Eyes of Spectators,
Was never yet seen in our Amphitheatres.
Our Commons and Peers from their several Places,
To half an Inch distance all pointed their Faces;
While the Rayes of old *Phœbus*, that shot thro' the Sky-light,
Seem'd to make on the Stage a new kind of Twilight;
And the Gods without doubt, if one could but have seen 'em,
Were peeping there thro' to do Justice between 'em.

## V.

*Figg* struck the first Stroke, and with such a vast Fury,
That he broke his huge Weapon in Twain I assure you;
And if his brave Rival this Blow had not warded,
His Head from his Shoulders had quite been discarded.
*Figg* arm'd him again, and they took t'other Tilt,
And then *Sutton*'s Blade run away from its Hilt;
The Weapons were frighted, but as for the Men,
In truth they ne'er minded, but at it again.

## VI.

Such a Force in their Blows, you'd have thought it a Wonder
Every Stroke they receiv'd did not cleave them asunder.
Yet so great was their Courage, so equal their Skill,
That they both seem'd as safe as a Thief in a Mill;
While in doubtful Attention Dame *Victory* stood,
And which Side to take could not tell for her Blood,
But remain'd like the Ass, 'twixt the Bottles of Hay,
Without ever moving an Inch either Way.

## VII.

Till *Jove,* to the Gods, signify'd his Intention
In a Speech that he made them, too tedious to mention;
But the Upshot on't was, that at that very Bout,
From a Wound in *Figg*'s Side the hot Blood spouted out.
Her Ladyship then seem'd to think the Case plain,
But *Figg* stepping forth with a sullen Disdain,
Shew'd the Gash, and appeal'd to the Company round,
If his own broken Sword had not given him the Wound.

## VIII.

That Bruises and Wounds a Man's Spirit should touch,
With Danger so little, with Honour so much!
Well, they both took a Dram, and return'd to the Battle,
And with a fresh Fury they made the Swords rattle;
While *Sutton*'s Right Arm was observed to bleed,
By a Touch from his Rival; so *Jove* had decreed;
Just enough for to show that his Blood was not Icor*,
But made up, like *Figg*'s, of the common red-Liquor.

## IX.

Again they both rush'd with as equal a Fire on,
That the Company cry'd, *Hold, enough of cold Iron,*
*To the Quarter Staff, now Lads.* So first having dram'd it,
They took to their Wood, and I'faith never shamm'd it:

---

\*    *Icor*: from the Ancient Greek: the liquid said to flow in place of blood in the veins of the gods.

The first Bout they had was so fair, and so handsome,
That to make a fair Bargain, was worth a King's Ransome;
And *Sutton* such Bangs to his Neighbour imparted,
Wou'd have made any Fibres but *Figg*'s to have smarted.


X.

Then after that Bout they went on to another —
But the Matter must end on some fashion, or other;
So *Jove* told the Gods he had made a Decree,
That *Figg* shou'd hit *Sutton* a stroke on the knee.
Tho' *Sutton* disabled, as soon as he hit him
Wou'd still have fought on, but *Jove* wou'd not permit him;
'Twas his Fate, not his Fault, that constrain'd him to yield,
And thus the Great *Figg* became Lord of the Field.[202]


## SUTTON vs. WELLS, 1726

At Mr. Figg's new Amphitheatre joining to his house, the sign of the City of Oxford in Oxford Road, Marybone Fields, tomorrow, being the 13th April 1726, will be performed a Trial of Skill by the following Masters.

Whereas I John Wells, from Bury St. Edmunds, master of the noble Science of Defence, do once more invite the reputed, famous Mr. Sutton to meet me and exercise the usual weapons fought on the Stage; when as skill consists in the judgment of the sword, I only desire that he will not, as before, lurk, but exert himself to the utmost, that the spectators may have an opportunity of seeing all he is master of, as also whose judgment and skill is superior, which that this battle may fully determine to the satisfaction of all encouragers and lovers of the science, shall, as always been, be the utmost care of their humble servant, John Wells.

I Edward Sutton, from Gravesend, Master of the said Science, will not fail to meet Mr. Wells as above, and I am resolved to answer him in every article of his request, and being amazed by what he means by lurking, I shall dispute in another manner not so liable to deception.

Note, they fight in white drawers, white stockings, shirts, and pumps. N.B. the doors win be opened at three, and the Masters mount at five exactly.[203]


## SUTTON & WELLS vs. PERKINS & BENNET, 1726

At Mr. FIGG's GREAT ROOM, at his House, the Sign of the City of Oxford, in Oxford-Road, Marybone-Fields, To-morrow being the 7th of September, will be perform'd a compleat Trial of Skill by the following Masters.

We Christopher Perkins, and Rowland Bennet, Champions from Ireland, having received several Affronts from the noted Mr. Edward Sutton and Mr. John Wells, with Regard not only to our Judgment in the Sword, but that of all the rest of our Countrymen; most arrogantly assuming to themselves a much better, and declaring that we ought not to appear upon the Stage but at Blunts; with several other Particulars that require the most publick Satisfaction, and for which in Honour and Vindication of ourselves and and Countrymen, we demand their Appearance at the Time and Place, abovesaid, to receive the just and due Reward of their Behaviour in Exercising the best they can at the usual Weapons practised or the Stage; either backwards or forwards, no Cuts ty'd up; that Side which gives most Wounds have half the Money in the Box; or as they and the Company please.

---

202 *Universal Mercury*, April 1726, 24-27.
203 *St James Evening Post*, April 12, 1726.

# G. R.

## At Mr. FIGG's New Amphitheatre.

Joyning to his House, the Sign of the City of *Oxford*, in *Oxford Road, Marybone Fields*, on *Wednesday* next, being the *8th* of *June*, 1726. *Will be Perform'd a Tryal of Skill by the following* Masters.

VVHereas I *EDWARD SUTTON*, Pipemaker from *Gravesend*, and *Kentish* Professor of the Noble Science of Defence, having, under a Sleeveless Pretence been deny'd a Combat by and with the Extoll'd Mr. FIGG; which I take to be occasioned through fear of his having that Glory Eclipsed by me, wherewith the Eyes of all Spectators have been so much dazzled: Therefore, to make appear, that the great Applause which has so much puff'd up this Hero, has proceeded only from his Foyling such who are not worthy the name of Swordsmen, as also that he may be without any farther Excuse; I do hereby dare the said Mr. FIGG to meet as above, and dispute with me the Superiority of Judgment in the Sword, (which will best appear by Cuts, &c.) at all the Weapons he is or shall be then Capable of Performing on the Stage.

I JAMES FIGG, *Oxonian* Professor of the said Science, will not fail giving this daring *Kentish* Champion an Opportunity to make good his Allegations; when, it is to be hop'd, if he finds himself Foyl'd he will then change his Tone, and not think himself one of the Number who are not worthy the Name of Swordsmen, as he is pleased to signifie by his Expression: However, as the most significant Way of deciding these Controversies is by Action, I shall defer what I have farther to Act till the Time above specified; when I shall take care not to deviate from my usual Custom, in making all such Bravadoes sensible of their Error, as also in giving all Spectators intire Satisfaction.

N.B. *The Doors will be open'd at Four, and the Masters mount between Six, and Seven exactly.* VIVAT REX.

*Fig. 18. Figg vs. Sutton, June 8, 1726. From William Hone's* Every-Day Book, Volume II, *1827*

We Edward Sutton, from Gravesend, and John Wells from St. Edmonds Bury, Masters of the Science of Defence cannot understand by the Style of this Challenge whether it came from Ireland or Smithfield, but believe from the latter, because it exactly agrees with one we receiv'd there the other Day from two Merry Andrews[*]; however since the abovesaid Champions (as they call themselves) can be spared from fro thence; and as they seem disposed for Blood and Wounds, we will not fail to meet them as above, at our Countryman Mr. Figg's, (the Stage we hope they intended to invite us to, as the only Place within the Bills of Mortality proper for Gentlemen of the Sword to appear and exercise at,) and maintain our superior Judgment, upon any Terms as they or the

---

[*]  "Merry Andrew is an old word of the Elizabethan era for a jester, or mountebank, not yet wholly obsolete." Mackay, 50.

worthy Spectators require, only desiring to insist upon having the best of Weapons, and if one one of either Side be disabled, his Companion to perform the Remainder of both Battles, or else to leave us, as we usually are, Masters of the Stage; which we claim as our just Right, and shall always do our utmost to support.

Note, Mr. Bennet fights Mr. Sutton, they having never fought yet. The Spectators are earnestly desired not to interpose or interrupt the Masters in any kind while they are performing.[204]

## LETTER by SUTTON, 1726

Whereas Mr. Figg's two Combatants, the great Mr. Wells and the renowned Mr. Banks, did not think it convenient to accept of Mr. Stokes's and my Invitation, to give a Specimen of their Aibilities, Gratis, at Mr. Stokes's Amphitheatre, on Wednesday last, I think proper in Resentment of the scurrilous Reflexion in their Bills, on the worthy Company that have hitherto appeared at Mr. Stokes's, and in Justice to my own Character as a Master of the Sword, to challenge any two from Mr. Figg's Amphitheatre to fight me at Mr. Stokes's Bout and Nout, either for the whole House or for Love, as they shall think proper to inform the Publick, in their Advertisements, and I doubt not but to make it appear, that the Applause they pretend to, never was given them by anybody but themselves.

EDWARD SUTTON.[205]

## "HAVING FOUGHT 182 BATTLES and NEVER YET BEEN DEFEATED", 1727

At Mr. Stokes's Amphitheatre, Joining to his House, in Islington Road, on Monday next the 27th of February, will be a Trial of Skill by the following Masters. I Hugh Macdonald, from Ireland, Master of the Noble Science of Defence, since my Arrival from that Kingdom, hearing of the Character of the invincible: Kentish Champion, Mr. Edward Sutton, and having fought the best of Masters in my own Country, and with good Success, they acknowledging me to be as good a Master as they can produce, do not question but I shall let the World see that an Irishman is to be brought in Competition with any Englishman whatsoever; and will fight the Weapons upon any Terms he pleases, although being a Stranger, and never mounted a Stage in London, shall not be dismay'd at this bold Hector, in order to let his Countrymen see he is not that mighty Man as they take him to be.

I Edward Sutton, from Gravesend, in the renowned County of Kent, Master of the said Science, will not fail complying with this bold Hector's Request, doubting not but I shall make him a Present of my usual Complements; and am strangely surpriz'd that any Man should have the Thoughts of being in Competition with me, I having given such plain Demonstrations of the Sword, and having fought one Hundred and Eighty Two Battles, and never yet been defeated; therefore, making no farther Apology it shall be as my usual Custom is to please the Gentlemen with a general Applause, there being some Wagers laid on the Battle.

Note, Attendance will be given at One, and the Masters mount at Three precisely. There is Three Pair of Gloves to be play'd for at Blunts before the Masters mount. No Person to be admitted under one Shilling.

N. B. Whereas Mr, John Wells, and Mr. William Gill, was to have fought for 20 Guineas, some of the Money being deposited, but the whole sum not being made up; now Mr. Gill desires, the said Mr. Wells to come at the Time and Place above-nam'd, when he will makeup the Money on the stage, and fight him for it directly.[206]

---

204 *Daily Post*, September 6, 1726.
205 *Weekly Journal or British Gazetteer*, October 22, 1726.
206 *Weekly Journal*, February 25, 1727.

## "CLOVE in the FOOT": SUTTON DEFEATS FIGG, 1727

LONDON, June 13.

The Company at Mr. Figg's Amphitheatre was agreeably entertain'd this Week; and pretty much at his own Expense; for there having been some private Disputes between him and Mr. Sutton, the Gravesend Champion; the last was determined to end them, in that publick Manner; so to it they went in Earnest; The Hero of the Day was Mr. Sutton, who came off Victorious; and his Opponent 'tis thought will not be fit for Action for some time, being wounded in the Belly, and, to use their own Term, made a Devil of; that is, Cloven in the Foot.[207]

## SUTTON vs. BRYAN BURN, 1727

AT his House, the Sign of the City of Oxford in Oxford-Road, Marybone Fields, this present Monday being the the 9th of October, will be perform'd a Trial of Skill by the following Masters.

Whereas I BRYAN BURN from the Kingdom of Ireland, Master of the Noble and Laudable Science of Defence, since my Arrival in this Kingdom have had the Honour of performing the Judgment of the Sword with the famous Mr. Figg at Oxford in his own County, and had the Approbation of the Gentlemen then present of not being any Ways inferior to him in Judgment or Courage; but being a Spectator on Wednesday Sept. 27, when the Battle was between Mr. Sutton and Mr. Macguire, at which Mr. Sutton was Victor by great Odds; but he scoffing and laughing at all the Country, and saying on the publick Stage he would serve them all so, I being a Master, thinking myself not inferior to any Master, do give Mr. Sutton a fair Invitation to exercise the usual Weapons practised on the Stage, and for the Honour of my Country and the Credit of myself, he shall not come off without knowing the Colour of his Blood, as I did to his Countryman Mr. Figg before he quitted the Stage at Oxford.

I EDWARD SUTTON from Gravesend in the renowned County of Kent, Master of the said Science, do willingly accept this Hibernian Champion's Request, but desire he would take Care not to be disabled at two Bouts at Sword as his Countryman was; but if he is not quick as I am nimble, I shall shew him such Play perhaps as will not be acceptable to him, any more than to the rest of those Hibernians which come to drive the World before them: I am resolved, as my Custom is, to please all Spectators with intire Satisfaction, which shall be to the utmost Care of their humble Servant, Edward Sutton.

N. B. The Doors will be open at Three, and the Masters mount between Four and Five precisely.[208]

## "THE TERRIBLE CHAMPION", 1727

At Mr. Stokes's Amphitheatre, in Islington Road, on Monday next, being the 13th of November, will be perform'd a Tryal of Skill by the following Masters.

Whereas I James Hughes, from the North of Ireland, known by the Name of the terrible Champion in those Parts, having already conqer'd all in my own Country, which the English Swordsmen are not Strangers to, was ambitious of extending my Reputation beyond the Limits of my own Country, whereupon I made a Tour into England, in order to engage the most celebrated Matters there, and hearing of the noble Exploits of Mr. Edward Sutton, the Kentish Champion, in cutting my Countrymen, and sending them home Lame, do challenge and defy the said Edward Sutton, to meet me and exercise the usual Weapons now in Esteem; and he being thought an excellent Man at Quarter Staff I desire to begin that first, flattering myself than whilst he, like the Carthaginian Hannibal, is puft up by his former Successes, with an over-bearing Opinion of himself, it will be my Lot, like the Roman Scipio, to put a final Stop to his further Progress.

---

207 *The Ipswich Journal, or, The Weekly-Mercury*, June 10, 1727.
208 *Daily Post*, September 9, 1727.

I Edward Sutton, from Gravesend in the County of Kent, think myself under an indispensable Obligation to accept, in every Article, the Invitation of this bold and triumphant Hibernian, notwithstanding his Height, which is Six Foot Three Inches, he being so fair a Mark cannot well mis him; and as for his Length and Strength I value not, for neither of them shall protect him from the utmost Severity of my Sword; bur I shall make no farther Apology, only that I make no doubt of proving him as weak in my Hands, as was of old the effeminate Persian Darius in those of Alexander. Attendance will be given at Twelve, and the Masters mount at Two.

N. B. They fight wet or dry, by reason there are several Irish Gentlemen who came over from Ireland on purpose to see it, and have laid great Sums of Money with some English Persons of Distinction.[209]

## "A TERROR to ALL the SWORDSMEN", 1728

*At Mr.* Stokes's Amphitheatre, *in Islington Road, this present Wednesday, being the 9th of October, 1728, will be perform'd a Tryal of Skill by the following Masters.*

Whereas I Michael Butler, from Kilkenny, in the Kingdom of Ireland, Master of the Noble Science of Defence, and in my own Country a Terror to all the Swordsmen there, and conquer'd all the Masters that I ever engaged with, which are Forty-seven, but having had a Battle with the famous Mr. Sutton, the Kentish Champion, in which, by an accident, he gave me a large Cut, tho' I think it not done by his Judgment; therefore I dare him to meet me once more at the Place above-mention'd, where I shall make him and his Votaries know that I shall retrieve my Character from that Misfortune, and remain Champion of Europe; and if the Gentlemen are not satisfy'd, I will fight the Weapons thro' till they are pleased, to shew that the Irish Blood is as good as the English.

I Edward Sutton, from Gravesend, in the County of Kent Master of the said Science, who never did nor will refuse any Master, am still proud to have the second Combat with this Hibernian Hero, tho' I did not by Judgment give him the last Cut, it may be his Lot to have double this time, which shall be by Judgment and Agility of Body. Making no farther Apology, I intend to the the best Means, which is usual my Custom to give intire Satisfaction to the Spectators.

Attendance to be given at Two, and the Masters mount a Four. There will be the usual Diversion of Cudgel-playing.[210]

## A FIGHT on SAINT PATRICKS DAY, 1729

At Mr. STOKES'S AMPHITHEATRE, *In* Islington-Road, *this Day, the 17th of March, being St.* PATRICK's *Day, will be a* Trial of Skill *by two Champions of Ireland, and two of England.*

Whereas I THOMAS ELMORE and I ANDREW MAC COLLEY, both from Ireland, Masters of the Noble Science of Defence, in Honour of the Day, and the Credit of our Country and Selves, knowing the famous Characters of Mr. Stokes and Mr. Sutton, the two Champions of England, we do thereby give them an Invitation to a Trial of Skill at the usual Weapons practis'd on the Stage, doubting not in the least but to let the English Swordsmen know that there is now arriv'd their Master-piece in the Noble Art of Defence. I the said Andrew Mac Colley have fought 106 battles, and was never defeated; and if any Gentlemen will lay any Wagers on the Battle there is some Irish Gentlemen will back Mr. Mac Colley for any Sum.

We JAMES STOKES and EDWARD SUTTON, Masters of the said science, being not afraid of any Hibernian Hectors whatsoever, will not fail complying with their Request, fearing not but to welcome these St. Patricks with a Cross, which will be very acceptable to them, and to maintain our Characters with Resolution we will not submit to any Irish Man whatsoever, being resolved to make it as smart a Batle as ever was fought in England.

---

209 *Weekly Journal or British Gazetteer*, November 11, 1727.
210 *Daily Journal*, Oct 9, 1728.

At Mr. FIGG's GREAT-ROOM,
At his House, the Sign of the City of Oxford,
in Oxford-Road, Mary-bone Fields, this present
Wednesday being the 2d of July, will be perform'd a
Tryal of Skill by the following Masters.

Hereas I JAMES HUGHES, from the North of Ireland, Master of the Noble Science of Defence (commonly call'd the Terrible Champion in my own Country, who never did engage any but the best Masters, as is well known) having ab.ut two Years ago had a Trial of Skill with the famous Mr. Sutton, and being in a bad state of Health, he had some small matter of Odds over me then: But being now strong and well, I desire him to meet me a second Time, and exercise the usual Weapons fought on the Stage, when, if he will, or dare, that Man that gives the most Cuts at Sword, and Blows at Staff shall take the whole Box, questioning not in the least but to convince him and all his Countrymen of their Opinions, and make him know that he has now met with his Master; and all the rest of the English Masters shall well understand the same before my Departure from this Kingdom, having already conquered all the Masters in the Kingdom of Ireland,

JAMES HUGHES.

I EDWARD SUTTON, from Gravesend in the County of Kent, Master of the aforesaid Science, will not fail meeting this terrible and undaunted Champion at the Place above-specified, in order to answer him in every Article of his Request; and altho' his Height be six Foot odd Inches, I value not his Length nor Strength, for neither of them shall protect him from the utmost Severity of my Sword and Staff, and those Gentlemen that will Honour me with their Company, shall see as good Performance as ever was seen in the Noble Art of Defence.

EDW. SUTTON.

There will be a famous Boxing Match between Joseph Thatcher, and one Jacob Belcher from Ireland, for ten Guineas.

The Box will be set at Three, and the Masters mount between six and seven.

*Fig. 19. Daily Post, July 2, 1729*

The Boxes to be set at Two, and the Masters mount between four and five, by Reason of a Double Battle.

N. B. There is six Pair of Gloves to be play'd for at Blunts between the English and Irish Gamesters, upon Account or the Day. Mac Colley fights Sutton, and Stokes fights Elmore.[211]

## SUTTON vs. SHERLOCK, SON of the "CHIEF MASTER", 1729

*At Mr.* FIGG'S GREAT-ROOM, *At his House, the Sign of the City of Oxford, in Oxford-Road, Marybone Fields, this present Wednesday, the 14th of May will be a Trial of Skill by the following Masters.*
Whereas I William Sherlock, Son of the famous James Sherlock, chief Master of the Science of Defence in the Kingdom of Ireland, lately put the Skill of the celebrated Mr. Sutton twice to the test in both Encounters, came off with Honour superior to that of any of his former Antagonists, especially in the last, which was on the 2d of May, when he received a Cut on the Head from me, which he was not able to return, I having a very visible Advantage over him, till we came to Quarter-Staff. I therefore invite him to another Engagement at the Time and Place above mentioned, at the following Weapons only. Six Bouts at Single Sword, Three Bouts at Sword and Dagger, Three Bouts at Sword and Buckler.

---

211 *Daily Post,* March 17, 1729.

I Edward Sutton from Gravesend, Master of the aforesaid Science, being always proud to meet such dexterous Heroes as this boasting Challenger, do in all Points accept his daring Invitation, desiring him to be very cautious, lest I prove him not invulnerable, since I design this for the decisive Battle wherein I hope to inlist him among his other Countrymen who have been vanquish'd by my Sword.          *Edward Sutton*[212]

## SUTTON vs. BENNET, 1729

At Mr. STOKES's AMPITHEATRE, Islington Road, on Monday next, being the 2d of June, will be a Trial of Skill by the following Masters.

Whereas I Rowland Bennet, from the Kingdom of Ireland, Master of the Noble Science of Defence, having fought Mr Figg 19 times, and disabled his Master Mr. Buck; an likewise fought Mr. Sutton two Years ago, and gave him a Cut on the Forehead, and only receiving a small Cut in the Leg, which was by Accident, was to have fought him the second Battle, but he declining, and left the Kingdom and went to North Britain, and made an Excuse he was sent for, I believe more for fear of my Sword than any thing else: I therefore desire him to meet me at the Place above specified where I shall give him to understand, with the utmost Severity, that I am not to be deem'd as the rest of my Countrymen.

I Edward Sutton, from Gravesend, in the renown'd County of Kent, Master of the Science, never did, or will refuse any Master in Christendom, will not fail meeting him a the Place he mentions, and to let him know I never will fly my County for fear of the Sword, making no further Apology but I will endeavour to maintain my Character as I have hitherto gain'd, and to the intire Satisfaction of the Spectators.          Edward Sutton.

The Doors will be open'd at 3 o'clock, and the Masters mount at 5 precisely.

There will be Cudgel-playing as usual.[213]

## "Mr. FIGG'S HEAD was THREATEN'D to be CUT OFF", 1730

*At* Mr. FIGG'S GREAT ROOM, *At his House, the Sign of the City of Oxford in Oxford Road, next Wednesday, the 17th of June, will be a Trial of Skill by the following Masters.*

WE Rowland Bennet from the City of Dublin, and Andrew Mac-Colley from Sligoe, both in the Kingdom of Ireland, so far Masters of the Science of Defence, as to believe the Solidity of our Judgment unquestionable, and that Britannia has not a Son to whom we ought to say Obeysance in respect of Valour, having more than once engag'd her Darling Figg, whose Fame, together with that of Mr. Edward Sutton's, seems to stagnate the Blood of Swordsmen, and fill the world with Wonders of their Performance tho in the End, like Æsop's teeming Mountain, a Mouse is the Product of the mighty Ball. If the said Gentlemen can Act, they lately took Occasion to Dictate, we do hereby desire then not to be sparing at the Time and Place above appointed, where the last Drop of Blood we may command, shall be spent, with Pleasure, in Hibernia's Cause, or her Honour be for ever lost, by our unexpected and meritorious Fall.

Rowland Bennet, Andrew Mac-Colley

We James Figg from Thame in Oxfordshire, and Edw. Sutton of Renowned Kent (the former having laid aside the Thoughts of fighting any more this Season, had not this Occasion offer'd) being so grossy affronted by the above Desperado's, that Mr. Figg's Head was threaten'd to be cut off by Mr. Mac-Colley, and Mr Sutton challenged in like Manner by Mr. Bennet; hereby promise to meet and entertain them at the Place and Time required, hoping they will candidly receive the bloody Banquet, since they so earnestly sollicit our just Indignation to

---

212 *Daily Journal*, May 2, 1729.
213 *Daily Journal*, May 31, 1729.

prepare it for them, sharp Sword, and no Favour, being the Fare they may expect; though in our humble Opinion, Sampson's jaw-bone would be of the same Service as Steel, to check their Pride, and make one a Conqueror over a Thousand such Philistines. All we crave, is, the Sight of their Face in Battle, taking no Pleasure in throwing at a Man's Breech, and making him sit uneasy, &c. promising, on our Part, that if one of us be cut down, the other shall fight his two Opponents.

James Figg, Edward Sutton.

Note, There is such a Demand for Vinegar this Mackarel Season, that the Captain can scarce procure Acids enough to pleasure the Taste of the Publick; but is promised a Reserve against the Time appointed, to oblige his best Customers, &c.

The Doors will be open'd at Three and the Masters mount at Five.[214]

## "AN UNPRECEDENTED TRIAL of SKILL": SUTTON vs. JAMES ROACH, 1730

At the Request of several of the British and Irish Nobility,
*At Mr. FIGG'S GREAT-Room, This present Wednesday, being the 18th Instant, will be shewn an unprecedented Trial of Skill in the Science of Defence, by the two following Masters; after which, Fighting of this Kind will be prorogued for four Months, especially if this Bill pass Nem. Con. in a full House, as it is expected, viz.*

I James Roach, late Corporal on Board his Majesty's Ship the Portmahone, from the City of Dublin in the Kingdom of Ireland, who never yet appear'd on a Stage in this Metropolitan City, declining those mighty Titles most of my ambitious Countrymen have too inadvertently coveted, tho', in Justice, I have acquired more Honour than any of my Predecessors, by fighting and defeating such Men as they were neither capable or willing to engage, notwithstanding the Blustre they have made of their Achievements of late Days, of which the Fly settling on a Coach Wheel as it went round, and crying out, What a Dust do I raise! is a just Simile. However, to avoid Prolixity, I shall only acquaint the Publick, It has been my good Fortune, among others, to vanquish the famous Sherlock, Jun, the growing Hope of my Native Country, and the Darling of Swordsmen; as also Brookes, the matchless Silver Baker, at Portsmouth: And that upon Advice of Mr. Edw. Sutton's, the famous and invincible Kentish Champion, having wounded two of my Countrymen on Wednesday last; Men, whose Actions, had they been proportionate with their Character, he could not have injur'd; I intend to fight him at the Time and Place above appointed, if he be pleas'd to accept this Invitation, and go through the Weapons with him backwards or forwards, for the Honour of his Country and the Benefit of the Box; for which I will bravely contend, while Nature's dread Decay shall slew the Hero is no more, &c.

I Edward Sutton, of unconquer'd Kent, Master of my Sword, and a Scourge to Pretenders, will not fail meeting this brave and bold Invitor, whom Fame has told me is a Tartar; and that to fall by his Arm would be more Glory than I have won from the conquer'd Troops of his vanquish'd Countrymen, a Recital whereof would be too tedious: But let him look to't that he does not add to the melancholy Catalogue, &c.

E. Sutton.

Note, That Gentlemen may not be imposed on, the Galleries will be set at 2 s. 6d. as usual; and 'tis hop'd they will be timely in securing Seats, the Masters being commanded to mount at Three precisely. The Box will be set at One.

Note also, There will be extraordinary good Diversion of Cudgel-playing, &c.[215]

214 *Daily Post*, June 15, 1730.
215 *Daily Post*, November 18, 1730.

## SUTTON vs. BUTLER, 1731

At the Sign of the George in St. Mathew's, on Thursday next being the 14th of this Instant January, will be the most smartest Trial of Skill known in the Memory of Man, by the Champion of England, and the Champion of Ireland, viz.

I MICHAEL BUTLER from Kilkenny in the Kingdom of Ireland, Master of my Sword in all its Branches, Offensive of Defensive, having had the Honour to perform at Windsor before his present Majesty twice, and likewise most Persons of Quality in the three Kingdoms with a general Applause with the invincible Kentish Hero, called the Champion of Europe, I do hereby invite him once more to a third Trial, and doubt not in the least but to Eclipse him of his Laurells which he has hitherto gain'd by the Sword, and to make him understand the Kingdom of Ireland can produce as good a Master as any in Europe.

MICHAEL BUTLER.

I EDWARD SUTTON of Gravesend in Unconquer'd Kent, Master of the said Science, which never yet knew the Scandal of a Defeat, or ever refused any Man in Christendom, viz. French, Dutch, or any other Nation whatsoever, will not fail Meeting this Hibernian Hector at the Place above mention'd; those Gentlemen that will honour me with their Company, may be sure to see as good Performance as was ever yet known in the Memory of Man; and do intend to let the World know I wear the Flag of Defiance at my Main-top-mast-head; making no farther Appology, but I intend to make the Town amends for my last Battle I fought in this Place, which shall be the utmost Care of your humble Servant,

EDWARD SUTTON.[216]

## "WITH the LEFT FOOT STRAPT DOWN to the STAGE", 1731

At the White Horse Tavern in Ipswich, on Thursday next, being the 28th of this Instant January, will be an extraordinary Tryal of Skill by the following Champions:

I MICHAEL BUTLER of the Kingdom of Ireland, Master of the Noble Art of Defence, having lately ingaged with Mr. Sutton, having been his Equal and Superior in all other Battles that I have Fought with him, except the last in this Town, (which was by the Force of his Arm and not by the Judgment of his Sword) was oblig'd by Persons of no skill in that Science to give way. This is to let him know, that I do give him a second Invitation and will Fight him at Length, at Sword and Dagger, and Sword and Buckler, with the Left Foot strapt down to the Stage, and the Single Sword and Quarter Staff not strapt. The Reason is to let the Gentlemen that will honour me with their Company, know that I do not but doubt to get the Victory over this Kentish Hero, and give him a Rowland for his Oliver. The best Man taking the whole Box, paying Charges.

MICHAEL BUTLER.

I EDWARD SUTTON of Gravesend in the County of Kent, Commander of my Sword, and the Scourge of my Enemies, knowing the abovesaid Champion rather to exceed in Words than Actions, will not fail meeting him; and the Conquest will be render'd more Glorious if it falls on my Side, as thro' Providence it hath hitherto done, by declaring Men of Merit, and disdaining iinterest for Balance with true Honour, which some of our Protection may or ought to contemplate and reflect on; and according to his desire I will answer him, and use him as a Stranger, in giving him his way, which is not common in this Art, or ever was done only twice, since the sword was in Request.          EDWARD SUTTON.

N.B. Attendance at One o'Clock, and the Champions mount between Three and Four.

Note, There will be other Diversions to divert the Gentlemen before the Masters mount the Stage,

Ipswich, Jan. 23, 1731.[217]

---

216 *Ipswich Journal*, January 2, 1731.
217 *Ipswich Journal*, January 16, 1731.

## "THE BEAUTY of the SWORD": SUTTON vs. BENNET, 1731

At Mr. FIGG'S GREAT-ROOM, *At his House, the Sign of the City of Oxford in Oxford Road, Tomorrow, the 21st Inst. the Beauty of the Sword, in all its Branches, Offensive and Defensive, will be display'd in the utmost Perfection, by the Two following Masters, and known Judges of the Science of Defence, viz.*

I Rowland Bennet, from the City of Dublin, and Kingdom of Ireland, who tho' I have not that Vanity to stile myself Head Master of my native Country, nor Inadvertency enough to harangue on too many Abilities; tho' it is obvious to the Gentlemen of these Parts, that I have as great a Right to the Title of Master, as any of my Predecessors, or Fellow Countrymen in Being can pretend to; having engaged the renowned Mr. James Figg in 23 memorable Battles, and come off with that Honour some have envy'd, and many vainly coveted, at the Expence of a small Effusion of Blood, and every Way vaftly different from the Case of others, who have tempted his superior Force; but turning my vindictive Sword the last Season upon Mr. Edward Sutton, and he not being satisfy'd with the Legacy I left him upon his Wrist, before my Departure, I hereby invite him on my Return, to prove that at the Point of his Sword, which he has given his Tongue the Liberty to utter; the Time and Place above, serving for that Purpose, when, and where, I expect him to meet me, and receive the Reward of his Demerits.

*Rowland Bennet.*

I Edward Sutton, of unconquer'd Kent, Master of my Sword, cannot but with some Astonishment behold the Improvement made by my Hibernian Brethren, of the present Age; I mean, in apologizing for lost Enterprizes, and so pathetickly introducing themselves to new ones; insomuch that it is as great a Crime now to give a Challenge or Invitation without a Preface to it, as it was formerly to do so, and decline it. However, the Purport of this Intention, any one may easily guess, and I shall acquiesce accordingly, entreating my Foreign Bravo to guard against that Arm, which so lately deny'd the great Mac-Guire the Liberty of blowing his Nose so easily, and will not fail to repay the illegal Legacy he mentions with double Interest, if it were but on the Account of immortal Buck, whom jilting Fortune caused to fall by his untimely Steel, which he has not yet sufficiently atton'd for: But may the rest be my Task, Courage, Skill, and Conduct, all conspire to hurl him from the British Stage, and fix my Fame above the Reach of such my Enemies.

*Edward Sutton.*

Note, It will be a general Field-Day, with Capt. Vinegar and his Forces, who will pass thro an extraordinary Exercise on this Occasion, and give uncommon Satisfaction.

Note also, If the Head Son, of the Head Master of all Ireland, namely Mr. Sherlock, who pretended an Uneasiness on Account of not fighting me in Bouts, alternately on Wednesday last, will be pleased to attend, and see one come off unhurt, which I doubt not, I will divert him in like manner and by taking the Extremity from his Face, send the Block home without a Byass.

Attendance will be given at two, and the Masters mount at four.[218]

## "OFOOT IS NOT a MASTER", 1732

At Mr. Stokes's Amphitheatre, in Islington Road, This Day, being the 3d Instant, will be perform'd a Tryal of Skill by the following Masters, viz.

Wm. Fenn, from the Kingdom of Ireland, Master of the noble and laudable Science of Defence, being willing to engage that Heroick Master now in Esteem Mr. Edward Sutton, if he accepts of my Invitation at the Place above-mention'd, the best Man take the whole Box, and the Money therein, and with a Resolution am resolv'd to let his Countrymen know he is not the Man they take him to be, and to give him and the Spectators to understand

---

218 *Daily Journal,* April 20, 1731.

I am not the Pretender of that noble Art called Defence, but a profound Master in all its Branches Offensive and Defensive. I hope all my Countrymen, called Masters, for the future will take Pattern by me to behave themselves like Men of Valour, and not to have a Stain in their Character, for the Honour of Hibernian Glory.

William Fenn.

N.B. Whereas Mr. Sibblis has inserted in his Advertisements of fighting me after a Fellow called Ofoot, from Canterbury, a Drummer of the Foot Guards, who does not know the Fort of the Sword from the Feeble, if he will come to the Place above-mention'd I will fight him my Left Leg ty'd up, if he does not I shall post him as a Coward.

I Edward Sutton, from Gravesend, in the Renowned County of Kent, Master of my Sword, will not fail meeting the abovesaid Gentleman at the Time and Place above specified, and doubt not in the least but to please the Spectators with that uncommon Satisfaction as was ever given, desiring all Judges and Encouragers of this Noble Art to be present, and to give their Approbation of this decisive Battle between these two Kingdoms, which is the best Master: If Satisfaction is not given to content the Company, the Weapons shall be display'd till then given.

Edward Sutton.

*Note*, Ofoot is not a Master, nor any Man in Kent, only myself, as the World can testify.

The Weapons are to be fought backward or forwards as the Gentlemen require.

There will be the usual Diversion of Cudgel-playing before the Masters mount.

Attendance will be given at Three, and the Masters mount at Six.[219]


## SUTTON vs. WILLIAM HANNA, 1732

At Mr. SIBBLIS's Great Room, (Late Mr. FIGG's)

*In Oxford-Road, To-morrow, being Wednesday, the 5th Instant, a Trial of Skill in the noble Science of Defence will be perform'd between the two following, Masters, viz.*

Whereas I William Hanna, from the Kingdom of Ireland, Master of my Sword in all its Branches, Defensive and Offensive, having perform'd on the publick Stage several Times and never yet could find any of the Champions to draw Blood from me, being desir'd by several Gentemen of the famous Kingdom from whence I came to engage that renowned Mr. Edward Sutton, the Kentish Hero, do hereby give him an Invitation to a Trial of Skill at all the Weapons now in Practice on the British Stage: He being thought the only Man at Quarter-Staff, if requir'd by the Gentlemen then present, I will fight the Weapons as they shall think proper.

WILLIAM HANNA

I EDWARD SUTTON, of unconquer'd Kent, never did or ever will refuse any Master in Europe, am very proud to embrace the abovesaid Gentleman at his Request, hearing a large Character of his private Merits by teaching the usual Weapons, and extoll'd by great Judges, will meet him at the Place and Time above-mentioned..

Gentlemen, your Humble Servant;

EDWARD SUTTON.

N. B. There will be much greater Diversion of Boxing and Cudgel-playing than usual, divert the Company.

Attendance will be given at Three and the Masters mount at Six precisely.[220]

---

219 *Daily Journal*, May 3, 1732.
220 *Daily Post*, July 4, 1732.

## At Mr. SIBBLIS's Great Room,
## (Late Mr. FIGG's)

*In Oxford-Road, To-morrow, being Wednesday, the 27th Instant, a Trial of Skill in the noble Science of Defence will be perform'd between the two following Masters, viz.*

**William King, from the** City of Dublin, Tobacconist, commonly known by the Name of the Black King of Morocco, lately arriv'd from the Kingdom of Spain, Swordsman, who have fought all those who I ever met with, and came off with great Applause, hearing of the Fame of Mr. Sutton, the Kentish Hero, do invite him to meet and fight me at the usual Weapons, not doubting to let him know, that there is still an Irishman alive that is able to convince him with the utmost Severity.

WILLIAM KING.

I Edward Sutton, from Gravesend in the renowned County of Kent, Master of the abovesaid Science, am very proud to embrace this Opportunity of meeting this bold Hibernian at the Place above-mentioned, where the Spectators may expect to see a good Battle, which is the firm Resolution of

Your humble Servant, EDWARD SUTTON.

Note, There will be much greater Diversion of Boxing and Cudgel-playing than usual to divert the Company.

Attendance will be given at Three and the Masters mount between Four and Five, by reason of the Shortness of the Days.

*Fig. 20. Sutton vs. "the Black King." Daily Post, September 26, 1732.*

### "FORTUNE IS A GAMESTER", 1732

At Mr. SIBBLIS's Great Room, (Late Mr. FIGG's)

*In Oxford-Road, To-morrow, being Wednesday, the 12th Instant, a Trial of Skill in the noble Science of Defence will be perform'd between the two following, Masters, viz.*

WILLIAM HANNA from Dublin in the Kingdom of Ireland, Master of the Noble Science of Defence, having on Wednesday last engag'd that renowned Champion Mr. Sutton, the Kentish Hero, to the entire Satisfaction of the Spectators then present...he receiving cuts from me and not returning any again, which he is pleas'd to say was by Accident, I do hereby give him the second Invitation to fight me six Bouts at single Sword, and six Bouts at the double Weapons, the Quarter-Staff excepted, doubting not but to give the Gentlemen Satisfaction. Satisfaction.                    WILLIAM HANNA.

I EDWARD SUTTON, from Gravesend in the renowne County of Kent, Master of the aforesaid Science, do acknowledge my receiving a small Cut, and had the Edge of my Sword take Place this Hibernian must have gone to the lower Regions; but Fortune is a Gamester, let him take Care of the second Game, making no farther Apology, I will meet him at the Time and Place appointed, and let him have a Care I do not bring the Crimson from every Part of him.                    EDWARD SUTTON.

N. B. There will be much greater Diversion of Boxing, and Cudgel-playing than usual to divert the Company.

Attendance will be given at Three and the Masters mount at Six precisely.[221]

---

[221] *Daily Post*, July 12, 1732.

## "THAT CUT CALL'D ACCIDENT": SUTTON vs. GILL, 1732

By Command of several Persons of Quality At Mr. SIBBLIS's Great Room, (Late Mr. FIGG's)
*In Oxford-Road, this present Wednesday the 21st Instant, a Trial of Still in the noble Science of Defence will be perform'd between the two following Masters, viz.*

Whereas I WILLIAM GILL from Gloucester, Master of the laudable Science of Defence, having fought Mr. Sutton, the unconquer'd Kentish Hero: long since, and not performing the Weapons through, by accidentally geting a Blow on the Left Arm, which render'd me incapable of going through the Weapons, having some Ailment in my Arm before, the Gentlemen were pleased to give him the whole Money therein: I do hereby give him the second Invitation to fight me twelve Bouts at single Sword, and those Gentlemen who will honour me with their Company, may depend on my Bravery; but Misfortunes will attend the best Men. I am resolv'd to put in Execution all the Severity of the Sword, if not to please the Spectators. Let the said Champion take the same Advantage as he had before, but it shall be with great Difficulty and Cost of Blood.

WILLIAM GILL.

I EDWARD SUTTON of unconquer'd Kent, Master of the aforesaid Science, do acknowledge that Mr. Gill was in great Terror when he received that Cut call'd Accident; but as for 12 Bouts at Sword finely is a hard Task, but what is good for the Goose is good for the Gander; and therefore I will not fail meeting the abovesaid Mr. William Gill at the Time and Place above-mentioned, where he shall meet with a warm Reception.

EDWARD SUTTON.

Note, There will be two Boxing Matches in particular by the abovesaid Command, and a full House undoutedly upon this grand Occasion.

N.B. There will be Boxing and Cudgel-playing as usual by Capt. Vinegar's Company.

Attendance will be given at Three, and the Masters mount at Six.[222]

## A CONTROVERSY regarding the QUARTERSTAFF, 1732

At Mr. SIBBLIS's Great Room, (Late Mr. FIGG's)
In Oxford-Road, To-morrow, being Wednesday, the 2d Instant, a Trial of Skill in the noble Science of Defence will be perform'd between the two following Masters, viz.

Whereas I JOHN HOMES, from the City of Cork in the Kingdom of Ireland, Master of the noble Science call'd Defence, was present on Wednesday last when Mr. Sutton and Mr. Hanna fought, to the Satisfaction of the Spectators; and as the Quarter-Staff has been excepted by most of my Countrymen, and Reflections cast on them for the same, do therefore invite Mr. Sutton to fight me at the usual Weapons practised on the Stage; and as he is approved of to be the best Man in England at Staff, am of Opinion that I shall hurt his Character, which shall be the intire Care of                                   JOHN HOMES.

I EDWARD SUTTON from Gravesend, Master of the above-said Science, am proud to embrace the Opportunity of this bold Hibernian, to exercise the Weapons now in practice, thinking Hibernia had forgot Crab, Hazle or Ash, being a Terror to them for some Time past, will not fail meeting him at the Place above-mentioned, where the Company shall be sure of seeing a good Battle, which shall be the utmost Care of

EDWARD SUTTON.

Note, There will be much greater Diversion of Boxing and Cudgel-playing than usual to divert the Company. Attendance will be given at Three and the Masters mount at Six precisely.[223]

---

222 *Daily Post,* June 21, 1732.
223 *Daily Post,* August 1, 1732.

## SUTTON vs. WILLIAM SHERLOCK, 1734

At Mr. SIBBLIS's Great Room:

*In* Oxford-Road, Mary le bone Fields, *this present Wednesday the* 3d *of* July 1734. *Will be performed a Tryal of Skill by the two following Great Masters in that Noble Art, call'd* D E F E N C E.

WHEREAS a great and famous Battle was fought the *Wednesday* before *Christmas* last in *Dublin*, between the two greatest Masters in *Europe*, at the same Time was present most of the Nobility, and Gentlemen at the Battle in that Kingdom.

I *Edward Sutton*, from *Gravesend*, in unconquered *Kent*, engaged Mr. *William Sherlock*, at the same Place and time above-mentioned, the Battle contained as such Mr. *Sherlock* received a large Cut on the Leg, I received one on mine the same Time; I not staying any longer in that Kingdom, came to *Great Britain*, to my Native Country, at my return I read the News Papers and and found myself very much wrong reported that the abovesaid Mr. *William Sherlock*, gave me three Cuts for One; but I utterly deny the same to do myself Justice, I do hereby invite the said *Hibernian*, at the Place appointed when I shall end all Disputes, and let the Swords tell their tails.

*Edw. Sutton.*

I *William Sherlock,* from *Dublin*, in the Kingdom of *Ireland*, do acknowledge it was inserted in the News Papers, and I do not believe it was a great mistake, however, since he is so forward, a will answer him at the Place and Time above-mentioned, as it is in his own country, I do not doubt but to let his Countrymen know he is not the greatest Hero as some Gentlemen and the Populice thinks, your obedient, the Flower of *Hibernia* of this Noble Art call'd defence. *Wm. Sherlock.*

*NB.* There will be particular Care taken as the Gentlemen may be well seated without any Interruption, desiring them to come timely by Reason of a full House expected, being two famous Masters.

Cudgel playing as usual by Capt. *Vinegars* Company, till the Masters mount, which will be at *Seven*.[224]

## SUTTON KILLS WILLIAM SHERLOCK, 1735

*From the* St. JAMES'S EVENING-POST, *Jan.* 10.

*Dublin, December* 30... On Saturday last died, William Sherlock the famous Gladiator, who received a Cut in his right Arm about ten Days ago from one Sutton an English Prize-fighter. Sherlock's Arm was cut off two Days before he died.[225]

## THE DEATH OF SUTTON, 1737

On Tuesday last died at his House at Gravesend, Edward Sutton, the famous Prize-Fighter.[226]

---

224 A single sheet. *On a duel between William Sherlock of Dublin and Edward Sutton of Gravesend* [1734]. The British Library, St. Pancras.
225 *Derby Mercury,* January 15, 1735.
226 *Daily Post,* October 22, 1737.

GUIRE, BANKS,

# At his MAJESTY's Bear-Garden.

In Hockly-in-the-Hole, *this present* Wednesday, *being the* 14th *of* May, 1735. *Will be performed a Tryal of Skill by the following Great Masters in that Noble Art,* call'd DEFENCE.

WHEREAS I *Felix Mac Guire*, from the Kingdom of *Ireland*, Master of the Noble and renown'd Science of Defence, who was challenged by Mr. *Elsegood*, at his Battle last *Wednesday* ; and he having since thought better on it, has declined the same; but rather than so Noble a Science should lie Dormant, I do challenge the celebrated Mr. *Banks* to face me, if he has Spirit to attempt it, and not triumph at the late Success of his Countrymen over *Hibernia*; for I'll shew them the Odds of that, and give them a Receipt in full for the Debts owing from my Country, and plainly shew that 'tis not by their Judgment, for that Misfortunes often attend the Great, the Generous and Wise. I have been indeed ill used by several *Englishmen*, and am now resolved to make all even by rectifying all Deficiencies. All this shall be perform'd by my Keen Sword, and the insulted Arm of your Humble Servant,

FELIX MAC GUIRE.

I *Richard Banks*, Master of the abovesaid Science of Defence, will not fail meeting this Desperado (being not in the least intimidated by his Threats) and dispute his Judgment in all Points ; and as to his Chat concerning the Success lately obtained by my Fellow Countrymen, he shall now find it by real Judgment, not but that I am sensible Misfortunes attend all Men. As for the ill Usage which he complains of, I'll rectify those Mistakes by as Keen a Weapon as he, and with as much Resentment. I hate a Multiplicity of Words, my anger'd Sword shall sound my Praise,

RICHARD BANKS.

Attendance to be given at Three, and the Masters mount at Six.
Cudgel-playing and Boxing as usual by Captain *Vinegar*'s Company of sower Crabs.

*Fig. 20. Detail of broadside announcing combat between Felix Macguire and Richard Banks, to be held on May 14, 1735. Image Courtesy of the National Library of Ireland, LO Folder 4/1735/2.*

# ix.

## FELIX MACGUIRE

*F*elix MacGuire, another of Ireland's most noted prize-fighters, first appeared at Figg's Amphitheatre in *August of 1727, having heard "of the Fame and wondrous Character of the much-admired Oxonian Champion..." His earliest known announcement claimed that he was formerly a "Serjeant in Sir J. Whitwrong's Regiment of Foot,"* and that he had "fought the best and most noted Masters in [Ireland] and several other Kingdoms with a general Applause":*

### MACGUIRE vs. JAMES FIGG, 1727

At Mr. FIGG'S GREAT ROOM,

At his House, the Sign of the City of Oxford, in Oxford-Road Marybone-Fields, To-morrow being Wednesday the 9th of August, will be perform'd a Trial of Skill by the following Masters.

Whereas I FELIX MACGUIRE, from Dublin, Master of the Noble Science of Defence, and Serjeant in Sir J. Whitwrong's Regiment of Foot, having fought the best and noted Masters in that and several other Kingdoms with a general Applause, and hearing of the Fame and wondrous Character of the much-admired Oxonian Champion Mr. James Figg, have made this Trip over on Purpose to undeceive these Gentlemen who are so much his Adorers; and do therefore invite him to meet me as above, and exercise the usual Weapons practised on the Stage

---

* Sir John Whitwrong's Regiment of Foot was stationed in various places in Ireland during the early eighteenth century. See *The Political State of Great Britain,* July, 1712.

with all the Skill and Cunning he is Master of, or he may happen to be eclipsed in his Glory, for the Honour of Hibernia, and to the entire Satisfaction of all the Spectators.

I JAMES FIGG, Oxonian Professor of the said Science, do very readily acquiesce with this Hibernian Hero's Invitation, and shall make no other Apology for myself, than that I will, according to my usual Custom, treat my Antagonist to his and all the Spectators agreeable Satisfaction.

Note, There will be a Lac'd Hat play'd for at Blunts by Six of Moorfields Gamesters against Six of Lincoln's-Inn Fields Gamesters.

Attendance will be given at Three, and the Masters mount at Six precisely.[227]

## MACGUIRE vs. PARKES, 1727

AT Mr. FIGG'S GREAT ROOM at his House, the Sign of the City of Oxford in Oxford-Road, Marybone Fields, this present Wednesday being the 6th Instant, will be perform'd a Trial of Skill by the following Masters:

Whereas I FELIX MACGUIRE, lately arrived from the Kingdom of Ireland, Master of the Noble Science of Defence, having fought Mr. Parkes several Times in that Kingdom, and came off with Honour; and since my Arrival here have fought Mr. Figg and Mr. Sutton with the same Applause; Mr. Parkes being a Spectator at the Battle on Wednesday last, and he talking much of his Judgment of the Sword, I do do invite him to meet and exercise me at the usual Weapons practised on the stage, not doubting but to give entire Satisfaction to all Gentlemen.

I JOHN PARKES from Coventry, thought I had given this bold Challenger Reason to believe me a Master of the same Weapons, but farther to convince him, will not fail to meet as above, to let him know, I talk nothing but what I can and dare perform.

Note, They fight in Pumps and Drawers.

N.B. The Moorfields Gamesters and Lincolns-Inn-fields play at Cudgels for a Lac'd Hat, for Diversion of the Gentlemen before the Masters mount.[228]

## "I WILL STILL BE THEIR MASTER": MACGUIRE vs. SUTTON, 1727

### At Mr. FIGG'S GREAT Room,

AT his House, the Sign of the City of Oxford in Oxford-Road, Marybone Fields, To-morrow being Wednesday the 27th of September, will be perform'd a Trial of Skill by the following Masters.

Whereas I FELIX MACGUIRE, from the Kingdom of Ireland, Master of the Noble Science of Defence, since my late Encounter with Mr. Sutton the famous Kentish Champion, in which I was Victor; but he having since reported, the Reason was, his attending the late Fire at Gravesend; therefore have given him this timely Notice, and desire him to make no further Excuse, but keep himself in Order, for I do now invite him to retrieve his Character at the Place and Time appointed, to the utmost of his Power, and the best Judgment he is Master of; and himself and all others shall know, before my Departure to the above-nam'd Kingdom, that as I have been hitherto, so I will still be their Master.

I EDWARD SUTTON, from Gravesend in the Renowned Couny of Kent, Master of the said Science, am very proud to embrace this Irish Hero's Request; and as for Retrieving my Character, I know not any I have lost, by having met once with an Accident: However, I shall not make any Excuse for myself, but am resolved to let all Gentlemen who will honour me with their Company see as smart a Battle as ever was seen on the British Stage and perhaps this second Engagement I may give him to understand, I shall serve him as I have done the rest of his Hibernian Race, send them to Ireland with cut Leg and Face.

---

227 *Daily Post,* August 8, 1727.
228 *Daily Post,* September 6, 1727.

I suppose he'll prove no puny Starter:

If he does this Time, he has met a Tartar.

Note, A Lac'd Hat will be fought for by Six of each Side.

N. B. Attendance will be given at Three, and the Masters mount between Four and Five, by Reason of a Black and an Irishman to go through the Weapons after our Battle, upon several Disputes they have had.[229]

## "HIS GENIUS, REGARD to TRUTH, and VALUE for HONOUR", 1730

At Mr. FIGG'S GREAT ROOM, At his House, the Sign of the City of Oxford, in Oxford Road, Tomorrow being Wednesday, the 23d of September, will be perform'd a Trial of Skill between the true following Masters, viz..

Felix Macguire, from the City of Dublin in the Kingdom of Ireland, Master of the Science of Defence, having fought most of the celebrated Swordsmen in the three Kingdoms, particularly Mr. James Figg, the British Alexander, the renowned Sparks, and the invincible Sutton; yet stand the same Man, bidding Defiance to the proudest of them all: But first Mr. William Gill, whom I invite to a Trial of Skill at the Time and Place above mention'd, entreating him then and there to use that Sincerity with which I ever fought, and will continue to do, condemning such as cannot wound 'till they themselves have smarted, and by a Temerity, or Fool-hardiness, which they mistake for Courage, throw at random, and trust to Fortune for the Event. This, all who know me will allow, I was never guilty of; and I am only sorry I am so unfortunate to see a Precedent of that Kind in one of my own Countrymen, whose Interest with mine, in all Things else, is inseparable. As it is beneath a Gentleman to reflect upon one Person for the Behaviour of another, I hope those whose Favour I have hitherto been thought worthy of, will be pleased to continue it, as I shall endeavour to deserve, &c.

Felix Macguire.

I William Gill, from Ducal Gloucester, late Scholar to Mr. James Figg, now taking upon me the Name of Master, and having my Sword at Command, promise to face and fight the above Champion according to Request, admiring his Genius, Regard to Truth, and Value for Honour, Things uncommon in such Cases, and not frequently found among his Countrymen. His being Second to Mr. Holmes on Wednesday last, against my said Master, and acting contrary to the Tenour of his Challenge, I must confess gave me Umbrage; and to shew my Resentment in its proper Colours, I hereby protest against his Proceedings in that Affair, assuring him I intend to take a Pocket-piece from his Scalp, as my Master did from that of his Antagonist; trusting to his Honour for not palming my Sword, and my own Judgment for his not hurting me, &c.          William Gill.

Note, Captain Vinegar's Company have promis'd to be very smart on the Occasion, besides which, there will be other good Diversion. The Doors will be open'd at Three, and the Masters mount at five precisely.[230]

## MACGUIRE vs. SUTTON, 1730

I Felix Maguire from the City of Dublin, finding the Rising Sun of y Native Country's Glory setting on Britannia's Orb, am fully determin'd to dissipate the melancholly Cloud hanging over Hibernia's drooping Head, by inviting Edward Sutton the Kentish Hero to meet me upon this Stage on the 21st of this Instant to fight, otherwise forfeit the Box. And calls to Remembrance the Song of an old Author, who sings,

Not Man, nor Sword I dread; but Winter's Frost,

Unless I fight, more than I'm worth will cost.

229 *Daily Post*, September 26, 1727.
230 *Daily Post*, September 22, 1730.

The Kentish Hero's A N S W E R

I will not fail to meet him, and as I find him to be a Son of the Muses as well as Mars, therefore to shew him I can pass a bill of Exchange, I answer him as Ben Johnson did the Highwayman.

> Wer't thou Great Holmes, or the revived Ghost
> Of famous B - - - k*, my Courage is not lost;
> For know, base Slave, that I am one of those,
> Can fight a Man as well in Verse as Prose:
> And when thou'rt dead, write this upon thy Hearse.
> Here lies a Swordsman that was slain in Verse.

N. B. Great wagers have been laid on both sides, but the Victor can't be known till next Week.."[231]

## "FOUR COMBATANTS (MALE and FEMALE)", 1730

### At Mr. STOKES'S AMPHITHEATRE,

*In Islington Road, this present Monday the 3d Instant, such of the Nobility, Gentry, &c. as shall be pleas'd to honour the same with their Appearance, will be diverted in a most extraordinary Manner, with the compleatest Trial of Skill in the Science of Defence that has been seen in the Memory of Man, by the four following Combatants (Male and Female) who are not to be parallel'd in Europe, &c.*

Felix Mac-Guire, first Master and Swordsman in Vogue in the Kingdom of Ireland, Tutor to the noted Mr. Holmes, who has four times fought the celebrated Mr. Figg this Season, with general Applause, the Last of which Battle: I was engaged with him myself, wherein I wounded the said Mr. Figg in the Belly, and gave him other convincing Proofs of my judgment therein, on Wednesday the 11th Instant, when, contrary to all Expectation, Mrs, Elizabeth Stokes, styl'd the invincible, matchless, unconquerable City Championess, took upon her to condemn the Method of Mr. Holmes's displaying or raising his Guard, &c. before a Grand Appearance then assembled, which with regret I was obliged to hear; and in regard the said Gentleman was my Pupil, I so far resent it, that I hereby Invite the said Mr. James Stokes, together with the said Elizabeth his Wife, at their own Seat of Valour, and at the Time Appointed, to face and fight me and a Woman I have train'd up to The Science from her Infancy, one of my own Country, and who, doubt not, will as far exceed Mrs. Stokes as the is said to have done those the has hitherto been concern'd with. As for my Part, Mr. Stokes may expect I shall at in the most offensive Manner I can and that the last Drop of Blood in my Body shall be Spent is Vindication of my Friend, and for the Honour of my Country; than which nothing is dearer to his humble Servant, &c.

I James Stokes, Citizen and Shagreen Case-maker of London, in Conjunction with Elizabeth my Wife, will not fail gratifying the Request of our formidable Invitors, on the Account of Mr. Mac Guire, who we know to be a Person of as good Conduct and Character as ever visited these Realms in his Capacity, being proud he has taken the indefatigable Pains to train up a Woman worthy my Wife's engaging, and who is likely to afford so much Satisfaction to the Publick; it is what we have often wish'd, as her Bravery will shine with greater Lustre in Conquest over so fine a Female, and will transmit her Name to latest Posterity, which has already been the Admiration of both Sexes; and gives me new Life on every fresh Occasion, as Mr. Mac-Guire shall find on this, when I am resolved so to demean, as to compel the astonish'd Audience to say, Man never did, nor Hero can do more, &c.

---

\* Master Timothy Buck, previously slain in the arena (See Chapter V.i.).
231 *Derby Mercury*, October 22, 1730.

Note, Gentlemen are desired to be timely in securing Seats, the Combatants being commanded to mount at Three precisely, by reason of the Shortness of the Days, and the Length of Time this Double Battle must inevitably take up, which is likely to be the last this Season, especially if this Bill pass. Nem. Con.* in a full House, as it is expected.

The Box will be set at One, and good Diversion, and Accommodation provided to fortify the inside from the Coolness of the Weather, &c.[232]

## "WHOM in COMBAT the UNIVERSE NEVER yet COULD PARALLEL"

### (undated)

At Mr. Figg's Great Room, at his house, the sign of the City of Oxford, in Oxford Road, to morrow, Wednesday Nov. 11, the Nobility and Gentry will be entertained (for the last time this season) in a most extraordinary manner with a select trial of skill in the Science of Defence, by the four following Masters; viz.

We, William Holmes and Felix Mac Guire, the two first and most profound Swordsmen in the Kingdom of Ireland, whom in combat the Universe never yet could parallel, being requested to return to our native country, are determined to make our departure ever memorable to Great Britain, by taking our solemn public leave of the renowned Mr. Figg and Mr. Sutton, at the time and place appointed; to which we hereby invite them, in order to prove we can maintain our titles, and claim a preference in the list of Worthies.

Tis not the accidental blow Mr. Holmes received on his metacarpus the last time he fought Mr. Figg, has shocked his courage, or given room to Mr. Mac Guire to decline his interest; no, it has been the fate of the best Generals to retreat, and yet to conquer; and the loss of a leg or an arm has augmented the glory of a commander, because blind fortune, and not the want of conduct, forfeited a limb which force nor envy e'er could take away.

We James Figg, from Thame in Oxfordshire, and Edward Sutton of renowned Kent, by the lofty language and pointed similies of the above bravo's, guess at their aspiring minds, and sincerely promise, since they covet to be great men, that, if at the time and place appointed they obtain a victory, by the sword, we will present them with our truncheons, being four feet longer than that with which Alexander was honoured at the head of his army, and far more serviceable in case of a rupture: on the other hand, if it be our fortune to deprive them of their intended glory in one sense, we will endeavour to be grateful in another, by sending them home, like Admirals Bembo or Carter, whose names the loss of a leg and an arm made ever memorable, and may serve for the copy of their departure, if blind Fortune (as they call it) act according to custom, &c.

Note, Mr. Holmes and Mr. Figg are to fight the first bout; Mr. Mac Guire and Mr. Sutton the second: Mr. Holmes alternately with Mr. Figg, Mr. Mac Guire and Mr. Sutton in like manner, and so successively during the battle; and, if one be disabled, his associate to go through the weapons with his two antagonists. A full house being expected, gentlemen are desired to meet sooner than usual, the masters being commanded to mount at three precisely, by reason of the shortness of the days, and the length of a double battle, &c.[233]

## SUTTON CUTS MACGUIRE'S NOSE, 1731

Mr. Macguire, the Prize-Fighter, had his Nose cut clear from his Face by Mr. Sutton, at Figg's Ampitheatre last Wednesday.[234]

---

*   Abbreviation of the Latin *nemine contradicente,* i.e., no-one in disagreement.

232 *Daily Post,* November 23, 1730.

233 John Nichols and the late George Steevens, *The genuine works of William Hogarth; illustrated with biographical anecdotes, a chronological catalogue, and commentary* (London: Longman, Hurst, Rees, and Orme, 1808-17) 108-109.

234 *Caledonian Mercury,* April 22, 1731.

I Edward Sutton, of unconquer'd Kent, Master of my Sword, cannot but with some Astonishment behold the Improvement made by my Hibernian Brethren, of the present Age; I mean, in apologizing for lost Enterprizes, and so pathetickly introducing themselves to new ones; insomuch that it is as great a Crime now to give a Challenge or Invitation without a Preface to it, as it was formerly to do so, and decline it. However, the Purport of this Intention, any one may easily guess, and I shall acquiesce accordingly, entreating my Foreign Bravo to guard against that Arm, which so lately deny'd the great Mac-Guire the Liberty of blowing his Nose so easily...[235]

At Mr. FIGG'S GREAT ROOM, *At his House the Sign of the City of Oxford in Oxford Road, on Wednesday next, being the 19th of this Instant May, a select Battle will be fought, on the Foot of a former Quarrel, between the two following grand Antagonists of the Sword, viz.*

I Felix Mac-Guire, from the City of Dublin and Kingdom of Ireland, by Nature prone, and by Skill qualify'd to encounter any Gentleman professing the Science of Defence, of which my Behaviour on the British Stage is an undeniable Proof, notwithstanding I received a fall Cut on the Nose by Mr. Sutton in a late Engagement with him, which he has taken Care to represent all he could to his own Advantage, by magnifying his Merits on that Score, and lessening mine to a degree of Insolence; tho' it happen'd he soon after met with the same Mischance, which at one time or other attends Mankind in general; therefore as nothing but Blood can palliate the gross Offence, I hereby intreat him again to face and fight me at the Time and Place above, when and where very Artery in my Body shall be drained, or my invincible Arm shall procure the desired Satisfaction, my Sword ever yet going the full Length of my Wishes, when push'd on with brave Revenge, which e'er to Mischief, pav'd the bloody Way, &c. Nor let him tempt me more, left by a too hot Pursuit of Conquest he fall a Sacrifice to the bold Attempt.

F. MAC-GUIRE.

I EDWARD SUTTON of unconquer'd Kent, Generalissimo of the Sword, and Comptroller of the Customs on the the British Stage, will not fail balancing Accounts with the above Knight-Errant, whose boasted Achievements rather animate than daunt glowing Breast, uneasy only that fleeting Time cannot double his Expedition in bringing us together; tho' be it when it will, my Opinion is I shall find him a perfect Don Quixote, who would needs have persuaded his Man Sancha Pancha, that he had slain Maximus and brought off his Helmet as a Trophy of the Conquest, tho at the same Time it was nothing but a Barber's Bason. Strange Infatuation! How far it may carry my Opponent I know not, but let him know, could this Battle reward the Conqueror with a Truncheon, I would not fear the Title of Belisarius, who under Justinian the Great, sent Terror thro' the World, and vanquish'd all that e'er opposed him, &c.          EDWARD SUTTON.

Note, A general Court Martial will be held to divert Company before the Masters mount, by Captain Vinegar, and other Field Officers, for the Trial of some new-listed Recruits and old Offenders, on Neglect of Duty, and for disobeying Orders and Wednesday last.[236]

## LETTER by SUTTON MENTIONING MAGUIRE, 1731

On Wednesday next I am to fight a much better Man at Mr.Figg's, namely Mr. Mac-Guire, if I come off well with him, as I do not doubt otherwise, I will fight the said Michael Buttler on the same Stage afterwards, upon his sincere Promise to stand to a close Engagement, and not to run off the Stage, fall backwards, and retreat upon the very Wind of a Sword, as he always has done, and I believe will continue to do. As to Mr. Wells, concern'd with him in endeavouring to reproach me, his Life has been too often in my Hands, and a Person I have already crippled, so that he is not worthy my Notice, farther than to say, I am sorry one of my own Countrymen should set up for an impostor, tho' the other prides in being so.          EDWARD SUTTON[237]

---

235 *Daily Journal,* April 20, 1731.
236 *Daily Post,* May 17,1731.
237 *Daily Post,* May 17,1731.

## BRITAIN vs. IRELAND—THREE vs. THREE, 1731

At Mr. STOKES'S AMPHITHEATRE, *In Islington - Road*,

On Wednesday the 21st of this Instant July, by the Command, and under the Direction of several British and Irish Peers, as well as Gentlemen of both Countries, the following Combat will be fought by three of the principal Swordsmen on each side, for the Honour of Great Britain against that of the Hibernian Terra Firma, the like of which was never attempted but once in these Realms. The Combatants for Ireland are *Felix Mac Guire, Andrew Mac Colley* and *Nicholas Hussey*, reputed the best product of that Country: and for Great Britain, the inimitable couragious *Sutton*, of Gravesend in Kent; *Joseph Johnson*, of Stapleton in Yorkshire, a Person of solid Judgment and intrepid Valour; and lastly, the all-conquering sincere *Gill*, of Gloucester; Men the nearest upon Ballance of any in Christendem, who are to fight on these Conditions, viz Each Man to change Swords every Hour, and when the Weapons are gone through, if the Company be dissatisfy'd, they shall appoint two of the best, or any other two, to fight for the Box, which will be set on the Stage for that purpose: And as this Battle requires a greater Length of Time than common, Gentlemen are desir'd to take Notice, that Attendance will be given at Three, and the Masters mount at Five.

Note, At the same Place, on Tuesday, being the 20th Instant, the Publick will be entertain'd with the greatest Variety of Bull, Bear, and Ass baiting, ever seen in Great Britain, Mr. Stokes being provided with the noblest and most docuble Creatures of each Specie, which, at a great Charge, he has so train'd to the sport, that they never fail giving the highest Satisfaction to the Populace, and are become the Admiration of the most curious. Attendance at Three, and the Sport to begin at Five precisely.[238]

## "AND DEFEATED THEM ALL", 1732

*At the particular Desire of several Persons of Quality,*
At Mr. SIBBLIS's Great Room, (Late Mr. FIGG's)
*In Oxford-Roud, Mary-le-bone-Fields, To-morrow, the 6th Instant,*
*will be perform'd a Trial of Skill by two great Masters of the Science of Defence.*

Whereas I Felix Mac-Guire, from the City of Dublin in the Kingdom of Ireland, Master of my Sword, having fought five of the greatest Heroes in Great Britain last Summer, and defeated them all; and, lately, that celebrated Master, Mr. Sibblis, by a Cut in his Belly, I do hereby invite him to dispute his Character, and his Country's Honour, at the Point of the Sword.

F. MAC-GUIRE.

I Thomas Sibblis, from Suckley in Worcestershire, now Citizen and Dyer, Professor of the said Science, the Request of the Noblemen that were present on Thursday last when I fought the celebrated Wm. Hannah, and gave the greatest satisfaction, will not fail meeting this vaunting Hero.

THOMAS SIBBLIS.

N. B. Mr. Robert Thomas from Dublin challenges any Man belonging to the Stage to fight him three Bouts at Quarter-Staff after the Battle is over.

Attendance at Three and the Masters mount at Six precisely. Cudgel-playing and Boxing as usual.

Note, On Monday next there will be a Boxing Match between Charles Raventon and John Broughton, for Twenty Pounds and the whole House.[239]

---

238 *Daily Advertiser,* July 19, 1731.
239 *Daily Post,* June 5, 1732.

## At Mr. SIBBLIS's Great Room,
### (Late Mr. FIGG's)

*In Oxford-Road, Mary-le-bone Fields, this present Wednesday, being the 18th Instant, will be perform'd a Trial of Skill by the four great Masters of the noble Art call'd Defence.*

## PREPARE.

WHEREAS we William Holmes and Felix Mac-Guire, both of the Kingdom of Ireland, and Masters of the Noble Science of Defence, with our usual and undaunted Resolution, do invite Mr. Sutton and Mr. Sibblis to meet and fight us at the Place above-mention'd, where every Nerve shall be employ'd in Vindication of our Country, and in Opposition to fruitless Pretences of our Antagonists, and to the Satisfaction of all Gentlemen who shall honour u- with their Presence. This being the last Time of Mr. Holmes's Appearance on the Stage for this Season he intends to exert his Judgment with the utmost Activity; and no less is expected from his Partner.

### Felix Mac-Guire and Wm. Holmes.

## ALWAYS READY.

We Edward Sutton and Thomas Sibblis receive this agreeable Invitation, hoping the Hibernians will fullfil the Promise made to meet and fight us, where defeated Resolution perhaps may serve instead of undaunted, when Kentish Terror and Worcestershire Might begin to appear on the Stage, where we hope both Courage and Skill will assist in giving our Beholders intire Satisfaction, and yield to Mr. Holmes a crippling Arrival in the boggy Climate, as before, which shall be earnestly endeavour'd by us,

### Edw. Sutton and Tho. Sibblis.

This Battle shall be superior to the Non-performance of Mr. Gill, who for his own Safety declin'd the Stage last Wednesday, though often call'd for by his impatient Adversary, F. Mac-Guire; then Mr. Sibblis was willing, for the Honour of his Country, after a long Journey from Oxford, to supply the Vacancy made by Mr. Gill on the Stage; but resolves at the next Meeting to repair what he then omitted, as being provok'd by Mr. Gill's Absence was oblig'd to fight in his Boots.

It is to be observ'd these four are the chief Masters in both Kingdoms, which will occasion an extensive Diligence for Superiority.

Attendance at Three and the Masters mount at Six precisely.

*Fig. 21.* Daily Post, *July 18, 1733.*

## FELIX and LÆTITIA MACGUIRE vs. THOMAS and SARAH BARRETT, 1733

At Mr. SIBBLIS's Great Room,
(Late Mr. FIGG's)

*In Oxford-Road, Mary-le-bone Fields, this present Wednesday, being the 8th Instant, will be perform'd a Trial of Skill in the noble Science of Defence, between the following Champions and Chapionesses, viz.*

Whereas I Thomas Barratt, and Sarah my Wife, Champion and Championess of Exeter, gave great Satisfaction to the Gentlemen that were present at our last Engagement which Felix Mac-Guire and his wife, which was then judg'd equal, we do a second Time invite them to fight us at the usual Weapons practis'd on the Stage, where they may expect to meet a warmer Reception than they ever yet had, which shall be the earnest Endeavour of their humble Servants.

THOMAS and SARAH BARRATT

I Felix Mac-Guire, and Lettice my Wife, well known by the name of the bold Quaker, will not fail meeting these daring Inviters at the Times and Place appointed, not doubting but to give Intire Satisfaction to the Spectators and them some Marks with our keen Weapons.

FELIX and LETTICE MAC-GUIRE.

Attendance will be given at Four and the Champions mount at Six precisely.

Cudgel-playing and Boxing as usual by Capt. Vinegar's Company.[240]

## "CHAMPIONS and CHAMPIONESSES", 1733

And on Wednesday next, at the same Place, will be perform'd a Trial of Skill in the Noble Science of Defence, between the following Champions and Championesses, viz. *Felix Mac-Guire*, Fencing-Master from Dublin, and *Lætitia his Wife*; with *Richard Banks*, and the *Unconquer'd City Championess*; the best Master and Mistress to have all the Money taken in the Box.

Boxing and Cudgel-playing by some of the best Men in the Town. Note, Mr. Carter, lately from Gibraltar, challenges Mr. Holmes to fight him the same way at any Weapon he is Master of.

N. B. Mrs. Sutton and Mrs. Barrett not being being able to give the Gentlemen any Satisfaction, the European Championess, it if she be not disabled by the abovesaid Lætitia Mac-Guire, will give them both five Guineas to fight her the same Day.

Mr. Stokes teaches the Art of Defence every Day. Good Horses and Chaise to be lett reasonably.[241]

## MACGUIRE vs. BANKS, 1735

At his MAJESTY's Bear-Garden.

*In* Hockly-in-the-Hole, *this present* Wednesday, *being the* 14th *of* May, 1735. *Will be performed a Tryal of Skill by the following Great Masters in that Noble Art, call'd* D E F E N C E.

WHEREAS I *Felix Mac Guire*, from the Kingdom of *Ireland*, Master of the Noble and renown'd Science of Defence, who was challenged by Mr. *Evegood*, at his Battle last *Wednesday*; and he having since thought better on it, has declined the same; but rather than so Noble a Science should lie Dormant, I do challenge the celebrated Mr. *Banks* to face me, if he has Spirit to attempt it, and not triumph at the late Success of his Countrymen over *Hibernia*; for I'll shew them the Odds of that, and give them a Receipt in full for the Debts owing from my Country, and plainly shew that 'tis not by their Judgment, for that Misfortunes often attend the Great, the

240 *Daily Post*, August 8, 1733.
241 *Daily Post*, August 20, 1733.

Generous and Wise. I have been indeed ill used by several *Englishmen*, and am now resolved to make all even by rectifying all Deficiencies. All this shall be perform'd by my Keen Sword, and the insulted Arm of your Humble Servant,

FELIX MAC GUIRE.

I Richard Banks, Master of the abovesaid Science of Defence, will not fail meeting this Desperado (being not in the least intimidated by his Threats) and dispute his Judgment in all Points; and as to his Chat concerning the Success lately obtained by my Fellow Countrymen, he shall now find it by real Judgment, not but that I am sensible Misfortunes attend all Men. As for the ill Usage which he complains of, I'll rectify those Mistakes by as Keen a Weapon as he, and with as much Resentment. I hate Multiplicity of Words, my anger'd Sword shall found my Praise.

RICHARD BANKS.

Attendance to be given at Three, and the Masters mount at Six.

Cudgel-playing and Boxing as usual by Captain *Vinegar*'s Company of sower Crabs.[242]

---

242 *At his Majesty's Bear-Garden. In Hockly-in-the-Hole, this present Wednesday, being the 14th of May, 1735.*

Have you not heard of fighting Females,
Whom you would rather think to be Males?
Of Madam *Sutton*, Mrs. *Stokes*,
Who give confounded Cuts and Strokes?
They fight the Weapons through complete,
Worthy to ride* along the Street.

Can Female Modesty so rage,
To draw a Sword, and mount the Stage?
Will they their Sex entirely quit?
No, they have not so little Wit:
Better they know how small our Shares
Of Pleasure—how much less than theirs.[243]

---

\*     Original note: "Prize-Fighters, on the Day of Battle, ride through the Streets with a Trumpet before them."
243 Henry Fielding, *Miscellanies* (London: Printed for A. Millar, 1743), 107.

Fig. 21. "Hudibras vanquish'd by Trulla", from Samuel Butler's Hudibras [1663-1678]. "Mean While the other Champion, Yerst / In hurry of the Fight disperst / Arriv'd, when Trulla won the Day..." Yale Center for British Art, Yale Art Gallery Collection.

114

# VI.

## "MISTRESSES *of the* SCIENCE *of* DEFENCE"

A man of bus'ness won't till ev'ning dine,
Abstains from women, company, and wine:
From Fig's new theatre he'll miss a night,
Tho' cocks, and bulls, and Irish women fight...[244]


### ELIZABETH WILKINSON vs. HANNAH HYFIELD, 1722

#### CHALLENGE.

I, Elizabeth Wilkinson, of Clerkenwell, having had some words with Hannah Hyfield, and requiring satisfaction, do invite her to meet me on the stage, and box me for *three guineas*; each woman holding *half* a *crown* in each hand, and the first woman that drops the money, to lose the battle.

#### ANSWER.

I Hannah Hyfield, of Newgate Market, hearing of the resoluteness of Elizabeth Wilkinson, will not fail, *God willing*, to give her more blows than words—desiring home blows, and from her no favour; she may expect a good thumping.[245]

---

244 James Bramston, *THE ART of POLITICKS, In Imitation of HORACE's ART of POETRY. Source: A Collection of Poems in Six Volumes. By Several Hands. Vol. I.* (London: printed by J. Hughs, for R. and J. Dodsley, 1763 [1st ed. 1758]).

245 *Sporting Magazine: Or, Monthly Calendar of the Transactions of the Turf, the Chase and Every Other Diversion Interesting to the Man of Pleasure, Enterprize, and Spirit, Volume 15* (London: Rogerson & Tuxford, 1800), 112.

## A FEMALE BOXING MATCH, 1723

Scarce a Week passes but we have a Boxing-Match at the Bear-Garden between Women, where one, who stiles herself *The City Championess*, gains the *Plaudits* of the Mob who assemble there. She is allowed to equal any of her Sex with her Tongue, as well as her Hands, there not being one in the *British Fishery* at Billingsgate that dares to attack her that Way.[246]

## ELIZABETH BEDFORD vs. THE CITY CHAMPIONESS, 1723

AT the Boarded House in Marybone Fields, on Thursday next, bring the 3d Day of October, will be perform'd a Tryal of Skill by the following Women.

Whereas I ELIZABETH BEDFORD from the Pindar of Wakefield, hearing of the Fame of the City Championess, do invite her to Fight me at the usual Weapons fought on the Stage, viz. Back-Sword, Sword and Dagger, Sword and Buckler, and Quarter-Staff.

Whereas Elizabeth Bedford will not be satisfy'd without Fighting me, the CITY CHAMPIONESS, but hath several Times said, that I would not, nor dare not Fight her: Now to let her see the contrary, as well as to satisfy the Desire of those Gentlemen, who are willing to see whether I am as well qualify'd in the Noble Science of Defence as I am in the Art of Boxing, I will and dare meet her at the Place and – *[all remaining text cut off in the original].*[247]

## "LIKELY ENOUGH to EAT HER UP", 1725

We hear that the gentlemen of Ireland have been long picking out an Hibernian heroine to match Mrs. Stokes, the bold and famous city championess. There is now one arrived in London, who by her make and stature seems likely enough to eat her up. However, Mrs. Stokes being true English blood (and remembering some of the late reflections that were cast upon her husband by some of the country folk) is resolved to see out *vi et armis.*[*] This being likely to prove a notable and diverting entertainment, it is not at all doubted but that there will be abundance of gentlemen crowding to Mr. Figg's ampitheatre to see this uncommon performance.[248]

## BONDUCA O'BRIEN vs. MRS. STOKES, 1725

AT Mr. Figg's New Amphitheatre, joyning to his House, the Sign of the City of Oxford, in Oxford Road, Marybone Fields, To-morrow, being the 24th of this Instant November, will be perform'd a Tryal of Skill by the following Combatants.

We Christopher Perkins, Taylor, from Dublin, Master of the Noble Science of Defence, and Champion of Ireland (who have lately fought the best English Masters with a general Applause) together with Bonduca O'Brian, the bold Female Hibernian Heroine, having heard of the Valour of the famous Mr. Stokes, and his much admired Consort the brave City Championess, do invite them at the following Weapons, viz. Back Sword, Sword and Dagger, Sword and Buckler, and Quarter-staff; and we don't doubt of giving convincing Proofs of the Hibernian Bravery, to the entire Satisfaction of all Spectators.

---

246 *Caledonian Mercury*, September 9, 1723.
247 *Daily Post*, October 1, 1723.
* *Vi et armis*, lit. "with force and arms," a legal term for the remedy brought by the plaintiff for an immediate injury committed with force.
248 *Guests Journal*, Nov. 20, 1725.

We James Stokes, Citizen of London, and his Wife the celebrated City Championess, having heard an extraordinary Character of Mr. Perkins, and his Heroical Countreywoman, do accept their Challenge with a hearty Good Will; and are resolved to make them know, that there is a great deal of Difference between the Irish Dear Joys[†], and a courageous Couple, who belong to the chief City of the most Warlike Nation in the World. Note, The Place of Exercise is dry over Head, being inclosed all round and all over.[249]

## A FIRSTHAND ACCOUNT of FEMALE GLADIATORS, 1725

I was sufficiently curious to wish to see the gladiators, and I will describe their manner of fighting.

The gladiators' stage is round, the spectators sit in galleries, and the spectacle generally commences by a fight with wicker staves by a few rogues. They do not spare each other, but are very skilful in giving great whacks on the head. When blood oozes from one of the combatants, a few coins are thrown to the victor. These games serve to pass the time till all the spectators have arrived.

The day I went to see the gladiators fight I witnessed an extraordinary combat, two women being the champions. As soon as they appeared on the stage they made the spectators a profound reverence; they then saluted each other and engaged in a lively and amusing conversation. They boasted that they had a great amount of courage, strength, and intrepidity. One of them regretted she was not born a man, else she would have made her fortune by her powers; the other declared she beat her husband every morning to keep her hand in, etc. Both these women were very scantily clothed, and wore little bodices and very short petticoats of white linen. One of these amazons was a stout Irishwoman, strong and lithe to look at, the other was a small Englishwoman, full of fire and very agile. The first was decked with blue ribbons on the head, waist, and right arm; the second wore red ribbons. Their weapons were a sort of two-handed sword, three or three and a half feet in length; the guard was covered, and the blade was about three inches wide and not sharp—only about half a foot of it was, but then that part cut like a razor. The spectators made numerous bets, and some peers who were there some very large wagers. On either side of the two amazons a man stood by, holding a long staff, ready to separate them should blood flow. After a time the combat became very animated, and was conducted with force and vigour with the broad side of the weapons, for points there were none. The Irishwoman presently received a great cut across her forehead, and that put a stop to the first part of the combat. The Englishwoman's backers threw her shillings and half-crowns and applauded her. During this time the wounded woman's forehead was sewn up, this being done on the stage; a plaster was applied to it, and she drank a good big glass of spirits to revive her courage, and the fight began again, each combatant holding a dagger in her left hand to ward off the blows. The Irishwoman was wounded a second time, and her adversary again received coins and plaudits from her admirers. The wound was sewn up, and for the third time the battle recommenced, the women holding wicker shields as defensive weapons. This third combat was fought for some time without result, but the poor Irishwoman was destined to be the loser, for she received a long and deep wound all across her neck and throat. The surgeon sewed it up, but she was too badly hurt to fight any more, and it was time, for the combatants were dripping with perspiration, and the Irishwoman also with blood. A few coins were thrown to her to console her, but the victor made a good day's work out of the combat. Fortunately it is very rarely one hears of women gladiators.

Two male champions next appeared. They wore short white jackets and breeches and hose of the same colour; their heads were bare and freshly-shaven; one of them wore green ribbons, the other yellow. They were hideous to look at, their faces being all seamed and scarred. They also commenced by paying each other grotesque and amusing compliments, and then fell on each other with the same sort of weapons the women had used; but they showed more strength, vigour, and ability, if not more courage. One blow rapidly followed another; it was really surprising neither man should be killed, but this never seems to happen. They fought five or six times running,

† *Dear Joy*: A term for an Irish person, often derogatory, popularized in the 1680s.
249 *Daily Post*, November 23, 1725.

and only stopped for the sewing up of a wound or when too exhausted to continue. After every round the victor was thrown money by his backers; but he had to exercise great skill in catching the coins, for he had a right only to those he caught in his hands; those that fell on the ground became the property of some of the numerous rascals that were standing about, who hastened to pick them up and appropriate them. The two combatants received several wounds, one of them having his ear nearly severed from his head, and a few moments later his opponent got a cut across the face, commencing at the left eye and ending on the right cheek. This last wound ended the fight and entertainment, and I went away regretting my half-crown and determined never to assist at one of these combats again.[250]

## MARY WELCH vs. ELIZABETH STOKES, 1726

*At the Request of several English and Irish Gentlemen.*

At Mr. STOKES's Amphitheatre, in Islington Road, near Sadler's Wells, on Monday next, being the 3d of October, will be perform'd a trial of skill by the following Championesses.

Whereas I Mary Welch, from the Kingdom of Ireland, being taught, and knowing the noble science of defence, and thought to be the only female of this kind in Europe, understanding there is one in this Kingdom, who has exercised on the publick stage several times, which is Mrs. Stokes, who is stiled the famous Championess of England; I do hereby invite her to meet me, and exercise the usual weapons practis'd on the stage, at her own amphitheatre, doubting not, but to let her and the worthy spectators see, that my judgment and courage is beyond hers.

I Elizabeth Stokes, of the famous City of London, being well known by the name of the Invincible City Championess for my abilities and judgment in the abovesaid science; having never engaged with any of my own sex but I always came off with victory and applause, shall make no apology for accepting the challenge of this Irish Heroine, not doubting but to maintain the reputation I have hitherto establish'd, and shew my country, that the contest of it's honour, is not ill entrusted in the present battle with their Championess, Elizabeth Stokes.

Note, The doors will be open'd at two, and the Championesses mount at four.

N.B. They fight in close jackets, short petticoats, coming just below the knee, Holland drawers, white stockings, and pumps.[251]

## MARY WELSH & ROBERT BARKER vs. ELIZABETH & JAMES STOKES, 1727

In Islington road, on Monday, being the 17th of July, 1727, will be performed a trial of skill by the following combatants.

We Robert Barker and Mary Welsh, from Ireland, having often contaminated our swords in the abdominous corporations of such antagonists as have had the insolence to dispute our skill, do find ourselves once more necessitated to challenge, defy, and invite Mr. Stokes and his bold Amazonian virago to meet us on the stage, where we hope to give a satisfaction to the honourable Lord of our nation who has laid a wager of twenty guineas on our heads. They that give the most cuts to have the whole money, and the benefit of the house; and if swords, daggers, quarter-staff, fury, rage, and resolution, will prevail, our friends shall not meet with a disappointment.

We James and Elizabeth Stokes, of the City of London, having already gained an universal approbation by our agility of body, dextrous hands, and courageous hearts, need not preambulate on this occasion, but rather choose to exercise the sword to their sorrow, and corroborate the general opinion of the town than to follow the custom of our repartee antagonists. This will be the last time of Mrs. Stokes' performing on the stage.

---

250 Saussure, 277-279.
251 *Weekly Journal, or The British Gazetteer,* October 1, 1726.

There will be a door on purpose for the reception of the gentlemen, where coaches may drive up to it, and the company come in without being crowded. Attendance will be given at three, and the combatants mount at six precisely. They all fight in the same dresses as before.[252]

## ELIZABETH BEDFORD vs. MARY WELCH, 1727

*At Mrs.* L E E 's *Great Booth.*

In Blue-Maid-Alley, near the Marshallsea-Gate, Southwark, on Monday next, being the 3d of April, will be perform'd a compleate Trial of Skill by the following Championesses. Whereas I ELIZABETH BEDFORD, from the Pindar of Wakefield, in Gray's-Inn-Lane, being taught, and knowing the noble Science of Defence, hearing of the famous Irish Championess, Mrs. Welch, I do invite her to meet me, and exercise the usual Weapons practis'd on the Stage, doubting not but to let her and the worthy Spectators see, that my Judgment and Courage is far beyond her's. I MARY WELCH, from the famous City of Dublin, being well known by the Name of the Invincible Irish Championess, for my Abilities and Judgment in the above-said Science, having never engaged with any of my own Sex, but I always acquir'd Applause, shall make no Apology for accepting the Challenge of this English Heroine, not fearing in the least, but I shall give entire Satisfaction, as I did when I fought Mrs. Stokes, and a so maintain the Character I have assum'd, and thew my Country, that the Contest of it's Honour is not ill entrusted in the present Battle with their Championess.  MARY WELCH.

Note, The Boxes will be set at Three, and the Championesses mount at Five precisely. N. B. They fight in close Jackets, short Petticoats coming just below the Knee, Holland Drawers, white Stockings, and Pumps.[253]

## MARY BARKER vs. ELIZABETH HUGHES, 1728

At Mr. FIGG's GREAT ROOM, AT his House the Sign of the City of Oxford in Oxford-Road, Marybone-Fields, on Monday next being the 22d of April, will be perform'd a Trial of Skill by the following Champions.

Whereas I ROBERT BARKER from Dublin, Master of the Noble Science of Defence, knowing the Fame of Mr. Gill, by seeing him so often prov'd, reckon myself as good, if not his superior, the which to decide, I do invite him to meet me and exercise the usual Weapons now in Esteem.

I WILLIAM GILL from Gloucester, Master of the said Science, will not fail of complying with this Bold Hector's Request, and without making any farther Apology, am resolved to meet him at the Place above specified, where I hope to please all Gentlemen, and give intire Satisfaction.

Whereas I MARY BARKER, Wife of the abovesaid Robert Barker, having receiv'd so many Affronts from Elizabeth Hughes, and she being taught by several Masters of the Sword, extols herself to a high Degree; but I believe the World is sensible I am the only Championess in Europe, I do now invite the abovesaid Heroine to meet me at the Place above, and exercise the usual Weapons now in Esteem, where I doubt not but to give entire Satisfaction.

I ELIZABETH HUGHES, thinking myself far superior to any of my Sex in the three Kingdoms, very willingly accept the Invitation of this Bold Championess, and will give such convincing Proofs of my Judgment and Boldness of the Sword, that the World cannot produce such a Woman now living. Note, The Doors will be opened at Three, and the Masters mount at Five precisely: There will be the usual Diversions of Cudgel-playing before the Masters mount.[254]

---

252 James Peller Malcolm, *Anecdotes of the Manner and Customs of London During the Eighteenth Century* (London: Longman, Hurst, Rees, and Orme, 1810), 170-171.
253 *Weekly Journal or British Gazetteer,* April 1, 1727.
254 *Daily Post,* April 20, 1728.

Fig 22. Detail from "The Female Bruisers" by John Goldar. Published by Heny. Parker, No. 82 Cornhill, and Thos. Bradford, No. 132 Fleet Street, 1770. Courtesy of The Lewis Walpole Library, Yale University.

## ANN FIELD, "ASS-DRIVER" vs. MRS. STOKES, 1728

Whereas I, Ann Field of Stoke-Newington, ass-driver, well known for my abilities in boxing in my own defence wherever it happened in my way, having been affronted by Mrs Stokes, styled the European Championess, do fairly invite her to a trial of the best skill in boxing, for ten pounds, fair rise and fall; and question not but to give her such proofs of my judgment that shall oblige her to acknowledge me Championess of the Stage, to the entire satisfaction of all my friends.

I, Elizabeth Stokes, of the city of London, have not fought in this way since I fought the famous boxing-woman of Billingsgate twenty-nine minutes, and gained a complete victory (which is six years ago); but as the famous Stoke-Newington ass-woman dares me to fight her for the ten pounds, I do assure her I will not fail meeting her for the said sum, and doubt not that the blows which I shall present her with, will be more difficult for her to digest than she ever gave her asses![255]

## "COURAGE is NO MORE to be TAUGHT than WIT", 1728

At Mr. Stokes's Amphitheatre, in Islington Road, on Monday next, being the 26th of August, will be perform'd a Trial of Skill by the following Championesses. Whereas I Mary Barker, from Ireland, (of which Kingdom I am always proud to own myself a Native) having in my former Encounters with Mrs. Stokes, the English Championess, been thought to have experienc'd the Superiority of her Skill in the Sword, to my Disadvantage, am prompted, as well in Regard to my own Character, as in Honour to my Country, to give her a new Invitation to exercise with me all the usual Weapons practis'd on the Stage; and having since my past Controversies with her, been assisted with the Instruction of the ablest Masters in the Science, doubt not but in this Battle to behave myself so, as to make her ample Retaliation for her past Insolence, and give entire Satisfaction to the Spectators. I Elizabeth Stokes, of England, (a Country of which I can boast myself a Native, with Pride beyond my Antagonist of Tipperary) very chearfully embrace this Challenge, and, as I have hitherto supported myself with Magnanimity and Success, in the Character I was encourag'd to assume of English Championess, question not but to shew this Hibernian Heroine, notwithstanding the Amendment she pretends to have receiv'd since our last Engagement, that Courage is no more to be taught than Wit. Attendance will be given at Two, and the Championesses mount between Four and Five. There will be a Gallery on purpose for Women. Note, A lac'd Hat will be Cudgel'd for before the Championesses mount, by the Gamesters of Moorfields and St. James's. N. B. There will be a Boxing Match for five Guineas after the Battle between two Brick-makers.[256]

## SARAH BARRET vs. MRS. STOKES, 1728

At Mr. STOKES's Amphitheatre, in Islington Road, Monday next, being the 30th Instant, will be perform'd a Trial of Skill by the following Champions and Championesses. Whereas I Thomas Barret, from Dublin, who has fought six hundred and odd Battles, and travell'd the three Kingdoms through to find and fight the principal Masters in those Parts, and hearing of the Fame of Mr. Stokes and his Wife being profound, have brought my Wife on purpose to give them a fair Invitation: The said Sarah Barret has fought thirty five Battles in Ireland, Scotland and England, and was, never yet defeated, and does not in the least Doubt but to have as good Success with this European Championess. James Stokes, and Elizabeth Stokes, of the City of London, thought not to fight in Publick any more, but being creditably informed both by Scotch and Irish Gentlemen of Note, of the Bravery of this new Irish Champion and Championess in North-Britain; but I am no-ways surpriz'd at this Encounter, and

255 *Daily Post,* July 17, 1728.
256 *Weekly Journal or British Gazetteer,* August 24, 1728.

will display the Judgment of the Sword to their Disadvantage, my Spouse not doubting but to do the same, and hopes to give a general Satisfaction to all Spectators. Attendance will be given at Eleven, and the Encounter begins at Two. There will be the usual Diversion of Cudgel-playing before the Encounter begins.[257]

## "LIKE INTREPID AMAZONS", 1729

Here, commonly once or twice a Week, is a Challenge between two Champions, who, like the Roman Gladiators, fight at Back-Sword and other Weapons, and very often cruelly wound one another. Here is also Wrestling and playing at Cudgels; and what is still more to be admired, Women often, like intrepid Amazons, appear upon the Stage, and with equal Skill and Courage fight with the same Weapons Men use. This commonly draws much Company; and in the lowest Part of Life here is seen the Skill, Generosity, and Courage of the English Nation.[258]

## "EXPOSE'EM for a PAIR of FAINT-HEARTED COWARDS", 1729

At Mr. STOKES's Amphitheatre,

In *Islington* Road, on *Monday* next, being the 26th of *May*, 1729, will be a Trial of Skill by the following Masters.

I Charles Wright from Dublin, Master of the noble Science of Defence, together with my Scholar Mary Waller, being thereunto incited by the earnest Desire of several Gentleman, and an insatiable Thirst of Glory, do challenge Mr. James Stokes the renowned City Champion, and his martial Spouse (hitherto accounted Britania's most puissant Heroine) to a Trial of Skill at the usual Weapons, for fifty Pounds; which if they refuse, we will post them in such a Manner, that every Gate of this great Metropolis shall testify their Ignominy, and expose'em for a pair of faint-hearted Cowards.

We James and Elizabeth Stokes, far from being intimidated by the haughty Rhodomontades of such Hibernian Boasters, having maintain'd our usual Character of Invincible against several of their Countrymen; will not disappoint their Expectations, but meet them to their Confusion, and to the entire Satisfaction of the Company, if it can be effected by their humble Servants James and Elizabeth Stokes.

The Doors will be open'd at Three, and the Masters mount at Five. There will be the usual Diversion of Cudgel-playing.[259]

## a FEMALE BOXING MATCH at the GREEN DRAGON, 1729

On Monday next, there is to be Boxing Match at the Green Dragon on St. Michael's Hill for 7 Guineas, by one Mary Buck of this City, and Mary Barker from London.[260]

## "IN ABOVE 40 BATTLES", 1730

At Mr. STOKES'S AMPHITHEATRE, in Islington-Road, this Day, the 16th Instant, will be a Trial of Skill in the Judgment of the Sword between the two following Heroines, viz., Sarah Barret, from Whitehaven, in the County of Cumberland, Mistress of the Science of Defence, who, in above 40 Battles, have distinguished the Power of my Sex, and shone like a Star of the first Magnitude in the Opinion of the Public, having defeated the famous Mrs.

257 *Weekly Journal or British Gazetteer,* December 28, 1728.
258 *The foreigner's guide: both for the foreigner and native, in their tour through the cities of London and Westminster* (London: Joseph Pote, 1729), 120.
259 *Weekly Journal or British Gazetteer,* May 24, 1729.
260 *Daily Journal,* June 3, 1729.

Mary Barker, and improved a former Quarrel with the celebrated Mrs. Elizabeth Stokes to such a Height, that only Blood can make us Friends, hereby invite her, at the Time and Place above, to fight me with the usual Weapons of the Stage, or disown her Title to the Sword, in which (like Woman ) I believe myself to have the Pre-eminence, and cannot be flatter'd Success should fail, when sweet Revenge to Mischief leads the Way,' &c.

ANNE BARRET.

I, Elizabeth Stokes, too much Mistress of my Sword to apprehend Danger in the above Challenge, assure my Northern Opponent I shall use my utmost Endeavours to eclipse her Starry Character, and by Deeds excelling words, show Mankind I am an Orb above my Sex; and that Britannia shall to Ages boast, London has robb'd Arabia of its ensign, the Phoenix, only lodging in my Jemmy's Breast, &c.

ELIZABETH STOKES.

Note.—Mr. Thomas Barret, husband of the above-named Sarah, having challenged Mr. James Stokes in a like manner, the Men are to engage in Bouts alternately, each in Behalf of his Wife—a Cause precarious! But, in this Age, meritorious.

The Passage for Gentlemen will be render'd commodious, and no Entertainment be wanting to yield desired Satisfaction.

The Doors will be open'd at Three, and the Heroes and Heroines mount at Six.[261]


## FOUR FEMALE CHALLENGERS, 1730

Mr. Stokes and his Wife being last Wednesday at Mr. Figg's, in order to receive some Money that was due from Mr. Gill, Mr. Mac Colley, and Mr. Sutton, which they refused to pay, and Mr. Stokes being challeng'd, fought at Staff, and Mrs. Stokes was likewise challeng'd, there having lately arrived in Town four Women on purpose to fight her, but the not intending to make a Practice of Fighting, dares the said four Women to come to her Seat of Valour on the above Day, before the Champions mount, and the will fight them Bout and Bout till she or they are defeated. The Doors will be opened at Three, and the Champions mount at Five.[262]


## SARAH BARRETT vs. MRS. STOKES, 1730

At Mr. STOKES's Amphitheatre,

In Islington Road, on Monday the 13th of July, 1730, the Judgment of the Sword will be shewn in the best Manner that has been perform'd in the Memory of Man, between two compleat Masters of the Science of Defence, and their accomplish'd Wives, who are not to be equall'd in Europe, viz.

We Thomas and Sarah Barrett, after a Tour of several Years abroad, on our Arrival in this Metropolitan City, having challeng'd and engag'd the famed Mr. James Stokes and his victorious Wife, at their own Seat of Valour, where our Arms gain'd Applause enough to recommend us to the Publick, considering the Fatigue we had under-gone, and the Advantage our Antagonists had over us, by mounting the Stage fresh at Home, against Persons faint and weary'd with Travel as aforesaid: Being now in a State of Health, sufficient to undertake such an Enterprize, once more invite them at the Time and Place above to shew what superior Power they command, not doubting to prove they are more fallible than ourselves, and that Fame has too lavishly bestow'd that Character on them, which we are of Opinion, justly belongs to us, &c.

Thomas and Sarah Barrett.

We James and Elizabeth Stokes, rather admiring the Vanity of the above presumptuous Challenge, than what Consequence must be drawn therefrom, assure our Opponents, not a single Fault shall escape our watchful Eyes,

---

261 *Daily Post,* June 16, 1730.
262 *Daily Journal,* June 22, 1730.

without due Correction from our vindictive Swords; and that they might as well have attempted the Chariot of the Sun, as to invade those Arms which nothing but Time itself can subdue, by paying that Debt of Nature to which Monarchs must submit, as well the meanest Subject: Being satisfied in this, we condescend to devote ourselves wholly at their Service as above, resolving to give them a final Answer in the most authentick Manner our Art can study, or Mankind desire, &c.

James and Elizabeth Stokes.

Note, As a numerous Concourse is expected, and good Diversion procured for the Day, by Cudgel-playing, &c. The Doors will be open'd at Three, and the Combatants mount at Six.[263]

## "THAT POWERFUL ENGINE WOMAN", 1730

At Mr. STOKES's Amphitheatre, *In* Islington Road, *on* Monday *the 20th of* July, 1730. *the Judgment of the Sword will be shown in a Trial of Skill between two Masters of the Science of Defence, and two Women, whose Genius renders them the Admiration of both Sexes, viz.*

Joseph Paddon, from the City of Exon, late of Coleman-street, London, finding Mr. James Stokes and his Wife, like two impregnable Fortresses, have oblig'd the Enemy twice to raise the Siege this Campaign have resolv'd to try my own Fortune in a grand Attack on those Citadels of Defence, wherein I shall make use of that powerful Engine Woman, one whose Courage dare face the most iminent Dangers, and train'd from the Cradle to the Toils of War, with whom I thus summon them at the Time and Place above to appear in Arms, and with united Force to try the Event of one Day, which shall crown the Conquerors with immortal Glory, and either let Paddon live a Julius of the Stage, or make Stokes, like him, lament the Fall of honest Brutus, &c.

Joseph Paddon, M. G.

We James and Elizabeth Stokes, of London, as the Power of Ireland has retir'd in a most precipirate Manner, not able to endure Britannia's superior Charge, our Arms shall be bent against these Western Heroes, not doubting they will retire with equal Disorder, and serve to adorn those Temples Ambition only tells them, are not worthy the Bays they wear, and which Time itself can only rob them of. We are so well acquainted with Mr. Paddon, that we confess his Judgment, but condemn his Rashness, in depending on an Engine which has ever depos'd more Emperors than it created, and lets no Prince reign longer than it is employ'd to ignoble Ends. It will therefore be no Wonder, if he fall by the same Machine being but a Subject, and the brightest Form of the whole Creation turn'd Enemy to a Man so weakly arm'd, and but a Cæsar to his fond Opinion, &c.

James and Elizabeth Stokes.

Note, The above Woman is the Person Mr. Sutton gave out, Mrs. Stokes was afraid of fighting, and whom the Publick are of Opinion, is not to be beaten, but by Accident: Therefore Mrs. Stokes is resolv'd to exert herself all she can, and by defeating one in a Week, reduce all the four Female Champions in a single Month, who have been some Years dignify'd with magnificent Titles, and came to Town to be taught Obedience to their own Sex. There will be the usual Diversion of Cudgel-playing, &c, The Doors will be open'd at Three, and the Combatants mount at Six.[264]

## SARAH BARRETT vs. LÆTITIA MACGUIRE, "THE BOLD QUAKER", 1733

At Mr. SIBBLIS's Great Room, (Late Mr. FIGG's)

In Oxford-Road, Mary-le-bone Fields, this present Wednesday, being the 8th Instant, will be perform'd a Trial of Skill in the noble Science of Defence, between the following Champions and Championesses, viz.

---

263 *Weekly Journal or British Gazetteer*, July 11, 1730.
264 *Weekly Journal or British Gazetteer,* July 18, 1730.

Whereas I Thomas Barratt, and Sarah my Wife, Champion and Championess of Exeter, gave great Satisfaction to the Gentlemen that were present at our last Engagement with Felix Mac-Guire and his Wife, which was then judg'd equal, we do a second Time invite them to fight us at the usual Weapons practis'd on the Stage, where they may expect to meet a warmer Reception than they ever yet had, which shall be the earnest Endeavour of their humble Servants..

THOMAS and SARAH BARRATT.

I Felix Mac-Guire, and Lettice my Wife, well known by the Name of the bold Quaker, will not fail meeting these daring Inviters at the Time and Place appointed, not doubting but to give Intire Satisfaction to the Spectators and them some Marks with our keen Weapons.

FELIX and LETTICE MAC-GUIRE.

Attendance will be given at Four and the Champions mount at Six precisely.

Cudgel-playing and Boxing as usual by Capt. Vinegar's Company.[265]


## LÆTITIA MACGUIRE vs. the UNCONQUER'D CITY CHAMPIONESS, 1733

And on Wednesday next, at the same Place, will be perform'd a Trial of Skill in the Noble Science of Defence, between the folowing Champions and Championesses, viz. *Felix Mac-Guire,* Fencing-Master from Dublin, and Lætitia his Wife; with *Richard Banks*, and the *Unconquer'd City Championess*; the best Master and Mistress to have all the Money taken in the Box.

Boxing and Cudgel-playing by some of the best Men in the Town.

Note, Mr. Carter, lately from Gibraltar, challenges Mr. Holmes fight him the same Day at any Weapon he is Master of.

N. B. Mrs. Sutton and Mrs. Barrett not being able to give the Gentlemen any Satisfaction, the European Championess, if she be not disabled by the abovesaid Lætitia Mac-Guire, will give them both five Guineas to fight her the same Day. Mr. Stokes teaches the Art of Defence every Day. Good Horses and Chaise to be lett reasonably.[266]

Oratory

---

265 *Daily Post*, August 8, 1733.
266 *Daily Post,* August 20, 1733.

ETOW OH KOAM, King of the River Nation.
Printed for Jn.º Bowles & Son, at the Black Horse in Cornhill, London.

I. Verelst Pinx.ᵗ                                                                    J. Simon fecit.

*Fig. 23. Portrait of Etow Oh Koam, one of the Four Indian Kings who visited the Bear Garden in 1711. Print made by John Simon, after John Verelst, ca. 1755. Yale Center for British Art, Paul Mellon Collection.*

# VII.

## NATIVE AMERICAN GLADIATORS

*In 1710, "Four Indian Kings" visited the Bear-Garden at Hockley-in-the-Hole to witness a gladiatorial stage combat held in their honor. These "Four Indian Kings" or "Four Kings of the New World" were three Mohawk chiefs from one of the Five Nations of the Iroquois Confederacy, plus a Mahican of the Algonquian tribe. The three Mohawk were: Sa Ga Yeath Qua Pieth Tow of the Bear Clan, called King of Maquas, with the Christian name Peter Brant; Ho Nee Yeath Taw No Row of the Wolf Clan, called King of Canajoharie ("Great Boiling Pot"), or John of Canajoharie; and Tee Yee Ho Ga Row, meaning "Double Life", of the Wolf Clan, also called Hendrick Tejonihokarawa or King Hendrick. The Mahican chief was Etow Oh Koam of the Turtle Clan. Five chiefs set out on the journey, but one died in during the passage across the Atlantic.*

*These four Native American leaders visited Queen Anne in London in 1710 as part of a diplomatic visit organized by Peter Schuyler, mayor of Albany, New York. They were received in London as diplomats, being transported through the streets of the city in Royal carriages, and were received by Queen Anne at the Court of St. James Palace. They also visited the Tower of London and St. Paul's Cathedral. Treated as celebrities by the local populace, they were written about in poems, ballads, and music.*

*The visit of the Four Kings to the Bear Garden was announced in print in May:*

For the Entertainment of the Four Indian KINGS.

A Tryal of Skill to be fought at the Bear-Garden in Hockley in the Hole, this present Wednesday being the 3d of May, between John Parkes form Coventry, and Thomas Hesgate a Berkshire-Man, at these following Weapons, viz. Back-Sword, Sword and Dagger, Sword and Buckler, Single Falchion, Case of Falchions, and Quarter-Staff.[267]

*Their visit to the Bear-Garden was described and commemorated in the following verse:*

> In the next Place each Soul,
> Went to *Hockly in the Hole,*
> Where the Bears and the fierce Gladiators
> Gave the Monarchs a fight,
> Of the Force and the Might
> Of such Raw-bon'd and Termagant Creatures.[268]

*Although no account of the Indian Kings' reaction to the combat has survived, they evidently thought little of the nature of English "spectator" sports and activities, as evinced by one of their few recorded statements:*

We were invited to one of their [the English's] publick Diversions, where we hoped to have seen the great Men of their Country running down a Stag or pitching a Bar, that we might have discovered who were the [Persons of the greatest Abilities among them;] but instead of that, they conveyed us into a huge Room lighted up with abundance of candles, where this lazy People sat still above three hours to see several Feats of ingenuity performed by others, who it seems were paid for it.[269]

## JOHN MAGAFFY, "THE BOLD INDIAN", 1719

*Nine years later, in 1719, a gladiator and self-described "Indian" named "John Magaffy" appeared at the Bear-Garden, where he took part in a number of challenges. Although Magaffy might have been from the West Indies, English gladiators who had lived in those regions (such as the Irishman George Gray) would typically state that as their specific region of origin, rather than describing themselves as "Indian." Likewise, in the language of the time, people of African descent from the West Indies were typically described as "black" or "negroe". However, natives of the Americas were almost universally described as "Indians". Therefore, the greatest likelihood is that Magaffy was a Native American—although his exact place of origin was never specified in print. His first known combat took place against Irish master of defence Thomas Barrett:*

AT the Old Bear-Garden in Hockley in the Hole, on Tuesday being the 1st of September, 1719, will be perform'd, between Thomas Barret, and John Magaffy, a Tryal of Skill.
I Thomas Barret, from Dublin, whom has Fought 260 odd Priz's, and having a Difference with Mr. Magaffy, upon the Account of his reporting, that when he Fought me last, that he could Cut me where he pleas'd, which I took in Disdain; upon the same Affront do Challenge him to Fight me for the whole House, without Shirt or Stockings.

|  |  |
|---|---|
| Back Sword, | Single Falchon, |
| Sword and Dagger, | Case of Falchion, And |
| Sword and Buckler, | Quarter Staff. |

---

267 *Daily Courant*, May 3, 1710.
268 *The Royal Strangers Ramble, / Or, The Remarkable Lives, Customs, and Character of the Four Indian Kings: / With the manner of their Daily Pastimes, Humours and Behaviours since their / first Landing in England. Render'd into Pleasant and Familiar Verse* (London: W. Wise in Fetter-Lane, Fleetstreet, 1710).
269 *The Spectator*, April 27, 1711.

I John Magaffy, Sailor, commonly known by the Name of the bold Indian, and Master of the said Science, will not fail, God willing, to meet this bold Challenger, at his Place and Time appointed, and upon the same Terms he proposes, and don't doubt but to make him know that the Indian will give him full Satisfaction as he requires. The Box will be set at Four, and the Masters mount at Six.[270]

## JOHN MAGAFFY vs. JAMES FIGG, 1719

*Magaffy seems to have done well in his contest against Barrett, for only one week later, the following appeared:*

AT the Old Bear-Garden in Hockley in the Hole, on Tuesday being the 8th of September, 1719, will be perform'd a Tryal of Skill.

I John Magaffy, commonly call'd by the Name of the bold Indian, Master of the noble science of Defence, who have fought several Masters since I came to England, and have come off with Honour with every Master, as not to be beat, do, at the Request of several Persons of Quality, invite Mr. Figg, knowing him to be one of the best Masters in the three Kingdoms, to meet me and exercise the usual Weapons fought on the Stage.

I James Figg, from Thame in Oxfordshire, Master of the said Science, did think to mount the Stage no more, but being desir'd, by several Persons of Quality, and Citizens of London, to fight this bold Indian Champion, who was never beat, will not fail, God willing, to meet him at the Place and Time appointed, this being the first time I every mounted the Stage in this Place.

The Doors will be open at Three, and the Masters mount at Five.[271]

*Unfortunately, no outcome of the above contest was recorded. However, the fact that Magaffy was described by Figg (the leading gladiator of the day) as "never beat" was extremely high praise. The outcome of this contest seems to be inconclusive, for two weeks later, Magaffy challenged Figg again:*

AT the Old Bear-Garden in Hockley in the A Hole, on Tuesday being the 22d of September, 1719, will be perform'd a Tryal of Skill, by two Masters of the Noble Science of Defence.

I John Magaffy, commonly call'd by the Name of the bold Indian, Master of the noble science of Defence, who lately fought Mr. Figg, do invite him once more to fight me in Holland Shirt, Holland Drawers, Thread Stockings, and Pumps, for the whole House, and he that gives the most Cuts to have all the Money in the Boxes, at the usual Weapons fought on the Stage.

I James Figg, from Thame in Oxfordshire, Master of the said Science of Defence, did think that I had given him sufficient Satisfaction as before, will not fail (God willing) to meet this bold Indian Champion, on the Terms abovemention'd. The Doors will be open at Three, and the Masters mount at Five, by reason of the Days being short.[272]

*Magaffy's last known combat took place the next year, in the spring of 1720, and is unfortunately brief:*

At His Majesty's Bear-garden in Hockley in the Hole, To-morrow, being the 5th of April, will be perform'd A Trial of Skill between John Magaffy, call'd the bold Indian, and Thomas Hays, Masters of the Noble Science of Defence. N.B. The Doors will be open at 3, and the Masters mount at 5.[273]

---

270 *Original Weekly Journal*, August 29, 1719.
271 *Weekly Journal*, Sept. 5, 1719.
272 *Original Weekly Journal*, September 19, 1719.
273 *Daily Courant*, April 4, 1720.

*Fig. 24. A fencer of African descent, executing an attack with the small-sword, circa 1750. From* The Art of Fencing, *London: John Bowles at the Black Horse in Cornhill.*

# VIII.

## BLACK GLADIATORS

*As far back as antiquity, there is evidence of martial artists of African descent testing their abilities in Europe. In ancient Rome, numerous African gladiators, mainly from Ethiopia, fought in the arenas made famous at Pompeii and the Coliseum. Most were brought to Rome as slaves; however, some gladiators were able to win their freedom due to their celebrated fighting ability, and even continued to fight in the arenas thereafter. A mosaic depicting an Ethiopian* retiarius, *or net-and-trident-wielding gladiator, is currently housed at the Musée Granet, in Aix en Provence, France. Likewise, the British Museum contains two ancient roman terracotta statues, probably from the 2nd or 1st century BC, depicting two African pugilists wielding the* cestus, *a fighting glove sometimes used in pankration. Made of leather strips,* cesti *were sometimes filled with iron plates or fitted with blades or spikes, and were devastating weapons. Later, during the Middle Ages and Renaissance, individuals of African descent began appearing in European treatises on swordsmanship and the martial arts, such as the works of Hans Talhoffer (1467) and Paulus Hector Mair (1542).*

*Given this history, it is not at all surprising that fencers of African descent would take part in the stage gladiator phenomenon during the first half of the eighteenth century. As early as 1657, the following highly detailed account of Africans practicing European swordsmanship in the Caribbean was sent down by Richard Ligon:*

Some of [the African servants], who have been bred up amongst the Portugals, have some extraordinary qualities, which the others have not; as singing and fencing. I have seen some of these Portugal Negres, at Colonel James Draxes, play at Rapier and Dagger very skillfully, with their Stookados [*Stoccatos*], their Imbrocados, and their Passes: And at single Rapier too, after the manner of Charanza [*Carranza*], with such comeliness; as, if the skill had been wanting, the motions would have pleased you; but they were skilful too, which I perceived by their binding with their points, and nimble and subtle avoidings with their bodies, and the advantages the strongest man had in the close, which the other avoided by the nimbleness and skillfulness of his motion. For, in this Science, I had bin so well vers'd in my youth, as I was now able to be a competent Judge. Upon their first appearance upon the Stage, they march towards one another, with a slow majestick pace, and a bold commanding look, as if they meant both to conquer and coming neer together, they shake hands, and embrace one another, with a cheerful look. But their retreat is much quicker then their advance, and, being at first distance, change their countenance, and put themselves into their postures and so after a pass or two, retire, and then to't again: And when they have done their play, they embrace, shake hands, and putting on their smoother countenances, give their respect to their Master, and so go off.[274]

*The site of the aforementioned combats was the Barbados sugar plantation of Colonel Sir James Drax (1609–1662), an English planter and military officer from Warwickshire. The fact that these combats took place on a "stage" within an English plantation suggests that they may have been either gladiatorial contests, or (as the time of occurrence was likely the 1650s) combats based on the earlier "prize playing" variety—a distinct possibility given the author's failure to mention either blood or wounds. Ligon's account provides evidence that despite their low social status, people of African descent living in the American colonies were sometimes allowed—even encouraged—to train with various weapons, including the rapier and dagger, and became skilled at multiple schools of fencing—including that of the Italian rapier, as well as the profound system of Spanish swordsmanship (La Verdadera Destreza) founded by Jerónimo de Carranza.*

*During the early eighteenth century, a number of gladiators of African descent traveled from the Caribbean to London's Bear-Garden to test their skill, and win fame and fortune. The earliest mention of a black gladiator in England appears in 1700, and is followed by several others:*

Cornelius was forced to give Martin sensible images; thus calling up the Coachman he asked him what he had seen at the Bear Garden? The man answered, he saw two men fight a prize; one was a fair man, a Sergeant in the Guards; the other black, a Butcher; the Sergeant had red Breeches, the Butcher blue; they fought upon a Stage about four o' Clock, and the Sergeant wounded the Butcher in the leg.[275]

## GEORGE NERVIL TURNER & WILLIAM TOMPSON, 1701

A Trial of Skill, at his Majesty's Bear-Garden in Hockly in the Hole. To be performed on Wednesday, the 28th of this instant May, 1701, at three of the Clock precisely. 1st. James Harris, from Lemster[*] in Herefordshire, who has fought Fourscore and eighteen Prizes, and never was worsted. 2d, George Nervil Turner, a Black, Master of the Small Sword, who has fought several Prizes. 3d. William Page, Butcher of Bristol. And 4th. William Tompson, a Black, both Masters of the Noble Science of Defence, do all four intend to fight a double Prize: James Harris and William Page against the two Blacks. Gentlemen are desired to come betimes, by reason each Man doth intend to exercise the six usual Weapons, if they be not disabled.[276]

## GEORGE NOVER TURNER, 1709

A tryal of Skill to be fought at the Bear Garden, Hockley-in-the-Hole, to-morrow, 17th instant, between John Padwin, belonging to Her Majesty's ship, the Chester, and George Nover Turner, black, for a considerable sum of

---

274 Richard Ligon, *A true & exact history of the island of Barbados* (London: Humphrey Moseley), 52.
275 John Arbuthnot, *Memoirs of the extraordinary life, works, and discoveries of Martinus Scriblerus* ([1700]), 50.
\* Probably Leominster.
276 *Flying Post or the Post Master,* May 27, 1701.

money. Note. That John Stokes fights James Harris, and Thomas Hesgate fights John Terrwest, three bouts at back-sword for love.[277]

## THOMAS PHILIPS from JAMAICA vs. CARTER, 1724

AT the usual Place at *Hockley* in the *Hole*, to-morrow, being the 15th of September, will be Perform'd a *Tryal of Skill*, by the following Masters.

Whereas I *Robert Carter*, Master of the Noble Science of *Defence*, have often been affronted by one *Thomas Philips*, a black, in saying he is as good a Master as myself: Therefore to convince him of his Opinion, I am resolv'd to see what Colour his Blood is of and whether there be any difference between a White and a Black, desiring him to exert his utmost Skill, I resolving to do the same.

I *Thomas Philips*, lately arriv'd from *Jamaica*, Master of the said Science, will not fail to meet Mr. *Carter* as above, and as for seeing what Colour my Blood is of I value him not, nor any other Master, but believe I shall find means to fetch as much Blood from him as he shall do from me; desiring no Favour from him, and not questioning in the least but to give entire Satisfaction.

N. B. On Tuesday last a Soldier got on the Stage, and was Sawcy; therefore 'tis expected he will be there to morrow, and he may depend upon being well Lick'd.[278]

## THOMAS PHILIPS vs. GEORGE BELL, 1725

*AT Mr. Figg's New Amphitheatre, joyning to his House, the Sign of the City of Oxford, in Oxford-Road, Marybone Fields, this Day, being the 1st of September, will be perform'd a Tryal of Skill by the four following Masters.*

Whereas I Joseph Hamlin, the bold Hibernian, and I Thomas Philips, the Black from Jamaica, Masters of the Noble Science of Defence; the former having by Misfortune receiv'd a Cut on the Face, fighting with Mr. Sutton, the largest that ever was given; and the latter having fought George Bell, Scholar to the Celebrated Mr. Figg, on Wednesday last: We do therefore invite the said Mr. Sutton and George Bell at the usual Weapons pratis'd on the Stage, not doubting but to give as general Satisfaction as ever was given. In white Drawers, white Stockings, and Pumps.

I Edward Sutton, from Gravesend, Master of the Noble Science of Defence, and I George Bell, Scholar to the Invincible Mr. Figg; the former a bold and applauded Hero, who fears no Man; and the latter, tho' Young, yet had the Honour of pleasing a great Number of worthy Gentlemen last Wednesday; will not fail meeting this bold Hibernian, and the Jamaica Black, as above specified, where nothing shall be wanting on our Parts to please all Gentlemen, and gain a general Applause. Mr. Sutton desires the bold Hibernian to take care of the other side of his Face; and George Bell desires the Black to take care of his Leg.[279]

## ANONYMOUS "BLACK" vs. IRISH, 1727

*[Appended to a challenge between Felix Macguire and Edward Sutton.]* Attendance will be given at Three, and the Masters mount between Four and Five, by Reason of a Black and an Irishman to go through the Weapons after our Battle, upon several Disputes they have had.[280]

---

277 *Daily Courant,* August 16, 1709.
278 *Parkers London News or the Impartial Intelligencer,* September 14, 1724.
279 *Daily Post,* September 1, 1725.
280 *Daily Post,* September 26, 1727.

# The Modern Champions:

## OR,

A Tryal of Skill to be Fought at Her Majesty's Bear-Garden, on Wednesday next, between a Jereboam Tory, and a Jerusalem Whig: With their two Seconds.

When Gospel Trumpeter surrounded,
- By long Ear'd Rout, to Battle Sounded:
And Pulpit Drum Ecclesiastick,
Was beat with Fist instead of a Stick.
Then did Sir Knight —————————— Prophetically sung by the Learned Hudibras.

Fig. 25. Satirical broadside, printed London in the year 1710.

# IX.

## SCOTTISH GLADIATORS

*T*he legendary Donald McBane of Inverness has, through history and memory, assumed prominence as the most famous Scottish gladiator of the eighteenth century, and rightly so. However, a number of more obscure Scottish gladiators also fought at the Bear Garden and other amphitheaters during the same period. Archibald Macgregor, in his Lecture on the Art of Defence, published in 1791 in the west central Lowlands of Scotland, recounted the following:

Those gladiators (vulgarly called bullies) used to travel from one place to another, challenging whole armies, towns and cities to produce a man who would fight them. There is a tradition to this day among us, that when any of these gladiators came to a place, the people were obliged to give so much money, or produce a man to fight them with the sword. With regard to their demand, and the town or city being obliged to comply with it, I will not take upon me to assert the truth of it at present, having never been furnished with materials to solve this tradition. But, be that as it will, 'tis a certain fact they were allowed to go about in the manner I have described, and no doubt but it was in order to create emulation and spirit in people to learn the art of defence. I have conversed with people, who were none of the oldest, that remembered of seeing many of these gladiators fight upon stages all over the three kingdoms.[†] From these circumstances it would appear that 'tis not above fifty years since such practices were abolished...

ENGLAND and Ireland have had many swordsmen likewise; Scotland too must not be forgotten, for it has produced many dextrous swordsmen. Among others, the noted D. Bain[‡], a renowned hero, who always came off

---

[†]   The Three Kingdoms: England, Scotland, and Ireland.
[‡]   Donald McBane.

victorious. Duncan Stewart, the famous broad sword player, who knew the cut and thrust sword well also. This man fought many battles on the stage, both in England and Scotland, and has left many good swordsmen behind him. Charles Stewart of the 56th regiment, son to the said Duncan Stewart, was the best swordsman I ever saw; he beat one of the first masters of Italy at Gibraltar. But in short 'tis needless to mention one more than another, for he served all alike that ever tried him, which hundreds at this present day can testify. He was alike good at both small and broad, understood spadroon well, sword and dagger, &c. &c. He has also left a goodly number of swordsmen behind him of his own teaching.

*Following are the handful of challenges by Scottish gladiators that we have been able to find:*

## JOHN ANDERSON, 1699

This present Tuesday being the 16th of September, will be Perform'd (at His Majesty's Bear Garden in Hockley in the Hole) a Trial of Skill, between John Anderson the Famous Highlander, and John Terrewest of Oundle in North-Hamptonshire, at all the usual Weapons.[281]

## JAMES MOOR, 1701

At his Majesty's Bear Garden in Hockley in the Hole, to Morrow being Wednesday the 24th Instant, will be perform'd a Tryal of Skill between these four following Masters, viz. James Moor, the famous Highlander, and William Carpenter from the City of Oxford; Also James Harris from Lemster in Herefordshire, and John Davis, Champion of the West. All Gentlemen are desire to come betimes, it being a double Prize.[282]

## ANDREW MACKLAUGLIN, 1710

A Tryal of Skill to be fought at the Bear-Garden in Hockley in the Hole, this day the 1st Instant, at Two of the Clock precisely, between Andrew Macklauglan, from the Highlands of Scotland, and belonging to her Majesty's Ship the Weymouth, and James Harris who formerly Rid in her Majesty's Second Troop of Horse-Guards.[283]

## WILLIAM HEATH, 1722

At the Boarded House in Marybone-Fields, to Morrow being Wednesday the 12th Day of September, will be performed a Tryal of Skill by the following Masters:

I WILLIAM HEATH, from Edinburgh in Scotland, Master of the Noble Science of Defence, who hath Fought most of the best Masters in that Country, and was never yet conquer'd by any one; and hearing of the Fame of Mr. James Figg, am come hither on purpose to invite him to meet and fight me at the usual Weapons fought on the Stage.

I JAMES FIGG, from Thame in Oxfordshire, Master of the said Science, being always ready to embrace and engage any fresh and good Master, shall not fail to meet this bold Inviter at the Place and Time appointed, with full Intent to give a general Satisfaction to all Spectators.

They Fight Wet or Dry.[284]

---

281 *Post Boy,* September 26, 1699.
282 *Post Boy,* September 20, 1701.
283 *Daily Courant,* February 1, 1710.
284 *Daily Post,* September 11, 1722.

## WILLIAM HANNA, 1728

AT Mr. Figg's Great Room, *at his House, the Sign of the City of Oxford, in Oxford Road, Marybone Fields, To-Morrow being Wednesday the 30th of October, 1728, will be a Trial of Skill by the following Masters.* Whereas I William Hanna (from the Shire of Galway in Scotland) profess'd Master of the Noble Science of Defence, having fought the best and most experienc'd Masters in the Three Kingdoms, and gained great Applause, especially by the noted Mr. Daniel Beane[†], with whom I had my last Combat, am now come to London, with an earnest Desire to fight the celebrated Mr. Figg; but he having try'd my Abilities, has approv'd me a bold and good Master, and being resolved to exert his Manhood no more this Season, has referr'd me to Mr. William Gill, Champion...[285]

## "CAMPBEL THE SCOTS", 1728

Campbel the Scots, and Clerk the Irish Gladiator, had a Trial of Skill in the Tennis Court; the first received a wound in his Face, the second seven in the Body.[286]

## RICHARD MAC-CREVE, 1729

*AT Mr. Figg's Great Room, At his House, the Sign of the City of Oxford, in Oxford-Road, Marybone Fields, this present Wednesday, the 18th of June, 1729, will be a Trial of Skill by the following Masters.*

Whereas I, Richard Mac-Creve, from Under-Lockey, in the Highlands of Scotland, Master of the Noble Science of Defence, having fought my Countryman Daniel Bean[*], and acquired great Reputation in my own Country, came here on purpose to fight the celebrated Mr. Figg, but, to my great Disappointment, found him in so ill a State of Health, as to render him utterly incapable of giving me the Satisfaction I desire; however, being very unwilling to return home without displaying my Skill and Courage, and understanding that Mr. Sutton bears a distinguish'd Name in the List of Honour, I do hereby challenge him to fight me at the usual Weapons, desiring him to exert his utmost Vigour, which I shall endeavour to repel in such a Manner, as to give intire Satisfaction to the worthy Spectators.

I Edward Sutton, from Gravesend, in the County of Kent, Master of the said Science, will not fail to meet this undaunted Highlander, and send him home with the Marks of my Valour upon his Scotch Carcass.

The Doors will be open'd at 3 o'Clock, and the Masters mount at 6 precisely.

N.B. There will be a Match of Cudgel-playing between 7 Countrymen and 7 Londoners, for 7 Guineas.[287]

## MR. MCDONALD, 1746

Wednesday Noon there was a severe Trial of Skill between Mr. Sherlock from Dublin, and Mr. M^cDonald from the Highlands of Scotland, at Broughton's Amphitheatre in Oxford Road, when the Highlander was entirely discomfitted at his own Weapons in a few Minutes.[288]

---

† A pseudonym for Donald McBane.
285 *Daily Journal,* October 30, 1728.
286 *Daily Post,* December 10, 1728.
* Another pseudonym for Donald McBane.
287 *Daily Journal,* June 18, 1729.
288 *Stamford Mercury,* May 22, 1746.

# A
# TRYAL of SKILL

Between a

## Court LORD, and a *Twickenham* 'SQUIRE

Infcrib'd to Mr. *POPE*.

*But can your Arm a Weapon lift,*
*To battle P----ney, P---pe, or S----ft?*
*In an ill Hour the Task you chofe,*
*Bep----s'd in Rhime, be----it in Profe:*
*'Tis Act the Second of the Farce,*
*Juft as you duell'd, you write Verfe;*
*A vanquifh'd Hero in the Field,*
*And on Parnaffus forc'd to yield:*
*Let P---pe or P----ney be the Man,*
*You quit your Sword, or drop your Pen.*

### *L O N D O N*:

Printed and fold by J. DORMER, at the Printing-Office, the
Green Door, in *Black* and *White* Court in the *Old Bailey*.
[Price One Shilling.]
M.DCC.XXXIV.

# X.

## WELSH GLADIATORS

### "BOTH WELSHMEN", 1700

Yesterday, a prize was fought at the Bear-garden, between one King and another, said to be both Welshmen: they no way counterfeited, but cut each other to that degree that they both jump'd off together, and gave great satisfaction to the company.[289]

### MR. JONES of NORTH-WALES, 1700

On Wednesday in the afternoon a tryal of skill was performed between Joseph Thomas, Master of the noble science of self defence, and one Mr Jones, a gentleman that came out of North-Wales on purpose to fight him, at the Theater in Dorset Gardens, where were abundance of the nobility and gentry; and between each bout was a very fine consort of musick; but in the conclusion Mr Jones gained the day, with great applause.[290]

---

[289] *True Protestant Mercury,* 21 June 21, 1700.
[290] *True Protestant Mercury*, April 24–26, 1700.

## JONES, the BOLD WELSHMAN, 1700

At his Majestys Bear Garden in Hockley in the Hole, is a Tryal of Skill to be performed between these following Masters, on Wednesday the 11th of this instant September, by two of the Clock precisely, viz. William King, of Tidbury in Gloucestershire, who lately fought Jones the bold Welshman at the Play house; and John Terrewest, who lately fought Hesgatt, both Masters of the Science of Defence, at the usual weapons: Also six young men to Fight to divert the Company.[291]

At his Majesties Bear Garden in Hockley in the Hole. A Trial of skill to be performed (wet or dry) on Wednesday next, being the 30th of this instant October, between these following masters, James Harris, a Herefordshire Man, Master of the Noble Science of Defence (who hath fought fourscore and seventeen Prizes, and never was worsted; also Master to Mr Jones the Bold Welshman and Mr King) and Francis Gorman, who lately cut down 3 famous men, Master of the said Science. All Gentlemen are desired to come betimes.[292]

## THOMAS SOON, the BOLD WELSHMAN, 1712-1713

A Tryal of Skill to be fought at the Bear-Garden in Hockley in the Hole, this present Wednesday being the 21st of May, at 2 of the Clock precisely, between Thomas Soon (the Bold Welshman) of Wraxham in Derbyshire, Master of the Noble Science of Defence, and John Terrewest, Master of the said Science.[293]

Wednesday 19 August, Thomas Soon, the bold Welshman, and Thomas Pidgeon, Champion of the West, two masters of defence, fought with six or seven sorts of weapons in the Queen's Arms and the spectators paid 12s . & 6d.[294]

## HENRY DAVIS from WREXHAM in WALES, 1719

At the Old Bear-Garden at Hockley in the Hole, this present Tuesday, being the 9th of June, will be perform'd a Tryal of Skill, between Henry Davis from Roxam in Wales, Master of the Noble Science of Defence, and Robert Waldron, Plumber, Master of the said Science. Note, the Boxes will be set at 3, and the Masters mount at 6.[295]

At the Old Bear-Garden at Hockley in the Hole, this present Tuesday, being the 7th of July, will be perform'd a Tryal of Skill, between Thomas Barrett from Dublin, Master of the Noble Science of Defence, and Henry Davis from Rixam in Wales, Master of the said Science. Note, the Doors will be open at 3, and the Masters mount at 6.[296]

At the Boarded-House in Marybone-fiels, this present Wednesday, being the 15th of July, will be perform'd a Tryal of Skill, between Henry Davis from Rixham in Wales, Master of the Noble Science of Defence, and Thomas Parkes from Coventry, Master of the said Science. N.B. The Doors will be open at Three, and the Masters mount at Six.[297]

---

291 *Post Man and the Historical Account,* September 9, 1700.
292 *Post Man and the Historical Account,* October 29, 1700.
293 *Daily Courant,* May 21, 1712.
294 John Lucas, *The Memoranda Book of John Lucas 1712–1750, Vol . 16* (Leeds: The Thoresby Society, 2006).
295 *Daily Courant,* June 9, 1719.
296 *Daily Courant,* July 7, 1719.
297 *Daily Courant,* July 15, 1719.

## JOHN CRUMPTON from MONTGOMERYSHIRE, 1727

At Mr . Stokes's Amphitheatre joining to his House in Islington Road, on Monday next, being the 13th of March, will be performed a Trial of Skill by the following Masters.

I John Crumpton, from Montgomeryshire in Wales, Master of the Noble Science of Defence, about 6 Years past, fought three Battles in London, with good Success, and since, the best Masters in the Kingdom of Ireland, and North of England, and most parts of Great Britain: In my long Absence there are some Upstarts and Pretenders of the Sword, who feed themselves full of Vanity. I do invite Mr Sutton, who, I understand, makes it his Business to fight such Persons that does not know the Hilt from the Point, to gain a Character, at the usual Weapons practis'd on the Stage, desiring him to be Smart in Time of Action, and to use his utmost Skill, and the best judgement he is Master of, with the most Severity.

I Edward Sutton, from Gravesend, in the County of Kent, Master of the said Science, making no Apology, will not fail meeting this bold Welshman at the place above specified: where I believe I shall learn him to take Care how he deals with such Pretenders and Upstarts, which shall be my utmost Care, to please the Gentlemen with intire Satisfaction, as my usual Custom is.

The Boxes will be set at Three, and the Masters mount at Five.

N .B . There will be the Diversion of Cudgel playing before the Masters mount.

No person to be admitted under one shilling.[298]

---

298 *Weekly Journal,* March 11, 1727.

*Fig. 26. Detail from* The stage medley representing the polite taste of the Town & the Poet G- - - Polly Peachum & Captn. Macheath, *[April, 1728]. Courtesy of The Lewis Walpole Library, Yale University.*

# XI.

## FOREIGN GLADIATORS

### MONSIEUR ONNEY, a FRENCH CHAMPION, 1726

At Mr. FIGG's New Amphitheatre, joining to his House, the Sign of the City of Oxford, in Oxford-Road, Marybone Fields, on Monday next being the 18ᵗʰ of April, will be perform'd a Trial of Skill by the following Masters. Whereas I Robert Carter of the City of London, Master of the noble Science of Defence, have had several Disputes in Words with Monsieur Onney the French Champion concerning the Judgment of the Small Sword; now to put a final Decision to any farther Arguments and to come to Blows, I do invite him to meet me and exercise the following Weapons, viz. Back Sword, Sword and Dagger, Sword and Buckler, Sword and Poniard. I John Onney, from the City of Mountinock in the Province of Languedoc in France, Master of the said Science, who never did intend to fight on a Stage; but being often forced and insulted by Mr. Carter to my Prejudice, will not fail to meet this bold Inviter; where I hope to reward him for his gross Affronts. N.B. The Doors will be open'd at two, and the Masters mount at five exactly.[299]

---

299 *Daily Post*, April 14, 1726.

## PATERISHEY COMER, a SPANISH CHAMPION, 1729

At the Sign of the Chequer in St. Matthew's in Ipswich on Tuesday next: being the 28th of this Instant January, will be performed a small Tryal of Skill, between the Spanish Champion, and the Champion for England.

Whereas I Paterishey Comer from the Province Andalusia, born in the City of Sivil [Seville], Master of the Noble Science of Defence, and Champion for Spain, known by the Name of the Bold Spaniard, having fought before King Philip and several Foreign Princes, and always came off Conqueror, and since my Arrival to England, fought Mr. Figg to the entire Satisfaction of the Spectators, and likewise Mr. Read the Norfolk Champion, at Yarmouth, and won the Stage; hearing Mr. Sutton, which is stil'd the Champion of Europe, is in these Parts, I came on purpose to Fight him, doubting not in the least but to make him know that I am his Master piece, and to let him knew that the Kingdom of Spain can produce as good a Master as any in Europe, and I will fight him the Weapons any way which the Gentlemen shall think proper.

I Edward Sutton from Gravesend, in the Renowned County of Kent, Master of the said Science, am not afraid of any Champion in Christendom, will not fail Meeting this undaunted Spaniard at the Place above specified, and to let him understand there is not any Man to be compared with a True Born Englishman, being a Novelty, I will endeavour to see whether Spanish Blood runs so free as English, and for the Honour of my Country and the Credit of myself, I will fill remain Champion as I have hitherto done, and the Company shall see the smartest Battle as ever was in these Parts, which had be to the utmost Care of their Humble Servant, EDWARD SUTTON.[300]

## A GERMAN GLADIATOR KILLED

In the memory of many, *Sherlock*, an *Irishman*, fought a *German* brought over by the late *Duke of Cumberland* for the special purpose of *prize-fighting*. The combat was on the stage of the Theatre in the *Haymarket*, and the fight was bloody. The *German* laid open the *Irishman's* cheek, from his ear to his mouth the wound was sewed and bound up and the second act terminated with the *German's* life; his antagonist with a backhand blow, cutting him from hip to hip, and so deep as to divide his bowels so that his exit from the stage and from the *world* were on the same instant.[301]

## BEAUGRAND, the FRENCHMAN, 1749-50

We are assured, and to the great Joy of the Gentlemen skilled in the Sword, that Mr. Sherlock has once more condescended to appear on the Stage, which nothing could have induced him to do, but to prevent Mr. Beaugrand the Frenchman's Progress.[302]

Yesterday was fought at Broughton's Amphitheatre in Oxford Road, the great Battle between Sherlock and Beaugrand the Frenchman; they fought nine Bouts, when Beaugrand received three Cuts; two small ones, one on the Leg, and a deep one under the Eye, and Sherlock none. They both behaved in a very genteel Manner, and fought with great Courage.[303]

Yesterday was fought at Broughton's Amphitheatre in Oxford road, the great Battle between Sherlock and Beaugrand, the Frenchman; they fought nine Bouts, when Beaugrand receiv'd five Cuts, and Sherlock none.[304]

300 *Ipswich Journal*, January 18, 1729.
301 Reprinted in *The Graphic: A Weekly Illustrated Newspaper*, Volume 40, July to December, 1889.
302 *General Advertiser*, February 7, 1749.
303 *Derby Mercury*, February 9, 1749.
304 *Ipswich Journal*, February 17, 1750.

# XII.

## A JEWISH GLADIATOR

Abraham-Meilck Moredecai, 1728

At Mr. STOKES's Amphitheatre, in Islington Road, on Monday next, being the 28th of October, 1728, will be perform'd a compleat Trial of Skill by the following Masters. I Abraham-Meilck Moredecai, the Jew, Master of the Noble Science of Defence, having had the Honour to fight several Masters in my Travels, and have lately had Disputes with Mr. Stokes about the Judgment of the Sword, am willing to give him a Specimen of my Abilities, and do therefore dare him to a Trial of his best Skill for Twenty Pounds and the whole House; which if he refuses, I will post him in all Gentlemen's Company wherever I come. I James Stokes, Citizen of London, Master of the said Science, did not intend to fight any more this Season, but having been imposed upon, and grossly affronted by the abovesaid Jew, he insisting to fight me for Twenty Pounds, will not refuse meeting him on his own Terms, as 'tis well known in this famous City that I never did refuse any Master of the Sword, I having fought Masters of several Nations, but never bled any of this, and will therefore shew the Difference of true Courage and Blood, for the Honour of my Country. Note, Attendance will be given at Two and the Masters mount at Four. There will be the usual Diversion of Cudgel-playing before the Masters mount.[305]

---

305 *Weekly Journal,* October 26, 1728.

Fig. 27. Detail from Feeling by John Nixon. London, 1784. Courtesy of The Lewis Walpole Library, Yale University.

# XIII.

## ESSAYS *and* POETRY

### *Of* PRIZE-FIGHTING, 1726

*S I R,*

IT is with Surprize I perceive that the antient and laudable Art of Prize-fighting has escap'd the Panegyrick of all our modern Brethren; and I confess my Want of Power to stifle my Indignation, while I observe the noble Science of Defence so overlook'd by those whose Duty and Interest it ought to be to record the Glories of their Cotemporaries, I mean the profound Journalists of the present Age.

I own I had it frequently in my Inclinations to celebrate the Merits of the gallant Fraternity of the Blade, but was deterred by my Despair of equalling the ingenious Mr. *Byrom*, whose Ode[*] upon this Subject will ever be remember'd to their Glory, and his; and nothing could have perswaded me to attempt the Theme but an After-thought, to wit, that as I only write in Prose, the Danger of the Comparison may be avoided: The Man who walks a-foot will be consider'd by himself, and never examined by, nor compared to him who keeps his Chariot; though, if he should pretend to a curule Equitation, his Horses, Coach, Painting, Liveries, and Servants, are all set in Opposition to his Brother Beaus, and he must expect his Character from the Result as that Examination.

This Art, than which none is, for its Antiquity, more illustrious, had long left the Stage, and been buried in Obscurity; while its Place in the World was usurp'd by a mischievous younger Brother of the same Family, but

---

[*]  For Byrom's diary entries and "Ode" on the famous Figg-Sutton contest, see Chapter V.viii, 85-88.

unworthy of the Name: Long had the noble Back-Sword and St. *George*'s Guard left the polite World, and given way to the paltry single Rapier, and Quart, and Tierce; till the publick-spirited Mr. *Figg*, out of meer Fondness for Antiquity, has lately undertook the *Restoring of the antient Gladiatory* of the Stage, and for that End has erected a *Gymnasium*, in which he instructs the young Gentlemen of this Age in the Weapons of their Ancestors. Happy Omen of the Revival of the Valour of their Ancestors! When our antient Way of Fighting is restored, well may we hope our antient Success! Then new *Guys* and new *Georges* shall arise, and new *Cows* be slaughter'd, and new *Dragons* demolished! Thrice happy present Age so fruitful in *Revivals!* now blest by the Restoration of two long-lost useful Arts, Elocution and Cudgel-playing! No more let it be said *cedant arma togæ*; but let our Revivors walk hand in hand to Fame, and be transmitted with equal Glory to Posterity! Let our Hero defend our Orator from Thumps, Thwacks, and Bangings; and let our Orator secure our Hero from Scorn, Calumny, and Revilings! Observe we another Instance of their Parity, in the Condition from which their several Sciences have been rescued: Oratory, upon its Banishment from the Pulpit, was forced to take Refuge in Booths and Play-houses, among Quacks, Mountebanks, Players, Dancers, and Tumblers; and *Gladiatory*, when it was driven from Court, flcd for Shelter to the Bear-Gardens and publick Streets: Porters, Apprentices, Pick-Pockets, nay even Taylors, those Usurpers of Man's Name, professed it; yet now Things have taken such a Turn, that I have seen a Member of the House of Commons gaping at a Lesson of Mr. *Henley*'s; and one of the other House condescending to take an instructive Knock of the Pate from Mr. *Figg*; nor am I without Hopes that I shall live to see a Kennel of Hounds called together by the Rules of a Declamation, and a Punctilio of Honour decided by the Laws of Back-Sword.

But to drop this Comparison, which my Readers will perceive was only a Digression, let us take a View of the magnanimous Behaviour of our Gladiators in Adversity, and from thence judge if they are not worthy of this Turn in their Favour, and their Art entitled to the Admiration and Practice of our noble Youth, whose Fineness of Taste prompts them to pursue this agreeable Study. The gallant Actions of *Robin Hood*, his great Sufferings, and his Excellence at Quarter-Staff, which is a Branch of the noble Science, are too well known to need a Repetition here: The Courage and Conduct of old *Jack Falstaffe*, who, by his Manner of *bearing* his *Point*, we may learn to have practised this Art; and the great Successes and famous Exploits of the late Hero little *Gorman*, whose Renown stands pickled for the Use of Posterity in the preserving Salt of modern Satyr;

> *'Tis* Shakespear's *Play; and if these Scenes miscarry,*
> *Let* Gorman *take the Stage.*———

and who, for all his Bravery and Glory, was, to the eternal Disgrace of our Laws, hang'd like a common Thief, for only taking the Freedom with some of his Neighbours to borrow a Horse, Add to these the great Numbers of gallant Souls still in being, whom Thirst of Fame sends, in Imitation of those antient Prize-Fighters *Hercules*, *Theseus*, &c. traversing the Globe in search of Victory and Bread and Cheese.

Whoever has been conversant in Romances, must observe a great Resemblance between the Behaviour of Knights Errant and strolling Gladiators; but whoever peruses the Challenges and Defiances, which are to be met with in such Books, and compares them with the Records of *Figg*'s Amphitheatre, and the *Hockley* Bear-Garden, must still find it greater. I cannot let slip this Opportunity, without offering my Praises and Thanks to the sublime Penners of these Compositions, by what Name or Title soever distinguish'd: Happy Genius's! Inventors of a Style, which, without fettering Words with Sense or Meaning, makes a sonorous rumbling Noise, exactly calculated to raise the Courage of the Combatants.

> Like the Trumpet and the Drum,
> Which make the Warrior's Stomach come,
> And sharpen Valour, like Small Beer
> By Thunder turn'd to Vinegar.

I hope whoever is the present Secretary may be immortal as his Works; but if there should happen to be a Vacancy in that high Office, I would beg leave to recommend to it my very good Friend the Author of *Busiris*, whom I think every way qualified for so important a Trust; but if the Brotherhood should imagine, upon reading his Play, that his Excellence in the Sublime-obscure is not sufficient, I can assure them that some of his Prose-performances are able to attone for that Want, by a Mastery in the Flat-unintelligible. I hope my Services to the Science will give me so much Interest amongst them, as will make me able to obtain this Favour; that I may comfort myself for the future in Possession of a Character which I always aspired to, that of a proportionate Rewarder of Merit.

I had like to have concluded without observing, for the Honour of Prize-Fighting, that it has been so much encouraged by our Laws, as to have been formerly a Method not only of deciding Honour, but Life and Property: In these Cases I meet with but two Methods of Fighting appointed by Law; the one, when two Persons drubb'd one another heartily with Bags fill'd with Sand; and the other, when they used Battoons, as I find them called; I own I am much puzzled by that ingenious Diversion with Sand-Bags, being out of Use at *Hockley in the Hole*; but I have written a Treatise in Folio, which shall appear in due Time, proving, against *Selden*, and all others, for the Honour of Prize-Fighting, that the Battoons were no other than the modern Quarter-Staves, or at least the Origin of them; and I give this timely Notice, that all Friends and Encouragers of the noble Science may be prepar'd to forward my Undertaking with their seasonable Subscriptions.

*August* 20, 1726.

*I am, S I R,*
*Yours,* &c.
F. O.[306]

## ANCIENT ROMAN GLADIATORS and the PRIZE FIGHTERS COMPARED, 1728

### ESSAY VII.

*Of the* GYMNASIA, THEATRES, AMPHITHEATRES, NAUMACHIÆ *and* STADIA *of the Antients*; *but particularly of the antique* CIRCUS, *and modern* BEAR-GARDEN: *A Comparison between the* GLADIATORS *and our* PRIZE-FIGHTERS...

I so far profess myself a bigotted Admirer of the *Antients*, and all their Performances that every Thing which bears the Authentick Mark, or boasts the least Resemblance of Antiquity, touches me with Veneration, Surprize, or Pleasure: Of Consequence, when we narrow-soul'd, half-witted Mortals, the Moderns, follow, tho' at the greatest Distance, or imitate in the aukwardest Manner, any Custom, Amusement, or Work of theirs, I own my self secretly prepossessed in Favour of that Affair, even to a Degree of Partiality.

HAVING in the Six former ESSAYS, gone thro' most of the Publick *Entertainments*, (at least those resorted to by the *Beau-monde*) this small INTRODUCTION was occasion'd by my recollecting a Diversion truly *English*, the last mention'd, because supported mostly by the Commonalty; but which I look upon with Veneration, and frequent with Delight: Nor can the rude, vulgar Apellation of the *Bear-garden* give any Distaste to my Ears, since it was certainly design'd with a clear View to the *Antique Circus.*

As our Bear-garden may be justly esteem'd no bad Copy of the *Antient Circus*, it plainly demonstrates, that the Souls of the lowest of our People are inspir'd with a natural Propensity to the greatest and finest *Entertainments* of Antiquity; and should be accordingly distinguish'd, by a particular Politeness in their *Gou* from all other Nations.

---

306 Originally appeared in the *British Journal* of August 20, 1726; reprinted in Mathew Concanen, *The speculatist. A collection of letters and essays, moral and political, serious and humorous: upon various subjects* (London: J. Walthoe, MDCCXXXII).

To set this Matter in a true Light, and give my Readers a just Notion of the Reasons for this Comparison betwixt two Places, which may seem at first View widely different, it will be absolutely necessary to run over, in an historical Manner, the various Shews which gave first Birth to so spacious a Building, and trace them Step by Step, thro' the several Ages and Parts of the World, where these Spectacles have been exhibited with greatest Splendor and Applause...

I shall at once proceed to consider the Diversions of our *Bear-garden*, upon a Parallel with those of the *Antique Circus*, as succinctly as a necessary Perspicuity will admit of.

I must here caution my Readers to remember, that under the general Title of the Shews of the *Circus*, or *Bear-garden*, I comprehend all those *Entertainments* I have spoke to in this ESSAY, as far as they related to the *Antients*, or that I shall speak to, as copied from them by the Moderns. And when I talk of either of these Places in the singular Number, that represents the rest of the Brotherhood in *Athens*, Rome or London. It will be altogether foreign to the Business in Hand, to recapitulate, or enlarge upon the Part the Grecians play'd at all Entertainments of this Nature. What I have already advanc'd on this Subject, is sufficient to shew, that the publick Exercises to which they train'd up their Youth, in order to appear as Candidates for Fame at all their Games, were undoubtedly the Noble Original of the *Roman Circus* and *British Bear-garden*.

THE Great *Circus in Rome*, was a very large Oblong Square, with Noble Galleries, of the finest Architecture and Materials for the Spectators of the Games, according to their several Degrees; and under them, the Caves and Dungeons for the Beasts and Malefactors, who furnish'd out the *Entertainments*. In the Middle were several Ornamental Pillars, Altars, &c. with the *Meta*, round which the Chariots in their Races turn'd; where they set out, and where the Race concluded. In the *Arena* (which was strew'd with Sand, to suck up the Combatant's Blood, and hinder their Feet from slipping) were all the usual Exercises perform'd.

To this, in Use, if not in Grandeur and Beauty, answers our *Bear-garden*; the same the Design, End and Form, tho' I cannot say much as to the Buildings, Ornaments, or Encouragement which the other boasted: Tho' I will venture to affirm, that our Copy is upon an equal Foot of Merit with their Original. We have indeed some sorry Balconies and wooden Galleries for the Use of the Spectators, and a Pit for the exhibiting our Shews; but all conformable to the Appearance of those who are the chief Support of these Amusements, the lowest of the Vulgar; which as it is a Shame, it is a pity, and as it is a Pity, it is a Shame.

IN the *Circus*, the chief Spectacles were Men against Men; Men against Beasts and Beasts against Beasts: Chariot, or Horse-races, Leaping, Wrestling, and other Exercises of the like Nature.

IN the *Bear-garden*, our *Prize-fighters* Tally with their *Gladiators*, shewing as much Sport, and spilling less Blood; our Courage being made manifest thus to the World, without their Cruelty.

MEN indeed seldom enter our Lists against Beasts, unless Butchers against Bull-dogs, in brotherly Alliance with their own Curs; whose Preservation and Honour are justly as dear to them as those of their Wife and Children.

BUT as for Beasts against Beasts I think we may modestly say, we equal, if not exceed any Thing they ever produc'd on that Head; our charming Bears, our noble Bulls, and nobler Mastiffs, must give those Spectators (who have Sense enough to frequent all publick Amusements, to be instructed as well as delighted) the truest Notions of an invincible Bravery, join'd to the most sagacious Conduct...

IF we cannot boast of their Chariot-races, we can, to the Immortal Honour of our Country shew, that the Noble Sports of Wrestling, Cudgel-playing, Fisty-cuffs, Leaping, &c. flourish in *Britain*, more, perhaps, than ever they did in *Greece*: Diversions that have more Humanity and Discipline in them, than the well-tim'd Crack of a Whip, or the nice Turning of a Post.

THESE should have been the principal Foundation of their *Circus*, as they were of the *Grecian* Games, and are of our *Bear-garden*: And tho' they have been the Admiration of Antiquity, not a Shadow of them now remains, but as happily preserv'd in their Original Parity by the *British* Nation.

As these publick Games were the Delight of Greece for many Ages; on which principally depended the Education of their Youth, and the Amusements of the Old, being maintain'd by the joint Consent of all the separate

*Fig. 28. Study for "The Combate", etched vignette by Gravelot, 1737. MET Museum, Fletcher Fund, 1944.*

States, tho' ever so much disunited on other Accounts; and this at a Time, when at their Height for Power, Learning and Magnificence.

So with the *Romans*, the Representations of the *Circus* were the Darlings of their People, when their Wit was clear, their Studies solid; their Pleasures polite, and their Sway universal. And in either Empire with these they flourish'd, and with them fell; bravely surmounting all Difficulties, and withstanding all Shocks, till swallow'd up in that of a general Ruin.

PEOPLE of Genius and Spirit may shew a reasonable Surprize, that the Amusements of the *Bear-gardens* are so strangely neglected by People of Sense and Distinction; especially, as they are prov'd just Copies of such Glorious Originals: But what will they say when. I shall plainly demonstrate, that they may be render'd of the utmost Importance to this Nation, by keeping up the true Old *English* Spirit, and training up every individual Briton to be a General! —a Hero!

IF the vast Disparity betwixt the *Circus* and *Bear-garden*, in the Articles of Grandeur and Expence, is objected to us, let us but confider the prodigious Encouragement given to their SHEWS by *Senators, Consuls, Dictators, Emperor*s, and their whole State: Nay, the World in Conjunction with them, strove who should add greatest Lustre to their Games.

AND as we can boast the same Foundation, I think our People of Quality, Fortune, and publick Spirit, should with the greatest Zeal promote these Diversions, if not with a View of pleasing or instructing themselves, yet with a due Regard to the Delight and Improvement of the *Populace*, and the Honour of their Country.

THUS will the In-bred Valour and Martial Genius of this Nation be rous'd up and fix'd: Thus will the lowest of the People be inurd to behold with Raptures, gash'd Faces, spouting Veins, goary Sculls, hack'd Limbs, &c.

will they be harden'd to the most fearless Contempt of Danger and Death: Thus will our Bulldogs, those Noble Creatures, our other selves. (Beasts by Nature appropriated to this Nation) be kept in perfect Order, and that valuable Race preserv'd: Thus will such Spectacles add to the Native Fierceness of both, and breath a new Soul into the whole Kingdom.

AND indeed, if we enter'd a little more particularly into the real Merits of the *Circus* and *Bear-garden,* we shall find, that in Variety, the Original Design, and desir'd End, they differ not widely, however we fall short in Point of Luxury and Magnificence.

FIRST, then, let us examine the antient State of the *Gladiators,* upon the Parallel with our Modern *Prize-fighters,* they being the main Pillars of the *Circus* and *Bear-garden.*

I have already shewn, that the Rise of the *Gladiators* was owing to that barbarous Custom practis'd in all Ages of Antiquity, of sacrificing Captives, or Slaves, at the Funerals and Tombs of great Men. The *Romans,* who exceeded in Humanity most other Nations, scorning such mean Butchery, commanded them to kill one another like Men. Their first *Gladiators,* tho' they were of the same Rank with those who grac'd the foreign Funeral Altars, being either Slaves by Birth, Captives of War, or Malefactors condemn'd by Justice to Death. The first fought for Liberty, the others for Life. As they came more into Reputation, People voluntarily enter'd themselves into the Service for Pay, were regularly enlisted as Soldiers, and an *Academy* establish'd for instructing them in the Art of cutting Throats cleverly and decently. At last, to oblige some of the Emperors, Persons of Figure and Distinction enter'd the *Circus* as *Gladiators,* greedy of Immortal Fame: And *Nero* once compell'd a Thousand *Knights* and *Senators* in one Day, to grace his SHEWS, and cut, slash and slay one another in the most beautiful Manner, for the Good of their Country...

THUS in Italy the *Gladiators* rose, flourish'd, fell, and for several Centuries lay bury'd, till luckily reviv'd in *England:* The only Nation upon Earth that can boast the raising from the Dead an Amusement in it self equally useful and genteel; an Amusement, which from its intrinsick Worth so long claim'd a due Respect from the Masters of the World...

IT remains for me now to speak to our Modern *Prize-Fighters* in a way of Comparison with the Antient *Gladiators*; and at the same time come to the material Design of this Essay, and shew that we can carry this *Entertainment* to a greater Height, both as to Pleasure and Profit, than has been known to former Ages; where there should no Cruelty appear but in the Way of Justice; no Blood shed but for Instruction and Life or Death only consider'd, as every Man is devoted to the Good of his Country.

OUR Modern *Prize Fighters,* those happy Copies of the Old *Gladiators,* shew a Spirit superior to the boasted Bravery of the *Romans*: For as they are not Slaves, of Consequence not oblig'd to Fight; they only Fight for Fighting's sake.

BUT as I would embellish the *Bear-garden* Scene with the greatest Variety of *Actors*; and have always in Reserve a Number sufficient, not only to amuse the People, but to answer the unexpected Exigencies of the State, in Case of a Rebellion, Invasion, etc. So we must not too far trust barely to Hirelings for that Service. All Ages and Nations have experienc'd that Supply to be precarious; and especially in a Country of Liberty and Property, will altogether depend upon Whim and Humour, Therefore I propose, as a Matter of the last Importance to this Nation, and as the greatest Promoter of beautiful Justice—First—That all our Malefactors condemned to Death, be forc'd to stab, hack and hew themselves to Pieces for the Good of their Fellow Subjects; then their Deaths will infallibly prove of a more general Use to their Country, than their Lives could have been pernicious. By this Means the most profligate Wretches may die the truest Patriots; and every *Blueskin,* or *Sheppard,* go off the Stage, a *Curtius,* or *Murtius Scævola.* Thus argued *Tully* himself, when the Charge of Barbarity was laid to the SHEWS of GLADIATORS. — *These* SHEWS, says he, *may seem to some People very inhuman; but where only guilty Persons compose the Number of the Combatants, tis impossible that any Thing should fortify us with more Success, against the Assaults of Grief or Death.* And he might have added or more effectually instill a warlike Disposition into the Minds of the People.

SECONDLY, — I would oblige all State Criminals adjug'd to Transportation, or other corporal Punishments, to List themselves in the Service of the BEAR-GARDEN, in order, by small Play, to be instructed themselves in the Rudiments of War. Thus a little Gash, Cut, or Thrust, will inure them to the bearing of greater Wounds; be a Punishment in some Respect adequate to their past Crimes, and at the same time delight the *Populace*; train them up to Martial Exercises, and arm them against all cowardly Ideas.

THIRDLY, — to encourage Spectators to come there with a sincere Design to improve, the Go———nt should allow any Man that is willing to be enroll'd as an Out-pensioner, to be call'd upon in Cases of Necessity, to be free of the BEAR-GARDEN, both as to Diversion and Instruction; and that he should be absolutely at Liberty to have a crack'd Skull, a Thump on the Ribs, or broken Shins, whenever he demanded them, *gratis*.

I have already shewn what particular Influences this Proposal, well executed, may have on the Minds of the Commonalty of *England* in general. I now beg Leave to hint at the principal Advantage to which the whole Scheme must naturally tend.

Fig. 29. Prize fighter pictured in La Guerre's Stage Mutiny.

As the Scituation of this Kingdom, the fundamental Constitution of our State, and the Temper of our People require not a great Number of Standing Forces, kept in constant Pay; so if, upon any Emergency, our Affairs should stand in Need of a larger Supply than is usually kept on Foot, where shall we find Recruits to answer the pressing Necessities of the State, and form, in a Hurry, a large Army? All Ages and Nations have experienc'd, and smarted for the Folly of trusting too far, to raw and undisciplin'd Troops: — Where then can we hope for a reasonable Relief in such a Scene of Distress, but from a well-regulated BEAR-GARDEN, whose Auxiliaries may prove new-rais'd Troops, but veteran Heroes? 'Tis evident, that it may be brought to that Pass, as to form an *Academy* for the Army, a Nursery for Infant-Warriors, as *Chelsea-College* is for the Old. Let but our Encouragement rise to an equal Height with that of the *Romans*, in the SHEWS of their GLADIATORS, and we should never be reduc'd to so low an Ebb as to beat up for Volunties: Several Regiments, at a short Warning, might be borrow'd from the BEAR-GARDEN UNIVERSITY; every Man at least a Batchelor of Arts in the Sciences offensive and defensive, and a sufficient Number always kept in *petto*, as a *Corps de Reserve*.

SOME People may sneer at my Project, as absurd or chimerical; but let those merry Gentlemen consider, how often the *Romans* were oblig'd to List their GLADIATORS, when their Legions out-stretch'd *Arithmetick*, and they were Masters of the World.

LET any Man but read over attentively the Bills of Defiance from any of our BEAR-GARDENS, or AMPHITHEATRES, and the brave Replies of their Antagonists; if there be the smallest Spark of Courage *latent* in his Soul, such intrepid Terms of Honour must blow it up to a Flame of Glory. The World may talk of

*Alexander, Scipio, Hannibal,* and *Julius Cæsar,* whilst I set fearless in their View, *Kned Sutton, Jack Fig, Tim Buck,* and *Bob Stokes.*

As I have before provided the Army with Of—rs from the *Mas——de;* so I have now furnish'd it with private Men from the BEAR-GARDEN, which will be a certain Fund upon all Emergencies, without any real Expence to the Nation.

WERE it thought necessary to cultivate the Genius of those design'd for Sea Affairs, in the same Method of Education, 'tis but turning our Eyes towards the *Naumachia* of the *Antients,* and observing nicely all the Rules establish'd in the BEAR-GARDEN only with Respect to the Difference between Sea and Land-service, I fancy we may then produce something on the *Thames,* which could not have been so well executed on the *Tiber.*

I must own, all the other *Entertainments* of the BEAR-GARDEN are prudently imagin'd, and becoming the Bent of a brave Peoples and all conduce to the great Design, of mixing Instruction with our Amusements: And, that Men may be instructed by Brutes, *Æsop, Lemuel Guliver,* and *Hockly in the Hole* shew us.. Who can view Dogs tearing Bulls, Bulls goaring Dogs, or Mastiffs throtling Bears, without being animated with their daring Spirits! And what is brutal Fierceness in them, may produce true human Courage in us. Were the BEAR-GARDEN once rightly establish'd, the Managers of it might venture to introduce Lions, Tygers, Unicorns and Rhinocero's in formal Combat: This, with an Elephant or two to shew Postures, and a Flying-dragon for the high Ropes, would give the justest Notions of, and put us upon a Level with Antiquity, in the Articles of Grandeur and Variety.

But not to dwell altogether on the Merits of the BEAR-GARDEN, or our AMPHITHEATRES for PRIZE-FIGHTERS, as founded on the Entertainments of the antique CIRCUS, before I entirely quit the Regions of fighting Men, and fighting Beasts, I must not pass by, unregarded, our fighting Fowls...[307]

### The PRIZE-FIGHTERS, *A SIMILE,* 1731

OFT have I seen in *weekly bill,*
From *Figg*'s or *Stokes*'s room,
The hardy champions boast their *Skill,*
And speak each other's *Doom.*

So *Osborne* loudly vapours out,
What *mighty feats* he'll do,
With *Caleb* in another *Bout,*
Whom weeks before he slew.

As *these,* their valour to *enforce,*
Talk loud of *sharpen'd swords,*
So *Osborne* boasts his *mighty force,*
And *energy of words.*

Their *steel* (they cry'd) shall *foes* controul,
And *bloody* passage find;
His *language speaks into the soul,*
And penetrates the mind.

---

307 Ralph James, *The touch-Stone, or, historical, critical, political, philosophical, and theological essays on the reigning diversions of the town* (London: booksellers of London and Westminster, 1728), 197-237.

As injur'd honour, thirst of fame
For battle's their *pretence*,
Tho' still the hero's *real* aim
Is *hope* of sordid *pence*;

So W----le's *virtues*, Briton's *rights*,
Sound *specious* in his lay,
Tho', just as Champion *Sutton* fights,
So *Osborne* writes, for --- pay.[308]

## A FRAGMENT, 1733

O fatal Appetite of Praise,
That ruins us ten thousand Ways;
For Thee, Bear-garden Hero bleeds,
Smit with the Love of gen'rous Deeds...[309]

## REFLECTIONS on the BEAR-GARDEN, 1739

Let me, from Scenes so dread, repair
Back to my Country's milder Air;
There visit fam'd *Bear-Garden* Heroes,
From whose sham Fights ne'er Cause of Fear rose,
Or trip to view some valiant *Hibern*,
At Sutton's---neighb'ring Seat to *Tyburn*;
Where gentle *Butchers* oft resort,
That Brotherhood's peculiar Sport.
Here may I sit, and fear no slaying,
Mid' those *meek* Masters of Sword-playing;
Lay Wagers, laugh at *Figg* and *Stokes*,
And all our harmless fighting Fo'ks.
*Rome*'s fencing Sparks, say what you please,
In Wit fell vastly short of these;
Those met *to kill*, or to be kill'd,
Ours---but to have their Pockets fill'd.----
Shame of their boasted *Roman* Sense!
To Wisdom they've the best Pretence,
Who ne'er in those Encounters fight,
To *die*---but get their Living by't.[310]

---

308 *The gentleman's magazine, or, Trader's monthly,* November, 1731.
309 Mary Masters, *Poems on several occasions* (London: T. Browne, 1733).
310 Moses Browne, *Poems on various subjects Many never printed before* (London: Edward Cave, 1739).

*Fig. 30. "The Conquest, or Hob's Triumph," by Gravelot, ca. 1737. MET Museum, Fletcher Fund, 1944.*

## AT SOUTHWARK FAIR, 1739

The HOCKLEY Brave* might I rehearse;
How scarr'd, how mounted, and how fierce:
And turn to various sprightly Scenes,
Where HUMOUR similes, or SATIRE grins:
Where Cheat and Whore Sir SIMON part
One picks his Pocket, one his Heart...

\* The HOCKLEY Brave.] A Gladiator, or, as it is usually phrased, a Master of the Science of Defence. HOCKLEY IN THE HOLE is a celebrated GYMNASIUM for Heroes of this Order.[311]

## THE MODERN FINE GENTLEMAN, 1746

Devoted thus to politicks, and cards,
Nor mirth, nor wine, nor women he regards;
So far is ev'ry virtue from his heart,
That not a gen'rous vice can claim a part;

---

311 John Bancks, *Miscellaneous Works, in Verse and Prose, Volume I* (London: James Hodges, 1739).

Nay, lest one human passion e'er should move
His soul to friendship, tenderness, or love,
To FIGG and BROUGHTON he commits his breast,
To steel it to the fashionable test.[312]


## a CRITIQUE of the GLADIATORS, 1747

### LETTER LXVI
To the Chevalier de B * *.

*Of the English prize-fighters. Stories of* FIGG, *sir* THOMAS PARKINS, *&c. Boxing, riding, running, as practised in England, with reflections.*

LONDON, &c.

SIR,

It was to the accident of casting my eyes to-day upon the public papers that you owe the letter I now write you. These papers, properly speaking, are the registers of the manners of the nation: very singular things are often found in them, and the article I now communicate appear'd to me one of that number. It contains the defiances of two heroes of a species unknown among us, and who perhaps are more regarded here than they ought to be,

### The CHALLENGE.

"Whereas I GEORGE BISHOP, of Shaftsbury in the county of Dorset, master of the noble science of defence in all its branches, have been highly affronted here by mr. MACGUIRE with respect to the use of the sword, I invite him to fight me the weapon thro' upon the stage, I desire no favour, and wait with impatience to meet him.

Your servant, GEORGE BISHOP,"

### The ANSWER.

"I, FELIX MACGUIRE, of the kingdom of Ireland, master of my sword, having as fought with the most illustrious men of this kingdom, to wit, mr. FIGG, mr. SPARKS, mr. SUTTON, mr. JOHNSON, mr. GILL, and other great men, will not fail to meet mr. BISHOP at the time and place that shall be appointed, and will endeavour to maintain against him the honour due to my sword and my country. And I warn him to take special care that I do not make him limp off with a pair of crutches, as I have already done by several of his countrymen.

Your servant, FELIX MACGUIRE."

What do you think, sir, of the hectoring language of these miserable gladiators? If they are couragious men, what pity that their courage is so ill employed! Does not the taste of the English for spectacles of this kind astonish you?

How great soever may be the fame of these champions, I believe you will pardon me if I am not so curious to be myself a witness of their high feats of arms. The English reproach us for our antipathy to these barbarous combats, as if it was an effect of our effeminacy have we not as much ground to interpret the delight they take in them to their disadvantage? Ought humanity to bear the fight of wretches who knock one another on the head with staves, or cut one another to pieces with swords? Without accusing the people who make it their amusement to be cruel, let us not blush to shun even the image of such cruelty.

---

312 Soame Jenyns, *The Modern Fine Gentleman. Written in the Year 1746. Vol. I* (London: printed by J. Hughs, for R. and J. Dodsley, 1763 [1st ed. 1758]).

It is very difficult to avoid being inspired with something of ferocity at these spectacles. After they had famil-iarised themselves at Rome to see lions and tygers tear each other to pieces, combats of that sort grew insipid to the people, and it was found necessary to make those savages fight with men, in order to give new satisfaction. The Romans diverted themselves with what we call at this day barbarity. They lov'd to see the spilling of blood, and contemplated with pleasure, in an expiring gladiator, the horrible spectacle of the pains and agonies of death. They had masters, or rather monsters of ferocity, who taught those unhappy wretches how to merit the applauses of the public, either by suffering with constancy, or dying with a good grace. But what does this example prove, except that the Romans had not so much politeness as they piqued themselves upon having, and that they were more cruel than they imagined themselves to be? After all, Greek or Roman, what is their example to us? Let us not suffer ourselves to be imposed upon by the authority of nations, but acknowledge only the laws of reason. Such fights are unworthy of reasonable beings, and can only be a shame to humanity: wife men always abhor'd them. *If he that suffers is culpable,* says SENECA, *he has no more than he deserves: but what have you done, that you should deserve to see him suffer?*

It must be owned that these battles of the English gladiators are not so much in fashion as they have been people of distinction have almost left frequenting them, and scarce any body is seen at these matches but the lowest of the populace, or that class of men who are perhaps more despicable than the dregs of the people, because they imitate them as much in their manners, as they are exalted above them by their birth.

I must not conceal from you, however, that some persons of the first rank here have such an esteem for this noble exercise, that they learn it themselves, and a few there are who look upon the science of defence as the chief merit of an accomplish'd gentleman. I know one, mr. **, the brother of lord **, who served an apprenticeship under the famous mr. FIGG, whom I mentioned above. This English nobleman confiders it as such an honour to have been educated under so great a master, that he often treats him at his table. The persons invited are promised what entertainment they shall have, as we promise at Paris a dish of pheasants or venison. You must not think this strange, because every country has its customs: in France the people sing to amuse themselves, and here they pass their time in boxing.

Mr. FIGG said one day to a gentleman of my acquaintance, who had the happiness to be at one of these suppers, *Sir, no man has more compassion than I for the poor and miserable: but when once I am upon the stage, if I see flesh, I must cut away.* Such is the table discourse with which this celebrated man entertains those who admire his talents, and it must certainly make the treat very agreeable.

With regard to boxing, the nobility in England do not excel in it less than the common people. One of the peers of the kingdom is at this day the terror of all the hackney coachmen in London. I knew in the country a baronet, who resides there, and who, tho' he is very antient, piques himself still upon being the first wrestler in Great-Britain.* Some years ago he published a book upon the usefulness of the art in which he so much excels, and not having been so happy as to have such eminent disciples as he could have wished, out zeal for the public good, as well as for his own diversion, he now teaches it gratis to those who will attend his lectures. A lord who lives in his neighbourhood went one day to pay him a visit, and as they were walking together, and discoursing of this marvellous art, with the advantages that may be drawn from it to society, the old baronet catches his man hold behind, and throws him upon his head. His lordship, a little discomposed by the blow, got up in a rage: but our artful wrestler, in a grave and important tone, interrupted him. *My lord, says he, you may take this for a proof that I have a great friendship for you: you are the only man to whom I ever shew'd that lock.*

As we should always view things on the most favourable side, I imagine the English are less pleased with these combats in themselves, than with the exercise they take in them; and in fact, exercises of all kinds are here very much followed. Consider mankind thro', how many are there who exercise their bodies, how few their understandings!

---

* An obvious reference to Sir Thomas Parkyns, mentioned in the title of the letter.

...Perhaps this taste which the English discover for all sorts of exercise, is a proof that exercise is necessary for them. Those of our pleasures which seem at first sight to be arbitrary, had often their rise from real necessities. Who knows but the quality of the air that is breathed in England, and the aliments on which the people live, may create more occasion here than in other countries for whatever will promote perspiration? These different exercises are most certain receipts against the spleen, and I believe contribute, generally speaking, to make the English more robust than the French. The more use men make of their strength, the stronger they are in proportion.

The Romans, who in the beginning of their state addicted themselves to bodily exercises to render themselves more war-like, continued to use them afterwards for their health: it was for this that AUGUSTUS play'd so often at foot-ball. But I cannot understand, how men can give themselves up to such exercises as degrade the dignity of our nature. How can beings who have any sentiment of humanity, make a diversion of seeing the engagements of these fencers, which puts them upon a level with the brutes whose fierceness they imitate.

   Í have the honour to be,

     Sir, your most humble, &c.[313]


## THE MAN OF TASTE, 1758

To boon companions I my time would give,
With players, pimps, and parasites I'd live.
I would with jockeys from Newmarket dine,
And to rough-riders give my choicest wine;
I would caress some stableman of note,
And imitate his language and his coat.
My ev'nings all I would with sharpers spend,
And make the thief-catcher my bosom friend.
In Fig the prize-fighter by day delight,
And sup with Colley Cibber ev'ry night.[314]


## A SONG on the STAFF, 1767 (excerpts)

I'll tell you a story will make you to laugh,
Of a sett of odd flicks that are turn'd to a Staff,
Made of young sappy alder, and old knotty yew,
And straggling Scotch fir, and spungy bamboo.
   *Derry down, down, hey derry down...*
 Sure now the proud French will acknowledge our yoke,
Ours is not a staff that is rugged or broke;
'Twill knock down our foes and secure all our friends;
'Tis a Quarter-Staff, loaded with lead at both ends.
 Now with our Staff merrily on let us jog,
To make it each country hath furnish'd a log;
And when 'tis laid by, may it glory still share,
And be cut out in truncheons for Bart'lmy Fair.[315]

---

313 Jean-Bernard Le Blanc, *Letters on the English and French Nations* (London: J. Brindley; R. Francklin; C. Davis; & J. Hodges, 1747).

314 James Bramston, *The Man of Taste. Occasion'd by an Epistle Of Mr. Pope's on that Subject. Source: A Collection of Poems in Six Volumes. By Several Hands. Vol. I* (London: printed by J. Hughs, for R. and J. Dodsley, 1763 [1st ed. 1758]).

315 *The Batchelor: Or Speculations of Jeoffry Wagstaffe, Esq; Vol. II* (Dublin: James Hoey, 1769), 82-83.

*Fig. 31. Plate from* Hobbinol, or the Rural Games. *1757 London edition from the author's collection.*

# XIV.

## EPIC POEM *of a* PRIZE-FIGHT

HOBBINOL, or the RURAL GAMES.

By William Somerville

(excerpts), 1740.

Prop'd on his Staff, with anxious Thought revolves
His Pleasures past, and casts his grave Remarks
Among the heedless Throng. The vig'rous Youth
Strips for the Combat, hopeful to subdue
The Fair one's long Disdain, by Valour now
Glad to convince her coy erroneous Heart,
And prove his Merit equal to her Charms.
Soft Pity pleads his Cause; blushing the views
His brawny Limbs, and his undaunted Eye,
That looks a proud Defiance on his Foes.
Resolv'd, and obstinately firm he stands;

Danger, nor Death he fears, while the rich Prize
Is Victory and Love. On the large Bough
Of a thick-spreading Elm TWANGDILLO sits:
One Leg on *Ister's* Banks the hardy Swain
Left undismay'd, BELLONA's Light'ning scorch'd
His manly Visage, but in Pity left
One Eye secure. He many a painful Bruise
Intrepid felt, and many a gaping Wound,
For brown KATE's Sake, and for his Country's Weal...

FORTHWITH in hoary Majesty appears
One of gigantic Size, but Visage wan,
MILONIDES the Strong, renown'd of old
For Feats of Arms, but, bending now with Years,
His Trunk unwieldy from the verdant Turf
He rears deliberate, and with his Plant
Of toughest Virgin Oak in rising aids
His trembling Limbs; his bald and wrinkled Front,
Entrench'd with many a glorious Scar, bespeaks
Submissive Rev'rence. He with Count'nance grim
Boasts his past Deeds, and with redoubled Strokes
Marshalls the Croud, and forms the Circle wide.
Stern Arbiter! like some huge Rock he stands,
That breaks th'incumbent Waves; they thronging press
In Troops confus'd, and rear their foaming Heads
Each above each, but from superior Force
Shrinking repell'd, compose of stateliest View
A liquid Theatre. With Hands uplift,
And Voice *Stentorian*, he proclaims aloud
Each rural Prize.

"To him whose active Foot
Foils his bold Foe, and rivets him to Earth,
This Pair of Gloves, by curious Virgin Hands
Embroider'd, seam'd with Silk, and fring'd with Gold.
To him, who best the stubborn Hilts can wield,
And bloody Marks of his Displeasure leave
On his Opponent's Head, this Beaver white
With Silver Edging grac'd, and Scarlet Plume.
Ye taper Maidens! whose impetuous Speed
Outflies the Roe, nor bends the tender Grass,
See here this Prize, this rich lac'd Smock behold,
White as your Bosoms, as your Kisses soft.
Blest Nymph! whom bounteous Heav'n's peculiar Grace
Allots this pompous Vest, and worthy deems
To win a Virgin, and to wear a Bride".

*Fig.32. Plate from* Hobbinol, or the Rural Games. *1757 London edition from the author's collection.*

THE Gifts refulgent dazzle all the Croud,
In speechless Admiration fix'd, unmov'd.
Ev'n he, who now each glorious Palm displays,
In sullen Silence views his batter'd Limbs,
And sighs his Vigour spent...

GORGONIUS now with haughty strides advanc'd,
A gauntlet seiz'd, firm on his guard he stood
A formidable foe, and dealt in air
His empty blows, a prelude to the fight.
Slaughter his trade; full many a pamper'd ox
Fell by his fatal hand, the bulky beast
Dragg'd by his horns, oft at one deadly blow,
His iron fist descending crush'd his skull,
And left him spurning on the bloody floor,
While at his feet the guiltless axe was laid.
In dubious fight of late one eye he lost,
Bor'd from its orb, and the next glancing stroke
Bruis'd sore the rising arch, and bent his nose;
Nathless he trumph'd on the well-fought stage,
*Hockleian* hero! nor was more deform'd
The CYCLOPS blind, nor of more monstrous size,
Nor his void orb more dreadful to behold,
Weeping the putrid gore, severe revenge
Of subtile ITHACUS. Terribly gay
In his buff doublet, larded o'er with fat
Of slaughter'd brutes, the well-oil'd champion shone.
Sternly he gaz'd around, with many a frown
Fierce menacing, provok'd the tardy foe.
For now each combatant, that erst so bold
Vaunted his manly deeds, in pensive mood
Hung down his head, and fix'd on earth his eyes
Pale and dismay'd. On HOBBINOL at last
Intent they gaze, in him alone their hope;
Each eye solicits him, each panting heart
Joins in the silent suit. Soon he perceiv'd
Their secret wish, and eas'd their doubting minds,

"YE Men of *Kiftsgate!* whose wide-spreading fame
In ancient days was sung from shore to shore,
To *British* bards of old a copious theme;
Too well, alas! in your pale cheeks I view
Your dastard souls. O mean, degenerate race!
But since on me ye call, each suppliant eye
Invites my sovereign aid, lo! here I come,
The bulwark of your fame, though scarce my brews
Are dry from glorious toils, just now achiev'd,

To vindicate your worth. Lo! here I swear,
By all my great forefathers' fair renown,
By that illustrious wicker, where they sate
In comely pride, and in triumphant sloth
Gave law to passive clowns; or on this spot
In glory's prime, young HOBBINOL expires,
And from his dearest GANDERETTA'S arms
Sinks to death's cold embrace; or by this hand
That stranger, big with insolence, shall fall
Prone on the ground, and do your Honour Right."

FORTHWITH the hilts he seiz'd; but on his arm
Fond GANDERETTA hung, and round his neck
Curl'd in a soft embrace. Honour and love
A doubtful contest wag'd, but from her soon
He sprung relentless, all her tears were vain,
Yet oft he turn'd, oft sigh'd, thus pleading mild:

"Ill should I merit these imperial robes,
Ensigns of majesty, by general voice
Conferr'd, should pain, or death itself avail
To shake the steady purpose of my soul.
Peace, fair one! Heaven will protect the man
By thee held dear, and crown thy generous love."

Her from the listed field the matrons sage
Reluctant drew, and with fair speeches sooth'd.

Now front to front the fearless champions meet:
GORGONIUS like a tower, whose cloudy top
Invades the skies, stood lowering; far beneath
The strippling HOBBINOL, with careful eye
Each opening scans, and each unguarded space
Measures intent. While negligently bold,
The bulky combatant, whose heart elate
Disdain'd his puny foe, now fondly deem'd
At one decisive stroke to win, unhurt,
An easy victory; down came at once
The pondrous plant, with fell malicious rage,
Aim'd at his head direct; but the tough hilts,
Swift interpos'd, elude his effort vain.
The cautious HOBBINOL, with ready feet
Now shifts his ground, retreating; then again
Advances bold, and his unguarded shins
Batters secure, each well-directed blow
Bites to the quick; thick as the falling hail,
The strokes redoubled peal his hollow sides.

Fig. 33. Hob Triumphs over Sir Thomas, *by John Laguerre. Courtesy of The Lewis Walpole Library, Yale University.*

The multitude amaz'd with horror view
The rattling storm, shrink back at every blow,
And seem to feel his wounds; inly he groan'd,
And gnash'd his teeth, and from his blood-shot eye
Red lightning flash'd, the fierce tumultuous rage
Shook all his mighty fabric; once again
Erect he stands, collected, and resolv'd
To conquer, or to die: swift as the bolt
Of angry JOVE, the weighty plant descends.
But wary HOBBINOL, whose watchful eye
Perceiv'd his kind intent, slip'd on one side
Declining; the vain stroke from such an height,
With such a force impell'd, headlong drew down
The unwieldy champion: on the solid ground

He fell rebounding breathless, and astunn'd,
His trunk extended lay, sore maim'd, from out
His heaving breast he belch'd a crimson flood.
Full leisurely he rose, but conscious shame
Of honour lost his failing strength renew'd.
Rage, and revenge, and ever-during hate,
Blacken'd his stormy front; rash, furious, blind,
And lavish of his blood, of random strokes
He laid on load; without design or art
Onward he press'd outrageous, while his foe
Encircling wheels, or inch by inch retires,
Wise niggard of his strength. Yet all thy care,
O HOBBINOL! avail'd not to prevent
One hapless blow; o'er his strong guard the plant
Lapp'd pliant, and its knotty point impress'd
His nervous chine; he wreathed him to and fro
Convolv'd, yet thus distress'd, intrepid bore
His hilts aloft, and guarded well his head.
So when the unwary clown, with hasty step,
Crushes the folded snake, her wounded parts
Groveling she trails along, but her high crest
Erect she bears, in all its speckled pride,
She swells inflam'd, and with her forky tongue
Threatens destruction. With like eager haste,
The' impatient HOBBINOL, whose excessive pain
Stung to his heart, a speedy vengeance vow'd,
Nor wanted long the means; a feint he made
With well-dissembled guile, his batter'd shins
Mark'd with his eyes, and menac'd with his plant.
GORGONIUS, whose long-suffering legs scarce bore
His cumbrous bulk, to his supporters frail
Indulgent, soon the friendly hilts oppos'd;
Betray'd, deceiv'd, on his unguarded crest
The stroke delusive fell; a dismal groan
Burst from his hollow chest, his trembling hands
Forsook the hilts, across the spacious ring
Backward he reel'd, the crowd affrighted fly
To' escape the falling ruin. But, alas!
'Twas thy hard fate, TWANGDILLO! to receive
His pondrous trunk, on thee, on helpless thee,
Headlong, and heavy, the foul monster fell.
Beneath a mountain's weight, the unhappy bard
Lay prostrate, nor was more renown'd thy song,
O seer of *Thrace!* nor more severe thy fate.
His vocal shell, the solace and support
Of wretched age, gave one melodious scream,
And in a thousand fragments strew'd the plain.

*Fig. 34. Study for "Hob's Defence", etched vignette by Gravelot, 1737. MET Museum, Fletcher Fund, 1944.*

The nymphs, sure friends to his harmonious mirth,
Fly to his aid, his hairy breast expose
To each refreshing gale, and with soft hands
His temples chafe; at their persuasive touch
His fleeting soul returns; upon his rump
He sate disconsolate; but when, alas!
He view'd the shatter'd fragments, down again
He sunk expiring; by their friendly care
Once more reviv'd, he thrice assay'd to speak,
And thrice the rising sobs his voice subdu'd;
'Till thus at last his wretched plight he mourn'd.

"SWEET instrument of mirth! sole comfort left
To my declining years! whose sprightly notes
Restor'd my vigour, and renew'd my bloom,
Soft healing balm to every wounded heart!
Despairing, dying swains, from the cold ground
Uprais'd by thee, at thy melodious call,
With ravish'd ears receiv'd the flowing joy.

Gay pleasantry, and care-beguiling joke,
Thy sure attendants were, and at thy voice
All nature smil'd. But, oh! this hand no more
Shall touch thy wanton strings, no more with lays
Alternate, from oblivion dark redeem
The mighty dead, and vindicate their fame.
Vain are thy toils, O HOBBINOL! and all
Thy triumphs vain. Who shall record, brave man!
Thy bold exploits? Who shall thy grandeur tell,
Supreme of *Kiftsgate?* See thy faithful bard,
Despoil'd, undone. O cover me, ye hills!
Whose vocal clifts were taught my joyous song.
Or thou, fair nymph, *Avona*, on whose banks
The frolic crowd, led by my numerous strains,
Their orgies kept, and frisk'd it o'er the green,
Jocund, and gay, while thy remurm'ring streams
Danc'd by, well pleas'd. Oh! let thy friendly waves
O'erwhelm a wretch, and hide this head accurs'd."

So plains the restless PHILOMEL, her nest,
And callow young, the tender growing hope
Of future harmony, and frail return
For all her cares, to barbarous churls a prey;
Darkling she sings, the woods repeat her moan.

*Fig 35. Plates I (top) and II (bottom) from Miller's 1738* Gladiatory Art of Defence *[see page 185].*

# XV.

## TECHNIQUES *of the* GLADIATORS

ANONYMOUS, 1712

This I take to be the Case of a New Pamphlet, which is just now come out among us, and which, as it enters the stage like a Gladiator at the Bear-garden, with a great Flourish, Brandishing its Weapons, carrying a fine Feather in its Hat, the shirt and Hair tied up with Ribbands, a bright Weapon in its Hand *in Terrorem*, and the like so it comes ushered in by the shouts and Huzza's of the Rabble, who, according to Custom, always attend it.

These Gladiators, tho' they think the shows and shorts useful, yet when they come to close, when they draw towards each other to fight, regarding neither the fine shirt tied up with Ribbands, the fine Feather in the Hat, or the glistering of the sword, the Business then is to keep a true Edge, keep their Eye upon their Enemy's Guard, see where he aims to Hurt, and where he lyes open to an Advantage.[316]

---

316 *A defence of the allies and the late ministry: or, remarks on the Tories new idol* (London: J. Baker, 1712), 3. Once attributed to Daniel Defoe, but now firmly disputed.

## SIR RICHARD STEELE, 1713

*No. 22. [Tuesday] November 24, [1713]*

Nihil agis Dolor: quamvis sis molestus, nunquam te esse confitebor malum.
Cic. Tus. Ques.

AS Health is reckoned one of the greatest Blessings, and Pain or Sickness the greatest Evil that attends Mankind, a Discourse that may tend to mitigate the last, will of Consequence heighten the first; which State we must enjoy with so much the more sincere Pleasure, as we are the less liable to Interruption from the other. If Pain were allowed to be really one of the greatest Evils, how miserable must the Condition of Man be, not only in the Instance of suffering, but in the Contemplation of being hourly liable to it? If we proceed in our Enquiry, we shall find that Pain, even thro' Custom and Use, has been made not only not formidable but familiar. We read that the Spartan Children were educated under the painful Extremities of Heat and Cold, Hunger and Thirst, at that Time when their Bodies and Minds were least fortified to digest the Philosophy of such hardy Virtue. If we look among the military Men, even those of the lowest Order, how many Instances of incredible Patience may we find in those, who go thro' the most painful Livelihood, more thro' Custom and Exercise, than the Reflection of any Honour or Profit? This Force, of Custom is still farther to be seen in that Race of modern Heroes the Prize-fighters, Fellows of the most infamous Lives and Conversations; nay even some of them so timorous in the common Incidents of Life, as to allow Pain the greatest Evil; and yet upon certain Periods to assume the Bravery of the Souldier, and the Constancy of the Philosopher. You may see these receive a Wound with the same steady uncontrouled Countenance as they give one, and appear less concerned than the Spectators at the Success of the Engagement. They are placed in such a View, where the least Action or Look that expresses an unmanly Concern must be taken Notice of, and therefore are in a constant Readiness rather to receive the Stroke of their Enemy than unhandsomely avoid it, knowing that their Reputation and Profit does not so much arise from their Skill in avoiding their Enemy, as their Patience in enduring; for this must be the Effect of Courage, but the other may be of Chance. How soever cruel and inhumane these Entertainments may be thought, the Doctrine of enduring Pain, and even Death it self, are represented more forcibly than in the finest Paintings of Poets and Philosophers. If Custom and base Hire can beget such Hardiness, as we have seen it do even in Children and Men of no Capacity or Education, as to enable them to work thro' frequent Pain and Anguish; what transcendent Proofs of Fortitude may not be expected from the Man supported by Reason and Philosophy, under the accidental Pressures of Pain or Sickness?[317]

## WILLIAM HOPE, 1715

*The author of the following pamphlet, while claiming to be the mysterious "H.B.", was likely the Scottish fencing master Sir William Hope, whose work is defended and promoted throughout the text. In the 1724 edition of Hope's* Vindication of the True Art of Self-Defence *(published the year of his death), following the preface, an advertisement mentions several other works by Hope, including one entitled* Observations on the Gladiators Stage-Fighting.[318] *As shall be seen, this text is highly critical of the gladiator's method of fencing. Likewise, in another of Hope's texts,* The Fencing-Master's Advice to His Scholar, *Hope expresses a similar disdain and disapproval of two English and Irish gladiators, whose skill he witnessed in a fencing school.[319]*

---

317 *The Englishman*, November 24, 1713.
318 Sir William Hope, *A Vindication of the True Art of Self-defence. With a Proposal to the Honourable Members of Parliament for Erecting a Court of Honour in Great-Britain. Recommended to All Gentlemen, But Particularly to the Soldiery: To which is Annexed, a Short, But Very Useful Memorial for Sword-men* (Edinburgh: William Brown, 1724).
319 Sir William Hope, *The Fencing-master's Advice to His Scholar* (Edinburgh: John Reid, 1692), 31.

*Fig. 36. Plate III from James Miller's* Treatise of yᵉ Gladiatory Art of Defence *(see page 185 for corresponding technical description).*

## A FEW OBSERVATIONS UPON THE FIGHTING FOR PRIZES IN THE BEAR-GARDENS:

by a

Lover and Well-wisher, not only to the True and Useful Art of the SWORD, but also to the Safety and Security of the Persons of those Brave, Courageous, and Bold Performers in these publick Places, for Trial of Skill in this Gentlemanly Art.

Ea enim tuta est potentia quæ Viribus suis modum imponit.
A N D,
That's an only sure and general Guard;
Whose Cross, the Blow, as well as Thrust doth ward.

# CHAPTER XV

## THE PREFACE.

*The following Observations being sent to me by a Friend, who is not only Curious, but also a great Lover of the Art of the* SWORD, *with a Liberty to me to print them, if I judged they might be any Ways useful to the Publick; I have thought fit to do it, not doubting but they will be of Use to all, but, especially to* SWORD-MEN, *who cannot fail to reap Benefit by the serious Perusal of them, and of the Book to which they relate; the only Design of which, is, no doubt, to put the true Art of Defence with the Sword, against all kind of edged or pointed Weapons, both on Foot and Horse-back, upon a right and solid Foot; for the Benefit and Safety of our Country-men, whether engag'd only Voluntarily for a Prize, or Unfortunately for their Lives.*

## OBSERVATIONS UPON THE
### *Fighting for* PRIZES, &c.

SIR,

BEING a Lover of all kind of Gentlemanly Exercises, particularly that of the Sword, I took the Opportunity (having had One or Two of the *Gladiator's* Bills thrust into my Hand, a few Days after I came to Town) to go along with one of my Acquaintance, who takes Delight in that Divertisement, to the *Bear-Garden* in *Marabone-Fields*, that I might observe if the Performers made good what they asserted in their publick Bills, viz. That they were *Masters of the Science* (as they term it) *of Defence*, or rather, *of the true Art of the Sword*; for that includes both the defensive and offensive Part, which are the Whole of the Art.

But, to my great Surprize, these Masters of true Defence, as they call themselves, after they were engag'd, did not above once or twice *Traverse*, or *go about* the Stage; or, in their own Terms, did not finish *One Bout*, when they cut one another; the one upon the Head, and the other in the Breast.

Thought I to my self, if this be the Effects of your Dexterity and Skill in the Art of Defence, a Man may be as well without it; for I am sure, Two who had never before handled a Sword, could not have cut one another sooner, nor more, in so short a Time, as these Two Pretenders to the true Art of Defence did.

This made me conclude, that I had all along been in a Mistake, in fancying that Two dextrous and adroit Sword-men could fight very smartly, and in good Earnest, and not receive, for a considerable Time, any Wound from one another, but what would be slight and no Ways disabling; and this Thought prevail'd with me for some Days, during which Time, I run down and undervalu'd in all Companies, nay, even in the publick Coffee-houses, the Art of the Sword, as ot no Use, because I had seen that those, who pretended to be Masters of it, could not, for above one Minute, defend themselves from one another's Blows.

This was the Effect and Consequence of what I observ'd, not only that Day, but also Two or Three Times since, when they likewise very soon cut one another; until being one Day in the City, and turning over some Books in Mr. *Strahan's* Shop, opposite to the *Royal-Exchange*, I by Chance see a Book of Fencing, writ by one Sir *William Hope*, which he calls his *New Method of Fencing*; and having the Curiosity to peruse it, I soon begun to alter my Thoughts, and change my Opinion, as to the Insufficiency of the Art, to defend a Man, for a considerable Time, in the Heat of an earnest Engagement, nay, even in a Rencounter or Duel, for one's Life.

For in the Book he makes it plain, that the Uncertainty these Masters Defence, proceeds not at all from the Imperfection and Insufficiency of the Art, but from the Openness and Uncertainty of the Guard they commonly make use of, which is the *Medium* Guard; a Guard liable and expos'd to all the Variety of Lessons, and Feints, that any Man can think of; and that it is no wonder, that not only pursuing from that very open Guard, but also drawing their Parades from it, they meet with that Uncertainty in their Defence, which any, who frequent that Place of Publick Tryal of Skill, may easily observe.

For, altho' Sword-men, as he says, *are neither infallible, nor invulnerable,* more than other People, yet it discovers a great Imperfection in those who profess the Art, when they cannot defend themselves, by their Dexterity, for a few Minutes; which he asserts a true Artist is capable to do, nay, even a great deal longer, if he

*Fig. 37. Plate IV from James Miller's* Treatise of yᵉ Gladiatory Art of Defence *[Note: there is a mistake in the original, this plate actually corresponding to the description for Plate V, "St. George's Guard"—see page 186 for description].*

makes use of such a true Defence, and cunning Dexterity, as Art can furnish him with; and which Defence, he says, he has improv'd to that Perfection to which it is brought in his *New Method*; and that is, the Defence which he draws from the Hanging Guard in Seconde with a sloping Point; because, from that Guard or Posture, he draws all his Defence or Crosses, as well against Thrusts as blows; (for he lays down as a Foundation, That all true Defence with any Weapon, depends upon the Cross it makes upon the Adversary's Weapon, whatever be the Position of the Sword-hand; and that the greater the Cross is, the more slow is the Adversary's Pursuit, which, by all possible Means, we should endeavour to render so, and consequently the more secure and certain a Man's own Defence, because, without a Cross, there's no true Defence; and to ward a Blow, or turn off a Thrust with the Sword-Hilt, or Shell, shows no more Art, than to do it with a Gauntlet, or Head-Piece, seeing the Blow is by both, not defended by Art, in forming a Cross, but received upon the Metal, which is Sword Proof,) and from hence asserts this seeming Paradox.

*That he has brought the Art of Defence, by the right forming of such good Crosses, to the utmost Perfection Humane Nature is capable of, because,* says he, *there cannot be a greater than a right Cross or Angle, formed by any Two Weapons; and that this right angled Cross, being frequently in ones Defence, drawn from this Guard in Seconde with a sloping Point, and the greatest Cross, making,* as has been said, *the most secure and safe Defence, therefore it is impossible for humane Nature to invent a better Defence, than what is drawn from this Guard,* because the greatest Cross that can be framed by Two Weapons, for a Man's Defence, is drawn from it; which is indeed a Demonstration, but what I did not so well take at first reading, until I more seriously reflected upon his Argument; *whereas most other Guards,* says he, *particularly those of the Small-Sword in Quarte and Tierce, in framing their Parades, make but small Crosses, which gives to the Adversary frequent Opportunities of making a Variety of Feints or falcifying Motions, whereby a Man's Defence is render'd more Uncertain, and consequently his Person more expos'd to his Adversary's Thrusts;* the very Reverse of which a Man meets with, who with Cunning and Dexterity makes use of his Defence and Crosses, from this excellent Hanging-Guard in *Seconde,* as he ought.

For, *says he,* There is a Cunning and Subtilty, as well as Dexterity, which belongs to the true Art of the Sword, and which but few, professing the Art, are Masters of Thrusts and Blows being to be avoided several other Ways, by a judicious and agile Artist, than by always meeting with, and obstinately opposing the Adversary's Sword; a Thing not known in the *Bear-Gardens,* where, at first engaging they come commonly close up to one another, and there with Fury discharge repeated Blows, whereby ensue *Contretemps* and grievous Wounds; which does indeed please the ignorant Mob, but ought to be abominate by all good Artists and Men of Judgement, seeing it is a most scandalous Disparagement to all true Art; which ought to be perform'd, not only with Calmness, but with a cautious Vigour and Judgment, otherwise such foolhardy Persons run headlong to their own Destruction, which, by a true Art is design'd to be prevented; Fencing being at first invented and design'd chiefly for Defending, and not for Offending; that falling in only by the Way, and mostly (except upon Necessity) to be made use of as a Means to effectuate the other main End, which is a Man's Defence and Preservation of his Life, when in good Earnest atack'd.

To which, *he says,* It may be objected; that what is to be done, had as good be soon done; and that Down-head, Slap, Thrust, and away with it, is much more manly, than to stand Shifting and Dalieing, as if a Man were afraid of his Skin, or could not endure the Sight of his own Blood.

To which he Answers in the Negative, for, *says he,* Whatever Backsword Masters may venture upon a publick Stage, where they run only the hazard of a few, many Times slight, Cuts in fighting for a Prize; yet the Case is quite different, when a Man has his Life at Stake, and is lyable to both Stroke and Thrust; and which, when gone, cannot be recall'd again; so that, if ever a Man ought to have his Wits about him, and keep himself free from Passion, it is, when he is engag'd for Life; that being his All, nay, his very Self; in respect whereof the Loss of the whole World is not so much as to be named, or put in the Ballance, especially when a Man runs the Hazard, of being in a few Minutes thrust into, and entring Eternity in violent Passion and Blood; A Damping and Dreadful Thought indeed, to any serious thinking Christian! And against which (as Matters go now a-Days amongst those who are call'd Men of Honour, who but too often make Trifles the Ground of bloody Quarrels) the true Art of the Sword is a most excellent Preservative.

For, *says he,* altho' when the most dextrous Sword-men in the World come to be engag'd, the one will certainly, if they continue a while fighting, have the better of, and Master the other; there being scarcely any such Thing to be found, as a perfect Equality amongst Men; yet, for the most Part, such dextrous Artists as are over-come, are commonly so, either by being commanded, or disarmed, or by receiving several slight Wounds, which, altho' not Mortal, yet are sufficient, at last, to disable them, that they are necessitate to succumb, and yeild to their conquering Adversary; whereas, when People engage without Art, they, commonly with Passion, rush so furi-ously and headlong upon one another, that the Wounds they receive, or exchange, are for the most Part Mortal; so that the true Benefit all Men reap by Fencing, is, that altho' they cannot always conquer their Adversaries, or even defend themselves from slight Wounds, yet they shall, by their Art, for the most Part, both of them save their Lives, by receiving only such Wounds, as are at first but Sight, altho' disabling; whereas those *Coups Fourrez,* as the *French* Term them, which are receiv'd full Tilt, and wholly Home, by Ignorants and Maladroits, when in Earnest engag'd, prove generally not only Disabling, but Mortal; which Disadvantage alone, ought, he says, to excite and encourage all Gentlemen, not only to the thorough Understanding of this most useful and saving Art, but also to endeavour to put it always in Practice, with Caution, Vigour, and Judgment; without which, a Man loses a great deal of the Benefit, which otherwise he would reap by his Art.

For, *He says,* he is also apt to believe, that the first Rise of People's making use of sharp Weapons did proceed from this: *That in the first Ages, slender and weak Men found themselves at a great Disadvantage, when they came to engage those who were strong and vigorous, either at Hand-blows or with other blunt Weapons; and to bring themselves to some Equality with such Robust and strong Persons, did invent first the* Sabre, *or* Broad-Sword, *whose Edges are mostly made use of; but still finding themselves at a Disadvantage, by reason of the other's great Strength, overpowering them in the Herculian Way of discharging their Blows against them, which they had not Strength to resist, they did next fall upon the Pointed Weapons, that is* Sheering *and* Small-Sword; *well concluding, that if they could but give a Thrust, it would do generally more Execution than the others Blows; to obviate which, the Strong and Vigorous Men did, upon the other Hand, invent the First Method to Cross, and put aside those dangerous Thrusts, which was the True Foundation, and Rise of the Art of Defence.*

At Last, when the Generality of People, who were ignorant of this new found out Art, of both Defending and Offending, found themselves also at a great Disadvantage, when they came to be engag'd with those Weapons, against such dextrous Artists; they, to render themselves still in more equal Circumstances with both strong and weak Sword-men, did, after the Invention of Gunpowder, endeavour to determine all their Quarrels with Fire-Arms, whereby they render'd the other Arts with the Sword of no Use; (a Method frequently taken by many even now a-Days) and which, by the way, shows how necessary it is for all Sword-men, to be good Marks-men with the Pistol, as well as dextrous Artists with the Sword, that they may not be surpris'd with the Atacks of either, but be in utrumque paratus, as we say, that is equally ready and knowing, to use their Pistol or handle their Sword; so, by what has been said, he thinks it very evident, that the Art did at first consist chiefly in the Defensive Part; by that People, when engag'd falling commonly in Passion, could not rest satisfy'd with only defending themselves, but did also, at the same Time, endeavour to return upon their Adversaries, what their Adversaries intended to put upon them, which was either Blow or Thrust: And thus they join'd, or added the Offensive Part of both Edge and Point, to the Defensive Part; both which together, do at this Day, contain and make up the whole Art of the Sword.

He also asserts Two other chief Advantages this *Hanging-Guard in Seconde* hath above all other Guards; which are *First,* That it is equally useful a Foot against the Thrust, as against the Blow; and *Secondly,* the only proper Guard a Horseback, against both small and sheering Sword; for it is hardly possible, *says he,* to defend a Blow, either a Foot, or Horseback, with any of the ordinary *Quart* and *Tierce Parades* of the Small-Sword; and if a Small-Sword Master shall pretend to defend a Blow with the Small-Sword, it will be found that he shall immediately (in Place of making use of a true ordinary *Quart,* or *Tierce Parade*) fall in to this in *Seconde,* which makes good all that this Author asserts of it; so that this Guard in *Seconde* being in all Cases and Circumstances, a general and most safe Posture, from whence such good Causes may be made, as will ward and defend, the Attacks of all kind of Weapons, whether only edged, as the Back-sword, or both edged and pointed, as the Sheering; he therefore earnestly recommends it to the Publick, and advises all Masters, both of the Back-sword and Small, to refrain from, and wholly quit their open and unsecure Guards, and uncertain and imperfect Parades, which they can only draw from them, and take themselves to this Natural, General, and most secure Guard in *Seconde* with a sloping Point, from whence may be drawn and formed such good Crosses, as cannot fail, when made use of by a dextrous and judicious Artist, to defend him from the Blows and Thrusts of all Weapons, and that as well on Horse back as a Foot.

And whereas it is commonly asserted by forward Ignorants, that they can easily Beat the best Sword-man from any nice and formal Guard he can put himself in, by a forward and violent Pursuit, *he says,* that however other Guards may be liable to this, when made use of by half skill'd Sword-men, yet, those forward Naturalists can never pretend to have that Advantage against this Guard in *Seconde,* because the more vigorously a Sword Man is attack'd, who makes use of it, the more he is forced to the true Posture of it, and so far from being Beat from it, that he is rather in a manner Beat and Forced to it, so safe and natural a Posture is it; so that this Assertion of

*Fig. 38. Plate V from James Miller's* Treatise of yᵉ Gladiatory Art of Defence *[Note: there is a mistake in the original, this plate actually corresponding to the description for Plate IV, "the Hanging-Guard"—see page 186].*

beating a Sword-man from his Guard or Defensive Posture, is at Bottom false, because, whatever Posture a Sword-man be in, if from that Posture he make and frame good Crosses upon his Adversary's Sword, whatever be the Position of the Sword-hand, he can never be said to be beat off his Defence; for when he is a performing of that, he is always upon his Guard or defensive Posture: A Guard being only the first Position of the Body, into which a Man places himself at first drawing of his Sword, and is always good when the Body is made thereby thin and short; for so soon as ever he enters into Action, he commonly goes from the nice Posture of his Guard, and falls in to the forming of good Crosses for his Defence; which Crosses are his only true Guard, and not the Posture he at first put himself into.

This Author has a great many other common Positions and Directions, quite contrary to what is commonly advised and put in Practice by the Generality of Fencing-Masters; such as, that in making use of the common Small-Sword Parades in *Quart* and *Tierce*, a Man is many Times obliged, for his better Defence, to frame the Cross upon his Adversary's Sword, close almost to his own Body, the better to meet with the foible or weak Part of it, otherwise he will be fair to have the Thrust forced home upon him.

That in thrusting a plain Thrust against the ordinary *Quart* or *Tierce* Guards, especially within the Sword, to make it the more swift, and to take the better, the Sword's Point should be carried Home upon the same Side it is presented, beyond the Adversary's Sword-hand, or Wrist, before ever the Thruster offer to disengage whereby the Thrust, especially by thrusting with the Hand in *Tierce*, will be a great deal more Surprizing and Swift, than when a Man disengages just as his Sword lyes (without this previous advancing Motion upon the same Side) and thrusting with his *Hand* in Quart upon the Weak of the Adversary's Sword, which is indeed a nice Direction.

That in Thrusting after Feints, and from Binding, a Man should thrust at some little Distance, and evite, or shun his Adversary's Sword as much as possible; which is quite contrary to the common Method, because, *says he*, As upon the defensive Part, or Parade, a Man ought always to endeavour to meet with, and oppose his Adversary's Sword; so upon the offensive Part, or pursuit, he ought to shun it, the better to prevent his Adversary's forming a Cross upon it; whereby his Defence and Parade will be the more uncertain.

That in planting any Thrust, a Man ought generally, unless the open he is to thrust upon, lye very near to him, so to plant it, that his Sword's Point may be as much as possible upon a Level with the Sword-Arm, near to the Shoulder-Joint; that being the straitest and longest Line, and consequently that which will reach furthest; and if he do it not, that it is the better for him, and more dangerous for his Adversary, to thrust low towards the Belly, as high at the Breast, because the lower Parts of the Body are not only more easily pierc'd and wounded, than those about the Breast, which are better fenced, by the Chests being Cartilagenous and Bony, but also lying so low, more difficult to defend, by the *Ordinary Quart* and *Tierce Parades.*

And for preventing of *Contretemps*, stragling Thrusts, exchanged Thrusts, Thrusts from the *Riposte*, and *Takeing of Time*, all which are different: He advises the constant Use of the left Hand, without which, *he says,* it is very difficult to prevent any of them, when engag'd with a forward half-skill'd Antagonist; upon which Account, he advises all good Sword-men when engaged with such Persons, to become, if possible, the Pursuers, because, when once Ignorants, or half-skill'd Persons, are forc'd to their Defence, they are commonly done with it; and this is the Reason why such Persons generally pursue at first most furiously when engag'd, knowing their own Weakness and Uncertainty in Defending; a very excellent Direction, and which all good Sword-men ought to engrave in their Memories.

That one of the chief Reasons, why the Art of the Sword is so much neglected and undervalued by many, proceeds from People's generally looking upon all Gentlemen, who have been but a few Months at School, to be good and dextrous Sword-men; and when such are engag'd and worsted by forward Ignorants, they immediately impute it to the Imperfection of the Art, and not to the unskillfulness and maladroitness of these young Sword-men; for to become a true and skillful Artist, requires a very frequent, long, and assiduous Practice in School-play, against all Kind of Constitutions and Tempers; a Calmness or Presence of Mind, a vigorous Agility, and what Crowns all, a solid Judgment; to make use, in an earnest Engagement, as well of the Cunning and Subtilty of the Art, as of the most Surprizing and Masculine Lessons, belonging to it; for, *says he,* by sometimes breaking a little Measure, making a Kind of Circular Motion, or yeilding a Foot or Two of Ground, until the Violence of ones Adversary's Pursuit be over, when a Sword-man has Room for it, he may many Times save his Life; when by obstinately opposing a most violent Pursuit, from a passionate and froward Adversary, by a continued Defending with the Sword, he may be so pressed upon as to fail in his Parade, or Cross, and thereby receive a mortal Wound; for whatever may be the mistaken Notion of some nice People, of breaking of Measure, and reasonably yeilding or giving a little Way upon Occasion; neither Art, nor Honour, oblige a Sword-man to stand an immoveable Butt, for his Adversary to strike and thrust at; notwithstanding of which, he very much disapproves of a too much, or constant going back, or rather timerous retiring. This is also very Good.

That the strong or weak Parts of a Sword, are not to be consider'd, so much with respect to the Ordinary Division of its Blade, into *Fort* and *Foible*, as with respect to the Cross it frames upon the Adversary's Sword, and Pressure it makes upon it; either by its own Weight only, or by the Impulse of the Sword-hand added to it; because, as these are, so, according to the nice Rules of Art, must the *Fort* or *Foible* of a Sword, when in Action, be reckon'd; the most Part of a Sword becoming sometimes thereby all Fort, as at other Times all Foible, whereby the *Fort* and *Foible* of a Sword, in Place of being fix'd and determin'd, as by the common and ordinary Division thereof, by the Middle, into *Fort* and *Foible*, become, in Action, altogether changeable and unfix'd and depend wholly upon the framed Cross, and Pressure or Impulse, or the Agent's Sword-hand; All which, at first View, seem very Odd, and contrary to the true Rules of Art, but upon second Thoughts and solid Reasoning, will be found to be as great Truths in the Art, as they are Niceties unknown to most Masters.

Again, after he has most particularly and convincingly answer'd all the Objections can be made, by the greatest Enemy, and most caviling Ignorant, against the Usefulness of the Art of the Sword, and which discovers this Author's Modesty and Ingenuity; he compares good and dextrous Sword-men to skillful Gamesters, who, altho' they may at first sitting down to any Game, have a bad Run, as they term it, against Bunglers, will certainly at last carry off their Money; so good Sword-men, not pretending to Infallibility, as has been said, may sometimes come to be worsted by bold unskillful Persons, but that upon the Main they have a very considerable Odds to the better, and will not fail, to succeed, once in many Times; which Uncertainty, *says he,* ought to humble good Sword-men, and prevent their too much presuming upon their Art and Dexterity, and also, rather make them cautious and backwards, as too hasty and forwards in engaging in any Quarrels, which, without impairing their Reputation and Honour, they can possibly prevent, or hansomely decline, at least endeavour to take up and accommodate, by the Interposition of judicious and honourable Seconds; The only true End for which they were at first design'd, and not (according to the unaccountable and most unfriendly present Custom) to encourage their Principals, and excite perhaps intimate Comarads, only disobliged for a rash Expression, or other Trifle, to kill and destroy one another, by engaging them in an illegal Duel, or which is no better, a premeditate Rencounter; This as to the Seconds.

And as to the Principals; he hopes that the unreasonable, as well as ungenerous Custom of suffering Seconds, perhaps not so much as Witnesses to the Quarrel, to engage with them, will be hereafter prevented, and discharg'd, their Business being only, first to accommodate Matters, and reconcile Parties, if possible, by proposing a just and honourable Satisfaction to the Person injur'd; or if that will not do, secondly, to stand by at a very little Distance, with their Swords drawn, to see fair Play, and that there be no dishonourable or ungentlemany Advantage taken by the Parties engag'd, so long as they are in Fight, and a determining the Quarrel; and always betwixt Bouts or Breathings, to endeavour, by all Means to persuade the Parties to an amicable Reconciliation, to prevent the sheding of more Blood, or perhaps the Loss of one of their Lives; but it is, *says he,* the Work of Principals more than Seconds, to prevent this unreasonable engaging of Seconds, to fight along with them; for a Second, who is a Man of Honor, cannot hansomly, nor will not decline engaging with his opposite Second, if he desire it of him; unless the Principals interpose and prevent it.

And for the more effectually taking up of Quarrels, and preventing of Duels and passionate Rencounters, which would be of such Advantage and Benefit to all the *British,* who are generally so Bold and Courageous, as to decline no Manner of Battle, when either provoked, or otherwise prompted to it; he lays down a most plain and easie Scheme, not only for establishing a Society of Sword-men, for the greater Encouragement, and better Improvement of the Art; but also, for a Court of Honour, so very necessary and useful; and which is so much desired by all peaceable, well natur'd, and truly honourable Persons of all Ranks, that he hopes it may, in due Time, be offer'd to the Consideration of King and Parliament, by some honourable Member, who is a Lover, not only of the Art of the Sword, but of the Preservation of his Country men's Lives; where he hopes it shall meet with that Encouragement, which the Importance and Nature of so good and honourable a Design may deserve, especially considering how many private Persons have of late lost, or rather thrown away their Lives, in most unaccountable and trifling Quarrels, which such a Remedy might, in all probability, have prevented.

Thus have I not only discover'd to you a few of the many uncommon Positions, and Directions, contain'd in this useful and curious Book, but also given an Account of the Behaviour of most of the Gladiators in the Bear-Gardens, and how deservedly they assume to themselves, the Gentlemany and Honourable Title of perfect Masters of the true Science of Defence; altho' this Author also acknowledges, that there are some of them very pretty and dextrous Sword-men, did they but make use of such a secure Guard, or Posture, as he recommends, from whence they could easily draw and frame good and safe Crosses, for their more certain Defence; he also approves of Gentlemens frequenting such Places of Tryal of Skill, because it accustoms them to the hearing the

*Fig. 39. Plate VI, "the Sword and Dagger", from Miller's* Gladiatory Art of Defence *[see page 186 for description].*

Clashing of Weapons, and the seeing Wounds given, and Blood drawn; (altho' I wish this last were seldomer done for the greater Reputation of the Art) which brings a Man, in a little Time, to value as little the Cut of a sharp Sword, as the Blow of a blunt Stick, or Cudgel.

But for the Fisty-Cuff-Battles, or trying of ones Manhood by Boxing, which is of late brought upon the publick Stages, he altogether disapproves of them, as appearing (besides their being Ungentlemany) not only Butcherly, but barbarous and inhuman, and therefore hopes they will be for the future discountinanced and discourag'd, by all Gentlemen of Generosity and Honour, seeing, at best, they can tend to nothing, but to throw those who engage in them, into Decays, or other lingring Diseases, by Reason of the grievous and violent Blows they receive from one another, upon their Heads, Bellies and Stomachs, so that it would grieve and draw Pity from any generous Man's Heart, to see them thus brutishly bruise and maul one another; nay, even to that Degree, that he says he has seen them sometimes carry'd off the Stage, without any Appearance of Life.

Now, this being so, and this Gentleman so earnestly recommending to all People, the Usefulness and Security of the hanging Guard in Seconde, from whence, to draw a general Defence, both a Foot and Horseback, whereby he puts the whole Art of the Sword upon a new Foot, as it were, by rendring the acquiring of it, not only plain and easie, but also short; reducing the defensive Part in a Manner to but Two Motions, for parrying of all Kind of Blows and Thrusts, and the Pursuit to only about half a Dozen very plain and easie Lessons, for offending by both

Blow and Thrust. I say, this being so; and that this Author can have no mean or selfish End in it; but upon the contrary, by improving of the Art, to preserve and save People's Honour and Lives when unfortunately engag'd in an Occasion with Sharps; is it not Matter of Wonder, and most unaccountable, that the Masters, to whose Hands this Book has come, do not either frankly follow this good Advice, which so much tends to the Preservation of Mens Persons, or otherwise offer sufficient Reasons (which I don't believe they well can, if they have seriously and with Attention perused his Book, the Author having answer'd in it all the material Objections can be brought against it) for discovering the Imperfection and Insufficiency of this new and safe Method of Defence, so generously and earnestly offer'd to them.

I confess, for my own Part, I can give no other Reason for it but this; That, as in Matters of Religion, Men are commonly fixt in that Persuasion, to which they are educated from their Youth, whether *Jewish*, *Mahometan*, or *Roman Catholick*; (for a *Mahometan*, or *Jew*, stick as close to, and believe, and depend as much upon the Certainty of their *Creeds*, as the most precisely head-strong and inflexible Fanatick, of either Whig, or Tory amongst us) and rest satisfy'd, that they are in the right Way to Salvation, without ever examining further, altho' there are other Systems of Religion, lying before them, and open to their View, which, if seriously examined, would be found more consonant and agreeable to both Reason and Scripture: so in all Arts and Employments, particularly, that of the Art of the Sword; These Masters having been taught the Common Method keep close to it, and never think either of improving it, or falling upon a better and safer, but jog on in the old imperfect and unsecure Road, from Master to Provo, and provided they get but a Livelyhood by it, trouble themselves very little either about the Improvement of the Art, or Safety of their Scholar's Persons; I always except the more curious Masters out of this *Category*.

This I take to be the true Reason of their continuing in their old Rot, and not thoro'ly examining the Importance and Usefulness of so very considerable and Improvement in the Art of Defence, as is so earnestly offer'd to them by this Gentleman, in his *New Method*; in Behalf of which, I could say a great deal more, were not my Letter already too long; but knowing you to be not only a great Lover of the Art, but also a very knowing and judicious Sword-man, I recommend the serious Perusal of the Book it self to you, with which I am persuaded you will be very well satisfy'd. If you judge these few Observations may be of Use to the Publick, I allow you to print them, and shall conclude with that very apposite Sentence, which the Author has in his Title Page. *Gladiatura, non solum ad Honoris, Vitæque Conservationem; sed etiam ad Corporis, atque Animæ Relaxationem, perquam necessaria.* Which I English thus:

> Fencing for Diversion does not only serve,
> It Life, as well as Honour, doth preserve;
> The Manly'st Exercise of Heroick Kind,
> To chear the Body, and relax the Mind.

London, Oct.      SIR,
29. 1714
                    I am your Obliged and
                         very Humble Servant, H.B.

*Fig. 40. Plate VII, "the Sword and Buckler", from Miller's* Gladiatory Art of Defence *[see page 186 for description].*

## DONALD MCBANE, 1728

*In his fencing treatise, McBane (a former champion gladiator) treats of a large variety of weapons in use during the period, while typically discussing them in the context of self-defense (against Game-Keepers, "rustical fellows", or attackers armed with other weapons) and for use in duels. However, he makes one exception with the so-called "Fauchion." McBane's reference to "Spectators where those Weapons are made use of" strongly suggests that he is speaking of this weapon in the context of its use by prize-fighters on the stage. Unlike James Miller's steel "falchion", evidence suggests that McBane likely refers to a wooden, dussack-like weapon, similar to those which can be seen in several gladiatorial images of the period.[320] An account from Dublin during the eighteenth century describes falchions as "oakstaves of casks hardened by smoking in chimnies, sharpened on one side, and a hole cut in one end to admit a hand to answer for a handle,"[321] while Bailey's English Dictionary of 1724 defines the word thus: "FAUCHION [Fauchon, F.] a sort of broad short wooden Sword."[322] A 1738 account from Virgina also refers to the falchion as a wooden weapon:*

---

320 See, for instance, the figures on pages 102 and 134 of this book.

321 Herbert, *Irish varieties, for the last fifty years: written from recollections* (London: William Joy, 1836) 77-88.

322 N. Bailey, *An Universal Etymological English Dictionary Comprehending the Derivations of the Generality of Words in the English Tongue* (London: E. Bell, 1724). [Unpaginated—see entry for "FAUCHION".]

In another Mat we found some *Indian* Tomahawks finely graved and painted. These resembled the wooden Faulchion used by the Prize-Fighters in *England*, except that they have no Guard to save the Fingers. They were made of a rough heavy Wood, and among these Tomahawks was the largest that ever I saw.[323]

*McBane likely used such a "fauchion" in his famous combat with Andrew O'Bryan. It is telling that, in his own account, McBane describes breaking (rather than cutting or wounding) the Irishman's arm with a falchion, once again suggesting that this may have been a blunt weapon. Regarding the weapon itself, McBane instructs:*

*Fauchions,* are Weapons that no Person can get any Credit by, for whoever understands the Back-Sword, must be Master of them, and whoever are Spectators where those Weapons are made use of, have Pleasure in seeing it, tho' single or double by Reason there is but one Guard belonging to them, and he who makes use of them, and can save his Knuckles without his Head is broake, may without control say, he was not hit at all.[324]

## JAMES MILLER, 1738

*Although its textual content is extremely brief, Miller's lavishly illustrated fencing treatise is the only one in existence that we currently know of that is solely devoted to the technique and weapons of the stage gladiators (Miller, of course, having been a gladiator himself).[325]*

### A short Treatise of yᵉ Gladiatory Art of Defence.

*My Lord,*

*Had not my King and Country demanded my service abroad, my Intention was, to have given the Public a short Treatise of yᵉ Gladiatory Art of Defence (a subject that few have handled) & to have all along Illustrated it with proper Sculptures and Figures. To have trac'd its first Rise and Origin, & pursued it through the several Degrees of its Advancement until it came to have Schools establish'd, Amphitheatres built, Stipends settled and Laurels and Largesses given to the Victors. To have specified and described the several Kinds of Weapons, and Arms, which Combatants, in different Ages, were wont to make use of, and by what skill and Manner of Address they might best be enabled to defend themselves, and annoy their Adversarys. But above all to have shown by very convincing Proffs and Arguments the great Usefulness of this science and the manly Exercises depending on it to every brave and warlike Nation; That Courage (under God) cannot be wanting, nor Conquest become a stranger to such People, as take delight in the Cultivation of the sword, but being ordered into another Country, I thought it not improper to present your Lordship with the Designs I have already made, and explained on the side of this sheet; as of Use to instruct the Learner, and remind the Proficient in this Art, and while I am gone, a small Memorandum of*

*My Lord,*
*Your most devoted servant*
*James Miller.*

323 *A Modern History, or the Present State of All Nations, Vol. XXXI* (London: Printed for the Author, 1738), 81.
324 McBane, 94.
325 For more on Miller's life and career, see Chapter V.v, pp. 66-72.

*Fig. 40. Plate VIII, "the Sword and Gantlet", from Miller's* Gladiatory Art of Defence *[see page 187 for description].*

*EXPLANATION.*

Plate I *shows you the* Outside-Guard, *which covers the outside of $y^e$ Body from Head to Toe, & to put yourself in a true Position, your* Sword Hilt *must be in a perpendicular Line with your right Toe, your right Heel in a Line with your left, and your Body resting a little upon the left Leg, the back part of your left Hand must be within half a span of the left side of your Face with your sword Arm a little bent and the distance between your Feet about 12 or 14 Inches, in proportion to your stature or Accommodation to your Ease.* [for plate, see top of page 170]

Plate II *is the* Inside-Guard *which covers the Inside of your Body and the Position is much the same with the first Plate only your right Heel must be in a Line with the middle of your left Foot, and $y^e$ back part of your left Hand half a span from the upper part of your Face, these are the two* Guards *upon which the whole Art depends.* [for plate, see bottom of page 170]

Plate III *is the* Medium-Guard, *which is not accounted so safe and therefore seldom or never practiced except by very expert Masters.* [for plate, see page 173]

*Fig. 41. Plate IX from Miller's* Gladiatory Art of Defence *[Note: there is a mistake in the original, this plate actually corresponding to the description for Plate X, "the Inside Fauchion", on page 187].*

Plate IV *is the* Hanging-Guard, *which is done by dropping y^r Point on a sudden clapping your Head to your Sword-Arm, looking directly under your Sword, and inclining a little towards your Adversary. This Guard is of excellent Use, when you are either pressed very hard, or have more than one to contend with.* [Note: there is a mistake in the original, and this description actually applies to Plate V, page 178]

Plate V *is* S^t. George's-Guard, *of singular Use on Horse back, and the only one indeed, that is proper upon that Occasion.* [Note: there is a mistake in the original, and this description actually applies to Plate IV, page 175]

Plate VI *is the* Sword *and* Dagger, *which (together with the rest of the double Weapons) depends altogether on your skill in the Back-sword, only, in the time of engaging, you are to look under your Guard without stooping, and keep your sword behind your Dagger, on which you are to catch your Adversary's Throws, while at the same time, you are annoying him with your sword.* [for plate, see page 181]

Plate VII *is the* Sword *and* Buckler, *which differs only in this, that, while you are engag'd, you must look above your Buckler and consequently be more expos'd.* [for plate, see page 183]

*Fig. 42. Plate X from Miller's* Gladiatory Art of Defence *[Note: there is a mistake in the original, this plate actually corresponding to the description for Plate IX, "the Faulchion or Hanger", below on this page].*

Plate VIII *is the* Sword *and* Gantlet, *which admits of the same Directions with Plate 6.* [for plate, see page 185]

Plate IX *the* Faulchion *or* Hanger, *the same with Plate 1.* [Note: there is a mistake in the original, and this description actually applies to Plate X on page 187]

Plate X *the* Inside Faulchion, *the same with Plate 2.* [Note: there is a mistake in the original, and this description actually applies to Plate IX on page 186]

Plate XI i*s the* Quarter-Staffe, *which must be held between your Fore-Finger and Thumb very loosely, for the Convenience of slipping, but high enough over your Head to cover it, having y$^r$ right Foot a little more forward than y$^r$ left you are to look under your Guard without stooping, and, when you throw at y Adversary, grasp y$^r$ Weapon.* [for plate, see page 188]

Plate XII *is the* Quarter-Staff *revers'd which varies from the former, only that y$^r$ left Foot must be more forward than y$^r$ right, & y$^r$ left Hand uppermost.* [for plate, see page 189]

*Fig. 43. Plate XI, "the Quarter-Staffe", from Miller's* Gladiatory Art of Defence *[see page 187 for description].*

Plate XIII *is the Figure of a Cut on y^e outside of the* Sword Arm. [for plate, see page 193]

Plate XIV *is the Figure of a Design to Cut the* inside *of the* Head. [for plate, see page 196]

Plate XV *the Figure of a Cut on the* outside *of the Leg.* [this plate is unfortunately missing in the extant original].[326]

## EXCERPTS from THOMAS PAGE, [1746]

*On the title page of his treatise on the use of the broadsword, Thomas Page proclaims to show "the True Method of Fighting with that Weapon as it is now in Use among the Highlanders; deduc'd from the Use of the Scymitar; with every Throw, Cut, Guard, and Disarm." However, in the middle of his text, following a lengthy section on "Lessons", Page surprisingly notes that, "The Gladiator upon the Stage is very exact in these Lessons, and generally plays an exact round of them with little or no Variation." Recently discovered evidence from 1782*

---

326 Captain James Miller, *Treatise of ye Gladiatory Art of Defence* (London: 1738).

*Fig. 44. Plate XII, "the Quarter-Staff revers'd", from Miller's* Gladiatory Art *[see page 187 for description].*

*suggests that, in his youth, Page was a student of the venerable gladiator Timothy Buck (Figg's teacher).* [327] *If this is true, then Page, who was born in 1713, would have been a mere teenager during his time training under Buck (who was mortally wounded in 1729, and who had died by 1730—see pages 34-35). Here follows Page's series of lessons which he claims were used by the stage gladiators.*

## The G U A R D S.

A *Guard*, which is the Position of the Sword, whereby a Blow is warded off from any Part of the Body, has four different Names from the four different Parts of the Body, which are defended by each of them seperately, and are thus denominated,

> The *Inside* Guard,
> The *Outside* Guard,
> The *Hanging* Guard,
> The *St. George's* Guard.

---

327 Keith Farrell, "Thomas Page and Timothy Buck", keithfarrell.net, August 20, 2018, https://www.keithfarrell.net/blog/2018/08/thomas-page-and-timothy-buck/

The Inside Guard is when you stand with each Foot on the Line of Defence and hold the Point of your Sword over against your Adversary's Left Temple, and the Hilt in a Line with his Right Hip, and the Middle of your Sword cutting the Line of Defence at acute Angles, by which the internal Parts of the Limbs on the Right Side, and the fore Part of the Face and Body, with the whole Left Side, will be defended from being Cut.

The Outside Guard is rais'd when you stand with your Body square, astride the Line of Defence with the Right and Left Foot at right Angles with it, holding the Point of your Sword over against your Adversary's Right Temple, and sinking the Hilt in a Line with his Left Hip, by which the external Part of the Right Side of the Head, Neck, Arm, Body, Thigh and Leg, and secured from being Cut. In this Guard, the Position of the Right Hand differs from all other Guards, for it is to be bent at the Wrest with the back of the Hand and the Knuckels, (which are always in a Line with the Edge of the Sword) turn'd upwards and outwards, which defends the Sword Arm from the Shoulder to the Wrist, without ever moving the Sword.

From this you go to the Hanging Guard, which is thus performed, with your Right Foot step a little backward and sideways, so as to make an acute Angle with the Line of Defence, and at the some Moment raising the Elbow of the Sword Arm, and present the Point of the Sword against your Adversary's Breast, and covering your own Head, till you can see your Adversary's Face clear under your own Fort: This Guard covers the Head, Shoulders, Face and Breast, and with the Point stops your Adversary from pressing too closely upon you, and keeps him at length when he is endeavouring to come up to half Sword, and is the dernier[*] Resort when you have retreated, or are push'd into a Corner from whence you are too weak to advance, and not enough room to Traverse.

The last Guard arises from this, and is called St George's Guard, which is perform'd by standing square across the Line, and holding the Sword a little rais'd above you own Head, parallel to your Shoulders, with the Edge turn'd upwards toward your Adversary; and is only used occasionally to stop a right down Blow aim'd at the Head of Shoulders. These are all the absolute Guards, and must be learn'd till you can raise them distinctly after each other, with a steady and erect Body, and a nimble and strong Arm; during the whole time of which the Left Hand is used as a Ballance to the Body, and by the Motion of which the Center of Gravity is kept over the standing Leg; as in the Inside Guard, by the fore Foot's being advanc'd, the Center of Gravity would be thrown too forward, if the Left Hand's being extended backward did not bring it over the Left Leg.

In the Outside Guard, the Left Hand is held before and close to the Body below the Navel, to bring the Center of Gravity perpendicular over the Middle of the Line, at the Ends of which the Feet are plac'd at right Angles with the Line of Defence: The same is done in the Hanging, and St. George's Guard.

When you are perfect in the Attitude and Position of the Limbs, and can dexterously raise the Guards, standing on the Line of Defence, the same Guards must be practised in the Advance, Retreat, and the Traverse. And to each Step of each Motion must be pitch'd a Guard, as in the Advance, to every Step you must change from an Inside Guard to an Outside, or from an Outside to an Inside, and as you go Step by Step change the Guard for Guard, nor are any other Guards made use of in the Advance, than the Outside and the Inside; but in the Retreat every Guard is made use of in its Turn, but must be chang'd Step by Step as in the Advance, except you choose to retreat under a Hanging Guard, which is really the best, if you lie only on the Defensive, and then instead of changing at every Step, point your Sword directly at your Adversary's Breast.

In the Traverse, also the Outside and Inside, with the Hanging Guard, are made use of. The Inside can only be used to the Step of the Right Foot, but in coming about with the Left Foot you must *stop* under an Outside or a Hanging Guard, as you see convenient.

In the back Traverse, the very reverse of every Motion and Guard is to be observed, as in the Traversing back with the Left Foot the Inside only is to be pitch'd and in the Step with the Right Foot the Outside or Hanging is to be used; and these Steps attended by these Guards are to be practis'd and compleated before you can begin to take the first Lesson, which is This.

---

[*]  *Dernier:* Last.

## L E S S O N the First.

What is called a *Lesson* in the Science of the Sword, is the Manner of attacking your Enemy, or defending your self, under some one or more or those Guards[§] which are already explain'd, and putting in practise the Rules already given; as for Example, this first Lesson teaches you to use the plain Guards, without the Advantages of Slips, Falsifies, Battering, &c. (all which will be explained hereafter) in the Manner following: With a steady Countenance looking full in your Adversary's Eyes, meet him boldly, and throw sharply at his Inside, and immediately stop an Outside, which you have no sooner received but throw again to his Inside with the utmost Vigour and Rapidity, an with the same Swiftness stopping an Outside. This is to be practis'd at first but slowly, till you are perfect in each Part of the two Throws, and then by Degrees increase the Swiftness of every Motion, till you can play A Bout upon the plain Guards perfectly; and then the same Lesson is to be practis'd over again in the Advance, the Retreat and the Traverse, till you are perfect in Offending your Adversary, and Defending your self with the Outside and Inside Guards, which will bring you to the,

## The Second L E S S O N.

Which begins where the last ends, and adds to the two former Guards, the Hanging, and the St. George's Guard; and having made use of the Outside and Inside as in the former Lesson, go directly from the Outside to the Hanging Guard, and lying a little while under that Cover, wait to see where your Adversary will Throw, which if he does not do immediately, Throw smartly at his Inside stop his Outside, recover to a Hanging again, and stopping with a St. George, Throw vigorously at his Head.

All this is to be practised slowly at first, 'till you are extreamly perfect in every Change and then play over the whole Lesson with Life and Spirit; and then as in the former Lesson, the whole is to be play'd over again upon the Advance, the Retreat and the Traverse, seperately and respectively.

These Lessons, when perfect, is what is call'd plain Playing.

Preparatory to the third Lesson is to be learn'd,

## The S L I P.

Which has been before explain'd, and is practis'd in the following Manner upon each of the Guards.

First on the Inside; When your Adversary Throws an Inside, instead of *Stopping* it with an Inside Guard, draw your Right Foot backward towards the Left, in the same Manner as in the Retreat, and at the same Moment withdraw your whole Body backward and Sideways to the right of the Line, letting your Adversary's Point pass by your Sword a little out of his Reach, and steping into your former Position, Throw home at his Outside, which can't but be open by his over throwing himself, which He will do the more by missing your Body, and not being receiv'd by your Sword, which he expected, to stop the effort of his Strength. This is the *Slip* upon the Inside. The same practis'd upon the Outside is as follows; Draw the Right Leg with the whole Body backwards and sideways a little out of the Line, towards the Left Hand, contracting your Arm a little, your Sword still in the Line, and under an Outside Guard; let your Adversary's Point slip past you, and at the same Moment reducing your Right Foot to its former Position, Throw smartly at the Outside of his Head, which will lie so forward by his over throwing himself, that he can neither recover nor stop with a Guard. The Slip is also call'd *Breaking Measure*.

The next Guard in which the Slip is us'd, and in which it is more proper than any of the rest, is the Hanging Guard, insomuch that every Throw that can be made at it is better slip'd than stop'd; which is done by stepping with the Right Foot quite out of, and at right Angles with the Line, and the whole Body beyond it towards the Right, so that your Adversary's Point slipping past you, leaves his Head, Neck, Shoulders and Breast, exposed to the full Force of your Inside, Throw. The same slip without any variation is practis'd upon a St. George's Guard, as in the Hanging. Being perfect in these Slips, you begin

## The Third L E S S O N.

Thus, Meet your Adversary full with a Throw at his Inside, and not stopping his Outside, slip it as above directed, and Throw smartly at his Inside again, which if He stops recover to an Outside, and under that wait for his throwing. Pitch to an Inside, and give an *Opening*, slip his Throw to the Inside, throw vigorously at the Outside and retreat under a Hanging Guard. This is to be practis'd as the former, in the Advance, the Retreat, and the Traverse.

## L E S S O N the Fourth.

Advance under a Hanging Guard; Throw an Inside; Stop an Outside; Slip an Inside; Throw at the Head; Recover to a Hanging; Retreat under an Outside Guard; change to an Inside; Slip and Throw the Inside, and Outside alternately, with three Throws and three Slips on each Guard advancing one Step after each Slip. This also must be practis'd upon the Retreat, and the Traverse, which when you are perfect in, you must begin to Falsify or make *Feints*.

To make a *Feint*, as was observed before, is offering towards an Attempt to Cut without Throwing home, and may be practis'd with Success from every Guard, but is most useful on the Inside and Outside; and is thus practis'd; When you lie under an Inside Guard, change with a quick Motion towards an Outside, with all the Appearance of resolutely Throwing Home, but stop short the Moment you have past your Adversary's Sword, and returning back with the utmost Swiftness, throw Home to an Inside where he has given you an Opening, by his attempting to stop an Outside, where he expected your Throw. The Reverse of this is the Feint to the Outside. When you lie under a Hanging Guard there are three Feints in use, because from thence you have three Throws either to the Outside, the Inside, or right down at the Top of the Head; if you Feint to the Inside, return your Sword round the Point of your Adversary's, and make a Cut at the Crown of the Head.

Or if you make a Feint at the Crown of the Head from the Hanging Guard, as if you were going to make a Cut in the very middle betwixt the Outside and the Inside, you must stop short at the half Throw, and returning quick throw Home either to the outside or inside of the Head which you see open.

## L E S S O N the Fifth.

Advance to your Adversary under the cover of an Outside; Feint to an Inside; Recover to an Outside; which will oblige your Adversary to open his Play, for he must either stand still without Motion, or make some offer at some of the three Openings you have given him; if he throws an Inside at you, slip him and throw home an Outside; and recovering the same, Feint to an Outside, and throw home an Inside.

If your Adversary should throw home an Inside, stop it, and throwing home an Outside, slip an Inside; Feint to an Outside, and with a double Feint come half way to the Hanging Guard, and from thence throw swiftly at the Crown of the Head. Practise this (as all other Lessons) at first very slow, repeating every Part often over, till you can go through the whole with Life and Spirit.

Before you come to the more loose and general Lessons, it will be necessary to know the *Lunge*, the *Bearing* the *Battering*, and their Uses.

## The L U N G E.

The Lunge (explained before) is annex'd to every Throw except the Outside, in which it is seldom us'd to Advantage. In all other Throws it is not only useful but necessary when you play at length, but at half Sword it is never to be attempted, because it throws your whole Head and Body under your Adversary's *Fort*.

*Fig. 45. Plate XIII, "a Cut on ye outside", from Miller's* Gladiatory Art of Defence *[see page 188 for description].*

When you meet your Adversary, instead of covering yourself under any Guard, throw briskly at his fairest Opening, whether it be Outside or Inside, and at the same Moment of your Throw step forward with your Right Foot, so that you may reach him home in your Throw, and yet be out of Reach of his Sword, upon your recovering from the Lunge, which must be with the utmost swiftness from the Moment of giving the Cut; this is to be practis'd with every Throw in loose Playing whilst you play at length, that is with your Body wholly out of the Reach or your Adversary's Sword, yet near enough always to command the Wrest of his Sword Arm, and consequently so as to cut any Part of the same Arm with the least Step forwards.

After you are perfect in the Lunge, and can use it readily to every Throw, begin to meet your Adversary's Fort with your Fort with a brisk Lunge at the same Time, both lying under an Outside Guard, and with a stiff Arm, pressing strongly against it, slip your Fort to his Foible, holding his Sword out of the Line, which is call'd

## BEARING.

This gives you his Head, Neck, Shoulder and Arms quite open, and at the same Time weakens his Arm, so as to prevent his stopping your Throw, which ever you use either Outside or Inside, and which must be thrown as quick as possible from your Bearing. The Reverse of this is Bearing upon an Inside.

Bearing upon the Hanging Guard is never safely to be practised, and always to be avoided, unless at the half Sword, and even there a Cut must be either given or received, before any Advantage can be made of it, and the only Advantage that can be propos'd is bearing upon your Adversary's Sword a little out of the Line and opening his Outside, though at the same time you open your own Head and inside much more, and if your Enemy be alert, he may easily slip from your Bearing, and Cut you infallibly.

Bearing is never to be used but in steady Playing, and not in the Advance, the Retreat, or the Traverse.

From *Bearing* you proceed to *Battering*, which is forcibly striking upon the Foible of your Adversary's Sword, either once, twice, or thrice, so as to beat him out of the Line, which will consequently lay him open to that Side on which you Batter. *The Batter* may be us'd to any Guard, but with different Success, for the Inside being by much the strongest Guard that is held, the Batter scarce ever break the Line upon it, except when your Adversary's Arm is extreamly weakened by long Play, and in the Hanging Guard by its Position the Batter is apt to slip of it. The St. George's Guard is not hurt by the Batter, because it is only used to stop a Blow, and never to lie under. The Outside therefore is the only Guard in which it can be used to any Advantage, tho' not always with the same Success; however, if it be thought useful, its Practice is to strike strongly upon your Adversary's Sword once, and if you find his Sword beaten ever so little out of the Line, repeat the Batter one, two.... or one, two, three, which may very likely drive his Sword quite out of the Line, (the Outside being the weakest Guard) and give you an Opportunity of throwing at the Opening, but beware at his feeling your first Batter, that he does not slip your second, and cut you more securely than if he had slipt your Throw.

When you are perfect in every one of these five Lessons, and can readily use every Guard, Throw, Feint, and Slip, the next and most material Part of Play, and upon which the Success of each depends, is *Timeing*, a Term not yet explain'd, and is as follows.

## TIMEING.

Is the exact and critical Throwing in you Sword upon every little Opening, that appears between the changing of your Adversary's Guards, Posture of Body or Position of Limbs. For no Change can possibly be made, either in the Sword, Body, or Limbs, without giving a transient Opening, easy to be hit by a sharp Eye and quick Hand; besides that Opening that is always left, and must be so when the Change is compleated; as for Example.

When you stand full guarded under an Inside, you have a clear Opening left on the Outside; and so under whatsoever Guard you lie, its Opposite is always open: Now besides this, whenever you change, as from an Inside to an Outside, there is a transient and temporary Opening of the Wrist, Arm, Breast, Face and Head, in the very middle between your Guards that is, in the middle of your Change from the Inside to the Outside, and when your Sword is properly in neither; now successively throwing upon this Opening whilst your Adversary's Sword is changing from the Inside, and yet not got fully to the Outside, is called *Timeing* an Inside. Thus throwing into the Opening which is made by changing from an Outside to an Inside, is called *Timeing* an Outside; and Throwing in to that Opening which is made in changing from the Outside which is made in changing from the Outside to the Hanging, which lays open the Ribs, Hip, Thigh, and under part of the Arm, tho' but for a Moment, is call'd *Timeing* the Hanging Guard.

In changing from the Hanging to the St. George's Guard, all the Parts of the Body below the Throat and the inside of the Sword Arm are expos'd, and taking the Advantage of that Opening is call'd *Timeing* to a St. George. This is the Practice of *Timeing* upon the plain Guard, and must be put in execution in advancing, retreating, and traversing, every Step of which gives the Openings more evident than when you are Stationary; besides other Openings arising from the changes of the Center of Gravity, which is continually altering by the Motion of every Step.

Timeing also is of the greatest use in the Defensive Part of the Science, and is the quick and judicious Change of your Sword from one Guard to another, in order to cover an open Part which is attack'd; and doing it so as to stop your Adversary's Sword full in the Line is call'd *Timeing a Guard*; for if you let his Sword pass the Line before you Stop it you can't avoid being Cut, and must give several new and defenceless Openings.

By these few Particulars the Usefulness of Timeing may partly be perceiv'd, but is Necessity and Excellence can never be thoroughly known till you come to play loose; and then so many Openings will plainly be seen upon every Change and Motion, that you will loose with regret such fair Opportunities of Cutting before you become a compleat Master of *Timeing*, which is not only necessary in Throws and Guards, but even in Stepping, Advancing, Retreating, Travelling, and Lunging; for if each Step of these be not exactly Timed with the Change of your Sword either from one Guard to another, or from a Defensive Guard to an Offensive Throw, or back from a Throw to a Guard again, you will by every step give fresh Openings, and may be cut twice before and after your own Change; and the Advantages and Disadvantages of Timeing will be shewn at large when you came to the loose Lessons, but before they are begun it will be necessary to teach the two Methods of Cutting the Leg, and the Disarming upon an Outside.

A Throw at the Leg is us'd only in single Combat, and is, if you go home, a disabling Throw. It's Practice is, in the first Method, to receive an Inside, and instead of throwing an Outside, step a little forwarder, sinking your Body at the same time you transfer your Weight from the Left to the Right Leg, bring the Point underneath your Adversary's Sword, and throwing swiftly at the Calf of his Leg, spring back as from a Lunge, under the Cover of a St. George's Guard. This Throw, tho' extreamly safe in itself, is never to be us'd to a Master of *Timeing*, for if he slips his Right Leg backwards and sideways cross his Left Leg, and *Time* you either to an Inside or an Outside, which he chooses, will cut you either in the Head or the Arm. The second way of going down to the Leg is by much the safest of the two, and is done by sinking the Body very low at half Sword under a St. George's Guard, make a Feint to the Leg, recover to a St. George, give an Opening at the Head, and at the same time Feint to the Leg again, but stoping fully with a St. George go swiftly down to the outside of the Leg, and spring off as before.

The *Disarm* upon the Outside (though there are others) is by much the best, safest, and the most in use of the Scymiter; and is, for that reason, commonly call'd the Turkish Disarm; and is thus perform'd.

Receive an Inside full, at the same Time stepping forward with the Right Foot to the half Lunge, change to the Outside; and in the Change, bear your Adversary's Sword out of the Line; and in the same Instant step nimbly about with your Left Foot up to your Adversary's Heel, and seizing the Shell of his Hilt with your Left Hand, quit your Bearing, and with your Point fixt to his Breast force the Sword from his Hand; which he must quit or stab himself upon your Point.

These are the single Lessons and the very Grounds of the Science of the Broad Sword, and a loose lesson is no more than these Grounds variously repeated, and these Principles differently combin'd; so as to make an easy Transition from any one Part of a regular Lesson to that of another as your Judgement shall best direct you, to offend your Enemy, or as necessary may oblige you, to defend yourself. And thus it is either in single Combat in publick Battle, that each of these Principles may be indifferently us'd as your Adversary presses upon you or you upon him.

The Gladiator upon the Stage is very exact in these Lessons, and generally plays an exact round of them with little or no Variation: But the Highlanders in the Field make use of but a few of those Principles; but having another Instrument of defence turns his Sword chiefly to the Offensive Part, the outside and inside Throws are the Principle Offensive Uses of his Weapon; whilst he receives every Cut from his Adversary upon his Target which is a Shield fixt upon his Left Arm.

*Fig. 46. Plate XIV, "a Design to Cut the inside", from Miller's* Gladiatory Art *[see page 188 for description].*

## JOHN GODFREY on PRIZE-FIGHING, 1747

### (excerpts)

I think I have had some of the Theory and Practice of the Sword: The following Reasons may be some Excuse for my Conceit. If I am mistaken, no man living has been more abominably abused by Flattery; for I have for many years been fed with that Notion from the Town, and have been told that I could execute what I knew, and give better reasons for what I did in the Sword, than most Men, by Men of Rank so far above me, that it is scarce to be supposed, that they would ever debase themselves by idly flattering one so insignificant. I believe it will be further acknowledged, that I have a considerable Time supported this Opinion of myself by proving it upon all, who were willing to dispute it with me. I have purchased my Knowledge in the Back-Sword with many a broken Head, and Bruise in every Part of me. I chose to mostly go to FIG, and exercise with him; partly, as I knew him to be the ablest Master, and partly, as he was of a rugged Temper, and would spare no Man, high or low, who took up a Stick with him. I bore his rough Treatment with determined Patience, and followed him so long, that Fig, at least, finding he could not have the beating of me at so cheap a Rate as usual, did not show such Fondness for my Company. This is well known by Gentlemen of distinguished Rank, who used to be pleased in setting us together.

I have tried with all the eminent Masters since Fig's Time, and I believe, made them sensible of what I could do; and it has been so publicly proved, that I cannot think that anyone will deny the Fact...

The Inside and Outside Throws are both very safe. I give the Preference to the Inside; because it goes with a surer Edge, and may be made with more strength and Velocity. This is very observable in Battles fought upon the stage, where you will find all the Inside Cuts to be much deeper and severer than the Outside. It must be allowed also, that they are more likely to hit the Face, which being so much more tender than the Head, will sooner carry the Battle. Indeed, the Outside Throw I would recommend for the Head and Face, when your Adversary makes to your Leg; it keeps clearer of his Blade, and if well timed, seldom meets with Interruption; but especially if it be made slanting, with a kind of back sweep, which, if your Antagonist be not very wary and quick in his Recover, must hit him in the Face, and this sweeping Turn carries a direct Edge. But in the whole, I should choose to be most familiar with the Inside, as I take it to be more faithful to the Line, and you certainly can recover quicker and more readily from it. Nature seems to have made it more a Friend to Time: For I believe it will be allowed, that a Man naturally can make an Inside Blow quicker and easier than an Outside, and certainly oftener, before the Wrist is fatigued, as the Turn of it that way is not so great a strain upon the Muscles, as the other; and I dare say a Man's Arm will be sooner strained and weakened by strong Blows to the Outside, than to the Inside, because in the Inside Blow the Muscles act in a true Line of Direction, but in the other are contorted or twisted, and their Power thereby weakened; for it is well known by every Anatomist skilled in  muscular Motion, that the two extreme Parts of a Muscle must answer a true Line of Direction, before the Muscle can act with Power...

We are allowed to be more expert in the Back-sword than any other Nation, and it would be a pity, if we were not to continue so. In FIG's Time, the spirit of it was greatly kept up; but I have been often sorry to find it dwindle, and in a Manner, die away with him. It must be allowed that those amphitheatrical Practices were productive of some ill, as they gave some Encouragement to Idleness and Extravagance among the Vulgar. But there is hardly any good useful Thing, but what leaves an Opening for Mischief, and which is not liable to Abuse. Those Practices are certainly highly necessary, and the Encouragement of Back-sword Fighting, and Boxing, I think commendable; the former for the Uses which have been mentioned; the latter, and both, to feed and keep up the British spirit. Courage I allow to be chiefly natural, probably owing to the Complexion and Constitution of our Bodies, and flowing in the different Texture of the Blood and Juices; but sure it is, in a great measure, acquired by Use, and Familiarity with Danger. Emulation and the Love of Glory are great Breeders of it. To what Pitch of daring do we not see them carry in Men? And how observable it is in Miniature among the Boys, who, almost as soon as they can go alone, get into their Postures, and bear their little bloody Noses, rather than be stigmatized for Cowards?

...WILLIAM GILL was a Swords-Man formed by FIG's own Hand, and by his Example turned out a complete Piece of Work. I never beheld anybody better for the Leg than GILL. His Excellence lay in doing it from the Inside; and I hardly ever knew him attempt it from the Outside. From the narrow Way he had of going down (which was mostly without receiving) he oftener hit the Leg than anyone; and from the drawing Stroke, caused by that sweeping Turn of the Wrist, and his proper way of holding his Sword, his Cuts were remarkably more severe and deep. I never was an Eye-Witness to such a Cut in the Leg, as he gave one BUTLER, an Irishman, a bold resolute Man, but an awkward Swords-Man. His Leg was laid quite open, his Calf falling down to his Ankle. It was soon stitched up; but from the Ignorance of a Surgeon adapted to his mean Circumstances, it mortified; Mr. Cheselden was applied to for Amputation, but too late for his true Judgement to interfere in. He immediately perceived the Mortification to forbid his Skill; and refused to be concerned in what he knew to be beyond his Power. But another noted one was applied to, who, through less Judgement, or Value for his Character, cut off his Leg above the Knee, but the Mortification had got the Start of his Instruments, and BUTLER soon expired...

Mr. JOHNSON is a staunch Swords-Man. I do not know anyone now who has so great a Share of Skill and undaunted Resolution, mixed together. He is a thorough MASTER of the true Principles of the Back-Sword; but I must take the Liberty to say, that his Joints are stiff and slow in Action; while I allow that his Judgement surpris-ingly makes up that Defect. JOHNSON fights most from the Hanging, and executes more from it, than any I ever saw from that unready Guard. I have often thought it a great Pity a Man of his sound Knowledge of the Sword, should have so much recourse to the Hanging. I own the Word Recourse fits not JOHNSON, because, as I said before, it is a kind of sheltering Guard, and in others mostly used to shift from Danger. I am sure that Fear pitches not his Hanging; and he has as little occasion for a Shelter from his Adversary, as any Man I have known. He fully proves it, as he differs from all the rest in using that Guard. The others use it in a Retreat, he advances with it, and maintains it through the whole Battle with unshaken Firmness.

Mr. SHERLOCK must be pronounced an elegant Swords-Man, with uncommon merit. His Designs are true and just, encouraged by an active Wrist and great Agility of Body. He pitches to the Small-Sword Posture, the Recommendation of which I here repeat. I know there are great Demures against it, but I will venture to justify him in it. He is certainly right to use that Guard, most properly called a Guard, which best stops the too near Approach of his Adversary, and at the same Time supplies him with more readiness to Action. But though I am willing to give every Man his due Merit, I cannot step into the Filth of Flattery; therefore must confess, Mr. SHERLOCK is not faultless. I will point out one Defect, and leave it to Judges whether I am right in my Observa-tion. It is his Subjection and Proneness to starting, by which he may evidently put himself in the Power of a Man of much inferior Judgement. I have often see Mr. SHERLOCK engaged with a Man of far less Abilities of himself, when upon a bare Stamp with the other's Foot, and Movement of his Sword, he has hurried back with Precipitation. Sure Mr. SHERLOCK must own he hereby gives his Opposer great Advantage; however, I leave him with this Acknowledgement, that if he had Mr. JOHNSON's firm stable Resolution, he would rival any I have mentioned.

I conclude with JOHN DELFORCE, and though he never fought with the Sword, I think it would be unpar-donable not to give him a Place among the best of them; for sure none more fit, more able to bring up the Train. he is a very proper Case, or Cover to the whole Picture, and may stand the guarding Sentinel of the Art. I venture to proclaim him the only Rival to FIG's Memory. He is so well known for a Cudgeller on the Stage, that I need not lose any Time in reviving him to Thought. He is an incontested Pattern among Spectators, and has made everybody sorely sensible of his Abilities with the Stick, who dared dispute it with him. My Head, my Arm, and Leg are strong Witness of his convincing Arm. As I said before, I have tried with them all, and must confess my Flesh, my Bones remember him the best. He strongly evinces with the Stick, what he would execute with the Sword. JOHN DELFORCE has every Ingredient to compound a perfect Swords-Man, proper Strength, unerring Judgement, and sufficient Experience. He has a Spring in his Wrist more ready and powerful than any I have seen, and FIG seems to have bequeathed to him Insight into *Time* and *Measure*.

# XVI.

## BOXING

*A round the midpoint of the eighteenth century, after many decades of serving as a mere preliminary, or sideshow attraction, to the more devastating sword contests (or, as a feature of feminine contests), boxing finally replaced swordsmanship as the main draw of the amphitheaters. As shall be shown, it then took on a very dangerous and fatal nature. Although many excellent histories of boxing already exist (the subject having received far more attention from historians than that of the gladiators), it would be remiss not to include some of the more vivid and descriptive challenges and accounts during, and immediately following, this period of transition. The subject is also one of historical importance, as many aspects of gladiatorial contests—such as the presence of seconds, the settings, the bills of challenge, and various rules—also applied to the boxing contests held at the Bear-Garden, and to those that followed in the decades thereafter. In that sense, gladiatorial prize-fights exuded significant influence on the origins of boxing, and on the history of combat sports for centuries to come.*

### ENGLISH BOXING & WRESTLING, 1706

Wrestling and Boxing is the peculiar faculty of the English Nation, no Men in the World fight with the Head, Hand and Foot like an English Man; nor could any Nation stand before them, if that were the Way of Fighting.[328]

---

328 *A Review of the State of the English Nation,* July 27, 1706.

## SIR THOMAS PARKYNS on BOXING TECHNIQUE, 1713

*Sir Thomas Parkyns (1664-1741) taught and demonstrated at Figg's amphitheatre from at least 1728 thru 1730 (see Chapter XVII, page 236-237). Although known primarily for his 1713 treatise on grappling and wrestling, entitled* Προγυμνάσματα. The Inn-play: Or, Cornish-hugg Wrestler, *Parkyns's writings include a short chapter on boxing. Involving head butting, eye-gouging, kicking, and grappling, it gives one an idea of the very different mode of boxing that was practiced during the period, and a taste of what Parkyns reportedly showed at Figg's:*

Boxing.

(G )

BY all means have the first Blow with your Head, or Fist at his Breast, rather than at his Face which is half the Battle, by reason it strikes the Wind out of his Body. Throw Pepper in his Eyes,

2. If you have long Hair soap it, the best Holds are the Pinnion with your Arms at his Shoulders, and your Head in his Face, or get your Right Arm under his Chin, and your Left behind his Neck; and let your Arms close his Neck strait, by holding each Elbow with the contrary Hand, and crush his Neck, your Fingers in his Eyes, and your Fingers of your right Hand under his Chin, and your left Hand under the hinder part of his Head, or twist his Head round by putting your Hand to the side of face; and the other behind his Head.

F I N I S.[329]

## ENGLISH BOXING TACTICS, 1719

Any Thing that looks like Fighting, is delicious to an Englishman. If two little Boys quarrel in the Street, the Passengers stop, make a Ring round them in a Moment, and set them against one another, that they may come to Fisticuffs. When 'tis come to a Fight, each pulls off his Neckcloth and his Waistcoat, (* Some will strip them-selves naked quite to their Wastes) and give them to hold to some of the Standers-by; then they begin to brandish their Fists in the Air; the Blows are aim'd all at the Face, they kick one another's Shins, they tug one another by the Hair, &c. He that has got the other down, may give him one Blow or two before he rises, but no more, and let the Boy get up ever so often, the other is oblig'd to box him again as often as he requires it. During the Fight, the Ring of By-standers encourage the Combatants with great Delight of Heart, and never part them while they fight according to the Rules: And these By-standers are not only other Boys, Porters, and Rabble, but all Sorts of Men of Fashion; some thrusting by the Mob, that they may see plain, others getting upon Stalls; and all would hire Places, if Scaffolds could be built in a Moment. The Father and Mother of the Boys let them fight on as well as the rest, and hearten him that gives Ground, or has the Worst. These Combats are less frequent among grown Men than Children, but they are not rare. If a Coachman has a Dispute about his Fare with a Gentleman that has hired him, and the Gentleman offers to fight him to decide the Quarrel, the Coach-man consents with all his Heart: The Gentleman pulls off his Sword, lays it in some Shop, with his Cane, Gloves, and Cravat, and boxes in the same Manner as I have describ'd above. If the Coachman is soundly drubb'd, which happens almost always, that goes for Payment, but if he is the Beator, the Beatée must pay the Money about which they quarrell'd. I once saw the late Duke of Grafton at Fisticuff in the open Street, with such a Fellow, whom he lamb'd most horribly. In France we punish such Rascals with our Cane, and sometimes with the flat of our Sword; but in England this is never practis'd; they use neither Sword nor Stick against a Man that is unarm'd; and if an unfortunate Stranger (for an Englishman would never take it into his Head) would draw his Sword upon one that had none, he'd have a hundred People upon him in a Moment; that would, perhaps, lay him so flat he would hardly ever get up again till the Resurrection.[330]

---

329 Sir Thomas Parkyns, *Προγυμνάσματα. The Inn-play: Or, Cornish-hugg Wrestler* (Nottingham: William Ayscouh, 1713), 27.
330 Henri Misson (de Valbourg), *M. Misson's Memoirs and Observations in His Travels Over England: With Some Account of Scotland*

*Fig. 47. Ticket design for Broughton's Amphitheatre, ca. 1742. Courtesy The Lewis Walpole Library, Yale University.*

## a FRENCHMAN DESCRIBES BRITISH BOXING, 1723

Their [the British's] Courage and Valor by Sea and Land are well known. They both in Town and Country are robust and laborious; and the Carpenters, Smiths, Sailors, Labourers, Gardeners, &c. after having worked hard and toiled all the Day, will divert themselves in the Evening in Wrestling, and other Exercises that require a great deal of Vigour, and are agreeable to the Humour of the Nation. 'Tis common to see them try their Strength against one another in boxing with their Fists, striking with their Heads, and employing the whole Force and Activity of their Legs and Arms, in a Word, without any Thing but their natural Weapons, and this only for the Pleasure of being Conquerors, or to decide any Difference that has happened between them; and as soon as Victory has

*and Ireland* (London: D. Brown, 1719), 304-306.

declared on any Side, the Vanquisher and the Vanquished embrace, go and drink together, and drown all Resentment and Animosities in a Glass of Wine, or a Pot of Beer, the most usual Liquor in this Country.[331]

## WHITAKER vs. THE VENETIAN, 1725

A certain English Gentleman who wagered lately with a Foreigner at Slaughter's Coffee-house in St. Martin's-Lane (as mentioned in our last) that he would find one of his Countreymen who should beat an Italian in Town, famous for Boxing and Victories that Way (on whose Side the foreign Gentleman made his Wager;) as soon as the Articles were signed, applied himself for a Man to the celebrated Mr. Fig, who has procured him a Grazier, known far and near for a stout Boxer; and he is now entertained at Mr Fig's House for Instruction and proper Diet till the Day of Battle. We are assured that some thousand Pounds have been laid on this Occasion, and that a great Body of Butchers, who have been Witnesses of the Grazier's Dexterity, have waited on the Gentleman, his Patron, with a Request, that he would let each of them go a Guinea with him: but the Gentleman is so satisfied with his Man, that their Request was not granted. The Combatants have had an Enterview, when the English Champion took the Italian by the Hand, and invited him to one Bout for Love (as he termed it) before hand; but he declined it. In a Word, the Publick daily enter into this Affair with so much Passion for the Event, and Gentlemen are so warm on both Sides, that it looks like a National Concern.[332]

London, Jan. 21. Yesterday, pursuant to several considerable Wagers laid between some Italian and English Gentlemen at Slaughter's Coffee-house in St. Martin's Lane, there came on a notable Boxing Match at Figg's celebrated Amphitheatre in Oxford Road, between Stopa l'Aqua, a Venetian Gondalier or Waterman, and John Whetacre an English Drover. The Battle was fought with equal Spirit and Resolution on both Sides, but not with equal Stature, Strength or Skill, the Italian being the tallest by several Inches, but the Englishman the most Sturdy, for he received all the Attacks of the Italian without much Hurt or Concern, gave him several terrible Falls without having one himself, and beat him so sorely, that he was forc'd at last to cry out 'Basta', which signify'd that he was basted enough. There was a numerous and uncommon Appearance of Spectators, Count Staremberg and other Foreign Ministers being present, together with several of the English Nobility and Members of Parliament, to see which Nation carry'd the Day.[333]

Yesterday was fought at Figg's Amphitheatre, a famous Boxing Match between a Venetian Gonalier, or Waterman, and one Whitaker an English Drover. The Wager was Twenty Guineas of a side, but the Betts amounting to many Hundred Pounds. The battle lasted 18 or 20 minutes, in the Presence of several English and Foreign Lords and a great Concourse of Gentlemen, and the Englishman beat his Adversary in a terrible manner.[334]

> We've entertain'd th'*Italian* Strollers here,
> We've lent their Music no unwilling Ear;
> *Cuzzoni* warbling mov'd our Youths' Desire,
> And *Senesini* set our Nymphs on Fire.
> We've recogniz'd their vocal Empire long,
> And dy'd obsequious to the dying Song.
> Their *Tramontani* Bubbles hence they spoil,

---

331 Aubrey de La Mottraye, *A. de La Motraye's Travels through Europe, Asia, and into parts of Africa: with proper cutts and maps* (London: Printed for the Author, 1723), 146.
332 *Caledonian Mercury*, January 25, 1725.
333 *Caledonian Mercury*, January 28, 1725.
334 *Stamford Mercury*, January 28, 1725

Hence the melodious Sharpers fleece our Isle;
Their Triumph This—But when our Arms they dare,
And clench the Fist, and tempt the Boxing War
Indignant Rage our warm Plebeians fires
(To sing's *Italian*, but to fight is Theirs!)
Stalls, Shambles, Shops they quit, and pour away,
Enquire the Challenger, and ask the Fray:
All ardent ask: but 'tis reserv'd for one.
The Champions enter'd, and the Fight begun.
    And what can now thy Skill, fond Stranger, do,
Thy boasted Skill, against a *British* Foe?
He moves intrepid, and resistless throws
From Feet, Hands, Head, at once, whole Storms of Blows,
And rushes on Thee, like an Host of Foes:
'Till fell'd, and rais'd, and baffled o'er and o'er,
Thou prostrate ly'st, and own'st the Victor's Pow'r.
While twenty thousand *Ios* round proclaim,
And echoing Domes resound the *Briton*'s Fame.[335]

## A DESCRIPTION OF BRITISH BOXING, 1726

Combats among the Men are another kind of Diversion, where the Spectators are more peacable. The Assailants begin with running against each other, Heads foremost, like Rams, and afterwards come to Boxing. By the Laws of the Play (as they call it) a Man is not to strike his Adversary on the Ground, but must give him time to rise; and the Standers-by take care to see these Laws strictly observed. They never part till one of them calls for Quarter, which they don't do till they are quite disabled. These Combats are in great esteem among the English and very diverting not only to the Men but to the Women likewise. One may see Mothers bring their Sons, and married Women encourage their Husbands to engage: And Persons of Quality lay aside their Swords, Wigs, and Neck-cloaths to box, when they are insulted by mean People, against whom they must not draw their Swords. For if a Man should happen to do so against any Person whatever, he would run the Risque of being knock'd down by the Mob, which is the Reason that there are no Bullies in London. And such as are pleased with Conflicts of this Kind, may easily indulge their Taste by turning Prize-fighters. There are now and then some of them in this City; but none since my coming, or at least I have not seen any.[336]

## GRETTON vs. "PIPES", 1729

### ADVERTISEMENTS
At Mr. Figg's Great-Room,
At his House, the Sign of the City of Oxford, in Oxford-Road, Marybone-Fields, on Tuesday next being the 22d of April,
WILL be a great Boxing Match between the famous Champions Mr. John Gretton and Mr. Thomas Allen, commonly known by the Name of Pipes, for an Hundred Guineas and the whole House, fair Fall fair Rise, and that Man that lyes on his Fall shall be kick'd up by his Antagonist. It will be the sharpest Battle that ever was

---

335 *A Latin Trologue spoke before one Terence's Plays at Westminster; on Occasion of a late Boxing-Match, between an Englishman and an Italian. from Miscellaneous Poem, by Several Hands. Published by D. Lewis* (London: J. Watts, 1726).
336 Béat Louis de Muralt, *Describing The Character and Customs of the English and French Nations* (London: T. Edlin, 1726), 42.

known, and the last Time of their Fighting. The Doors will be open'd at Three, and the Champions mount at Six. There will be the usual Diversion of Cudgel playing before the Champions mount.[337]

We are inform'd, that Mr. Allen, well known by the Name of Pipes, was this Day to engage with Mr. Greton, at Mr. Figg's Great Room; but being now indispos'd, desires it may be deferr'd 'till this Day Fortnight, at which Time he hopes to give a general Satisfaction to the honourable Assembly then present.[338]

## NEWELL vs. PATEN, 1729

At Mr. Figg's Great-Room, At his House, the Sign of the City of Oxford, in Oxford-road, Marybone-Fields, this present Tuesday the 1st Day of April, will be a Trial of Manhood by the Following Champions.

Whereas I Robert Newell, Butcher, having received a great many Affronts from John Paten, the

*Fig. 48. Detail from* The stage medley representing the polite taste of the Town, *1728. Courtesy of The Lewis Walpole Library, Yale University.*

Windsor Bargeman, one in particular when Mr. Gretton and Mr. Allen fought, the latter of which I was Second to, and he to the former; whereupon I give him this Invitation to Box me for Twenty Guineas, fair Fall and Rise, and I doubt not but to give him as warm a Reception as ever he met with, which I hope will will discourage him from engaging any more with me

I John Paten, will not fail meeting this brave Fellow at the Place above-mention'd, where, if he does not perform what he promises, he may expect ever after to be posted for a Coward; and if he thinks fit I'll fight him for double the Sum.

The Doors will be open'd at Three, and the Champions mount at Five.[339]

---

337 *The Daily Post,* Feb 19, 1729.
338 *The Daily Post,* Feb 25, 1729.
339 *The Daily Post*, April 1, 1729.

## NEWELL vs. WHITAKER, 1729

At Mr. Stokes's Amphitheatre, In Islington Road, this present Tuesday the 13th of May, will be a Trial of Manhood by the following Champions.

Whereas I Robert Newel, Butcher, lately fought and vanquish'd John Patten, the famous and strenuous Windsor Bargenan, to the entire satisfaction of the worthy Spectators, and have since been match'd to fight John Whitaker, the celebrated Lincolnshire Drover, who fought and defeated the renowned Italian Boxer, that came over in purpose to try his Manhood with him, and since overcame the noted Mr. Gretton, and Geofry Burch, from Harrow on the Hill; I do hereby challenge him to box me for Fifty Pounds, as the sear of Valour above mention'd, being a Place adapted for such Conflicts. The Conqueror to have the Wagers laid and the Benefit of the House.

I John Whitaker, Lincolnshire Drover, having defeated the abovenamed Boxing Champions, thought to have faredown contented with my Share of Glory, and never more to appear upon a publick Stage; but being challeng'd by his daring Champion, I shall not fail to meet him at the Time and Place above mention'd, where I shall endeavour to give both him and the Company full Satisfaction.

The Doors will be opened at Three, and the Champions mount at Five. There will be the usual Diversion of Cudgel-playing before the Champions mounts.[340]

## "BRIGHT KEY" vs. JOHN SMITH, a.k.a. "BUCKHORSE", 1729

At Mr. Stokes's Amphitheatre, *In Islington Road, this present Monday, being the 21st of July, will be perform'd a Trial of Manhood by the following Champions,*

WHEREAS I James Cheesebrook, Butcher of Clare-Market, commonly known by the name of Bright Key, and universally celebrated for my Dexterity in Boxing, being lately a Spectator at Mr. Stokes's Amphitheatre, saw the famous John Smith vanquish those two renowned Heroes, rugged and Tough, and the West Country Champion, when, tho' he seem'd to be vastly elevated with his Victory, I affirm'd myself to have more Judgment in Boxing than he, which issu'd in a hot Dispute between us, which being as yet undetermined, I challenge him to meet and Box me for 20 l. and the whole House.

I JOHN SMITH, Paviour, of Broad St. Giles's, willingly accept the abovesaid Challenge, not doubting but I shall knock down this bold Butcher, as I have several others, which will, I hope, be a great Satisfaction to him, and to all the worthy Spectators.[341]

## ONE WOMAN vs. FIVE, 1730

At Mr. Stokes's Amphitheatre, in Islington Road, this present Monday, being the 22d Inst. Two Select Trials of Manhood will be shewn in the utmost Perfection, by the four following Proficients in the Art of Boxing, viz.

John Whitacre, the famous Lincolnshire Drover, Thomas Allen, vulgarly called Pipes, James Taylor, Waterman of Hungerford, and Thomas Day of St. James's: The First renown'd as the extensive Fenns, and look'd upon as the Dimmock of his Country; the second, like the London 'Prentice, admir'd and fear'd by all that have hitherto engaged him; the Third rides Triton of his Siler Thames; and the Fourth has not a less Share of Bravery than the other Three: So that 'tis hard to say which will bear away the Bell.

As these Champion are nominated for the surest Cards in the pack, by several Gentlemen who made the Match, there is no Danger of fighting a Crib, as they call it, neither of them knowing whom he is to engage with,

340 *The Daily Post*, May 13 1729.
341 *The Daily Post*, July 21, 1729.

till they meet on the Stage, when that Point is to be determined by a Majority of the Audience, which 'tis expected will be very numerous on the Occasion.

Conditions of the Combats are, Fair Fall, Fair Rise, and those shewing foul Play to be jointly sued according to Law &c.

Note, Some Bye Matches will also be fought, and as good Diversion of Cudgel-Playing, &c. before the Masters mount, as can be desired: And as the whole Entertainment will take up more Time than usual, 'tis hoped the Company will not lose any Part thereof, but honour the House with their Presence so much the sooner.

Mr Stokes and his Wife being last Wednesday at Mr. Figg's, in order to receive some Money that was due from Mr. Gill, Mr. Mac Colley, and Mr. Sutton, which they refused to pay, and Mr. Stokes being challeng'd, fought at Staff, and Mrs. Stokes was likewise challeng'd, there having lately arrived in Town four Women on purpose of Fighting, dares the said four Women to come to her Seat of Valour on the above Day, before the Champions mount, and she will fight them Bout and Bout till she or they are defeated.

The Doors will be opened at Three, and the Champions mount at Five.[342]

## BROUGHTON vs. "PIPES", 1730

At Mr. Stoke's Amphitheatre, In Islington Road, this present Monday, being the 19th Instant,

Will be the compleatest Trial of Manhood that has been for some Years past, between the two famous Champions, John Broughton, who won the Coat and Crest of Liberty the 1st of August last, and Tho. Allen, Pipe-Maker, for several considerable Sums of Money. They fight wet or dry, and he that is not ready to mount the Stage with his Second, at 4 o'Clock, forfeits 10 l. so those that intend to have good Places, are desired not to delay their coming. There need be no Encomium to recommend those Champion to the Publick, they having an establish'd Character; Pipes, by beating Burch of Harrow on the Hill, and the Lincolnshire Drover, who beat the Italian Boxer. Broughton, by beating Gretton, who has for several Years reign'd Champion.

Attendance will be given at 12 o'Clock, with suitable Accommodation for the Reception of the Quality and others.[343]

## EDWARDS vs. BROUGHTON, 1731

At Mr. FIGG's Great Room,

*This present Tuesday the 15th of this Instant June, will be a Boxing-Match between the two following Antagonist,* THOMAS EDWARDS *of Standgate, Waterman, and* JOHN BROUGHTON *of Hungerford, Bargeman, for Fifty Pounds, viz.*

I *Thomas Edwards,* commonly known by the Name of Counsellor *Lear,* a Waterman at Standgate, who carried Counsellor Lear off from the Messenger's House, &c. has since fought the famous *Broughton,* a Bargeman of Hungerford-Stairs, 37 Minutes in St. George's Fields. I do now Invite the abovesaid *John Brouhghton,* to fight me at Mr. Figg's on Tuesday next for Fifty Pounds, fair Rise, and fair Fall, and that he shows foul play to lose the Money.          *T. Edwards.*

I *John Broughton,* Bargeman, who defeated the famous *Thomas Allen,* commonly call'd by the Name of *Pipes;* I do intend to meet and fight the abovesaid *Thomas Edwards,* commonly call'd Counsellor *Lear,* of Standgate, for Fifty Pounds on Tuesday next, on the same Terms he proposes; or for 100 l. if any Person will lay the Wager, &c.          *J. Broughton.*

Note, *The Box will be set at Three, and the Antagonists mount at Six precisely. Mr.* Figg *has wholly declin'd*

---

342 *London Daily Journal*, June 22, 1730.
343 *Daily Journal*, October 19, 1730.

## At Mr. STOKES's AMPHITHEATRE,

*In Iflington Road, this prefent Monday, being the 22d Inft. two Select Trials of Manhood will be fhewn in the utmoft Perfection, by the Four following Proficients in the Art of Boxing, viz.*

OHN WHITACRE, the famous Lincolnfhire Drover, THOMAS ALLEN, vulgarly called PIPES, JAMES TAYLOR, Waterman of Hungerford, and THOMAS DAY of St. James's: The Firft renown'd as the extenfive Fenns, and look'd upon as the Dimmock of his Country; the Second, like the London 'Prentice, admir'd and fear'd by all that have hitherto engaged him; the Third rides Triton of his Silver Thames; and the Fourth has not a lefs Share of Bravery than the other Three: So that 'tis hard to fay which will bear away the Bell.

As thefe Champions are nominated for the fureft Cards in the Pack, by feveral Gentlemen who made the Match, there is no Danger of fighting a Crib, as they call it, neither of them knowing whom he is to engage with, till they meet on the Stage, when that Point is to be determined by a Majority of the Audience, which 'tis expected will be very numerous on the Occafion.

Conditions of the Combat are, Fair Fall, Fair Rife, and thofe fhewing foul Play, to be jointly fued according to Law, &c.

Note, Some Bye Matches will alfo be fought, and as good Diverfion of Cudgel-Playing, &c. before the Mafters mount, as can be defired: And as the whole Entertainment will take up more Time than ufual, 'tis hoped the Company will not lofe any Part thereof, but honour the Houfe with their Prefence fo much the fooner.

Mr. Stokes and his Wife being laft Wednefday at Mr. Figg's, in order to receive fome Money that was due from Mr. Gill, Mr. Mac Colley, and Mr. Sutton, which they refufed to pay, and Mr. Stokes being challeng'd, fought at Staff, and Mrs. Stokes was likewife challeng'd, there having lately arrived in Town four Women on purpofe to fight her, but fhe not intending to make a Practice of Fighting, dares the faid four Women to come to her Seat of Valour on the above Day, before the Champions mount, and fhe will fight them Bout and Bout till fhe or they are defeated.

The Doors will be opened at Three, and the Champions mount at Five.

*Fig. 49.* Daily Journal, *June 22, 1730. Of particular note are the "Conditions of Combat", suggesting boxing rules earlier than those of Broughton and Queensbury.*

*the Stage, and taken a House in Poland-street near Great Marlborough-street, St. James's, in order to teach Gentlemen only; and will be fix'd in a Week's time. There will be the usual Diversion of Cudgel-playing, by Captain Vinegar and his Company.[344]*

## a BOXER KILLED, 1732

*John Adams,* who unfortunately kill'd a Man in a Boxing-Match, was found guilty of *Manslaughter,* and was burnt in the Hand and discharged.[345]

## ANOTHER BOXER KILLED, 1734

*Joseph Greenfield*, who was try'd for the Murder of *John Jones*, at *Hampstead*, in a Boxing-Match, was found guilty of *Manslaughter.*[346]

## YET ANOTHER BOXER KILLED, 1734

James Firth, tried for the Murder of Valentine Clark, in a Boxing-Match, was found guilty of Manslaughter.[347]

## and ANOTHER BOXER KILLED, 1734

*Perkins* the Gardiner was tried for the Murder of his Wife, and *James Williman* for the Murder of one *Bridges* in a Boxing-Match, and were found guilty of *Manslaughter:* One other Criminal was burnt in the Hand, two ordered for Transportation, and one to be whipt.[348]

## YET ONE MORE BOXER KILLED, 1734

Yesterday a man was killed in a boxing match at Kensington common.[349]

## "the FIGHTING LAWYER", 1735

Last Tuesday a great Boxing Match was fought at Mr. Stokes's in Islington Road, between Nathaniel Miller, the famous Uxbridge Champion, and William Atkins of Gray's-Inn-Lane, commonly known by the Name of the *Fighting Lawyer*. They fought an exceeding good Battle about 15 Minutes, and the Uxbridge Man was beat.[350]

344 *Daily Advertiser,* June 15, 1731.
345 *Weekly Register or, Universal Journal,* July 8, 1732.
346 *Weekly Register or, Universal Journal,* June 1, 1734.
347 *Weekly Register or, Universal Journal,* July 13, 1734.
348 *Weekly Register or, Universal Journal,* August 24, 1734.
349 *Grub-Street Journal,* August 29, 1734.
350 *Daily Gazetteer,* July 11, 1735.

## AN AUDIENCE MEMBER KILLED, 1738

Yesterday was a great Boxing Match between the famous Broughton and one Stephenson, a Coachman, for a Hundred Pounds, which was won by the former. One Mr. Maynar, a Barber and Perukemaker in Dean-street, Soho, was squeez'd to Death as he attempted to get into the Great Booth at Tottenham Court to see the said Battle.[351]

## THE DEATH OF "PIPES", 1738

Last Friday Night was buried, Thomas Allen, commonly called Pipes, particularly famous for his Art and Bravery in Boxing; He was Gallery Door keeper to Drury-Lane Playhouse; and the Funeral (which was extraordinary decent) was, for his faithful Services, defray'd by his Master. It was remarkable, that his Pall was supported by John Broughton, Nathaniel Peartree, George Taylor, George Stevenson, Benjamin Boswell, and Thomas Dimmack. Six of the most celebrated Boxers that this or perhaps any Age has produced. To see half a Dozen such brave Fellows affectionately and decently attending him to his Grave is an Instance (as in their Scene of Life he was often their Antagonist) of the innate generous Love of Valour for which Englishmen are so justly distinguish'd.[352]

## SMALLWOOD KILLS DIMMOCK, 1740

Yesterday a great Boxing Match was fought at the Great Booth at Tottenham-Court, between the two acted Champions, Smallwood a Chairman, and Dimmock a Carman; and the latter was by a Fall, which dislocated his Collar-Bone, kill'd on the Spot. They endeavour'd to bleed him, and used all proper Means, but to no Purpose.[353]

## CAPTAIN VINEGAR'S REVENGE, 1740

Last Week there was a great Boxing-match at his Majesty's Bear-garden at Hockley in the Hole, at which the Author of the *Champion* being present, Capt. Vinegar, after the Battle was over, ordered him to be toss'd in a Blanket, for the Diversion of the Company, for presuming to prefix his Name to such a Heap of Scurrility, Impudence and Nonsense.[354]

## "ONE of the MOST SEVERE BOXING MATCHES", 1742

*November* 22, 1742.

THIS is to acquaint all true lovers of manhood, that at the Great Booth, Tottenhamcourt, to-morrow, being the 23d instant, it is believed there will be one of the most severe boxing matches that has been fought for many years, between

RICHARD HAWES, Back-maker,
and
THOMAS SMALLWOOD,
for Fifty Pounds.

351 *Daily Gazetteer,* March 31, 1738.
352 *Derby Mercury,* May 11, 1738.
353 *Daily Gazetteer,* January 30, 1740.
354 *Daily Gazetteer,* June 17, 1740.

The known hardiness and intrepidity of these two men will render it needless to say any thing in their praise, Gentlemen are desired to come soon, for as this battle has been deferred a fortnight, *at the particular desire of several Nobleman and Gentlemen*, a full house is early expected.

There will be several bye-battles as usual; particularly one between *the noted Buckhorse* and *Harry Grey*, for two guineas. And a good day's diversion may be depended upon.[355]

## "THE FIGHTING QUAKER", 1742

*April* 26, 1742.

At the Great Booth at Tottenham Court, on Wednesday the 28th instant, will be a trial of manhood between the following champions,

Whereas I William Willis (commonly called by the name of the *Fighting Quaker*), having fought Mr. Smallwood about twelve months ago, and bruised and battered him more than ever he encountered before, though I had the ill fortune to be beat by an accidental fall; the said Smallwood, flushed with the success blind Fortune had then given him, and the weak attempts of a few Irishmen and boys that have of late fought him for a minute or two, makes him think himself unconquerable: To convince him of the falsity of which, I invite him to fight me for £10, at the time and place above mentioned, when I doubt not but shall prove what I have asserted, by pegs, darts, hard blows, and cross-buttocks.

WILLIAM WILLIS.

I, Thomas Smallwood, known for my intrepid manhood and bravery on and off the stage, accept the challenge of this *puffing Quaker*, and will shew him, that he is led by a *false Spirit*, that means him no other good, than that he should be chastised for offering to take upon him *the arm of flesh*.

THOMAS SMALLWOOD.

N. B. The doors will be open at ten, and the combatants mount at twelve.

There will be several bye-battles as usual, particularly one between John Divine and John Tipping, for £5 each.[356]

## "THE JUMPING SOLDIER", 1742

*May* 4, 1742.

AT the Great Booth, in Tottenham Court, to-morrow, May the 5th instant, will be a trial of manhood between the following champions, vis.

Whereas I John Francis (commonly called by the name of the *Jumping* Soldier) who have always had the reputation of a *good fellow*, and have fought several bruisers in the street, &c. nor am ashamed to mount the stage, when my manhood is called in question by *an Irish braggadocio buffer*, whom I fought same time ago at Tottenham-Court (in a *bye-battle*) for twelve minutes, and though I had not the success due to my courage and ability in the art of boxing, do invite him to fight me for two guineas, at the time and place above-mentioned, where I doubt not I shall give him the truth of a good beating. JOHN FRANCIS.

I Patrick Henly, known to every one for the truth of *a good fellow*, who never refused any one, on or off the stage, and fight as often for the diversion of gentlemen as for money, do accept the challenge of this *Jumping Jack*, and shall, if he don't take care, give him one of my *bothering* blows, which will convince him of his ignorance in the art of boxing. PATRICK HENLY.[357]

---

355 Henry Lemoine, *Modern Manhood: Or, the Art and Practice of English Boxing* (London: J. Parsons, 1788), 40-41.
356 Ibid, 42-43.
357 Ibid, 44-45.

# BROUGHTON'S AMPHITHEATRE
## and SCHOOL, 1743

*January* I, 1742-3.

PROPOSALS for ERECTING
an AMPHITHEATRE
For the Manly Exercise of
BOXING,

By John Broughton, *Professor of Athletics.*

*Multa Viri nequicquam inter se vulnera jactant:*
*Multa cavo lateri ingeminant & pectore vastos*
*Dant sonitus, erratque aures & tempora circum.*
*Crebra manus; durocrepitaut sub vulnere malœ.*

VIRGIL.

ATHLETICS have ever been encourag'd in those Countries where Strength and Valour have been the Characteristicks of the Inhabitants, at *Greece*, particuarlarly among the *Spartans*, the most Heroic of that People, and at *Rome* these Exercises were held in such high Estimation, that even *Princes* and *Nobles* have not disdain'd to enter the List as Competitors. BRITONS then who boast

*Fig. 48. John Broughton by John Hamilton Mortimer, 1767. Yale Center for British Art, Paul Mellon Collection.*

themselves Inheritors of the *Greek* and *Roman* Virtues, should follow their Example, and by encouraging Conflicts of this magnanimous Kind, endeavour to eradicate that *foreign Effeminacy* which has so fatally insinuated itself among us, and almost destroy'd that glorious Spirit of *British Championism*, which was wont to be at once the *Terror* and *Disgrace* of our Enemies.

While Authority serves to recommend this Practice, Reason likewise convinces us of its Usefulness, for as Exercise is the Nurse of Strength and Activity, and these are the natural Perfections of the Body, what can be more Rational than Encounters which manifestly tend to this End? Especially when the Promotion of them may conduce to the *public Utility* as well as *private Recreation;* for if the Prowess of the People is the natural Bulwark of a Country, the Encouragement of this Quality will excite every one to an Emulation and Improvement of it; and as Experience convinces us that Foreigners tremble less at the *Firelock* than the *Fist* of a Briton, we may by a laudable Incitement of this Species of natural Fortitude, become as formidable to other Nations, as the Poet describes *Entellus* to have been to his Antagonist, when he says,

> *Nunc dextra ingemimans ictus, nunc ille sinistra;*
> *Nec mora, nec requies, quam multa grandine nimbi*
> *Culminibas crepitant: Sic densis ictibus Heros*
> *Creber utraque manu pulsat, versatque Dareta.*

and what Enemy would dare the Vengeance of an Arm that must reduce him to the melancholy Condition of

*————————————genua Aegra trahentem,*
*Jactantemque utroque caput, crassumque cruorem*
*Ore ejectantem, mislosque in sanguine dentes.*

THE principal Reasons that have occasioned the Decay of *British* Championism, it is apprehended are

The Want of a convenient and elegant Place for the Exhibition of these Ceremonies

The present Indiscrimination there between Persons of the first Rank and Condition, and those of the meaner and lowest Class.

The exorbitant Charge of an Amphitheatre.

The great Imposition on the Spectators by those who, merely for Lucre's Sake enter the Lists, tho' entirely unqualified for such arduous Conflicts.

The Want of a Manager well skill'd in the Direction of such Solemnities.

To Remedy all which the Undertaker proposes

I. To erect in some Place, most commodious for this Metropolis, a *magnificent Amphitheatre*, to be dedicated to the Exercise of that Manly *Art of Boxing.*

II. That this Building shall be so contriv'd as entirely to prevent the Gentry's being incommoded by the Populace; and as Servants will be admitted to keep Places, the Inconvenience of Attendance or Disappointment will be avoided.

III. That the Consideration to be paid by the Champions for the Use of the Amphitheatre, shall be determin'd either by Agreement between the Parties, or left to the Decision of the Gentlemen present.

IV. That the Public may not be imposed on by any *fictitious* or *unequal* Battles, none shall be permitted the Benefit of a House but those who have signalized themselves to the Satisfaction of of the Spectators, or are notoriously famous for their Bravery and Skill in this noble Art; nor will the Undertaker spare any Pains in procuring such From all Parts of this Kingdom, and *farther* he apprehends all Search would be *useless*.

V. That it is with the utmost Deference the Undertaker proposes himself as Manager of these Solemnities; and as he has been so long conversant therein, and hitherto remain'd invincible, he humbly hopes he shall be esteem'd properly qualified for that important Office, more especially as the Preservation of *Decency* and *Decorum* at such Ceremonies requires a *manual Authority* in the Person who presides.

As an Affair of this Nature must unavoidably be attended with a very large Expence, the Undertaker hopes to be assisted in it by the *generous Contributions* of those Noblemen and Gentlemen who are Lovers and Encouragers of this heroic Art; and, in Return of their Favours, assures them no Diligence shall be wanting, on his part, in the Propagation of the Science, the Oeconomy of its Exhibitions, and the Support of that Dignity which is suitable to an Undertaking of such *noble* and *national* Importance.

Mr. BROUGHTON proposes, with proper *Assistants*, to open an Academy, at his Amphitheatre, for the Instruction of those who are willing to be initiated in the *Mystery* of Boxing; where the whole *Theory* and *Practice* of that truly *British* Art, with all the various *Stops, Blows, Cross-Buttocks,* &c. incident to Combatants, will be fully taught and explain'd ---- And that Persons of *Quality* and *Distinction* may not be deterr'd from entering into a *Course* of these Lectures, they will be given with the utmost *Tenderness* and Regard to the *Delicacy* of the *Frame* and *Constitution* of the *Pupil;* for which Reason, *Mufflers* are provided that will effectually secure them from the Inconveniency of *black Eyes, broken Jaws,* and *bloody Noses.*

N. B. *Any Gentleman may have a private Course of Lectures at bis own House, and those who honour Mr.* BROUGHTON *with their Contribution towards his Amphitheatre will be admitted to the Public Ones* gratis.[358]

---

358 John Broughton, *Proposals for erecting an amphitheatre for the manly exercise of boxing, by John Broughton* [London : s.n., 1743].

*Fig. 49. George Taylor, undated.*

## "The TRUE ART of BOXING", 1743

*March* 10, 1743.

AT Broughton's New Amphitheatre in Oxford Road, the back of the late Mr. Fig's, on Tuesday next, the 13th instant, will be exhibited, The true Art of Boxing, by the eight famed following men, viz. Abraham Evans, Sweep, Belos, Glover, Roger Allen, Robert Spikes, Harry Gray, and the Clog-maker. The above eight men are to be brought on the stage, and to be matched according to the approbation of the gentlemen, who shall be pleased to honour them with their company. Note, There will be a battle-royal between the noted Buckhorse and seven or eight more; after which there will be several bye-battles by others. Gentlemen are desired to come by times, by reason of the number of battles.

The doors will be open at nine, and some of the champions mount at eleven.

No person to pay more than a shilling.[359]

## A CONTROVERSY BEWTEEN TAYLOR & BROUGHTON, 1743

*To all Encouragers of the Manly Art of Boxing.*

WHEREAS Mr. Broughton has maliciously advertised several battles to be fought at his amphitheatre, on Tuesday next, the 13th of March, in order to injure me, who am to fight Mr, Field the same day at Tottenham-court, I think it incumbent on me to undeceive the public, by informing them the greatest part of the persons

---

359 Lemoine, 49-50.

mentioned to fight there, never intended any such thing, or were ever acquainted with it; therefore hope this assertion will be understood (as it really is) a spiteful undertaking.

Mr. Broughton has likewise inserted in his bills, that he never practised any imposition on the champions who fought at his amphitheatre, and has in vain eneavoured to make it appear, which gentlemen will be sensible of, when an account of his exactions are set forth at large in print, which will be done with all expedition.

And to convince Mr. Broughton that I have no disgust to his amphitheatre, I am willing to meet him there and fight him for £100, whenever he pleases, not in the least regarding (as he expresses himself) the valour of his arm.

*March* 12, 1743.    GEORGE TAYLOR.[360]

## BROUGHTON'S RULES, 1743

Rules to be observed in all Battles on the Stage, as agreed to by several Gentlemen, at Mr. Broughton's, August 16, 1743.

I. THAT a square of a yard be chalked in the middle of the stage; and on every fresh set-to after a fall, or being parted from the rails, each second is to bring his man to the side of the square, and place him opposite to the other, and till they are fairly set to at the lines, it shall not be lawful for the one to strike the other.

II. That in order to prevent any disputes, the time a man lies after a fall, if the second does not bring his man to the side of the square within the space of half a minute, he shall be deemed a beaten man.

III. That in every main battle no person whatever shall be upon the stage, except the principals and their seconds; the same rule to be observed in bye-battles, except, that in the latter, Mr. Broughton is allowed to be upon the stage to keep decorum, and assist gentlemen to get to their places; provided always he does not interfere in the battle: and whoever pretends to infringe these rules, to be turned immediately out of the house. Every body is to quit the stage as soon as the champions are stripped, before they set-to.

IV. That no champion be deemed beaten, unless he fails coming up to the line within the limited time; or that his own second declares him beaten. No second is to be allowed to ask his man's adversary any questions, or advise him to give out.

V. That in bye-battles the winning man to have two-thirds of the money given, which shall be publicly divided upon the stage, notwithstanding any private agreement to the contrary.

VI. That to prevent disputes in every main battle, the principals shall, on their coming on the stage, choose from among the gentlemen present, two umpires, who shall absolutely decide all disputes that may arise about the battle; and if the two umpires cannot agree, the said umpires to choose a third, who is to determine it.

VII. That no person is to hit his adversary when he is down, or sieze him by the hair, the breeches, or any part below the waist: a man on his knees to be reckoned down.[361]

## SLACK vs. JAMES, 1743

LONDON, October 15.

Yesterday was fought the grand Boxing-Match, in the Great Booth at Tottenham-Court, between Mr. John Slack the Champion of Norfolk, and Mr. John James the most famous Boxer of London: The Betts were Twenty Pounds to Five, and Ten Pounds to Two, on the Head of Mr. James; as he was the best Boxer publickly known in London, having beat all that he had fought: But the Londoners were prodigiously let in, having laid great Sums of Money; for Mr. John Slack beat their famous Hero in less than eight Minutes, though there were great Odds laid

360 Idib, 50-51.
361 *The Ranger's Magazine: Or the Man of Fashion's Companion. Vol. 1. For the Year 1795 London: J. Sudbury, 1795.* 113-114.

that Mr. James would beat Mr. Slack in two Minutes. Slack gave James such Falls by Cross-Buttocks as quite demolished him, and his Blows with his Hands were such as James shrunk at every Time. In short Mr. James was, within Eight Minutes Time, by several Men carried off the Stage for dead. The said Mr. Slack a few Days before boxer a famous Irishman in Morefields, and beat him blind in less than four Minutes. Norwich Gazette.[362]

## JOHN GODFREY on the "BLOWS" of BOXING, 1747

Let us now examine the most hurtful Blows, and such as contribute most to the Battle. Though very few of those who fight know why a Blow on such a Part has such Effects, yet by Experience they know it has; and by these evident Effects, they are directed to the proper Parts; as for instance hitting under the Ear, between the Eyebrows, and about the Stomach. I look upon the Blow under the Ear to be as dangerous as any, that is, if it light between the Angle of the lower Jaw and the Neck; because in this Part there are two Kinds of Blood Vessels considerably large; the one brings the Blood immediately from the Heart to the Head, whilst the other carries it immediately back. If a Man receive a Blow upon these Vessels, the Blood proceeding from the Heart to the Head, is partly forced back, whilst the other Part is pushed forward vehemently to the Head: The same happens in the Blood returning from the Head to the Heart, for part of it is precipitately forced into the latter, whilst the other Part tumultuously rushes to the Head: whereby the Blood Vessels are immediately overcharged, and the Sinuses of the Brain so overloaded and compressed, that the Man at once loses all Sensation, and the Blood often runs from his Ears, Mouth, and Nose, altogether owing its Quantity forced with such Impetuosity into the smaller Vessels, the Coats whereof being to tender to resist so great a Charge, instantly break, and cause the Effusion of Blood through these different Parts.

This is not the only Consequence, but the Heart being overcharged with a Regurgitation of Blood (as I may say with respect to that forced back on the succeeding Blood coming from its left Ventricle) stops its Progress, whilst that Part of the Blood coming from the Head, is violently pushed into its right Auricle; so that as the Heart labours under a violent Surcharge of Blood, there soon follows a Cardiaca or Suffocation, but which goes off as the Parts recover themselves and push the Blood forward. The Blows given between the Eyebrows contribute greatly to the Victory: For this Part being contused between two hard Bodies, viz. The Fist, and Os frontale, there ensues a violent Ecchymosis, or Extravasation of Blood, which falls immediately into the Eyelids; and they being of a lax Texture incapable of resisting this Influx of Blood, swell almost instantaneously; which violent Intumescence soon obstructs the Sight. The Man thus indecently treated, and artfully hoodwinked, is beat about at his Adversary's Discretion.

The Blows on the Stomach are also very hurtful, as the Diaphragm and Lungs share in the Injury. The Vomitations produced by them I might account for, but I should run my anatomical Impertinences too far...[363]

## CHARACTERS of the BOXERS by JOHN GODFREY, 1747

ADVANCE, brave BROUGHTON! Thee I pronounce Captain of the Boxers. As far as I can look back, I think, I ought to open the Characters with him: I know none so fit, so able to lead up the Van. This is giving him the living Preference to the rest; but, I hope, I have not given any Cause to say, that there has appeared, in any of my Characters, a partial Tincture. I have throughout consulted nothing, but my unbiased Mind, and my Heart has known no Call but Merit. Wherever I have praised, I have no Desire of pleasing; wherever decried, no Fear of offending. BROUGHTON, by his manly Merit, has bid the highest, therefore has my Heart. I really think that all will poll with me, who poll with the same Principle. Sure there is some standing Reason for this Preference. What can

362 Ipswich Journal, Oct 22, 1743.
363 Godfrey, 50-52.

Fig. 50. *A bare-knuckle boxing match in the street, attended by an enthusiastic crowd. Detail from Hogarth's* The March to Finchley, *printed in London by Luke Sullivan circa December 1750.*

be stronger than to say, that for seventeen or eighteen Years, he has fought every able *Boxer* that appeared against him, and has never yet been beat? But not to build alone on this, let us examine further into his Merits. What is it that he wants? Has he not all that the others want, and all the best can have? Strength equal to what is human, Skill and Judgement equal to what can be acquired, undebauched Wind, and a bottom Spirit, never to pronounce the Word ENOUGH. He fights the Stick as well as most Men, and understands a good deal of the Small-Sword. This Practice has given him the Distinction of Time and Measure beyond the rest. He stops as regularly as the Swords-Man, and carries his Blows truly in the Line; he steps not back, distrusting of himself to stop a Blow, and piddle in the Return, with an Arm unaided by his Body, producing but a kind of flyflap Blows; such as the Pastry-Cooks use to beat those Insects from their Tarts and Cheesecakes. No—BROUGHTON steps bold and firmly in, bids a Welcome to the coming Blow; receives it with his guarding Arm; then with a general Summons of his swelling Muscles, and his firm Body, seconding his Arm, and supplying it with all its Weight, pours the Pile-driving Force upon his Man.

That may not be thought particular in dwelling too long upon BROUGHTON, I leave him with this Assertion, that as he, I believe, will scarce trust a Battle to a waning Age, I never shall think he is to be beaten, till I see him beat.

About the Time I first observed this promising Hero upon the Stage, his chief Competitors were PIPES and GRETTING. He beat them both (and I thought with Ease) as often as he fought them.

PIPES was the neatest Boxer I remember. He put in his Blows about the Face (which he fought at most) with surprising Time and Judgement. He maintained his Battles for many Years by his extraordinary Skill, against Men of far superior Strength. PIPES was but weakly made; his Appearance bespoke Activity, but his Hand, Arm, and Body were but small. Though by that acquired Spring of his Arm he hit prodigious Blows; and I really think, that at the last, when he was beat out of his Championship, it was more owing to his Debauchery than the Merit of those who beat him.

GRETTING was a strong Antagonist to PIPES. They contended hard together for some Time, and were almost alternate Victors. GRETTING had the nearest Way of going to the Stomach (which is what they call the Mark) of any Man I knew. He was a most artful Boxer, stronger than PIPES, and dealt the straightest Blows: But what made PIPES a Match for him, was his rare Bottom Spirit, which would bear a deal of Beating, but this, in my Mind, GRETTING was not sufficiently furnished with; for after he was beat twice together by PIPES, *Hammersmith* JACK, a mere Sloven of a Boxer, and everybody that fought him afterwards, beat him. I must, notwithstanding, do that Justice to GRETTING'S Memory, as to own that his Debauchery very much contributed to spoil a great Boxer; but yet I think he had not the Bottom of the other.

Much about this Time, there was one WHITAKER, who fought the *Venetian* GONDOLIER. He was a very strong Fellow, but a clumsy *Boxer*. He had two Qualifications, very much contributing to help him out. He was very extraordinary for his throwing, and contriving to pitch his weighty Body on the fallen Man. The other was, that he was a hardy Fellow, and would bear a deal of Beating. This was the Man pitched upon to fight the *Venetian*. I was at *Slaughter's* Coffee-House when the Match was made, by a Gentleman of an advanced Station; he sent for FIG to procure a proper Man for him; he told him to take care of his Man, because it was for a large Sum; and the *Venetian* was a man of extraordinary Strength, and famous for breaking the Jaw-bone in *Boxing*. FIG replied, in his rough Manner, I do not know, Master, but he may break one of his own Countrymen's Jaw-bones with his Fist; but, I will bring him a Man, and he shall not break his Jaw-bone with a Sledge Hammer in his Hand.

The Battle was fought at FIG'S Amphitheatre, before a splendid Company, the politest House of that kind I ever saw. While the GONDOLIER was stripping, my Heart yearned for my Countryman. His Arm took up all Observation; it was surprisingly large, long, and muscular. He pitched himself forward with his right Leg, and his Arm full extended, and, as WHITAKER approached, gave him a Blow on the Side of the Head, that knocked him quite off the Stage, which was remarkable for its Height. WHITAKER'S Misfortune in his Fall was then the Grandeur of the Company, on which account they suffered no common People in, that usually sit on the Ground and line the Stage round. It was then all clear, and WHITAKER had nothing to stop him but the bottom. There was a general foreign Huzza on the Side of the *Venetian*, pronouncing our Countryman's Downfall; but WHITAKER took no more

Time than was required to get up again, when finding his Fault in standing out to the Length of the other's Arm, he, with a little Stoop, ran boldly in beyond the heavy Mallet, and with one *English* Peg in the Stomach (quite a new Thing to Foreigners) brought him on his Breech. The Blow carried too much of the *English* Rudeness for him to bear, and finding himself so unmannerly used, he scorned to have any more doings with his slovenly Fist.

So fine a House was too engaging to FIG, not to court another. He therefore stepped up, and told the Gentlemen that they might think he had picked out the best Man in *London* on this Occasion: But to convince them to the contrary, he said, that if they would come that Day se'ennight, he would bring a Man who should beat this WHITAKER in ten Minutes, by fair hitting. This brought very near as great and fine a Company as the Week before. The Man was NATHANIEL PEARTREE, who knowing the other's Bottom, and his deadly way of Flinging, took a most judicious Method to beat him.—Let his Character come in here—He was a most admirable *Boxer*, and I do not know one he was not a Match for, before he lost his Finger. He was famous, like PIPES, for fighting at the Face, but stronger in his Blows. He knew WHITAKER's Hardiness, and doubting of his being able to give him Beating enough, cunningly determined to fight at his Eyes. His Judgement carried in his Arm so well, that in about six Minutes both WHITAKER's Eyes were shut up; when groping about a while for his Man, and finding him not, he wisely gave out, with these odd Words—Damme—I am not beat, but what signifies my fighting when I cannot see my Man?

We will now come to Times a little fresher, and of later Date.

GEORGE TAYLOR, known by the Name of GEORGE the BARBER, sprang up surprisingly. He has beat all the chief Boxers, but BROUGHTON. He, I think, injudiciously fought him one of the first, and was obliged very soon to give out. Doubtless it was a wrong Step in him to commence a Boxer, by fighting the standing Champion: For GEORGE was not then twenty, and BROUGHTON was in the Zenith of his Age and Art. Since that he has greatly distinguished himself with others; but has never engaged BROUGHTON more. He is a strong able Boxer, who with a Skill extraordinary, aided by his Knowledge of Small and Back-Sword, and a remarkable Judgement in the Cross-Buttock-Fall, may contest with any. But please or displease, I am resolved to be ingenuous in my Characters. Therefore I am of the Opinion, that he is not over-stocked with that necessary Ingredient of a Boxer, called a Bottom; and I am apt to suspect, that Blows of equal Strength with his, too much affect him and disconcert his Conduct.

Before I leave him, let me do him this Justice to say, that if he were unquestionable in his Bottom, he would be a Match for any Man.

It will not be improper, after GEORGE the BARBER, to introduce one BOSWELL, a Man, who wants nothing but Courage to qualify him for a complete Boxer. He has a particular Blow with his left Hand at the Jaw, which comes almost as hard as a little Horse kicks. Praise be to his Power of Fighting, his excellent Choice of *Time* and *Measure*, his superior Judgement, dispatching forth his executing Arm! But fie upon his dastard Heart, that mars it all! As I knew that Fellow's Abilities, and his worm-dread Soul, I never saw him beat, but I wished him to be beaten. Though I am charmed with the Idea of his Power and Manner of Fighting, I am sick at the Thought of his Nurse-wanting Courage. Farewell to him, with this fair Acknowledgement, that, if he had a true *English* Bottom (the best fitting Epithet for a Man of Spirit) he would carry all before him, and be a Match for even BROUGHTON himself.

I will name two Men together, whom I take to be the best Bottom Men of the modern Boxers: And they are SMALLWOOD, and GEORGE STEVENSON, the Coachman. I saw the latter fight BROUGHTON, for forty Minutes. BROUGHTON I knew to be ill at that Time; besides it was a hasty made Match, and he had not that Regard for his Preparation, as he afterwards found he should have. But here his true Bottom was proved, and his Conduct shone. They fought in one of the Fair-Booths at *Tottenham* Court, railed at the End toward the Pit. After about thirty-five Minutes, being both against the Rails, and scrambling for a Fall, BROUGHTON got such a Lock upon him as no Mathematician could have devised a better. There he held him by this artificial Lock, depriving him of all Power of Rising or Falling, till resting his Head for about three or four Minutes on his Back, he found himself recovering. Then loosed the Hold, and on setting to again, he hit the Coachman as hard a Blow as any he had given him in the whole Battle; that he could no longer stand, and his brave contending Heart, though with Reluctance, was forced to yield. The Coachman is a most beautiful Hitter; he put in his Blows faster than BROUGHTON, but then one of the latter's told for three of the former's. Pity—so much Spirit should not inhabit a stronger Body!

SMALLWOOD is thorough game, with Judgement equal to any, and superior to most. I know nothing SMALLWOOD wants but Weight, to stand against any Man; and I never knew him beaten since his fighting DIMMOCK (which was in his Infancy of Boxing, and when he was a perfect Stripling in Years) but by Force so superior, that to have resisted longer would not have been Courage but Madness. If I were to choose a Boxer for my Money, and could but purchase him Strength equal to his Resolution, SMALLWOOD should be the Man.

JAMES I proclaim a most charming Boxer. He is delicate in his Blows, and has a Wrist as delightful to those who see him fight, as it is sickly to those who fight against him. I acknowledge him to have the best Spring of the Arm of all the modern Boxers; he is a complete Master of the Art, and, as I do not know he wants a Bottom, I think it a great Pity he should be beat for want of Strength to stand his Man.

I have now gone through the Characters of the most noted Boxers, and finished my whole Work. As I could not praise all in every Article, I must offend some; but if I do not go to Bed till everybody is pleased, my Head will ache as bad as Sir Roger's. I declare that I have not had the least Thought of offending throughout the whole Treatise, and therefore this Declaration shall be my quiet Draught.

Let me conclude with a general Call to the true British Spirit, which, like purest Gold, has no Alloy. How readily would I encourage it, through the most threatening Dangers, or severest Pains, or Pledge of Life itself! Let us imitate the glorious Example we enjoy, in the saving Offspring of our King, and blessed Guardian of our Country. Him let us follow with our keen Swords, and warm glowing Hearts, in Defence of our just Cause, and Preservation of *Britain's* Honour.[364]

## SLACK vs. TAYLOR, 1748

At Mr. Broughton's Amphitheatre in Oxford-Road, on Wednesday next, the 10th instant, will be a decisive Trial of Manhood between

John Slack, from Norwich,

and

George Taylor.

Tickets will be deliver'd at the Door for the Matted Gallery at Five Shillings each.

The Doors to be opened at Nine.

Note, For the more convenient Reception of the Sporting Gentlemen, Mr. Broughton has greatly enlarg'd his Gallery.

N. B. Mr. Broughton proposes, with proper Assistants, to open an Academy at his House in the Hay-Market, for the Instruction of those who are willing to be initiated in the Mystery of Boxing; where the whole Theory and Practice of that truly British Art, with all the various Stops, Blows, Cross-Buttocks, &c. incident to Combatants, will be fully taught and explain'd; and that Persons of Quality and Distinction may not be deterr'd from entering into a Course of these Lectures, they will be given with the utmost Tenderness and Regard to the Delicacy of the Frame and Constitution of the Pupil, for which Reason Mufflers are provided, that will effectually secure them from the Inconveniency of black Eyes, broken Jaws, and bloody Noses.[365]

---

364 Godfrey, 55-66.
365 *The London Daily Advertiser*, February 4, 1748.

## SLACK vs. FIELD, 1748

London, February 11.

Thursday was fought at Broughton's Amphitheatre in Oxford-Road, the famous and long expected Battle between John Slack and James Field, for fifty Guineas, which lasted one Hour and Thiry-one Minutes, and at last was won by the former.[366]

## TAYLOR vs. SLACK, 1748

Norwich, Feb. 13.

At Broughton's Amphitheatre in London on Wednesday last, was decided the third Battle between George Taylor the Barber and John Slack, which ended in Favour of the Barber in twelve Minutes, in which not above three were employed in Fighting, both being very circumspect, and trying to make each other Fight. There were very few Blows or Falls: The Barber was in very fine Order, and not only fixed a severe Blow on Slack just below his Ribs (where he had stopped several before with his Elbows) which he could not get rid of, but followed it with two or three more desperate

*Fig. 51. A Boxing Academy. Detail from* The Present Age 1767.

ones in the same Place, which forc'd Slack to give up.---The Truth is, that Strength and Weight must be served, and there was a great Superiority in both on Taylor's Side.---The Box was 117 l.[367]

## JAMES vs. SLACK, 1748

Yarmouth, July 5.

Yesterday was a trial of Manhood, at our Fort, between Joseph James and John Slack, when the latter got the Advantage, and beat James in three Minutes; Also John Simpson was beaten by John Curtis. There were near a Thousand spectators.[368]

## THE DEATH of JAMES, 1748

A few Nights since was buried John James, particularly famous for his Art and Bravery in Boxing, the Funeral (which was extraordinary decent) was defrayed by his Father. It was remarkable, that his Pall was supported by

---

366 *The Derby Mercury,* February 10, 1748.
367 *The Ipswich Journal,* February 20, 1748.
368 *The Ipswich Journal,* July 9, 1748.

Broughton, Taylor, Stevenson, Smallwood, Slack, and Field, six of the most celebrated Bruisers that this, or perhaps any Age has produced.[369]

## SLACK vs. "THE NOTED JAW-BONE-BREAKER", 1748

On Wednesday was fought, at Broughton's Amphitheatre, a severe Trial of Manhood, between Mr. John Slack and Mr. Boswell, the noted Jaw-Bone-Breaker, which lasted 17 Minutes, and ended in Favour of Mr. Slack. The Box amounted to 57 Pounds.[370]

## SLACK vs. FIELD, 1749

Norwich, Feb. 18. On Thursday the 9th Instant, our Country man John Slack, fought the longest and bloodiest Battle in London, with Field the Sailor, ever seen at Broughton's Ampitheatre: It lasted an Hour and thirty-two Minutes, at Sheer Boxing, without Hugging, standing Still, or above four Falls in the whole; and it was very remarkable, that as the Betts were even at Setting to, the Fight was so equally maintain'd, that not 5 to 4 could be got, any Time during the Battle: Two Cross-Buttock Fall, excellently well-timed, but very seldom to be got so late in the Day, gave Slack the Victory. As this was judg'd to be a very near Match, and a great deal of Money was depending upon it, the House was fill'd very early with Persons of the first Distinction, who express'd the utmost Satisfaction and Applause of the uncommon Bravery and Skill exhibited on this Occasion: The Event shewed how necessary (to use the Fighting Phrase) Keeping is, to carry a Man thro' in Labours of this Kind; for tho' strict sobriety is not the Characteristick of either of these Heroes, yet Slack may fairly be said to have won, from a Restraint and Regularity, which nothing but the Importance of the Undertaking could have made tolerable to him, and which even the Thirst of Glory, or the Love of Wealth, could not prevail on his Antagonist to submit to. There was near 100 l. in the Box.[371]

## BROUGHTON vs. SLACK, 1750

The grand Boxing-Match between Broughton and Slack, which has been the Subject of so much Conversation among the modern English Heroes of all Rank, was fought Yesterday. The House was full very early. At Eleven the Champions mounted; and Broughton was fairly beat in 14 Minutes and 11 Seconds, as near as could be computed. The first two Minutes the Odds on Broughton's Head were 20 to 1, but Slack soon recovering himself changed the Betts, by closing the Eyes of his Antagonist, and following him close at the same Time, gained a complete Victory, to the no small Mortification of the Knowing ones, who were finely taken in. Before they began, Broughton gave Slack the Ten Guineas to fight him, according to his Promise, which Slack immediately betted against a hundred Guineas offered by a Gentleman against him.—The Money received at the Door amounted to 130 l. besides 200 Tickets at a Guinea and Half a Guinea each. So that it is thought, what with the Money received at the Door, that for the Tickets, (as they fought for the whole house) and the Odds Slack took, that he did not clear less than 600 l.[372]

Extracts from the Norwich Papers, concerning the Battle between Boughton and Slack. *From Norwich Gazette*
------Altho' none were admitted under double Price, the House was full be Half an Hour after Eight, and the

---

369 *The Whitehall Evening-Post Or London Intelligencer,* November 26, 1748.
370 *The Ipswich Journal,* December 31, 1748.
371 *The Ipswich Journal,* February 25, 1749.
372 *Derby Mercury,* April 13, 1750.

Champion mounted the Stage (by his Royal Highness the Duke's Command) at Ten. Broughton gave Slack Ten Guineas to fight for the whole House, and not divide it, as usual, which amount'd to upwards of 200l. The Odds before Fighting were ten to one; and when Broughton went on the Stage, he treated his Antagonist with the greatest Contempt and Disdain, and even laughed at the Blows Slack gave him.

*From Norwich Mercury*

Soon after the first Onset, Broughton threw Slack a dreadfull Fall, which entirely depriv'd him of his Senses and Strength for some time; when as he was put upon his Legs, he either fell down, or was with ease knocked down by his Antagonist, and it was, generally, thought impossible for him to recover: Yet when it was least expected, he revived, and as Broughton was attacking, Slack by great Luck planted a straight Blow directly in his Eye, which gave a Check to his Fury. This was soon after followed by several severe Blows of the like kind, and tho' Broughton was by much the strongest and heaviest Man, yest Slack shifted

*Fig. 52. Slack, based on an older bust. From Egan's* Boxiana.

so artfully, and avoided the Falls so dexterously (even when laid hold on) that there was very little Advantage got by Broughton in this respect: In short, after a most bloody Fight, which lasted exactly Fourteen Minutes, in which the Odds from Ten to One, and in common from Six to One, were more than once brought even, Mr. Broughton after exerting the utmost Effort and Arts that Nature could put forth, or Judgment devise, was forced to yield to the Younger Heroe, not in Words indeed, for he was past Utterance.[373]

## "THERE WAS NEVER FASTER FIGHTING", 1751

Norwich, Feb. 9. At Broughton's Amphitheatre, on Wednesday last, after the most bloody Battle that ever was seen for the time it lasted, which was just sixteen Minutes, George Taylor beat his Antagonist John Slack, from this City. The House was full before Nine, and the Fight over by Ten o'Clock. The Odds before setting to were Two to One on Taylor. For the first six Minutes there never was faster Fighting, or more terrible Blows and Falls, but Slack had the worst of it, and the Odds were greater against him than at the Beginning; but in the next five Minutes, which were employed in hard Boxing, without a Fall, the Battle was brought even, and both of them seemed equally tired, and out of Wind; from this time, Slack's straight Blows began to take Place, and he had greatly the Advantage, both in Fighting and Falls, insomuch that the Odds were at 14 Minutes more in his Favour than they had ever been against him; 'till unluckily, when it was impossible for him to have lost but by an Accident, by a Twist of his Leg to disengage himself from his Adversary's Lock, and in which he succeeded so as to give the Fall, he had the Misfortune to put out his Knee, which lost him almost a certain Victory. Taylor, who may be truly said, to have won this Battle out of the Fire, has declared he will appear no more on the Stage, so

373 *Ipswich Journal,* April 12, 1750.

that our Countryman is now the first Fighting Man in England. There was above 200 l. in the boxes, besides Tickets.[374]

## LEA "THE CHAIRMAN" vs. SLACK, 1752

I George Lea, who fought Mr. John Slack at the Corner of Bow-Street, Covent-Garden; the sole Reason of my not beating, was owing to my being so much in Liquor, not having been in Bed for three Nights before; and I have since challenged to fight him for Twenty Pounds, or any Sum he likes, on the Ground, which he refuses: I hereby give the second Challenge to fight him for Twenty Pounds on the publick Stage, being resolv'd to fight him the second Time, with two Seconds that never were Seconds on the publick Stage.[375]

LONDON, February 11.
    Yesterday Slack defeated the Chairman at Broughton's Amphitheatre in about three Minutes, in the Presence of a dignified and crowded Audience. Just before the Heroes mounted the Stage, there was an Alarm given, the Gallery was falling down, which put the Spectators into the greatest Confusion.[376]

LONDON, February 13.
    On Monday, when Slack the Butcher fought Lea the Chairman, there was such a Crowd, that it was computed there was 150 l. in the House; such is the Encouragement given to the Gentlemen of that Polite Art, besides a considerable Reward, flung by the Gentlemen of Taste, to their ingenious Pupils, who exhibit before their Masters mount, which often prevents some of them from picking of Pockets for some Days afterwards.[377]

## "THEY COULD HARDLY LIFT UP THEIR ARMS to STRIKE a BLOW", 1752

Yesterday Slack beat Falkner, after an Engagement of 27 Minutes. It was allowed by the Spectator to be the greatest Battle that was ever fought and though the Odds before setting too were three to one on Slack, yet during the Battle, the Betts came about two to one on Falkner. Two Minutes before it was ended, it was generally thought that the next fall would determine the Victory, and they were both so weak, that they could hardly lift up their Arms to strike a Blow, but a Fall ensuing from their closing, Falkner was the undermost, which determin'd his Fate; and his Conqueror, when attempted to be lifted off from the vanquish'd Hero, Flipt out of the Second's Arms, and lay on the Stage as flat as his Antagonist, and they were both obliged to be carried off the Stage, The Seconds were George Taylor, and Tom-Boy; the former to Falkner, and the latter to Slack.[378]

## SLACK vs. GODDARD, 1752

Extract of a Letter from London, dated Nov. 15.
    'This Day at Broughton's Amphitheatre, came on the Boxing-Match between Slack and Goddard, on the first Set to, 50 l. to 20 l. was laid on Slack, and several Pounds laid 3 to 1; Slack gave the two first Falls, but Goddard gave the Third, which made the House ring; after that, Goddard (who is much stronger than Slack) endeavored all he could to close with Slack and buttock him, rather than stand fair Boxing, by which Means he falled Slack

374 *Ipswich Journal*, February 16, 1751.
375 *London Daily Advertiser*, January 21, 1752.
376 *Derby Mercury*, February 7, 1752.
377 *Derby Mercury*, February 14, 1752.
378 *Derby Mercury*, May 15, 1752.

often, and within 14 Minutes and a half our Norwich Hero was obliged to submit, and to all Appearance was very much beaten.'[379]

### *The* BRUISER's PROGRESS, 1752

A Link-boy once I stood the *grin*,
  At Charing Cross I plie'd;
Here, light your honour for a *win*,
  To every *Cull*, I crie'd.

On Sundays, oft I *loung'd* the *gag*.
  And *shul'd* at the Church-door,
Good people pray bestow a *mag*,
  I'm *panumless* and poor.

In Leis'ter-Fields, as most can tell,
  Come black your honour I;
But *dirty work*, I lik'd not well,
  And *gaffling* then did try.

At Tottenham-Court, I first sat out,
  With lusty Jumping Jack,
With Hunt and others had a bout,
  And carried off the *wack*.

With Slack at Broughton's once I fought,
  And there gave him his fill;
His *twenty guineas*, vict'ry bought,
  And I'm the fame man still.

But these professions all are bad,
  They bring so little *bit*;
So I'm turn'd *Roadsman* on the *pad*,
  My eyes! a lucky *hit*.

Ye Jockies *rum*, and *blowings queer*,
  Of whatsoever fame,
Depend upon it never fear,
  Die when I will, I'm *game*.

And if I should my exit make,
  At Tyburn's fatal tree;
Poor Field, my master did partake,
  The self same destiny.[380]

---

379 *Ipswich Journal,* November 25, 1752.
380 Lemoine, 72-73.

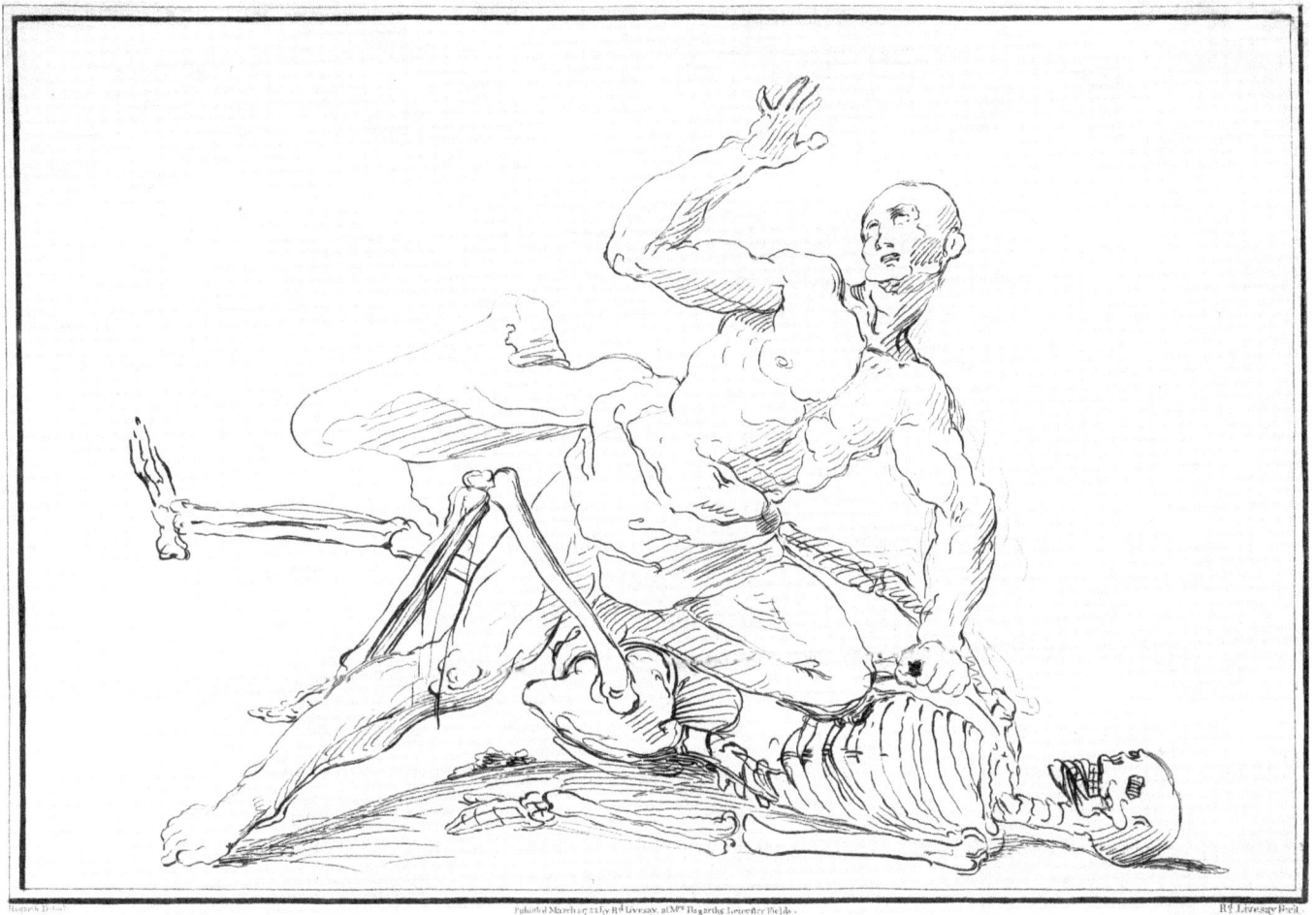

*Fig. 53. George Taylor and Death, by Hogarth [1764/1782]. Courtesy of The Lewis Walpole Library, Yale University.*

## "THIS DREADFUL COMBAT", 1754

*Harlston in Norfolk, July 30.* Yesterday in the afternoon Slack and Pettit met and fought. At the first SET-TO, Pettit seized Slack by the throat, and held him up against the rails, and GRAIN'D him so much as to make him turn extremely black; this continued for half a minute before Slack could break Pettit's hold; after which for near ten minutes Pettit kept fighting and driving hard at Slack, when at length Slack clos'd with his antagonist, and gave him a very severe fall, and after that a second and third; but between these falls Pettit threw Slack twice off the Stage, and indeed Pettit so much dreaded Slack's falls, that he ran directly at his hams, and tumbled him down, and by that means gave Slack an opportunity of making the falls very easy; when they had been fighting eighteen minutes, the odds ran against Slack a guinea to a shilling; whereas on first setting out, it was three or four to one on his head; but after this time Slack SHORTENED Pettit so, as to disable him from running and throwing him down in the manner he had done before, but obliged him to stand to close fighting. Slack then clos'd one of his eyes, and beat him very much about the face. At twenty minutes Pettit grew weaker, Slack stronger; this was occasioned by Slack's strait way of fighting. At twenty-two minutes the best judged allow'd Slack to have the advantage over Pettit very considerably, as he was then recovering his Wind, which was owing to Game; when they had box'd twenty-four minutes, Pettit threw Slack again over the rails. This indeed Slack suffered him to do, as by that means he fixed a blow under Pettit's ribs, that hurt him much. Whilst Slack was again getting upon the stage (it was not half a minute before he was remounted) Pettit had so much the fear of his antagonist before his eyes, that he walk'd off without so much as civilly taking leave of the spectators, or saying any thing to any person.

This the ****ers call roguing of it; for it is thought Pettit run away full strong. The whole time of their fighting was twenty-five minutes; and this morning the Battle was given to Slack, who drew the first ten guineas out of the box." Thus ended this dreadful combat.

Every man, who has the honour of the British fist at heart, must look with admiration on the Bottom, the Wind, the Game, of this invincible champion Slack. How must they applaud his address in fighting strait; and with what detestation must they look upon his dastard antagonist, who could so shamefully rogue it!

I cannot but lament the cruelty of that law, which has shut up our Amphitheatres: and I look upon the professors of the noble art of Boxing as a kind of disbanded army, for whom we have made no provision. The mechanics, who at the call of glory left their mean occupation, are now obliged to have recourse to them again; and coachmen and barbers resume the whip and razor, instead of giving black eyes and cross-buttocks. Some have been forced to exercise their art in knocking down passengers in dark alleys and corners; while others have learned to open their fists and ply their fingers in picking pockets. Buckhorse, whose knuckles had been used to indent many a bruise, now clenches them only to grasp a link; and Broughton employs the muscles of his brawny arm in squeezing a lemon or drawing a cork. His Amphitheatre itself is converted into a Methodist Meeting-house! and perhaps (as laymen are there admitted into the pulpit) those very fists, which so lately dealt such hearty bangs upon the stage, are now with equal vehemence thumping the cushion.

The dextrous use of the fist is truly British exercise: and the sturdy English have been as much renowned for their Boxing as their Beef; both which are by no means suited to the watery stomachs and weak sinews of their enemies the French. To this nutriment and this art is owing that long-established maxim, that one Englishman can beat three Frenchmen. A Frenchman, who piddles on a fricassee of frogs, can no more encounter with an Englishman, who feeds upon beef, than the frog in the fable could swell her little body to the size of an ox.

Our present race of spindle-shanked beaux had rather close with an orange wench at the playhouse, than engage in a bye battle at Tottenham Court. It is therefore no wonder, that they should object to this manly practice, for which they are so ill fitted. How can we imagine, that they could stand against the buffets of a bruiser when they might be patted down with the fan of a lady? An attempt was once made by Broughton to bring this study into vogue, by establishing a School for Boxing, in which he himself was to be the Lecturer. He invited the young gentlemen of the army, and all other men of spirit, to engage under his directions; and promised to arm their feeble wrists with mufflers, so that nothing might be apprehended by the softest head or tenderest skin. A few indeed were hardy enough to try a fall with him: but most of our young fellows gave up the gauntlet for scented gloves; and loathing the mutton fists of vulgar carmen and porters, they rather chose to hang their hands in a sling, to make them white and delicate as a lady's. I cannot but regret, that this design was not generally encouraged, as it might perhaps have abolished almost the only use, that is at present made of the sword; and men of honour, instead of tilting at each other, might have had satisfaction in a tight Set-to behind Mountague House.

The amusement of Boxing I must confess is more immediately calculated for the vulgar, who can have no relish for the more refined pleasures of whist and the hazard table. Men of fashion have found out a more genteel employment for their hands in shuffling a pack of cards and shaking the dice: and indeed it will appear upon a strict review, that most of our fashionable diversions are nothing else but different branches of gaming. What lady would be able to boast a route at her house consisting of three or four hundred persons, if they were not to be drawn together by the charms of playing a rubber?

To this polite spirit of gaming, which has diffused itself through all the fashionable world, is owing the vast encouragement that is given to the Turf; and horse-races are esteemed only as they afford occasion for making a bet. The same spirit likewise draws the knowing ones together in a ****-pit; and ****s are rescued from the dunghill, and armed with gaffles, to furnish a new species of gaming. For this reason among others I cannot but regret the loss of our elegant amusements in Oxford Road and Tottenham Court. A great part of the spectators used to be deeply interested in what was doing on the stage, and were as earnest to make an advantage of the issue of the battle, as the champions themselves to draw the largest sum from the box. The Amphitheatre was at once a school for boxing and gaming. Many thousands have depended upon a match; the odds have often risen at a black eye; a large bet has been occasioned by a cross-buttock: and while the house has resounded with the lusty bangs of the combatants, it has at the same time echoed with the cries of five to one, six to one, ten to one.

The loss of this branch of gaming is a publick calamity; and I doubt not but the gentlemen at White's, and all others whom it concerns, will use their endeavours to have it restored. The many Plates given all over the kingdom have undoubtedly improved our breed of horses; and if the diversion of Boxing was to meet with equal encouragement, we should certainly have a more stout and hardy race of bruisers. It might perhaps become a fashion for gentlemen, who were fond of the sport, to keep champions in training, put them in sweats, diet them, and breed up the human species with the same care as they do ****s and horses. In course of time this branch of gaming, like all others, would doubtless be reduced to a science; and Broughton, in imitation of that great genius Hoyle, might oblige the publick with a treatise of the Fist, and Calculations for laying the Odds at any Match of Boxing.[381]

## SLACK vs. HARRIS, 1755

London, Feb. 28.

Thursday last was decided at Bristol, the great Boxing Match between John Slack and Cornelius Harris. The Battle lasted upwards of twenty Minutes and was carried on with great Vigour on both Sides; but at last Mr. Harris was obliged to confess he could fight no longer. It is said, he is so much bruised that he cannot recover. On this Battle centred all the Hopes of that Family, who have now lost their boasted Honour of having never been beat.[382]

## STEPHENS "THE NAILOR" vs. SWAFFORD, 1760

The old Broughtonian spirit, or manly exercise of boxing, is not yet extinct amongst us, since a bloody and desperate battle was fought yesterday in the fields, near Marybone, between one Stephens, a nailor, and one Swafford, a butcher, which lasted about fifteen minutes, and ended in favour of the former. A press-gang, who attended, secured several useful hands, who, possibly, may be of more service to their country than being idle spectators at a boxing match.[383]

## STEPHENS "THE NAILOR" KILLS TAPLIN, 1760

Tuesday was fought in the Fields, near Mary-le-Bon, a most severe Battle, between Stephens, a famous Boxer, by Trade a Nailer, and one Taplin, a Carman, in whose Favour the Odds ran Three to One; the Fight was managed with great Skill and Dexterity on both Sides for about 12 Minutes, when Victory at length declared for the Nailer, to the no small Mortification of the knowing ones. Taplin had two of his Ribs broke, and received so many Bruises that it is though he can not recover. It is computed not less than 10,000 Persons were present.[384]

Taplin the Carman, who fought the desperate Battle with the Naylor the other Day, in Marybone Fields, is since dead of his Bruises.[385]

---

381 *Jackson's Oxford Journal,* September 7, 1754.
382 *Jackson's Oxford Journal,* March 15, 1755.
383 *Public Ledger,* January 16, 1760.
384 *Derby Mercury,* February 15-22, 1760.
385 Ibid.

## SLACK vs. STEPHENS "THE NAILOR", 1760

*LONDON, May 8.*

We hear that the Nailer, the noted Bruiser, flushed with the Success he has already obtained, has, at the Request of some Gentlemen, sent a formal Challenge to Mr. Slack, now settled at Bristol, to meet and fight for any Sum.[386]

Yesterday, at the Tennis-Court near the Haymarket, after three bye Battles (one of which those versed in the Science deemed a remarkable good one) the Heroes, Slack and Stevens the Nailor, mounted the Stage; On their first Appearance, the Odds were twenty to one on Slack's Head; but in three Minutes the Nailor proved Conqueror, to the great Disappointment and Loss of the not Knowing Ones. This Battle, it is thought, may occasion, if the Civil Power permit, two more; one between the Heroes themselves, and the other between their Seconds.[387]

*LONDON, May 29.*

The Heroes of the Fist are likely to come into Play again. Hero Slack is matched for a considerable Sum against Stevenson the Nailer, to fight on Monday next at the Tennis-Court in James-street, near the Hay-market. If the latter should hit the right Nail on the Head, that no Doubt will occasion a second Trial of Skill, in which Butcher must come off victorious; This will be productive of a third Combat; the Event of which none knows, except those in the Secret.[388]

*LONDON, June 5.*

On Monday the famous Battle was fought between Slack and Stephens, the Nailer, at the Tennis-Court in James-Street, Haymarket, at which were present several Noblemen and Persons of Distinction. The Combatants had only three Bouts; in the first Slack struck his Antagonist a violent Blow on the Side of his Head; at the second, Stephens hit Slack under the short Ribs, and gave him a desperate Fall; and finally pursuing his Advantage, gave him so dreadful a Blow on his Stomach, that he lay for some Time senseless on the Stage, and was obliged, after about three Minutes and a half Contest, to submit to the superior Strength of his Adversary. The Streets were crowded with Spectators to see the Combatants pass and repass.

We hear that upwards of 10,000 l. has been won and lost by the last Battle between Slack and the Nailer.

It is said that Slack very kindly advised the Nailer to make his Will, and get his Coffin ready, for he had but a short Time to live. Great Men like others are sometimes mistaken.[389]

## MAGGS vs. STEPHENS "THE NAILOR", 1761

Monday last the Trial of Skill between George Maggs, of Pensford in this County, and Stephens the Nailer, was decided at the Tennis-Court in St. James-Street, near the Hay-Market, London. There were assembled the greatest Concourse of Nobility, Gentry, &c ever known on the like Occation. The Champions mounted the Stage between Twelve and One. At first setting to, Maggs struck the Nailer down; afterwards the Nailer knocked him down twice; and for ten Minutes he seemed to have the Advantage: However, the heroic Maggs, by his great Skill, uncommon Strength, unequal'd Courage, and matchless Agility, soon changed the Scene; struck the Nailer down six Times successively; and finally stript him of all Laurels he had acquired by his many former Victories.--- Smallwood was Second to Maggs, and Faulkner to Stephens.---

386*Newcastle Courant*, May 17, 1760.
387*London Evening Post*, May 31, 1760.
388*The Leeds Intelligencer,* June 3, 1760.
389*Derby Mercury,* June 6, 1760.

*Fig. 54. George Taylor beaten by Death. Designed by Hogarth before 1764, and printed March 1, 1782. Courtesy of The Lewis Walpole Library, Yale University.*

According to the most exact Accounts, the Battle lasted just seventeen Minutes and a half.

A certain Royal Personage was present, and won large Sums. 'Tis said upward of 50,000l. depended on the Issue of this Battle: One Nobleman lost above 2000l.

We hear that Maggs and the Nailer were weighed a few Days before they fought; and that there were only five Pounds Difference, which was in Maggs favour.[390]

## SLACK vs. WYBURNE, 1764

We hear that there will be shortly a Trial of Skill in the most noble and antient Art of Boxing, between the celebrated Mr. Slack (who some Years ago defeated the redoubted Hero, Mr. Broughton) and one Wyburne of this City.- Several considerable Betts are depending upon this Occasion, and the Gentlemen Gladiators expect excellent Diversion.[391]

---

390 *Bath Chronicle and Weekly Gazette*, March 5, 1761.
391 *Dublin Courier*, December 10, 1764.

## THE DEATH OF BUCKHORSE, 1772

*Nov. 1772:* Thursday night the famous Buckhorse, well known for upwards 40 years last to the nobility and gentry at New Market and other public places of resort, fell down dead in Covent Garden, where he was attending, as usual, with his link, to call coaches for the people coming out of the play house. This famous hero of the "bruising stage" in his youth, used to divert the company before the champions mounted by boxing anyone who chose to attack him, in order to pass away the time. He was so very hardy that he could bear a great deal of drubbing, and often beat a much bigger and stronger boxer than himself; at last he had one of his eyes totally beat out, and of late years the poor wretch was greatly reduced so as to carry small twigs and walking sticks about for a livelihood, notwithstanding he was merely so great a favorite with the lord Windsor, that he had him sit for his picture in miniature, which he outfitted round with diamonds and gave it to an acquaintance.[392]

## DEATH OF GEORGE TAYLOR, 1782

To the Memory of George Taylor whose Skill and Courage in the Manual Combat would have done Honour to the Roman Circus / Incorruptable and Unconquerable / Learn Heros of a higher Class from his Example to render British Bravery Invincible.

> Vain all the Honours of my brow,
> Victorious Wreaths farewell,
> One Trip from Death has laid me low,
> By whom such Numbers fell.
> Still bravely I'll dispute the Prize,
> Nor yield—tho' out of breath,
> 'Tis but a fall, I yet shall rise,
> And vanquish even—Death.

---

392 Note by Thomas Bowen, 1772. Perkins School for the Blind, Samuel P. Hayes Research Library,
https://www.digitalcommonwealth.org/search/commonwealth:vx021v23n

*Fig. 55. John Smith, alias "Buckhorse", depicted in later years. Published between 1768 and 1772 by Thomas Bowen.*
*Courtesy of The Lewis Walpole Library, Yale University.*

*Fig. 56. Cudgel fencers, one with wrapped head and hand. Detail from Collet's* Holland Smock, *London, 1770.*
*Royal Collection Trust.*

# XVII.

## LATER ACCOUNTS, *and the* END *of the* GLADIATORS

*A*s *the eighteenth century progressed, gladiatorial contests began to wane in favor of boxing matches. Those gladiatorial combats that did take place in the 1730s and 1740s featured increasingly sensational set-ups (for instance, pitting multiple opponents of different nations against one another) and unusual weapons, perhaps in an attempt to draw publicity and stay relevant. The custom likely suffered from the deaths of its greatest proponents, James Figg and Edward Sutton, during the 1730s, as well as from the constant barrage of condemnation, negative publicity, and ridicule from the British press and* literati. *The last true gladiatorial combats took place in the 1750s. During the several decades that followed, and towards the end of the century, martial prize contests using antiquated weapons continued to take place in rural settings—possibly exhibiting a lingering influence from the gladiators—but by that time, the extant historical accounts suggest that these weapons were blunt.*

### GLADIATORS PRAISED, 1718

Men of a Liberal Education should scorn to be outdone in Gallantry by the Prize-Fighters. Their Challenges are conceived in the most civil Language; and the Tryal of Skill is performed for the most part without Enmity, though with great Spirit.[393]

---

393 *The Free Thinker,* June 20, 1718.

## a TRIAL at TWO-HANDED SWORD, 1725

On Monday last was performed at the Great Booth in Southwark, a Trial of Skill at two Handed Sword, between Robert Carter of London, a noted Master, and John Hancaw a French Fencing Master in Spittlefields, and the latter got much the better on't.[394]

## WILLIAM GILL vs. the BOLD SPANIARD, 1727

### ADVERTISEMENT.

At Mr. STOKES's Amphitheatre, Joining to his House, in Islington Road, on Monday the 6th of March, will be performed a Trial of Skill by the following Masters. I William Johnson, commonly called the bold Spaniard, having heard of the great Fame William Gill has acquired by the Noble Science of Defence, tho' he cut me once before, I have like a mettled Horse, an Ambition not to let another go before me, do invite him to meet me on the Stage, to fight with the usual Weapons, not doubting but to shew, for the Honour of my Country, that a Spaniard can wield a Sword as well as the best English Hero, Scotch Bragadocio, or Hibernian Gladiator, I William Gill, having received a Challenge from a bold Spaniard, whom I thought I had given enough before, but he, like his Countrymen before Gibraltar, has the Insolence to offer at another Attack, tho' the last was so unsuccessful: I shall not fail of meeting at the Place aforesaid, not doubting but to maintain the Honour of the English Stage, only desiring sharp Swords and no Favour.

> I William Gill, my Honour will maintain,
> Against this huffing Bully come from Spain;
> I'll maim him, cut him with my Sword, and hack him,
> And with my Quarter-Staff I'll soundly thwack him.

The Doors will be opened at two, and the Masters mount at four. N.B. No Person to be admitted under one Shilling.[395]

## A TRYAL of SKILL with the FLESHING FLAIL (undated)

A Tryal of Skill is to be fought &c. between John Parkes of Coventry, and John Terrewest. Note— They fight at the Ancient Weapon called the Threshing Flail.[396]

## A BOUT at FLESHING FLAIL, 1727

At STOKES's and SUTTON's Amphitheatre,

In Islington Road, near Sadler's-Wells, this present Wednesday the 16th of April, will be perform'd a Trial of the noble Science of Defence between the following Masters.

I CHRISTOPHER CLARKSON, the bold old Soldier from Lancashire, having fought Mr. Stokes on Monday the 3d Instant, to the entire Satisfaction of the Company, but it being at that Time undetermin'd which of us had the Advantage, give him this second Invitation to exercise with me at the aforesaid Place the following Weapons, Back-Sword, Sword and Dagger, Sword and Buckler, Threshing-Flail, and Quarter-Staff.

---

394 *Caledonian Mercury,* March 5, 1729.

395 *Weekly Journal or British Gazetteer,* March 4, 1727.

396 John Ashton, *Social life in the reign of Queen Anne: taken from original sources* (New York : Scribner and Welford, 1883), 241.

*Fig 57. Man using a threshing-flail in a melee. Detail from Hogarth's* Chairing of the Members, Plate 4, *London, 1758.*

I JAMES STOKES, Citizen of London, do accept of this Challenge, and doubt not but in this Battle to put all future Debates of my Superiority out of the Question.

N. B. Attendance will be given at Four, and the Masters mount at Six precisely, by Reason of the Additional Weapon. The Threshing-Flail has not been exercised on a Stage these seven Years.[397]

## A TRIAL at PUSHING with the SMALL-SWORD, 1727

In Islington Road, on Monday next, the 31st of July, will be perform'd a Trial of Skill by the following Masters.

Whereas I CHRISTOPHER CLARKSON, call'd the bold old Soldier, from Preston in Lancashire, having mounted the Stage for these many Years with universal Approbation, and always came off with Satisfaction to the

397 *Daily Post,* April 26, 1727.

Spectators and Renown to myself, am unwilling that my Lawrels should wither thro' Inaction, and having heard of the unparalleled Character of Mr. Oliver, for his Skill in the Small Sword, as well as his Abilities in the Weapons usually practis'd on the Stage, thinking him a proper Subject to give a now Lustre to my Sword, do therefore dare him to a Trial at Pushing with the Small Sword three Bouts, and likewise to the Exercise of the usual Weapons, where I doubt not but to manifest to all the worthy Company, that I am able in Age to maintain the Honour of my Youth.

I JOHN OLIVER, from the City of Carfargos, perceive that no Reputation, how well soever establish'd, is sufficient to secure one from the Emulation of some Cavillers, and therefore find myself under a Necessity of accepting the Invitation of this batter'd Hero in every Article of it; and if his Genius should happen to fail him in this Battle, and instead of adding to his former Trophies, entirely impair them, I flatter myself I shall rest easy from all rash Challenges of this Nature for the future,

Note, There will be a Boxing Match for 10 Guineas by a noted Weaver, and a young Man who never appear'd on any Stage before. N. B. Attendance will be given at Four, and, to prevent the Company's waiting, the Men which Boxes will mount at Six, and the Masters at Seven precisely. Beginning with the Small-Sword.[398]

## "SLASHING and CUTTING of THROATS", 1728

Look you, the *Bear-Garden* is preparing, and the *Gladiators* coming out to entertain the People. And here every thing is dull without Mischief, the Blood must run about to give satisfaction; and all the Pleasure lies in slashing and cutting of Throats. For this purpose these wretched Fencers are fed high for the Exercise, fatted for the Shambles, and treated for Destruction at no small Expence. Thus Men are stabbed to divert those of their own Kind; and to kill handsomely goes for Skill, Commendation, and Improvement. Thus Barbarities are not only practised, but taught as a Science: It is an Art to be well prepared, and a Glory to execute the Murder...[399]

## SIR THOMAS PARKYNS at FIGG's, 1728

### ΠΡΟΓΥΜΝΑΣΜΑΤΑ:

THE INN PLAY: Or, CORNISH-HUGG WRESTLER: Digested in a Method which teacheth to break all Holds; and throw most Falls mathematically; easy to be understood by all Gentlemen, &c. and of great Use to such who understand the Small-Sword in Fencing; and by all Tradesmen and Handicrafts that have competent Knowledge of the Use of the Stilliards, Bar, Crove Iron or Lever, with their Hypomochlions, Fulciments or Baits.

By Sir THOMAS PARKYNS of Bunny Park, Bart.

Lactamur Achivis doctius unctis.

Hor. Ep. Lib. 2- Ep. I. ad Aug.

The Third Edition corrected, with large Additions.

Printed for Thomas Weekes, at the White Hart in Westminster-Hall; and sold by Humphry Wainwright, at Bunny in Nottinghamshire.

N. B. This Third Edition being called for, if any Masters with their Scholars have a Mind to see the Book exercised over Paragraph by Paragraph, for their better Information, as they may be able to go thro' every Paragraph by themselves, and leave Notice with the Publisher, Sir Thomas will fix a Day for that Exercise at Mr. Figg's Amphitheatre in Oxford Road before his Return into the Country, which will be in a Fortnight's Time.[400]

---

398 *Weekly Journal or British Gazetteer,* July 29, 1727.
399 Jeremy Collier, *Essays upon several moral subjects, Vol. III* (London: George Strahan, 1728).
400 *Daily Journal,* January 10, 1728.

## SIR THOMAS PARKYNS at FIGG's, 1730

*That it may no longer remain a* SECRET, *This is to give Notice,*

THAT at Mr. FIGG's Amphitheatre in Oxford Road, on Monday, the 28th Inftant, Sir Thomas Parkyns, of Bunny Park in the County of Nottingham, Bart. the Author of a Book on that curious Subject, call'd, The Inn-Play, or Cornish Hugg.Wreftler, propofes to explain and exercife over every Rule and Pofture mentioned in his Book.

N. B. The Book is to be had of Stephen Auften, Bookfeller, at the Angel and Bible in St. Paul's Church-yard.

## "SWORD and PINNION", 1729

At the Request of several Gentlemen that saw the last Engagement of Mr. Figg's and Mr. Bennett's, do desire they should have the other Engagement once more to decide the Cause.
At Mr. FIGG's Great-Room,
At his House, the Sign of the City of Oxford, in Oxford-Road Marybone-Fields, To-morrow being Wednesday the 10th of September, 1729, will be a Trial of Skill by the following Masters.

WHEREAS I Rowland Bennett, from Dublin, Master of the Noble Science of Defence, who engag'd that bold and mighty Hero the famous Mr. James Figg on the 30th of July last, when I receiv'd several Cuts, yet I am proud that I gave general Satisfaction to the Gentlemen then present, and do now give him a second Invitation to meet as above, not doubting but to give him a Return for his last, as well as an agreeable Satisfaction to all the Spectators.

I James Figg from Thame in Oxfordshire, Master of the said Science, thought to have declin'd practising the Sword on the publick Stage, but to satisfy the World once more will not fail meeting the abovesaid Mr. Bennett, and will put in execution the best of my Skill, which shall be the earnest Endeavour of James Figg.

Note, A Man from Taunton-Dean and another from Staffordshire, are to Wrestle for three Guineas a Man, the first two Falls in three, and two old Sword's Men are to fight three Bouts at single Sword and three Bouts at Sword and Pinnion.

'Tis expected that his Royal Highness the Prince of Wales will be there to see the Performance.[401]

## "A DOUBLE BATTLE": IRELAND vs. ENGLAND, 1729

At Mr. STOKES'S AMPHITHEATRE, *In* Islington-Road, *this Day, the 17th of March, being St.* PATRICK'*s Day, will be a* Trial of Skill *by two Champions of Ireland, and two of England.*

Whereas I THOMAS ELMORE and I ANDREW MAC COLLEY both from Ireland, Masters of the Noble Science of Defence, in Honour of the Day, and the Credit of our Country and Selves, knowing the famous Characters of Mr. Stokes and Mr. Sutton, the two Champions of England, we do thereby give them an Invitation to a Trial of Skill at the usual Weapons practis'd on the Stage, doubting not in the least but to let the English Swordsmen know that there is now arriv'd their Master-piece in the Noble Art of Defence. I the said Andrew Mac

---

[401] *St James's Evening Post,* September 9, 1729.

## At Mr. Stoke's AMPHITHEATRE,

*In Iflington Road, this prefent Monday, being the 6th Inft. will be a Trial of Skill by the following Mafters.*

WHEREAS feveral Gentle-men, Judges in the Science of Defence, have made a Wager of thirty Guineas, do particularly defire WILLIAM GILL from Gloucefter, Pupil to the Famous Mr. Figg, and JOSEPH JOHNSON from Yorkfhire, (who has fought Mr. Figg three Battles, to the Satisfaction of the Spectators) Mafters of the faid Science, to ufe their utmoft Skill in Fighting Ten Bouts at Sword and Dagger, for Two Guineas each Bout, and Three Bouts at Staff for Ten Guineas, and whoever is the Conqueror fhall, for his Encouragement, have half the Money:

We WILLIAM GILL and JOSEPH JOHNSON, to exprefs our Willingnefs to oblige, will not fail, at the Place and Time appointed, to ufe our utmoft Skill, as we above are defired, which we hope will prove to the entire Satisfaction of the Gentlemen who have laid the Wager, and to the reft of the worthy Spectators.

W. G. J. J.

The Doors will be open'd at 2 o'Clock, and the Mafters mount at 5 precifely.

There will be the ufual Diverfion of Cudgel-playing.

*Fig 58. William Gill vs. Joseph Johnson.* Daily Journal, *April 6, 1730.*

Colley have fought 106 Battles, and was never defeated; and if any Gentlemen will lay any Wagers on the Battle there is some Irish Gentlemen will back Mr. Mac Colley for any Sum.

We JAMES STOKES and EDWARD SUTTON, Master of the said science, being not afraid of any Hibernian Hectors whatsoever, will not fail complying with their Request, fearing not but to welcome these St. Patricks with a Cross, which will not be very acceptable to them, and to maintain our Characters with Resolution we will not submit to any Irish Man whatsoever, being resolved to make it as smart a Battle as ever was fought in England.

The Boxes to be set at Two, and the Masters mount between four and five, by Reason of a Double Battle.

N. B. There is six Pair of Gloves to be play'd for at Blunts between the English and Irish Gamesters, upon Account or the Day. Mac Colley fights Sutton, and Stokes fights Elmore.[402]

### SIX BOUTS at "DOUBLE SWORD", 1730

At Mr. STOKES's Amphitheatre,

*In* Islington Road, *on* Monday *next being the* 4th Day of *May 1730, will be a Trial of Manhood by the following Masters.*

I Richard Banks from Lancashire, Professor of the most noble Art and Science of Defence, having had some dispute with Joseph Paddon from Exeter in Devonshire, concerning the Judgment of the Sword, do invite him to

---

402 *Daily Post,* March 17, 1729.

## At Mr. Stokes's AMPHITHEATRE,

*In Iflington Road, this prefent Monday, being the 1ft Inft. will be a compleat Trial of Skill, in the Judgment of the Sword, between the two following Mafters, viz.*

Thomas Farrel, from the City of Dublin, in the Kingdom of Ireland, Mafter of the Science of Defence, having fought moft of the glittering Heroes with which the Stage is adorned, and refolving to purchafe Fame, tho' at the Expence of Blood, hereby tender a Challenge to the mighty Combatant Mr. John Needs, frequently call'd, the Green Knight, expecting him to meet and fight me at the Time and Place above, in order to maintain his Title, adjuft our late Quarrels by the Sword and Staff, which knows not the Difference between Honour and true Merit, for which laft I fhall contend, and hope to fhew the World, how cleverly an Irifh Gladiator can metamorphofe an Englifh Gentleman; and, of a Dubb'd Knight, make a forrowful Weft-Country Hic, &c.                Thomas Farrel.

I John Needs, from Frome in Somerfetfhire, in Defence of that Honour a grateful World has beftow'd on my fuccefsful Arms, affure my talkative Antagonift, I fhall not fail meeting him, being too well acquainted with his Judgment to rely on his Word for the Performance of the leaft Article in his Foggy Epiftle. On the contrary, if Dear Honnee does not look about him, he may find both his two Cheeks fhplit down the Middle of hifh Faufh, and be after running from the Weft-Country Hic (as he calls it) as his valiant Countrymen did from the Great Naffau, at the Battle of the Boyne, &c.
John Needs.

Note, For the Entertainment of the Company before the Mafters mount, there will be Diverfion of Cudgel-playing, Wreftling and Boxing; and every thing fo order'd, that nothing may offend, or interrupt the Evening's Recreation.

Fig. 59. Thomas Farrel vs. "the Green Knight." Daily Journal, *June 1, 1730.*

exercise six bouts at Single Sword, and six the Double, and three bouts at Staff, and he that gives the most Cuts at Sword and Blows at Staff, to have the Benefit of the House; and all Gentlemen that will Honour me with their Company, may expect to see as smart a Battle as ever was fought on the Stage, with sharp Swords, and expect no Favour from my Antagonist,

Your humble Servant, Richard Banks.

I Joseph Paddon from Exeter, Master of the said Science, do willingly accept of his Invitation, in hopes to convince my Antagonist ard his Abbettors, that I am capable to dictate him or any Man that presumes to fight me, and will not fail to meet him at the Place above-mentioned, and I am in hopes to frustrate him in his Design, and will give the worthy Spectators entire Satisfaction, which shall be the whole Care of their humble Servant,

Joseph Paddon.

The Doors will be open'd at Three, and the Masters mount at Six.

There will be the usual Diversion of Cudgel-playing before the Masters mount.[403]

---

403 *Weekly Journal or British Gazetteer,* May 2, 1730.

## PADDON vs. STOKES, 1730

At Mr. STOKES's Amphitheatre, In Islington Road, on Monday next being the 27th of July, 1730, will be perform'd a Tryal of Skill in the Judgment of the Sword; between the two following Masters, for the Benefit of the whole House.

WHEREAS on Monday the 20th Instant, I Joseph Padden from the City of Exon, late of Coleman-street, London, proficient in the Science of Defence, fought the Grand Master of this Metropolis, Mr. James Stokes, at his own Seat of Valour, before a numerous Appearance of worthy Spectators, to whom I refer for the Deportment of that Day, the Satisfaction they then express'd, promising a Character sufficient to reward my utmost Endeavours, and fit me for the most dangerous Enterprize, commanding me once more to try my Fortune with the said Gentleman, in single Combat, at the Time and Place first above-mention'd, for the Benefit of the whole House: Accordingly I do hereby invite him then and there to fight me on that Condition, without any Seconds, (his Wife particularly excepted) and as little Favour. This granted, Conquest will adorn my blooming Genius, and Fame to distant Worlds convey a Name that shall never die. Hoping my valiant West-Countrymen will honour me with their Appearance on this extraordinary Occasion, I am, &c.         Joseph Padden.

I James Stokes, Citizen and Shagreen Case-maker of London, Master of the Sword, having defeated many Alexanders, Cæsars, Pompeys, and other Stage Monarchs of their own Creation, by the philosophical Rule of correcting those who deserv'd it, still find Transgressors enough to tire the Thoughts of a Socrates, and weary the Arm of slaugging Bu----y. I shall therefore lay aside the dull Motion of Dignities, and turn Fabulist, desiring the above Gentleman to remember Æsop, viz. *A Boy groping for Eels laid hold of a Snake, the Snake perceiving it was Ignorance, and not Malice, cry'd, keep yourself well whilst you are well; for, in meddling with me, you'll have a bad Bargain on't.* I dare say, had he consulted the little School Author, he had not given me the above Challenge; but as it is, he must get off as he can, being resolv'd to maintain that Honour greater Hands have vainly attempted, &c.         James Stokes.

Note, There will be the usual Diversion of Cudgel-playing; and the two young Men who fought so long and brave a Battle on Monday last, are to box again for Ten Pounds, a Bett made by some contending Gentlemen, who as well as every Body else, admir'd their Behaviour. *N. B.* A Hat being left in Mr. Stokes's Gallery on Monday last, it is carefully kept for the Owner, if he pleases to describe and receive it. The Doors will be open'd at Three, and the Masters mount at Six.[404]

## ST. GEORGE, ST. PATRICK, and ROBIN HOOD, 1732

In Honour of St. *George* and St. *Patrick.*
*At Mr.* STOKES's AMPHITHEATRE, *In Islington Road, this present* Tuesday *the 14th Instant,*

WILL be his great Diversion of Bull, Bear, and Ass-baiting, the finest that has ever been seen in this Kingdom: Two Dogs fight for three Guineas.

And To-morrow, being the 15th Instant, will be the great Match made for Twenty Pounds, between Capt. Elmore, Head Fencing-Master of the Kingdom of Ireland, and James Stokes, Fencing-Master and Citizen of London.

N. B. The Conditions of Battle are as follows, viz. Three Bouts at Single Sword, three at Sword and Dagger, three at Sword and Buckler, and three at Robin Hood's Weapon, Quarter-staff.

Note, No Seconds are to be admitted on the Stage: There will be Fires kept in the Rooms, for the better Reception of the Gentlemen. Attendance will be given at One, and the Masters mount at Five.[405]

---

404 *Weekly Journal or British Gazetteer,* July 25, 1730.
405 *Daily Post,* March 14, 1732.

*Fig. 60. Study for "Hob's Defence", etched vignette by Gravelot, 1737. MET Museum, Fletcher Fund, 1944.*

## A QUARTERSTAFF CONTEST, 1734

PUBLICK DIVERSION *without Expence.*

*At Mr.* William Flanders's, *at the George Inn in New Brentford, on Wednesday the 9th Instant, will be perform'd the following Exercise, viz.*

JOSEPH JOHNSON of York, formerly a favourite Scholar of Mr. John Sparks, and excellent in the Exercise of the Quarter-staff, will fight Mr. Flanders, Master of the abovesaid Inn, who has always been particularly eminent in the Use of that Weapon, six Bouts: The Wagers on this Battle being so considerable between Gentlemen of Distinction and Fashion, there will be no Occasion to require any Money of the Spectators.

N. B. There is a Stage built in the great Yard of the Inn for that Purpose, and the Gates will be open'd at Eleven o'Clock, to admit the Gamesters in Cudgeling, Boxing, and other manly Exercises, to divert the Gentlemen before the Masters mount, which will be exactly at Two, that those Gentlemen who come from London, and other distant Places, may be at Home before Dark.[406]

---

406 *London Evening Post,* January 1, 1734.

## "I AM FOR... ANCIENT ROME, GLADIATORS and LIBERTY", 1735

I was present at a Diversion extremely different from the Opera, of which I have given thee a description, and they tell me is peculiar to this Country. The Spectators were placed in Galleries of an open Circus, below them was an Area fill'd not with Eunuchs and Musicians, but with Bulls and Bears, and Dogs, and Fighting Men. The Pleasure was to see the Animals worry and gore one another, and the Men give and receive many Wounds for so much Money. I had great Compassion for the poor Beasts which were forcibly incens'd against each other, but the human Brutes, who, unexcited by any Rage or Sense of Injury, could spill the Blood of others, and expose their own, seem'd to deserve no Pity. However I look'd upon it as a Proof of the martial Genius of this People, and imagin'd I cou'd discover in that Ferocity & Spirit of Freedom. A Frenchman that sate near me was much offended at the Barbarity of the Sight, and reproach'd my Friend who brought me thither with the sanguinary Disposition of the English in delighting in such Spectacles. My Friend agreed with him in General, and allow'd that it ought not to be encourag'd in a civiliz'd State. But a Gentleman who was placed just above them cast a very sour Look at both, and did not seem at all of their Opinion. He was drest in a short Black Wig, and his Boots on, and held in his Hand a long Whip, which when the Fellow fought stoutly, he would crack very loud by Way of Approbation. One wou'd have thought by his Aspect that he had fought some Prizes himself, or at least that he had received a good Part of his Education in this Place. His Discourse was as rough as his Figure, but did not appear to me to want Sense. I suppose, Sir, said he to my Friend, that you have been bred at Court, and therefore I am not surpriz'd that you do not relish the Bear Garden: But let me tell you, that if more People came hither, and fewer loiter'd in the Drawing Room, it wou'd not be the worse for Old England: We are indeed a civiliz'd State, as you are pleas'd to call it, but I could wish, upon certain Occasions, we were not quite so Civil. This Gentleness and Effeminacy in our Manners will soften us by Degrees into Slaves, and we shall grow to hate fighting in Earnest when we don't love to see it in Jest. Your fine Gentlemen are for the Taste of modern Rome, squeaking Eunuchs and Corruption, but I am for that of ancient Rome, Gladiators and Liberty. And as for the Barbarity which the Foreigner there upbraids us with, I can tell him of a French King whom their Nation is very proud of, that acted much more barbarously; for he shed the Blood of Millions of his Subjects out of downright Wanton-ness, and Butcher'd his innocent Neighbours without any Cause of Quarrel, only to have the Glory of being esteem'd the greatest Prize Fighter in Europe.[407]

## GLADIATORIAL COMBAT in ENGLAND, 1737

That amiable Freedom which reigns in *England* gives the People an Air of Gaiety that is to be met with no where else so universally: The Nobility, the Citizens, and the lower Rank of People have all their Recreations; and whereas in other Countries the Rich alone seem to have a Right to Pleasures, the *English* Nation has Diversions for all Classes; and the Mechanic, as well as his Lordship, knows how to make himself merry, when he has done his Day's Work. The *English* are very much for Shows; Battles especially, of what nature soever, are an agreeable Amusement to them, and of these they have all Kinds...

The Battles of Animals are not the only ones to be seen in *England*, there being very often Combats of Gladia-tors, when the Wretches for pitiful Lucre fight with one another at Swords, and very often wound each other cruelly: The *English* delight very much in this sort of Prize-fighting: They shout loud Applauses when either of the Two wounds his Antagonist, and when the Battle is over, the Two Combatants shake Hands, and make each other a low Bow, to shew they don't bear one another any Malice: I can't conceive how they find any Fellows to take up such an Exercise; the rather, because 'tis liable to very fatal Consequences; for they say, that by their Laws, he who wounds his Adversary, shall be at the Expence of curing him, and he that kills him, is to be hang'd without Mercy.

---

407 Baron George Lyttelton, *Letters from a Persian in England, to His Friend at Ispahan* (London: J. Millan, 1735), 7-9.

There's another sort of Prize-fighters, who fight every Evening in the Summer in a Square near *St. James's*, with no other Weapons but Quarter-staves, or wooden Swords, with which they break one another's Ribs, or knock one another on the Head, and the Victor is generally regal'd by some or other of the Spectators. I have also seen, as I have been going over the Square, a pack of Wrestlers, that endeavour'd to throw one another down, and when one of the Two has tripp'd up his Adversary's Heels, he politely gave him his Hand to help him up again: At all these Performances considerable Wagers are laid, as I have already had the Honour to tell you.[408]

## "FAIR PLAY" AMONG the GLADIATORS, 1741

IT is a Caution generally given to young Gentlemen much addicted to violent Exercises, to have a Care of over-strainings because an Accident of this Sort may be, and indeed is but too commonly, attended by Consequences which no Art can remedy. Naturalists tell us, that some of the rations in Physick were taught us by Animals; that the Virtues of a certain Herb were discovered by Goats, that the Bird *Ibis* gave the first Hint of a Glyster, and that Bathing was borrow'd from the Practice of a Domestick Brute. Hence I conceive it not at all amiss to adopt this boyish Maxim in Politicks, and to lay it down as a Rule for all such as will venture boisterous Kind of Publick Wrestling stiled *Opposition*, to be cautious of pushing too far, because if they have any Generals among them they may be informed it is in such Cases impossible to make a good Retreat. This is so consonant to Reason, and hath been so frequently, I had like to have said lately, confirmed by Experience, that I am not without Hopes Capt. *Vinegar* will admit that mine is a right Rule; and that for once he has met a good Thing in the Gazetteer; provided always that he be not out of Humour about what he said t'other Night concerning a BEAR and the DOGS, since if he should, to be sure nothing I can say (however good natur'd and obliging) could please him.

The Dispute between Parties this polite Writer, the first who equall'd the Merit of the Cause in which he engaged, has frequently compared to the *Ring* at *Moorfields;* and for once therefore the Consideration of it in that Light may be indulged me. Amongst the Heroes in that Part of the World Fair Play is a Thing always insisted upon; and how warm soever the Combatants may be, it is expected nevertheless that Rancour should never mix with Courage; for in that Case there would be no sport. But will any Retainer to the *Champion's* venture to assert that they have steadily adhered to this rule, that they have observed so much as *Hockley in the Hole* Decorum, or shewn a proper Respect to Good-Manners, as it is practised at present in the *Bear-Gardens* about this great City? I am perswaded there is not a *Cudgel-Player* of the whole CORPS who could be brought to say such a Thing, because the contrary is so very well known. Such a Failing however is of great consequence, and, if I am rightly informed, it has been something of this Sort which has been fatal to our AMPHITHEATRES, Of which *several* have *come* to *nothing* within the *Memory* of MAN. This methinks ought to be a Caution to the whole Fraternity, the rather because *Interest*, and a *Full* HOUSE seems to *be* their *ruling* Passion.

In the Days of the illustrious *Figg*, who, as I have been informed, had the Honour to instruct some PATRIOTS well as *Prize-fighters*, such strange Proceedings are now common, would by no Means have been allowed. He always insisted, that as the *Diversions* of his *House* were peculiar to the *English* as a *People*, so there should happen nothing there, which might discredit the Nation. His Challenges were drawn with Smartness, but no Scur-rility; and he never thought any MAN such a *Hero* as to be expected to dispute on two Stages the same Day: But since *Death* tripp'd up his heels, alas she never has overtaken the Noble Science of Defence. Every Fellow that can but flourish and hack, takes himself for a Master, and expects the best Swordsman in the Kingdom should engage him whenever the fighting Fit is upon him; and if the other betrays an Unwillingness to cut off his Ears, talks of posting him for a Coward. This is a vast Grievance in the Judgment of all Lovers of Back-Sword, because they apprehend it contrary to the Maxims of the Theatre, which require that the Combatants should be equally match'd; and not that every *high* spirited *young* Fellow, who has just learned to handle a Quarter-staff, should be

---

408 Baron de Pollnitz, *The Memoirs of Charles-Lewis, Baron de Pollnitz. Being the observations he made in his late travels from Prussia thro' Germany, Italy, France, Flanders, Holland, England, &c. Volume 4* (London: Printed for D. Browne, 1737-38).

encouraged to insult the *oldest* Brethren of the Blade.

All the knowing Part of the World agree there is a mighty Difference between the Modern and the Ancient Stage, to which they say 'tis owing that Strangers have entertain'd such odd Notions of our Amusements in this Way, as if they spoke us rather a barbarous than a free People. I should think therefore that when Cap. *Hercules*, Squire *Caleb,* or honest Mr. *Common sense* had an Afternoon to spare, it could not be better employ'd than in penning a smart Paper on the Laws relating to Combat, the rather because themselves being esteem'd a Kind of Gladiators, they may well be thought to understand the Subject, and to have it at heart; to say the truth, it is a kind of common Cause, and nothing could be more advantageous for the *querulous* Part of his Majesty's Subjects than that some Regulation in the Conduct of Debate in general was thought of and introduced. Otherwise, tho' I am as my Enemies say no Conjurer, yet I can foresee, that *Abuse* without *Licence* may be fatal to all *Sorts* of *Champions*, what kind of Weapons soever they use, and whether in their Warfare they shed Ink or Blood, I confess it is my Foible to grow grave on all Subjects; but as I am sensible of it, and ask Pardon for this: unseasonable Sobriety, I hope the Publick will pass it by, and my Brethren (to whom I have given so opportune a Caution) will not throw it in my Dish.

But to resume my Subject —— There is one thing exceedingly to the Honour of the *Spectators* at our *Amphitheatres*, that no sooner they discern a Mixture of *Malice* in the Heart of any Combatant, but immediately their Wishes incline another Way. The *English* are too *generous* to abet so foul a Passion as *Envy*, especially in *publick Contests*, and therefore see with Indignation such Practices as may give *Fumblers* in *Exercise* the Advantage over, the best M A S T E R of the Age. They look 'tis true with Delight on a Trial of Skill, when it is really such; but when a few *boistrous People* break in and are for being declared Conquerors without any Trial at all, they can't forbear *hissing* the Attempt, and *hooting* these *Darby Captains* from the Stage. I know a *Foreign Author* has made this Observation before me, but as it is just it will bear repeating. Besides, it is for the Honour of our Couutrymen that the Love of Justice is universal amongst them, and that they abhor in every Sense of Life, whatever has the Air of arbitrary Authority or barefaced Oppression. In other Countries Men of Rank will not suffer this, but 'tis in Britain only where the very Mob are equitable, and can discern and explode Foul Play as soon as the politest Assembly abroad. I say, 'tis here and here only; and long may they retain this Noble Spirit.

R. FREEMAN.[409]

## "A LARGE PIECE CUT OUT of his HEAD", 1742

Sept. 6, 1742.

AT the Great Booth at Tottenham court, on Wednesday next the 8th instant, there will be a severe trial of strength by the following Masters.

Whereas there was a a severe battle fought between Mr. Johnson and Mr. McArty, who has had the ill fortune to have a large piece cut out of his head, which has so much enraged this Hibernian hero, that he has vowed revenge—and said he could never leave London without another trial with the said Johnson, in which combat he would either retrieve his loss, or otherwise submit to a fate he has been a stranger to; the undaunted Johnson, not having the least regard to this bold sailor's threats, has agreed to fight him on the following terms, viz. to begin the weapons backward, and he that gives the most bleeding wounds at sword, and most blows at quarterstaff, to have the first 5 1. out of the box, and the rest to be shared as usual.

Attendance given at three o'clock, and the Masters mount the stage at half after four, by the reason the days are short.

To entertain the gentlemen while the house fills, there will be a hat played for at cudgels, which will be given to him that breaks the most heads.[410]

---

409 *Daily Gazetteer,* February 18, 1741.
410 Lemoine, 40-45.

*Fig. 61.* Hob Selling Beer at the Wake *by John Laguerre. British, ca. 1725. Yale Center for British Art, Paul Mellon Collection.*

## A MASONIC GLADIATOR, 1743

*At the Request of several Gentlemen of the worshipful Society of Free and Accepted* M A S O N S.

AT Mr. Broughton's new Amphitheatre, near the late Mr. Figg's, in Oxford-Road, on Friday next, the 16th instant, will be a Trial of Skill by the following Masters, viz. William Holmes, from the Kingdom of Ireland, Master of the Sword in all its different Branches, having since my Arrival here from Jamaica fought Mr. Johnson two Battles, in the first of which I had by far the Advantage, and he valuing himself in getting the better of the latter, (as he says) do invite him to fight a decisive one for the whole House, at three Bouts at the following Weapons, viz. Single Sword, Sword and Dagger, Sword and Buckler, single Falchon, Case of Falchons, and

245

desire Mr. Johnson to have his Sword in good Order; for he may expect a warm Reception than ever he met with, this being the last Time I ever propose to mount a publick Stage.

*William Holmes.*

Note, I will appear on the Stage with my White Apron as the Imperial Banner of the Free Masons Company under which I fight.

I Joseph Johnson, from Yorkshire, who never refused to fight a profess'd Master, will meet Mr. Holmes at the Time and Place above-mention'd, where I intend he shall feel the good Order of my Sword, by the Depth of its Penetration; I willingly agree to what he thinks his Advantage, fighting three Bouts at Falchons instead of Quarter-Staff, though it is a Weapon quite out of Practice in our Way; as to fighting for the whole House, 'tis what I expected, or else I would not have fought him at all, for I had resolv'd to give it quite over.

*Joseph Johnson.*

Note, It is agreed that he which gives the most bleeding Cuts, shall be entitled to the whole House, and likewise to leave no Bandage or Wounds dress'd till the Battle is over.

There will be Cudgel Playing for a Hat to divert the Gentlemen till the House fills.

Attendance will be given at Ten o'Clock, and the Masters mount at Twelve precisely.

There will be several Bye Matches of Boxing before the Masters mount.[411]

## MARTIAL PRACTICES in ENGLAND, 1744

The favourite Diversions in England, peculiar to itself, are generally such Exercises as suit best with Men of robust Constitutions, and some of them require a Share of Courage in the Performers, as Wrestling, Cudgels and Quarter-Staff: Others again are only Trials of Strength and Agility, such as pitching the Bar, throwing the Hammer, &c. Running, Leaping, Foot-Ball, Ringing of Bells, &c. As to that severe Trial of Manhood called Boxing, the engaging of Animals in Fight, as Bears, Bulls, Dogs, Cocks, the superficial flashing of the Masters of the noble Science of Defence, and the like, it must be acknowledged they are the Remains of the rough, perhaps savage, Disposition of the antient Inhabitants of this Island, and which ought not to meet with so much Encouragement, as they generally do, from the better sort.[412]

## A LETTER from a GLADIATOR, 1745

REMARKS *on an Address to the Publick in the Daily Advertiser on Wednesday and Thursday last, and sign'd* W. Flanders.

The first Thing worthy Notice is his boasted Defeat of Mr. Rowland Bennett, in half a Bout; bless us! What mighty Atchievements might have been expected from a whole Bout? It's well known that Mr. Bennett has gone through the Weapons with the late Mr. James Figg, and near disabled him. If Mr. Flanders's Vanity leads him to imagine he is to be named on the same Day with the said late Mr. James Figg, all who are now that knew both, know the contrary. I shall take no Notice of the formal Bib and Band Part of the Address, as where he lives and teaches, &c. but descend to the grand Point in Contest between us, viz. of his being fearful to reingage me. First then, previous to the late Battle between Mr. Smallwood and Mr. Slack at Mr. Broughton's, he appointed and enjoined me to meet him at the same Place to settle the Time we should next make our decisive Engagement, where he indeed came, but slipt away without taking the least Notice. A little time after I went to his House, and receiv'd for Answer he would let me know in a Day or two, but have not receiv'd one Word of Answer since. These are not the only Shuffles he has been guilty of before to me in the Delay and many Put-offs in our former

411 *Daily Advertiser,* December 15, 1743.
412 *The Geography of England: Done in the Manner of Gordon's Geographical Grammar* (London: R. Dodsley, 1744), 19.

Battles, after the Time agreed on for Performance, which Blame, I am well inform'd, he loaded me with, as being timorous; and now truly, after violating all his Agreements, he is determined (which by the Bye he ought to have been before) not to engage any more in a lucrative Way, and as is plain in no way at at all, as the World may judge, when I call'd and dar'd him to it in his own Shop, and in the open House after the Battle was over last Wednesday, when he slunk away without one Word of Answer; if these are not certain Indications and Demonstrations of Trepidity, I know not what are. *Joseph Johnson.*[413]

### a STAGE FIGHT INTERRUPTED, 1745

WHEREAS I Richard Banks, being Second to Mr. Johnson in his last Engagement with Mr. Sherlock, Mr. Hodgkins came on the Stage, drew a Sword, and made several Cuts at me, which I defended with with my Staff, and likewise paid him well with it after their Battle was over: If Mr. Hodgkins thinks he has made any Improvement lately, I desire he would meet me at Mr. Broughton's Amphitheatre, and fight six Bouts at single and double Weapons, and likewise six Bouts at Quarter-Staff, in order to prove himself a Master, otherwise I shall be of the Opinion, he is only a noisy Pretender. *Richard Banks.*[414]

### a CONTROVERSY REGARDING the SMALLSWORD, 1745

*To Mr.* F R A N C I S   S H E R L O C K.
*S I R,*
Remember you declin'd my Challenge at Bristol six Years ago; and as I burn with the same Thirst of Glory, I am still the more provok'd at your now trifling and Excuses since my Arrival at London, I would have you to understand, all your Judgment and Delicacy at the Line and Posture of the Small Sword, only serve to enflame the Spirit and Courage of a true Englishman; therefore, Mr. Sherlock, if you are not for letting the World judge of our Success, chuse the most obscure Corner, Hedge, or Ditch, where we shall decide in real Flesh and deep Wounds of the best Master; or if you deserve the Character the Town affords you, and be any ways, thro' Excess of Valour, prodigal of Blood, I shall be ready to divert the Spectators, with three Bouts at the Broad Sword, at Broughton's Ampitheatre, gratis.
*Anthony English.*[415]

Mr. ENGLISH,
I AM somewhat surpriz'd at your Advertisements, and the more so, because they seem to insinuate my Want of Courage and Resolution to meet you at Bristol, which Place you very well know I was oblig'd to leave, upon the sudden Departure of a Vessel I had contracted for a Passage in. To convince you how great a Regard I have, both for your's and my own Reputation, I here desire you to meet me at Mr. Broughton's on Friday next, at half an Hour after Four in the Evening. Your Hedge and Ditch fighting I scorn and detest, and am desirous the whole World may be Spectators of that Skill in the Sword which I expect from you, and which you may depend upon from me in the mean time be assur'd, that no Opponents, such as you, can ever alarm, much less dispirit me; for I hereby challenge the best Master in Europe to fight me nine Bouts at Back Sword, provided he gives me the Invitation a before next Christmas, for I am determin'd, after that Time, never to appear upon the Stage again. Yours,
*Francis Sherlock*[416]

---

413 *Daily Advertiser,* July 8, 1745.
414 *Daily Advertiser,* August 19, 1745.
415 *Daily Advertiser,* August 31, 1745. See also challenge from "Anthony Inglish, from Cork, in the Kingdom of Ireland," in the *Weekly Journal,* March 14, 1730.
416 *Daily Advertiser,* September 2, 1745.

CHAPTER XVII

## SWORD & TARGET, 1745

This Day there will be a great Trial of Skill at Mr. Broughton's Amphitheatre, near the late Mr. Figg's, in Oxford-Road, between Mr. William Johnston, from Limerick in Ireland, and Mr. Joseph Johnson, from Yorkshire, wherein will be exhibited the true Judgment of the Sword.

N. B. By the Request of several Gentlemen of Distinction, they begin at Sword and Target, in order to let the Spectators see the Nature of the Highlanders fighting. There will be Cudgel playing and Boxing as usual, to divert the Gentlemen till the Masters mount the Stage, which will be precisely at 4 o'Clock.

Our Yorkshire Champion freely offers himself, Horse and Sword, to join any worthy Gentleman in behalf of his King and Country, and will ready at an Hour's Warning.[417]

## HIGHLAND WEAPONS, 1746

Wednesday Noon there was a severe Trial of Skill between Mr. Sherlock from Dublin, and Mr. McDonald from the Highlands of Scotland, at Broughton's Amphitheatre in Oxford Road, when the Highlander was entirely discomfited at his own Weapons in a few Minutes.[418]

## A HOLLANDER, 1747

LONDON, October 10.

Yesterday was the great Trial of Skill at Broughton's Amphitheatre in Oxford-Road, between Mr. Sherlock and the Hollander, at the usual Weapons fought on the Stage, when Mr. Sherlock beat his Antagonist. It was a smart Battle.[419]

## WITH GAUNTLETS, 1752

Mr. Sherlock and another Fencing-Master, are once in a Month to fence for one hundred Pounds with an half Inch Gauntlet.[420]

## THE LAST GLADIATOR KILLED in COMBAT, 1753

Thomas Barritt. From the many cuts in his face called Old Chopping Block, a noted Prize Fighter; lost his life in single combat in Dublin about the year 1753, supposed to have been the last man in these kingdoms who made prize fighting his profession, his weapons were the broad sword & quarter staff, & at times used the target, he taught the use of the broad sword for the army, and the quarter staff for Park Keepers, Woodmen, and others.[421]

---

417 *Penny London Post or the Morning Advertiser,* October 9, 1745.
418 *Stamford Mercury,* May 22, 1746.
419 *Derby Mercury,* October 9, 1747.
420 *General Advertiser,* April 1, 1752.
421 Thomas Barritt, *Ancient Armour and Weapons in the possession of Thomas Barritt* [1793-1811], MS.

## SWORD, DAGGER, and BACKSWORD, 1766—1768

1766.—This is to give Notice to all Gentlemen Gamesters and Others, that are well skilled in those noble and manly Exercises of Sword and Dagger, and Back-Sword—That on Monday 22$^{nd}$ September will be played for at Sword and Dagger, at Bruton in the County of Somerset, a Lac'd Hat and Knot, valued one Guinea and Half. He that breaks the first Head to have the Knot, and he that Breaks the most Heads to have the Hat. And on Tuesday will be play'd for at Sword and Dagger one Guinea and Half. The first best Man to have a Guinea, the second best Man Half a Guinea. And on Wednesday will be played for at Back-Sword, one Guinea and Half, &c. The Play to begin each day at Ten o'Clock. N.B.—There will be greater Encouragement than usual to all Gamesters.

### SWORD and DAGGERS and BACK-SWORD.

On Thursday, 16th June next, will be played for at Sword and Dagger, at the White Horse in Langport, in the County of Somerset, a Purse of Two Guineas; and on Friday the 17th in the Morning, will be Back-Sword Playing for One Guinea; and in the Afternoon playing with Sword and Dagger for one Guinea more. The Players to comply with the Articles then to be proposed, and to begin Play each Morning precisely at Ten O'Clock. Suitable encouragement will be given to compleat Gamesters. Dinner on Table One O'Clock each day.—May 28, 1768.

### SWORD and DAGGER.

Sherborne, Dorset, on Wednesday and Thursday the 10th and 11th of August Instant, 1768, will be played for at Sword and Dagger at the Half Moon in this Town, one Guinea each day for him who breaks most Heads, and HALF a GUINEA for the second best Gamester. Good Encouragement will be given to the other Players. To mount the Stage precisely at Three in the Afternoon.[422]

## QUARTERSTAFF vs. SWORD, 1779

Harry Smith, well known by the appellation of 'The Squire'...was a complete sportsman of the Old School—skillful in the use of the cross and long bows, and at all athletic exercises—an adept at the single stick and quarter-staff, which last he would, till lately, turn with astonishing celerity. A well-known fact of his prowess in the last named exercise we subjoin: In 1779, a Sergeant of Elliott's Light Horse being then at Chichester, and who was reputed one of the best swordsmen of the day, challenged his sword against the Squire's staff, to draw the first blood; many are living who saw the encounter; when, at the expiration of four minutes, 'the Squire' gave his adversary the end of his staff in his forehead, which laid him flat on his back, and gained the victory. The staff, which is seven-feet ten-inches in length, is now preserved, and has thirteen cuts of the sword in it.[423]

## SWORD & DAGGER, 1786

On Thursday there was a smart contest at sword and dagger, between the gamesters of Dorset and Somerset, in which both prizes were adjudged to two of the Dorsetshire heroes.[424]

# FINIS.

---

422 *The Western Antiquary, or Note-Book for Devon & Cornwall.* No. 12. June, 1889. Vol. VIII, 231-232.
423 *The Gentleman's Magazine* (Westminster: John Nichols and Son, 1822), 286.
424 *Salisbury & Winchester Journal,* September 4, 1786.

*Fig 62. "John Broughton, Prize Fighter", holding a cane or staff. Engraved by F. Ross after William Hogarth. The Miriam and Ira D. Wallach Division of Art, Prints and Photographs: Print Collection, The New York Public Library.*

# BIBLIOGRAPHY

Arbuthnot, John. *Memoirs of the extraordinary life, works, and discoveries of Martinus Scriblerus.* [1700].

*The Art of Fencing.* [London]: John Bowles at the Black Horse in Cornhill, [1750].

*At his Majesty's Bear-Garden. In Hockly-in-the-Hole, this present Wednesday, being the 14th of May, 1735.*

*The ancient honour of the famous city of London restored and recovered by the noble Sir John Robinson knight & baronet, Lord Maior for this year 1663, in the truly English and manly exercises of wrestling, archery, and sword & dagger: with the speeches of Mr. William Smee (master of the game pro hac vice, and clerk of the market) upon this solemn occasion.* London: Printed for R.L., 1663.

Ashton, John. *Social life in the reign of Queen Anne: taken from original sources.* New York: Scribner and Welford, 1883.

Aylward, J.D.. *The English Master of Arms.* London: Routledge & Paul [1956].

Berry, Herbert. *The Noble Science: A Study and Transcription of Sloane Ms. 2530.* Newark, DE.: University of Delaware Press, 1991.

Bailey, N.. *An Universal Etymological English Dictionary Comprehending the Derivations of the Generality of Words in the English Tongue.* London: E. Bell, 1724.

Bancks, John. *Miscellaneous Works, in Verse and Prose, Volume I.* London: James Hodges, 1739.

Barritt, Thomas. *Ancient Armour and Weapons in the possession of Thomas Barritt.* [1793-1811], MS. From Manchester Libraries, Information and Archives, Manchester City Council, reference number BR MS f 399 B13.

*Bath Chronicle and Weekly Gazette.*

Betagh, William. *A voyage round the world. Being an account of a remarkable enterprize, begun in the year 1719, chiefly to cruise on the Spaniards in the great South ocean.* London: Printed for T. Combes [etc.] 1728.

Bramston, James. *The Man of Taste. Occasion'd by an Epistle Of Mr. Pope's on that Subject. Source: A Collection of Poems in Six Volumes. By Several Hands. Vol. I.* London: printed by J. Hughs, for R. and J. Dodsley, 1763 [1st ed. 1758].

Brooks, Baylus C.. *Dictionary of Pyrate Biography.* Lulu Press [S.l.], 2020.

Broughton, John. *Proposals for erecting an amphitheatre for the manly exercise of boxing, by John Broughton* [London : s.n., 1743].

Browne, Moses. *Poems on various subjects Many never printed before.* London: Edward Cave, 1739.

John Byrom, *The private journal and literary remains of John Byrom.* [Manchester]: Chetham Society, 1854.

*Caledonian Mercury.*

Castle, Egerton. *Schools and Masters of Fence.* London: George Bell and Sons, 1885.

Castle. Thornbury. W. R. Chambers, W. R. *Chambers's journal of popular literature, science and arts, Volume 59.* London: W. R. Chambers, 1882.

*A Challenge, from Richard Gravener Gentleman and Souldier, Against Thomas Blunne Shoomaker, to be Performed at the Red Bull in St. Johns Street, on Tuesday Next, the 20. of October, 1629.* Eliot's Court Press, 1629

*Chambers' Edinburgh Journal.*

William Chetwood, *A General History of the Stage.* London: W. Owen, 1749.

Clinch, George. *Marylebone and St. Pancras: Their History, Celebrities, Buildings, and Institutions.* London: Truslove, 1890.

Collier, Jeremy. *Essays upon several moral subjects, Vol. III.* London: George Strahan, 1728.

Concanen, Mathew. *The speculatist. A collection of letters and essays, moral and political, serious and humorous: upon various subjects.* London: J. Walthoe, 1732.

*Craftsman.*

*Daily Advertiser.*

*Daily Courant.*

*Daily Gazetteer.*

*Daily Journal.*

*Daily Post.*

Dalton, Michael. *The Countrey Justice: Containing the Practice of the Justices of the Peace.* London: G. Sawbridge, 1677.

*Dawks's News Letter.*

Danckaerts, Jasper. *Journal of Jasper Danckaerts, 1679-1680.* New York: Charles Scribner's Sons, 1913.

*A defence of the allies and the late ministry: or, remarks on the Tories new idol.* London: J. Baker, 1712.

*Derby Mercury.*

*Dublin Courier.*

D'Urfey, Thomas. *Wit and mirth: or, Pills to purge melancholy.* London: W. Pearson, 1720.

Drake, Peter. *The Memoirs of Capt. Peter Drake: Containing, an Account of Many Strange and Surprising Events, which Happened to Him*

*Through a Series of Sixty Years, and Upwards; and Several Material Anecdotes, Regarding King William and Queen Anne's Wars with Lewis XIV of France, Volume I.* Dublin: S. Powell, 1755.

Egan, Henry Pierce. *Boxiana; Or Sketches of Ancient and Modern Pugilism.* London: G. Smeeton, 1812.

*Englishman.*

*Fables of Æsop and Other Eminent Mythologists: with Morals and Reflections. By Sir Roger L'Estrange, Kt. The Sixth Edition Corrected, Volume 1.* London: R. Sare, 1714.

Farrell, Keith, "Thomas Page and Timothy Buck", keithfarrell.net, August 20, 2018, https://www.keithfarrell.net/blog/2018/08/thomas-page-and-timothy-buck/

Fielding, Henry. *Miscellanies.* London: Printed for A. Millar, 1743.

*Flying Post or the Post Master.*

*The foreigner's guide: both for the foreigner and native, in their tour through the cities of London and Westminster.* London: Joseph Pote, 1729.

*Free Thinker.*

*General Advertiser.*

*Gentleman's Magazine, or, Trader's Monthly.*

Goodwin, Thomas. *The Works of T. G. [With Preface to Vol. 1. by T. Owen and J. Barron.], Volume 3.* London: J. Darby, 1692.

Godfrey, Capt. John. *A Treatise Upon the Useful Science of Defence, Connecting the Small and Back-Sword, And showing the Affinity between them.* London: T. Gardner, 1747.

*The Geography of England: Done in the Manner of Gordon's Geographical Grammar.* London: R. Dodsley, 1744.

*The Graphic: A Weekly Illustrated Newspaper.*

Green, Mary Anne Everett. *Calendar of State Papers, Domestic Series 1652-1653, Volume 5.* London: Longman & Co., 1878.

*Grub Street Journal.*

*Guests Journal.*

Halfpenny, William. *Perspective made easy: or, a new method for practical perspective. Shewing the use of a new-invented senographical protractor; together with the draughts of several remarkable places, in and about the cities of Bristol and Bath; in twenty-six copper plates.* London: John Oswald, 1731.

Harland, John. *Collectanea Relating to Manchester and Its Neighborhood, at Various Periods, Vol. II.* Chetham Society, 1847.

Herbert. *Irish varieties, for the last fifty years: written from recollections* London: William Joy, 1836.

Hodgkin, John Eliot. *Rariora; being notes of some of the printed books, manuscripts, historical documents, medals, engravings, pottery, etc., collected (1858-1900).* London: S. Low, Marston & Co., Ltd., 1902.

Hone, William. *Every-Day Book, Or: Everlasting Calendar of Popular Amusements, Sports, Pastimes, Ceremonies, Manners, Customs, and Events, Volume II.* London: Hunt and Clarke, 1827.

[Hope, Sir William]. *A Few Observations Upon the Fighting for Prizes in the Bear Gardens, By a Lover and Well-wisher, not only to the True and Useful Art of the SWORD, but also to the Safety and Security of the Persons of those Brave, Courageous, and Bold Performers in these publick Places, for Trial of Skill in this Gentlemanly Art.* London: 1715.

—. *The Fencing-master's Advice to His Scholar.* Edinburgh: John Reid, 1692.

—. *A New, Short, and Easy Method of Fencing.* Edinburgh: James Watson, 1707.

—. *A Vindication of the True Art of Self-defence. With a Proposal to the Honourable Members of Parliament for Erecting a Court of Honour in Great-Britain. Recommended to All Gentlemen, But Particularly to the Soldiery: To which is Annexed, a Short, But Very Useful Memorial for Sword-men.* Edinburgh: William Brown, 1724.

Hutton, Alfred. *Sword and the Centuries.* London: G. Richards, 1901.

*Ipswich Journal.*

*Jackson's Oxford Journal.*

James, Ralph. *The touch-Stone, or, historical, critical, political, philosophical, and theological essays on the reigning diversions of the town.* London: booksellers of London and Westminster, 1728.

Jenyns, Soame. *The Modern Fine Gentleman. Written in the Year 1746. Vol. I.* London: printed by J. Hughs, for R. and J. Dodsley, 1763 [1st ed. 1758].

*Journal of Sport History.*

*A Latin Trologue spoke before one Terence's Plays at Westminster; on Occasion of a late Boxing-Match, between an Englishman and an Italian. from Miscellaneous Poem, by Several Hands.* London: J. Watts, 1726.

Le Blanc, Jean-Bernard. *Letters on the English and French Nations.* London: J. Brindley; R. Francklin; C. Davis; & J. Hodges, 1747.

*The Leeds Intelligencer.*

Lemoine, Henry. *Modern Manhood: Or, the Art and Practice of English Boxing.* London: J. Parsons, 1788.

Richard Ligon, *A true & exact history of the island of Barbados.* London: Humphrey Moseley.

*London Evening Post.*

Lucas, John. *The Memoranda Book of John Lucas 1712–1750, Vol . 16.* Leeds: The Thoresby Society, 2006.

Lyttelton, Baron George. *Letters from a Persian in England, to His Friend at Ispahan.* London: J. Millan, 1735.

Mackay, Charles. *New Light on Some Obscure Words & Phrases in the Works of Shakespeare and his Contemporaries.* London: Reeves & Turner, 1884.

Malcolm, James Peller. *Anecdotes of the Manners and Customs of London during the Eighteenth Century; Vol. II.* London: Longman, Hurst, Rees, and Orme, 1810.

Masters, Mary. *Poems on several occasions.* London: T. Browne, 1733.

Maynard, Josias and Swinnow. William. *A Tryall [of] Skill, Betwen Josias Maynard Citizen, and Cutler of London, and Master of the Noble Science of Defence ... of the House of White Friers, and William Swinow, Alias Scot, Citizen and Cooke of London, and Master of the Noble Science of Defence, of the House of Tower Royall.* 1652.

McBane, Donald. *The Expert Sword-man's Companion.* New York: Jared Kirby Rare Books, 2017.

Menzer, Paul, ed. *Inside Shakespeare: Essays on the Blackfriars Stage.* Susquehanna University Press, 2006.

Miller, Ben. *Irish Swordsmanship: Fencing and Dueling in Eighteenth Century Ireland.* N.Y.: Hudson Society Press, 2017.

Miller, Captain James. *Treatise of ye Gladiatory Art of Defence.* London: 1738.

Misson (de Valbourg), Henri, *M. Misson's Memoirs and Observations in His Travels Over England: With Some Account of Scotland and Ireland.* London: D. Brown, 1719.

*Mist's Weekly Journal.*

*A Modern History, or the Present State of All Nations, Vol. XXXI,* London· Printed for the Author, 1738.

*Modern Language Review.*

Mottraye, Aubrey de La. *A. de La Motraye's Travels through Europe, Asia, and into parts of Africa: with proper cutts and maps.* London: Printed for the Author, 1723.

Muralt, Béat Louis de. *Describing The Character and Customs of the English and French Nations.* London: T. Edlin, 1726.

*Newcastle Courant.*

Nichols, John, and Steevens, George. *The genuine works of William Hogarth; illustrated with biographical anecdotes, a chronological catalogue, and commentary.* London: Longman, Hurst, Rees, and Orme, 1808-17.

*On a duel between William Sherlock of Dublin and Edward Sutton of Gravesend* [1734]. Single sheet. The British Library, St. Pancras.

*Original Weekly Journal.*

*A Pacquet from Will's: or a New collection of original letters on several subjects. Written and collected by several hands.* London: Sam. Briscoe, 1701.

Palmer, Samuel. *St. Pancras: being antiquarian, topographical, and biographical memoranda, relating to the extensive metropolitan parish of St. Pancras, Middlesex.* London: S. Palmer, 1870.

*Papers of the Masters of Defence of London, Temp. Henry VIII to 1590.* Newark, DE: University of Delaware Press, 1991.

*Parkers London News or the Impartial Intelligencer.*

Parkyns, Sir Thomas. Προγυμνάσματα. *The Inn-play: Or, Cornish-hugg Wrestler.* Nottingham: William Ayscouh, 1713.

*Penny London Post or the Morning Advertiser.*

Pepys, Samuel. *Diary and correspondance of Samuel Pepys, F.R.S.,secretary to the admiralty in the Reigns of Charles II and James II, Vol. III.* London: H.G.Bohn, York Street, Convent Garden, 1858.

—. *Diary and correspondance of Samuel Pepys, F.R.S.,secretary to the admiralty in the Reigns of Charles II and James II, Vol. IV.* London: H.G.Bohn, York Street, Convent Garden, 1858.

—. *The Diary of Samuel Pepys, M.A., F.R.S., Clerk of the Acts and Secretary to the Admirality, Volume 3, Part 1.* New York: Croscup & Sterling Company, 1893.

Pollnitz, Baron de. *The Memoirs of Charles-Lewis, Baron de Pollnitz. Being the observations he made in his late travels from Prussia thro' Germany, Italy, France, Flanders, Holland, England, &c. Volume 4.* London: Printed for D. Browne, 1737-38.

*The Post Man and The Historical Account.*

Preston, Mr.. *Æsop. At the Bear-Garden: a Vision. By Mr. Preston. In Imitation of the Temple of Fame, a Vision, by Pope.* London: Sold by John Morphew near Stationers-Hall, 1715.

Prévost d'Exiles, Antoine François. *The Memoirs and Adventures of the Marquis de Bretagne and Duc d'Harcourt: The wonderful Vicissitudes of Fortune, exemplified in the Lives of those Noblemen, To which is added The history of the chevalier de Grieu and Moll Lescaut. Translated from the Original French by Mr. Erskine, Volume II.* London: T. Cooper, 1743.

*Proceedings of the Massachusetts Historical Society, 2nd Series, Vol. XIII.*

*Public Ledger.*

*The Ranger's Magazine: Or the Man of Fashion's Companion.Vol. 1. For the Year 1795.* London: J. Sudbury, 1795.

Reader, William. *New Coventry Guide: Containing the History and Antiquities of that City.* Coventry: Rollason and Reader, 1824.

*Read's Weekly Journal.*

*Renaissance Quarterly.*

*Review of the State of the English Nation.*

*The Royal Strangers Ramble, / Or, The Remarkable Lives, Customs, and Character of the Four Indian Kings: / With the manner of their Daily Pastimes, Humours and Behaviours since their / first Landing in England. Render'd into Pleasant and Familiar Verse.* London: W. Wise in Fetter-Lane, Fleetstreet, 1710.

*Salisbury & Winchester Journal.*

Salmon, Thomas. *Modern History: or the Present State of all Nations. Describing Their Respective Situations, Persons, Habits, Buildings, Manners, Laws and Customs, Religion and Policy, Arts and Sciences, Trades, Manufactures and Husbandry, Plants, Animals and Minerals.* Dublin: Geo. Grierson, 1733.

Saussure, Cesar de. *A foreign view of England in the reigns of George I and George II: The letters of Monsieur Cesar de Saussure to his family.* London: John Murray, 1902.

Sewall, Samuel. *The Diary of Samuel Sewall, 1674-1729. Newly edited from the ms. at the Massachusetts Historical Society by M. Halsey Thomas, Vol. 1.* New York: Farrar, Straus and Giroux, 1973.

Silver, George. *Paradoxes of Defence: Wherein is Proved the Trve Grounds of Fight to be in the Short Auncient Weapons, and that the Short Sword Hath Aduantage of the Long Sword Or Long Rapier. And the Weakenesse and Imperfection of the Rapier-fights Displayed. Together with an Admonition of the Noble, Ancient, Victorious, Valiant, and Most Braue Nation of Englishmen, to Beware of False Teachers of Defence, and how They Forsake Their Owne Naturall Fights: with a Briefe Commendation of the Noble Science Or Exercising of Armes.* London: Edvvard Blount, 1599.

Sorbière, Samuel. *A voyage to England: containing many things relating to the state of learning, religion, and other curiosities of that kingdom. Done into English from the French original.* London: J. Woodward, 1709.

*Spectator.*

*Sporting Magazine: Or, Monthly Calendar of the Transactions of the Turf, the Chase and Every Other Diversion Interesting to the Man of Pleasure, Enterprize, and Spirit, Volume 15.* London: Rogerson & Tuxford, 1800.

*St James Evening Post.*

*Stamford Mercury.*

Stiles, Ezra. *A history of three of the judges of King Charles I. Major-General Whalley, Major-General Goffe, and Colonel Dixwell: who, at the restoration, 1660, fled to America; and were secreted and concealed, in Massachusetts and Connecticut, for near thirty years. With an account of Mr. Theophilus Whale, of Narragansett, supposed to have been one of the judges.* Hartford: Elisha Babcock, 1794.

Stocking, Charles. *Ancient Greek Athletics.* Oxford: Oxford University Press, 2021.

Swetnam, Joseph. *The schoole of the noble and worthy science of defence.* London: Printed by Nicholas Okes, 1617.

Thornbury, George. *Old and new London: a narrative of its history, its people and its places, Volume 2.* London: Cassel, Petter & Galpin, 1880.

Thornbury, Walter. *Old and New London, a Narrative of Its History, Its People, and Its Places.* London: Cassell, Petter, Galpin & Co., 1881.

*True Protestant Mercury.*

*The Tyburn chronicle: or, villainy display'd in all its branches. Containing an authentic account of the lives, adventures, tryals, of the most notorious male factors. From the year 1700, to the present time.* London: J. Cooke, [1768].

*The Unfortunate Fencer; or The Couragious Farmer of Gloucester-shire.* P. Brooksby, J. Deacon, J. Blare, J. Back, [1675-1696].

*Universal Mercury.*

*Universal Spectator and Weekly Journal.*

Ward, Edward. *The London-Spy Compleat, in eighteen-parts.* London: J. How, 1703.

—. *The London-Spy Compleat, in eighteen parts. The second volume of the author's writings.* London: J. How, 1709.

Watts, Isaac. *A Defense Against the Temptation to Self-murther.* London: J. Clark and R. Hett, 1726.

*Weekly Journal.*

*Weekly Journal or British Gazetteer.*

*Weekly Journal with Fresh Advices.*

*Weekly Register or, Universal Journal.*

*Western Antiquary, or Note-Book for Devon & Cornwall.*

*The Whitehall Evening-Post Or London Intelligencer.*

# About the Author

BEN MILLER is an American filmmaker and author. He is a graduate of New York University's Tisch School of the Arts, was the winner of the Alfred P. Sloan Foundation Grant for screenwriting, and has worked for notable personages such as Martin Scorsese and Roger Corman. For the last nineteen years, Miller has studied fencing at the Martinez Academy of Arms, one of the last places in the world still teaching an authentic living tradition of classical fencing. He has served as the Academy's *chef de salle*, and has authored articles and lectured for the Association for Historical Fencing. He is the author of *Irish Swordsmanship: Fencing and Dueling in Eighteenth Century Ireland* (Hudson Society Press, 2017), and one of the authors of *Scottish Fencing: Five 18th Century Texts on the Use of the Small-sword, Broadsword, Spadroon, Cavalry Sword, and Highland Battlefield Tactics* (Hudson Society Press, 2018), co-authored by Maestros Jared Kirby and Paul Macdonald. He is the editor of *Self-Defense for Gentlemen and Ladies: A Nineteenth-Century Treatise on Boxing, Kicking, Grappling, and Fencing with the Cane and Quarterstaff* (North Atlantic Books, 2015), containing the writings of the noted duelist and fencing master, Colonel Thomas Hoyer Monstery. He wrote the foreword to the republication of Donald McBane's classic martial arts treatise, *The Expert Sword-Man's Companion: Or the True Art of Self-Defence* (New York: Jared Kirby Rare Books, 2017). He introduced, edited and annotated *King of the Swordsman* (Hudson Society Press, 2019) by Colonel Monstery. He has taught the German wand exercise and the use of the Germanic club at Combatcon in Las Vegas, where he has also lectured on topics relating to fencing history and physical culture. Miller's articles about fencing and martial arts history can be found on the websites *martialart-snewyork.org* and *outofthiscentury.wordpress.com*. His videos about physical culture and historical physical fitness methods can be found on his YouTube channel *Physical Culture Historians*.

## WORKS BY THE SAME AUTHOR

SELF-DEFENSE FOR GENTLEMEN AND LADIES: A NINETEENTH-CENTURY TREATISE ON BOXING, KICKING, GRAPPLING, AND FENCING WITH THE CANE AND QUARTERSTAFF (2015)

IRISH SWORDSMANSHIP: FENCING AND DUELING IN EIGHTEENTH CENTURY IRELAND (2017)

(WITH MAESTROS KIRBY & MACDONALD)
SCOTTISH FENCING: FIVE 18TH CENTURY TEXTS ON THE USE OF THE     SMALL-SWORD, BROADSWORD, SPADROON, CAVALRY SWORD, AND HIGHLAND BATTLEFIELD TACTICS (2018)

KING OF THE SWORDSMEN (2019)

METHODS OF USING THE CLUB FOR SELF-DEFENCE AND EXERCISE IN 19TH CENTURY GERMANY (2022)

## FORTHCOMING

INTRODUCTION TO PHYSICAL CULTURE

HISTORY OF THE INDIAN CLUB

THE WAND EXERCISE

## ONLINE

WWW.PATREON.COM/PHYSICALCULTUREHISTORIANS

YOUTUBE.COM/@PHYSICALCULTUREHISTORIANS

www.ingramcontent.com/pod-product-compliance
Lightning Source LLC
Chambersburg PA
CBHW062016090426

42811CB00005B/873